Eyes on China

An Intermediate-Advanced Reader of Modern Chinese

我看中国

现代汉语中高级读本

Princeton Language Program: Modern Chinese

Princeton University Press is proud to publish the Princeton Language Program in Modern Chinese. Based on courses taught through the Princeton University Department of East Asian Studies and the Princeton in Beijing Program, this comprehensive series is designed for university students who wish to learn or improve upon their knowledge of Mandarin Chinese.

Students begin with *First Step, Chinese Primer,* or *Oh, China!* depending on their previous exposure to the language. After the first year, any combination of texts at a given level can be used.

PROGRAM OVERVIEW			
FIRST YEAR	SECOND YEAR	THIRD YEAR	ADVANCED
First Step (For beginners with no previous knowledge of Chinese)	*A New China*	*All Things Considered*	*A Kaleidescope of China*
Chinese Primer (For beginners with no previous knowledge of Chinese)	*A Trip to China*	*Eyes on China*	*Anything Goes*
Oh, China! (For students who speak and understand some Chinese, especially "heritage" students who speak the language at home.)	*An Intermediate Reader of Modern Chinese*		*China's Peril and Promise*
			Literature and Society
			Readings in Contemporary Chinese Cinema
			A Reflection of Reality: Selected Readings in Contemporary Chinese Short Stories

Eyes on China

An Intermediate-Advanced Reader of Modern Chinese

我看中国

现代汉语中高级读本

周质平　Chih-p'ing Chou

刘锦城　Jincheng Liu

邹昕　Xin Zou

Princeton University Press
Princeton and Oxford

Copyright © 2019 by Princeton University Press
Published by Princeton University Press, 41 William Street, Princeton, New Jersey 08540
In the United Kingdom: Princeton University Press, 6 Oxford Street, Woodstock, Oxfordshire
OX20 1TW

press.princeton.edu

Library of Congress Control Number: 2018957745

ISBN 978-0-691-19094-5
ISBN 978-0-691-19095-2 (pbk.)

British Library Cataloging-in-Publication Data is available

Editorial: Fred Appel and Thalia Leaf
Production Editorial: Nathan Carr
Jacket/Cover Design: Layla MacRory
Production: Erin Suydam
Publicity: Tayler Lord and Kathryn Stevens

The publisher would like to acknowledge the authors of this volume for providing the
camera-ready copy from which this book was printed.

This book has been composed in STKaiti and Times New Roman

Printed on acid-free paper ∞

Printed in the United States of America

3 5 7 9 10 8 6 4 2

我看中国
Eyes on China

目录
Table of Contents

《我看中国》
序

　　《我看中国》（*Eyes on China*）是普林斯顿大学对外汉语教研室在高年级教材编写上的又一个新尝试。本书主要的对象是在大学里学过一年华裔汉语或两年现代汉语的学生，供一学年两学期使用，我们将本书水平定为"中高级现代汉语"。

　　过去 20 多年来，我们编写过多种不同形式的高年级对外汉语教材，有以现代思想史为选题的《中国知识分子的自省》（*China's Own Critics*, 1993）；有以《人民日报》为选材的《人民日报笔下的美国》（*The USA in the People's Daily*, 1993）；有以五四时期及三十年代文选为主题的《中国的危机与希望》（*China's Peril and Promise*, 1996）；有以社会分析及幽默小品合编的《文学与社会》（*Literature and Society*, 1999; 2016 Revised）；有教材体的文章与报刊文选合编的《事事关心》（*All Things Considered*, 2001; 2011 Revised）；有全书选自报刊杂志的《无所不谈》（*Anything Goes*, 2006; 2011 Revised）和《中国社会百态》（*A Kaleidoscope of China*, 2010）；有以电影为选材的《中国侧影》（*Readings in Contemporary Chinese Cinema*, 2008）；也有当代短篇小说的选读《文学中的现实》（*A Reflection of Reality*, 2014）等。《我看中国》在这一系列的教材中，是唯一一本全书课文由我们自己执笔写定的教科书。

　　我们之所以决定自己动手写课文，主要是多年来在教学的实践中，深感语言难易合适，主题生动有趣，能引起外国学生讨论兴趣的材料少之又少；我们似乎过分强调所谓"真实语料"的价值，而忽略了这些"真实语料"中夹带着过多不规范的结构，或不相干的话题。给只学过两年汉语的外国学生使用，不但难度过大，而且所谈的主题往往离他们的生活经验太远，上课时无从讨论。

　　就教材的编写而言，相对于"真实语料"，并非"虚构"或"人造"，而是在遣词造句上规范，在选题编排上有趣。对外国学生来说，一本理想的汉语教科书不但可以提高他们的语言能力，也可以增进他们对当代中国的了解。

　　在汉语教学界里，中级到高级教材之间，往往出现断层现象，也就是教材难度的跨越太大。一个刚学了两年汉语的学生是看不懂选自报刊的所谓"真实语料"的。结果，学生完全感受不到阅读的乐趣，只是挣扎在生词和句型之间，进行死记硬背。我们有鉴于此，动手编写了《我看中国》。

　　在这本书里，我们特别强调"当代中国"，因为坊间有太多的汉语教科书所介绍的中国，往往是古代中国，从阴阳八卦到太极五行，从牛郎织女、嫦娥奔月到节气、茶道、书法、气功、剪纸、中国结，真是无奇不有，唯独不讲的是当下中国的社会民生。我们这一界的一个有趣现象是"现代汉语教科书"，在内容上，并不"现代"。

《我看中国》所讲的，与其说是"当代"中国，不如说是"当下"的中国，是外国学生可以听到、看到的中国，是他们一旦到了，必须寝馈其间的中国。我们不忽略中国改革开放以来飞跃的进步，我们也不粉饰中国社会的黑暗、腐败与矛盾，同时也不回避政治上的敏感、禁忌与尴尬。我们用相对简单的语言，尽可能如实地反映当下中国的一个侧面，其中有可喜的，也有可忧的；有光明的，也有黑暗的；有得体的，也有不很得体的。于是，雾霾、中国梦、龙与熊猫、反腐败、顺口溜儿、共享单车、高铁、山寨产品、城乡差距、留守儿童、农民工、软实力、小鲜肉、海峡两岸等等都成了课本中的话题。在这些话题的陈述中，有的是从中国人的角度来看，有的是从外国人的视角而言。我们相信，这本教材所呈现出来的中国是一个真实有趣，城乡结合，多样并存的社会，而中国人则是一个努力工作而又充满幽默感的民族。

许多对外汉语教科书为了顾及中美两国的国情，一方面不能触碰到中国政府的言论禁忌，一方面又要符合美国人的"政治正确"，结果，许多富有争议的话题都进不了对外汉语课本。然而，这些表面上也许不很得体的话题，讨论起来不仅有趣，而且饶富深意。《我看中国》在这方面做了尝试性的探索。

本书 2016-2018 年在普林斯顿大学及普林斯顿北京暑期中文培训班试用，深得师生喜爱。

全书在编排上，仍采课文与生词同页互见的形式，并辅之以词语搭配，句型结构，词语辨析及练习等部分。为适应港台地区背景的学生，我们将 20 世纪中期以前之旧体汉字课文置于每篇之末，以备参考。

在成书过程中，哥伦比亚大学的刘乐宁教授、纽约州立大学的何瞻(James Hargett)教授，普大的王静老师、耶鲁大学的张永涛老师就本书的内容与结构提出了许多宝贵的改进意见。同事赵扬（Henry Zhao）先生、欧颖老师曾细校英语部分，黄鸾凤老师、董澍潭老师以及我们的多位同事也在教学过程中指出了书稿中的不少问题，杨玖老师在最后的编辑排版过程中不厌其烦地解答了各种技术问题。我们在此向他们深致谢忱。当然，书中如有任何错误，都是作者的责任。

周质平、刘锦城、邹昕

在普林斯顿大学东亚系

2018 年 6 月 2 日

Eyes on China

Preface

Eyes on China represents a new effort at compiling an intermediate-advanced level teaching resource made by Princeton University's Chinese Language Program. This textbook is primarily geared toward the student with two years of modern Chinese experience, and its contents can cover one academic year (two semesters). The difficulty of this textbook can be categorized as "intermediate-advanced" contemporary Chinese.

For the past 20 years, we have created a diverse collection of advanced-level textbooks, including *China's Own Critics* (1993), which uses the history of modern thought in China as its topics, *The USA in the People's Daily* (1993), which uses articles from The People's Daily as its topics, *China's Peril and Promise* (1996), which uses essays from the May Fourth period and the 1930s as its topics, *Literature and Society* (1996, 2016 Revised), which was comprised of a combination of social analysis and humorous short stories, *All Things Considered* (2001, 2011 Revised), which uses academic essays and news articles as its content, *Anything Goes* (2006, 2011 Revised) and *A Kaleidoscope of China* (2010), both of which are entirely comprised of newspaper articles, as well as *Readings in Contemporary Chinese Cinema* (2008), which focuses on Chinese cinema in its chapters, and *A Reflection of Reality* (2014), which uses contemporary short stories as its selected readings. *Eyes on China* stands out as the only textbook in this series of textbooks that was entirely written ourselves.

Our decision to write all the chapters ourselves primarily arose from the fact that in our many years of teaching experience, we deeply felt that there was a lack of teaching material that was suitable in difficulty, interesting and vivid in content, and conducive to debate among international students. At the same time, we seemed to overemphasize the value of so-called "authentic content", ignoring the irregular grammar structures, as well as irrelevant topics, nestled in such "authentic content". Should such material be given to a student with only two years of Chinese learning experience to use, the material would not only be too difficult, but the disconnect between the subject matter discussed in the topics and the students' personal experiences would be too great, and thus, not very conductive for discussion during class.

In terms of creating teaching material, the opposite of "authentic content" is not necessarily "imagined" or "man-made" content, but rather, content that is precise in vocabulary and grammar, and creative in topic selection and arrangement. The ideal Chinese textbook for an international student not only improves their language skills, but also enhances their understanding of contemporary China.

In the field of Chinese pedagogy, there is oftentimes a rift that opens between Intermediate Level and Advanced Level, a too wide of a gap in difficulty between the two levels in terms of teaching material. A student who has just completed two years of Chinese learning would undoubtedly find the so-called "authentic content" in a newspaper article incomprehensible. The result is a student unable to derive any pleasure in reading, who instead struggles with vocabulary and sentence structures, and is ultimately relegated to rote memorization. Considering such an outcome, we created *Eyes on China*.

In this textbook, we especially emphasized "contemporary China", because more often than not, the China introduced in many publications is traditional China; from Yin-Yang and the Eight Trigrams to Taiji and the Five Elements, from the folktales of The Cowherd and Weaver Girl and The Legend of Chang'e to solar terms, tea ceremonies, calligraphy, *qigong*, paper-cutting, and Chinese knots, all manners of wonders are covered with the notable exception of the livelihood of contemporary Chinese society. An interesting phenomenon in this field is that the "contemporary Chinese textbook" is anything but contemporary.

As for the contents of *Eyes on China*, what is covered is not just "contemporary" China, but rather "present-day" China. It is the China that a student, should they study abroad there today, can actually see and hear; the China that they would spend their days in today. We do not ignore the leaps and bounds made in progress since China's "Reform and Opening Up", but we also do not downplay the dark side of Chinese society, with its corruption and contradictions, and we do not shy away from the sensitive, taboo, and awkward subject of Chinese politics. By using relatively easy to understand language, we strive to reflect all sides of present-day China: the likeable and the regrettable, the light and the dark, the decent and not-so-decent. Thus, topics in this textbook include: air pollution, the Chinese Dream, "Dragon" and "Panda", anti-corruption, jingles, bike-sharing, high-speed trains, knock-off goods, differences between city and countryside, left-behind children, migrant workers, soft power, boy-toys, Taiwan and Mainland China, and more. Approaches to these topics include viewpoints of Chinese people and viewpoints of foreigners. We believe that this textbook depicts China as a multi-dimensional, multi-faceted society, and Chinese people as hard-working, yet humor-loving.

By taking into consideration certain social habits and customs of the East and West, namely, the inability to broach the topic of freedom of speech in China, and a need to be "politically correct" in the West, many interesting topics brimming with the potential for debate are left out of Chinese textbooks. These topics, which may seem indecent at face value, are not only rife with the potential for interesting debate, but can lead to profound understandings. A goal of *Eyes on China* is to seek out and push the lines on such taboos.

This textbook was field tested at Princeton and the Princeton in Beijing summer program from 2016 to 2018, garnering extremely favorable reviews from students and teachers alike.

In terms of this textbook's structure, chapters are arranged so that the lesson and relevant vocabulary appear on the same page, and are bookended with vocabulary collocation, sentence structures, synonym differentiation, review, homework and more. To accommodate students of Hong Kong or Taiwanese background, lessons appear in traditional Chinese at the end of each chapter for reference.

We are very grateful to Professor Liu Lening (Columbia University), Professor James Hargett (SUNY Albany), Dr. Wang Jing (Princeton University), and Dr. Zhang Yongtao (Yale University) for their insightful comments and constructive criticism during the development of this textbook. In addition, our colleagues, Mr. Henry Zhao and Ms. Ou Ying, proofread the English portions and provided valuable suggestions. We would also like to extend our sincerest thanks to Ms. Huang Luanfeng, Ms. Dong Shutan, and many other colleagues who helped improve this textbook in one way or another. Also, Ms. Joanne Chiang was invariably patient, helpful and generous with her time in providing us with technical support. Of course, any errors in the final work are the authors' own.

Chih-p'ing Chou
Jincheng Liu
Xin Zou

Department of East Asian Studies
Princeton University

June 2, 2018

English Translation by Henry Zhao

略语表
List of Abbreviations

adj.	....	adjective
adv.	....	adverb
aux.	....	auxiliary
conj.	....	conjunction
idm.	....	idiom
interj.	....	interjection
m.w.	....	measure word
n.	....	noun
N.P.	....	noun phrase
obj.	....	object
part.	....	particle
phr.	....	phrase
pref.	....	prefix
prep.	....	preposition
pron.	....	pronoun
p.w.	....	place word
suffix	....	suffix
t.w.	....	time word
v.	....	verb
v.-c.	....	verb-complement
v.-o.	....	verb-object
V.P.	....	verb phrase

Eyes on China

An Intermediate-Advanced Reader of
Modern Chinese

我看中国

现代汉语中高级读本

第 1 课

雾霾

　　"雾霾"的"霾"字很难写，而且不常用，连很多中国人都不认得，不会写。但是近几年，这个罕见的字，却成了到中国来的外国人第一个必须学习的汉字！

　　雾霾就是比较严重的空气污染，看起来有点像雾，可是又不是雾。有雾霾的时候，一天 24 小时都是灰蒙蒙的，看不清楚远处的东西。最严重的时候，连学校的高楼都看不太清楚。

　　据说，雾霾对健康有害，在雾霾严重的环境里生活一天，比一天抽两包烟对身体更不好。有时候，我从外面跑步回来，觉得喉咙很不舒服，咳

雾霾	wùmái	n.	smog, haze
认得	rèndé	v.	to know; to recognize (negation：不认得)
近几年	jìn jǐ nián	t.w.	in recent years
罕见	hǎnjiàn	adj.	seldom seen; rare
空气	kōngqì	n.	air
污染	wūrǎn	n./v.	pollution
雾	wù	n.	fog
灰蒙蒙	huī méngméng	adj.	dusky; overcasting; (cannot be modified by degree adverbs, e.g. 很, 非常, 有点儿.)
远处	yuǎnchù	n.	a distant place
高楼	gāo lóu	n.	tall building; skyscraper
抽烟	chōuyān	v.-o.	to smoke (a cigarette or a pipe)
喉咙	hóulong	n.	throat

嗽 咳得很厉害。我的中国朋友都劝 我戴 口罩，但我倒不太担心，因为中国八九十岁的老人很多，显然，雾霾对健康的伤害 并没有那么严重。而且，我在美国从来没戴过口罩。戴了口罩，看起来很奇怪，也很不舒服。

在街上戴口罩的人还真不少。戴了口罩把脸遮 住了，有的时候连老朋友也认不出来 了！所以，在北京有不少跟雾霾有关的笑话。像放学 的时候，家长接错了孩子。恋人约会，认错了对象，甚至跟陌生人 亲了嘴；当然，这样的笑话很夸张，但也表现 了中国人的幽默。中国人是个很有幽默感

咳嗽	késòu	v.	to cough
劝	quàn	v.	to urge; try to persuade
戴	dài	v.	to put on (eyewear, headgear, clothing accessories)
口罩	kǒuzhào	n.	gauze mask
显然	xiǎnrán	adv.	obviously; evidently
伤害	shānghài	n.	harm
遮	zhē	v.	to cover
认	rèn	v.	try to recognize
放学	fàngxué	v.-o.	(of school) let out or close; school ends
家长	jiāzhǎng	n.	parent or guardian of a child
接	jiē	v.	to pick up (from school, airport, etc.)
恋人	liànrén	n.	loved one; girlfriend or boyfriend
约会	yuēhuì	v.-o.	to date
对象	duìxiàng	n.	target; a potential marriage partner
陌生人	mòshēng rén	n.	stranger
亲嘴	qīnzuǐ	v.-o.	to kiss (no object; use "跟 sb.亲嘴" instead.)
夸张	kuāzhāng	adj.	exaggerated; overstated
表现	biǎoxiàn	v.	to display; to show

的民族，他们往往可以在非常恶劣的环境下苦中作乐，用一种无奈又风趣的态度来面对问题。

　　北京的雾霾，遇到有重要活动的时候，往往可以在短时间之内，突然变成蓝天白云。像 2008 年的奥运会、2014 年的 APEC 会议在北京举行的时候，北京人享受了几天难得的好天气，大家都很意外，也很高兴，把这样的蓝天叫做："奥运蓝"，或"APEC 蓝"。老百姓都说："你瞧，还是咱

幽默	yōumò	adj./n.	humorous; humor
幽默感	yōumò gǎn	n.	sense of humor
民族	mínzú	n.	a people; nationality
恶劣	èliè	adj.	hostile
苦中作乐	kǔzhōng zuòlè	idm.	to have fun amidst hardships
无奈	wúnài	adj.	grudgingly; have no alternative
风趣	fēngqù	adj.	witty
态度	tàidù	n.	attitude
面对	miànduì	v.	to face; to confront
遇到	yùdào	v.	to encounter
活动	huódòng	n.	event; activity
突然	tūrán	adv.	suddenly; abruptly
蓝天	lántiān	n.	blue sky
白云	báiyún	n.	white cloud
奥运会	Àoyùn huì	n.	Olympic Games
会议	huìyì	n.	conference; meeting
举行	jǔxíng	v.	to hold (a meeting, ceremony, etc.)
难得	nándé	adj.	rare, hard-earned (chance, opportunity)
意外	yìwài	adj.	be surprised; be taken by surprise
瞧	qiáo	v.	Look! (used to direct someone's attention to

们共产党 行！要蓝天，有蓝天；要白云，有白云！连天气都得听党 的领导！"

据科学 研究分析，形成 雾霾的主要原因是工业 污染和汽车排放 的废气 。近几年，中国汽车的销售量 已经超过 了美国。结果，造成了城市交通瘫痪 和空气的严重污染。这样的改变到底是进步还是退步？ 如果经济的发展必须用生活品质 的恶化 来作为 代价，这样的经济发展值得 吗？

			something or someone)
咱们	zánmen	pron.	we; us (including both the speaker and the listener)
共产党	Gòngchǎndǎng	n.	The Communist Party
行	xíng	adj.	capable; competent
党	dǎng	n.	political part; here it is short for the CPC
领导	lǐngdǎo	v./n.	lead; to exercise leadership
科学	kēxué	n.	science
分析	fēnxī	v./n.	to analyze; analysis
形成	xíngchéng	v.	to form; to come into being
工业	gōngyè	n.	industry
排放	páifàng	v.	to emit; to discharge
废气	fèiqì	n.	waste gas or steam; exhaust
销售量	xiāoshòu liàng	n.	sales
超过	chāoguò	v.	to exceed; to surpass
瘫痪	tānhuàn	v.	to be paralyzed
退步	tuìbù	v.	retrogress; to lag behind
品质	pǐnzhì	n.	quality (of life, of a product or service)
恶化	èhuà	v.	deteriorate; worsen
作为	zuòwéi	prep.	as
代价	dàijià	n.	cost
值得	zhídé	v.	be worth

I. 词语搭配 *Collocation*

1. 严重的污染/问题

   severe pollution/ problem

2. ……对健康/身体/环境+有害

   be detrimental to one's health/body/environment

3. 病得很厉害/疼得很厉害/咳嗽咳得很厉害/拉肚子拉得很厉害

   to be gravely ill/to be in extreme pain/to cough severely/to have severe diarrhea

4. 把……遮住

   to cover, to overlay

5. … a concrete example…表现……的幽默/热情/特点/态度

   to show…a good sense of humor/one's passion/the characteristics of…/one's attitude

6. 恶劣的环境/条件/天气

   (a) hostile environment/conditions/weather

7. 活动/会议+在 place 举行

   (of an event/conference) to take place (at a certain place)

8. 享受+生活/好天气/周到的服务

   to enjoy life/good weather/full and thorough service

9. 难得的机会/好天气/人才

   rare chance/good weather/talented person

10. 排放+废气/污染物/污水

    to emit emissions/pollutant/polluted water

11. A 的销售量/数量/成绩/水平+超过 B

    sales/amount/grade/level of A exceeds that of B

12. 交通/身体/电脑+瘫痪

    Traffic at a standstill/one's body is paralyzed/computer completely dies

13. 社会/经济+进步（Attention："进步"doesn't take any object.）

    to advance social/economic progress

14. 环境/关系/生活品质/……问题+恶化

deterioration of environment/relationship (between two countries)/quality of life/ [some sort of] problem

II. 句型结构 *Sentence Pattern and Structure*

1. Subj. + phrase 1，而且 phrase 2

   "而且" is a conjunction often used to connect two predicates, whereas "和" usually connects two nouns or noun phrases.

   "雾霾"的"霾"字很难写，而且不常用。

   骑自行车可以锻炼身体，而且对保护环境有好处。

   In the two examples below, "和" cannot be replaced by "而且" 比如：

   老师和学生都喜欢这个饭馆。

   中国文化和美国文化有很大的不同。

2. …statement (high degree)…，连 extreme example 都……

   The "连…都" pattern, meaning "even," is often used to stress an extreme example that lends support to the preceding statement.

   "雾霾"的"霾"字很难写，而且不常用，连很多中国人都不认得，不会写。

   他的朋友非常有钱，连飞机都买得起。可是他却穷得要命，连汉堡包都买不起。

3. Subj.+…，(但是)……却…… contrary to what is expected

   The clause after 却 introduces an unusual situation that comes contrary to what was expected.

   "雾霾"的"霾"字很难写，而且不常用，但是近几年来却成了到中国来的外国人第一个必须学习的汉字！

   他很老，但是走路却走得比年轻人快。

   他是个中国人，但是却不喜欢吃中国菜。

4. Object 看起来+ (有点儿／很) 像＋noun (phrase)

This pattern is often used to make a judgment or conjecture based on initial observation, which may or may not turn out to be true (please note that "像" cannot be omitted in this structure).

雾霾看起来有点儿像雾，可是又不是雾.

他虽然已经三十岁了，可是看起来还像二十岁的大学生。

5. (B 很 adj./有点儿 undesirable adj.)，A 比 B 更 adj.

This is a comparative structure, emphasizing that although B displays a certain trait, A is *even* greater in amount, number, size, degree, etc. The trait raised in the first part of this pattern, which often can be omitted, is acceptable for both speaker and the listener.

在雾霾严重的环境里生活一天，比一天抽两包烟对身体更不好。

（日本社会很发达，）美国比日本更发达。

（张三有点儿矮，）他的弟弟比他更矮。

6. A 劝 B +V.P./不要 V.P.

This pattern is used to give a mild warning.

我的中国朋友都劝我戴口罩。

现在北京的污染很严重，我的家人都劝我不要去北京学中文。

7. Others……，(但) 我倒……

This pattern is used to bring up an opinion, usually opposite to what is popularly or generally expected or believed, but in an agreeable and inoffensive way.

北京有雾霾，我的中国朋友都劝我戴口罩，但我倒不太担心。

他常常不上课，大家都说他是一个坏学生，可是我倒觉得他不一定有错，有可能他的老师教得不好，所以他不喜欢上课。

很多人都不喜欢麦当劳,觉得他们的东西不健康,但我倒比较喜欢在麦当劳吃饭,因为至少他们的东西比较卫生。

8. …phenomenon…，显然，…reasoning…（point out a reason/inference/conclusion）

The clause after *xiǎnrán* 显然 introduces an obvious explanation for the preceding phenomenon.

中国八九十岁的老人很多，显然，雾霾对健康的伤害并没有那么严重。

运动员的身体一般都很好，显然，运动对身体是有好处的。

9. Subj. 从来没 V 过（O）

This pattern means that the subject has never had the experience of doing something before (The aspect marker "过" cannot be omitted).

我在美国从来没戴过口罩。

他从来没去过中国。

Compare：Subj. 从来不 V.P.

Subj. 从来不 V.P., meaning the subject never does something, suggests that the subject does not like, or is not interested in, doing something.

他觉得酒吧太吵，从来不去酒吧。

他吃素，从来不吃肉。

10. 认/看/吃/听/闻+得/不+出来

(able/unable) to determine (what/who it is) by looking/tasting/listening/smelling

戴了口罩把脸遮住了，有的时候连老朋友也认不出来了！

你看得出来这是一个什么东西吗？

11. 跟……有关的 noun

This is a noun phrase, meaning "concerning/regarding."

戴了口罩把脸遮住了，有的时候连老朋友也认不出来了！所以，有不少跟雾霾有关的笑话。

跟学习有关的问题，你可以问老师。跟生活有关的问题，你应该去问你的同学。

12. V+错+object

   Cuò 错 is a verb complement in this pattern, to emphasize that what is done has been done mistakenly.

   因为看不清楚，恋人约会的时候认错了对象；放学的时候，家长接错了孩子。

   汉字很难记住，所以学生常常写错汉字。

13. 在……环境/情况/制度/ +下，……

   This pattern, meaning "under certain conditions/circumstances/situations/rules and regulations," is used to describe the conditions under which an event occurs.

   中国人是个很有幽默感的民族，他们往往可以在非常恶劣的环境下苦中作乐。

   在以前的制度下，中国人不用自己找工作，他们靠政府分配工作。

   在人少的情况下，老师可以给学生更多的帮助。

14. ……的时候/在……下，……往往……

   This pattern is used when the subject exhibits an inclination or tendency under certain circumstances or at a certain time.

   中国人是个很有幽默感的民族，他们往往可以在非常恶劣的环境下自己取乐。

   在游客过多的情况下，旅游景点往往会想办法限制游客的数量。

   下雨的时候，我往往在家里看书，不喜欢出门。

15. Subj.在 time duration 之内+achieve a goal

   (To achieve a goal or to complete a task) within a short period of time

   北京的雾霾遇到有重要活动的时候，往往可以在短时间之内，突然变成蓝天白云。

   别人考试得考三个小时，可是他在一个小时之内就可以做完，真是聪明。

16. 还是 sb./organization 行

This pattern is an implicit comparison and is often used when the speaker, after further reflection, finally realizes or comes to the conclusion that a person or an organization is more capable than originally thought.

你瞧，还是咱们共产党行！要蓝天，有蓝天；要白云，有白云！别的国家的政府怎么可能有这种能力？

还是你哥哥行，别人都不会做的作业，他半个小时就做完了。

那次比赛以后我发现，还是我们的学生行。别的学校的学生都不如我们的学生。

17. ...statement..., 要 A，有 A；要 B，有 B

This pattern is usually used to describe a person, an organization, or a country that is rich in resources, money, possessions, etc.

你瞧，还是咱们共产党行！要蓝天，有蓝天；要白云，有白云！

以前中国人吃不饱，穿不暖；但现在，中国人要房子有房子，要汽车有汽车，生活水平提高了很多。

现在中国要钱有钱，要人才有人才，所以发展得特别快。

18. 据 source of information 分析/研究/报道，...information...

This pattern introduces the source of information, lending credence to the information provided.

据科学研究分析，形成雾霾的主要原因是工业污染和汽车排放的废气。

据《纽约时报》报道，去年中国汽车的销售量已经超过了美国。

19. ...unfavorable situation in the past..., 结果，...undesirable result...

Jiéguǒ 结果 is often used to narrate an action in the past as well as its result and impact, which is often undesirable and negative.

这几年，中国汽车的销售量已经超过了美国。结果，造成了城市交通瘫痪和空气的严重污染。

他上个星期没好好准备考试，结果，他考得很不好。

10

20. ……造成…undesirable…的问题

To cause or produce something negative (i.e. problem, negative effect, etc.)

汽车越来越多造成了城市交通瘫痪的问题。

空气污染造成很多人出现咳嗽和喉咙不舒服的问题。

21. A 的成功/发展/提高/进步…以/用 B(来)作为代价

用/以 B 作为 A 的代价　　　to do one thing at the cost of something else

经济的发展需要用环境作为代价。

成绩的提高需要用健康作为代价吗？

22. Subj. 到底 + interrogative sentence / A 不 A/ A 还是 B？

Dàodǐ 到底 can be added before an interrogative sentence to show that the speaker is profoundly confused (as in Example 1) or to express the speaker's eagerness to know the answer (Example 2).

汽车虽然让我们的生活更方便，但汽车太多，造成交通瘫痪和空气污染，这样的改变到底是进步还是退步？

你到底有什么计划？快点儿告诉我。

23. ……，这样做值得吗？ Is it worth it?

如果经济的发展必须用生活品质的恶化来作为代价，这样做值得吗？

花两个月时间和几千美元来北京学中文，这样做值得吗？

III. 词语辨析 *Synonym Differentiation*

1. 成了+noun：to become (change in function or role, but without change in nature)

变成+noun：to turn into, to transform (usually a dramatic change)

雾霾的"霾"字本来是个罕见的字，可是现在却成了到中国来的外国人第一个必须学的汉字。

北京的雾霾遇到有重要活动的时候，往往可以在短时间之内突然变成蓝天白云。

11

2. 生活：to live (to live in a specified place; to spend your life or part of your life)

　　住：　to dwell, to occupy a home

　　在雾霾严重的环境里生活一天，比一天抽两包烟对身体更不好。

　　你在北京生活过吗？/ 我在北京住过三年。

3. 往往：　a habitual tendency or an inclination exhibited under a specific circumstance

　　常常：　a high frequency

　　晚上不上课的时候，学生往往去喝酒。

　　我常常去喝酒，每个星期都要去 3 次酒吧。

霧霾

　　"霧霾"的"霾"字很難寫,而且不常用,連很多中國人都不認得,不會寫。但是近幾年,這個罕見的字,卻成了到中國來的外國人第一個必須學習的漢字!

　　霧霾就是比較嚴重的空氣污染,看起來有點像霧,可是又不是霧。有霧霾的時候,一天 24 小時都是灰濛濛的,看不清楚遠處的東西。最嚴重的時候,連學校的高樓都看不太清楚。

　　據說,霧霾對健康有害,在霧霾嚴重的環境裏生活一天,比一天抽兩包煙對身體更不好。有時候,我從外面跑步回來,覺得喉嚨很不舒服,咳嗽咳得很厲害。我的中國朋友都勸我戴口罩,但我倒不太擔心,因為中國八九十歲的老人很多,顯然,霧霾對健康的傷害並沒有那麼嚴重。而且,我在美國從來沒戴過口罩。戴了口罩,看起來很奇怪,也很不舒服。

　　在街上戴口罩的人還真不少。戴了口罩把臉遮住了,有的時候連老朋友也認不出來了! 所以,在北京有不少跟霧霾有關的笑話。像放學的時候,家長接錯了孩子;戀人約會,認錯了對象,甚至跟陌生人親了嘴。當然,這樣的笑話很誇張,但也表現了中國人的幽默。中國人是個很有幽默感的民族,他們往往可以在非常惡劣的環境下苦中作乐,用一種無奈又風趣的態度來面對問題。

　　北京的霧霾,遇到有重要活動的時候,往往可以在短時間之內,突然變成藍天白雲。像 2008 年的奧運會、2014 年的 APEC 會議在北京舉行的時候,北京人享受了幾天難得的好天氣,大家都很意外,也很高興,把這樣的藍天叫做:"奧運藍",或"APEC 藍"。老百姓都說:"你瞧,還是咱們共產黨行! 要藍天,有藍天;要白雲,有白雲! 連天氣都得聽党的領導!"

　　據科學研究分析,形成霧霾的主要原因是工業污染和汽車排放的廢氣。近幾年,中國汽車的銷售量已經超過了美國。結果,造成了城市交通癱瘓和空氣的嚴重污染。這樣的改變到底是進步還是退步? 如果經濟的發展必須用生活品質的惡化來作為代價,這樣的經濟發展值得嗎?

课后习题
第1课

一、词语搭配 (Please pair the term in the left column with the most appropriate term in the right column. Then use the completed phrases to complete the sentences. You can change the order of the words and add more information if needed.)

（1）

(B) 享受　　　A 恶化
(D) 严重的　　B 生活
(A) 生活品质　C 幽默
(C) 表现　　　D 污染

Example：（　D　）：严重的 + 污染
很多人离开大城市主要是因为 大城市的污染太严重了 。

1. 很多中国人只知道工作赚钱,不会_____ B _____。

2. 为了_____ C _____,他常常讲笑话,可是他讲的笑话有时候一点儿都不好笑。

3. 虽然人们的收入提高了,但是因为污染越来越严重,_____ A _____。

（2）

(B) 交通　　A 机会
(C) 排放　　B 瘫痪
(A) 难得的　C 污染物

1. 能去美国留学,对年轻的大学生来说,_____ A _____。

2. 一场大雨以后,这个城市的_____ B _____,路上的车都排着长长的队。

3. 政府关掉了很多工厂,因为_____ C _____。

14

（3）

(C) 社会　　　　A 条件
(A) 恶劣的　　　B 会议
(B) 举行　　　　C 进步

1. 这个地方_____A_____,不但冬天很长,而且有严重的污染问题。
2. 我们怎么知道____C____还是在退步?是不是应该看人们的思想观念的改变?
3. 为了加强与其他国家的经济交流,中国决定_____B_____。

二、选择填空 (Complete the sentences by choosing the most appropriate term.)

1. 成了　　变成

   他 2000 年进入这家公司。一年以后,他____A____公司的领导。

   老虎怎么可能____B____狮子呢?我不相信!

2. 生活　　住

   你____B____几楼?

   我父母不喜欢在美国____A____,因为他们没有朋友。

3. 往往　　常常

   我搬到北京以后,请你____B____来我家玩儿。

   下雨的时候,人们____A____选择坐公共汽车。

三、完成句子 (Complete the sentence or dialogue with the given item in parentheses.)

1. A:夏天这么热,中国人也都喝冰水吧?
   B:不是这样的,虽然夏天很热,但是中国人却不喜欢喝冰水。(...但是...却...)
2. A:美国这么发达,我觉得美国政府一定很有钱。
   B:你错了。美国政府花很多钱,但是它却有很多债务。(...但是...却...)

3. 很多人都觉得离婚是一个道德问题,但我倒有时离婚是最好选择。(但我倒…)

4. 我的朋友都劝我不要选中文专业,但我倒中文专业又有趣又有用。(但我倒…)

5. 抽烟的人常常觉得喉咙不舒服,显然他们应该戒烟。(显然)

6. 这里的天总是灰蒙蒙的,显然污染染很严重。(显然)

7. A: 雾霾严重的时候,人们应该怎么做?

B: 在这个情况下,人们应该戴口罩。(在…情况下)

8. A: 学生可不可以要求改变期末考试(final exam)的时间?

B: 在期末考试学生着手反情况下,不可以改变。(在…情况下)

9. A: 期末考试的时候,学生有多长时间来完成考试?

B: 学生应该在两个小时之内来完成考试。(在…之内)

10. A: 你觉得中国的经济会超过美国吗?

B: 在短时间之内,中国经济不会超过美国的。(在…之内)

11. 现在的中国很发达,要工作有工作。(要 A 有 A,要 B 有 B)

12. 苹果公司是世界上最厉害的公司之一,要员工有员工。(要 A 有 A,要 B 有 B)

13. A: 你会为了变成有钱人而跟不喜欢的人结婚吗?

B: 对,变成有钱人需要用幸福作为代价。(用…作为代价)

14. A: 我觉得发展经济比保护环境重要,你觉得呢?

B: 我不愿意故让发展经济用环境作为代价。(用…作为代价)

15. 汽车给人们的生活带来了方便,但也造成了很多问题。有时候,我常常想:

汽车到底值得的? (到底)

16. 我昨天去找了你好几次,可是你都不在。你到底在哪儿? (到底)

四、回答问题 (Answer the questions.)

1. 什么是雾霾?雾霾对老百姓的生活有什么影响?

2. 北京的雾霾严重吗?有哪些例子可以说明?

3. 为什么中国的雾霾问题这么严重?

4. 雾霾这么严重,中国人是不是每天都很难过?

5. 遇到重要的活动,北京的空气质量会有什么改变?老百姓对此有什么看法?

6. 用生活品质的恶化来作为经济发展的代价,这样做到底值不值得？为什么？

7. 只有中国存在环境污染的问题吗？什么样的国家比较容易出现严重的污染问题？为什么？

8. 在历史上,欧美发达国家出现过严重的污染问题吗？污染问题是不是发展经济一定会遇到的问题？

9. 作者对中国政府的态度是什么样的？你觉得中国政府能解决雾霾问题吗？

10. 你觉得中国政府会不会喜欢这篇课文？为什么？

第 2 课

龙与熊猫

中国人常喜欢用龙来代表中国。

　　龙是一种传说中的动物，看起来有点儿像长了四条腿的蟒蛇，眼睛突出，张着嘴巴，嘴巴上长着胡子，有时还喷着火，张牙舞爪，样子可怕极了。可是，中国人很喜欢龙，常说他们是"龙的传人"。龙在古代中国也

龙	lóng	n.	dragon
熊猫	xióngmāo	n.	panda
代表	dàibiǎo	v./n.	to represent; representation
传说	chuánshuō	n.	legend; folklore
蟒蛇	mǎngshé	n.	serpent; python
突出	tūchū	v.	to protrude; to stick out
张	zhāng	v.	to open (one's mouth/eyes)
嘴巴	zuǐbā	n.	mouth
长	zhǎng	v.	(of hair, beard or mustache) to grow
胡子	húzi	n.	(in this context) barbel; beard; mustache
喷	pēn	v.	to shoot; to spurt; spout
火	huǒ	n.	fire
张牙舞爪	zhāngyá wǔzhǎo	idm.	(lit.) to bare fangs and brandish claws; to make threatening gestures
样子	yàngzi	n.	appearance
可怕	kěpà	adj.	fearful; terrifying
龙的传人	lóng de chuánrén	n.	Descendants of the Dragon
古代	gǔdài	adj.	ancient

是皇帝 的象征，一般老百姓是不许随便把龙绣 在衣服上的。

　　如果中国给外国人的印象 就像一条龙，瞪 着大眼睛，张牙舞爪，我觉得那是不幸 的，也是一种误导。我希望中国给人的印象更像熊猫——可爱，温和，但并不软弱，就像电影《功夫熊猫 》里的熊猫。要是有人欺负 他，他的"中国功夫"足够 自卫 。熊猫不是宠物，但他是大家的朋友，不伤害别人。他不像老虎、狮子，凶猛 而且带着攻击性 。

皇帝	huángdì	n.	emperor
象征	xiàngzhēng	v./n.	to symbolize; symbol
绣	xiù	v.	to embroider
印象	yìnxiàng	n.	impression
瞪	dèng	v.	to stare; to glare
不幸	búxìng	adj.	unfortunate; sad
误导	wùdǎo	v./n.	to mislead; to misguide
温和	wēnhé	adj.	mild; gentle
软弱	ruǎnruò	adj.	weak; soft (of character)
功夫熊猫	Gōngfu Xióngmāo		Kung Fu Panda, a 2008 American animated film produced by DreamWorks Animation
欺负	qīfu	v.	to bully
足够	zúgòu	adj./adv.	enough; sufficient; sufficiently
自卫	zìwèi	v./n.	to defend oneself; self-defense
宠物	chǒngwù	n.	pet
凶猛	xiōngměng	adj.	(of an animal) fierce
攻击性	gōngjī xìng	n.	aggressiveness; combativeness

　　除了龙以外，中国形象的另一个代表大概是长城。长城是人类历史上最伟大的建筑之一，为了防御北方的敌人，古代中国人在群山之间建了一道长达万里的城墙，这是人类建筑史上的奇迹。中国人应该感到自豪。可是，城墙毕竟代表封闭，城墙一方面使外面的敌人进不来，但另一方面也让里头的中国人出不去。

　　我希望现代的中国是一个开放的中国，一个包容的中国。所以，我觉

形象	xíngxiàng	n.	image
长城	Chángchéng	n.	the Great Wall
人类	rénlèi	n.	humans; mankind
伟大	wěidà	adj.	great (worthy of the greatest admiration)
建筑	jiànzhù	n.	structure; building; architecture
防御	fángyù	v.	to defend; to guard
敌人	dírén	n.	enemy
群山	qúnshān	n.	mountain range
建	jiàn	v.	to build
道	dào	m.w.	measure word for doors, walls, etc.
里	lǐ	n.	traditional unit of length, equal to 0.5 kilometers
城墙	chéngqiáng	n.	city wall
--史	shǐ	suffix	the history of...
奇迹	qíjì	n.	miracle; wonder
自豪	zìháo	adj.	be proud (of one's identity, country, etc.)
毕竟	bìjìng	conj.	after all (used to point out an undeniable fact)
封闭	fēngbì	adj.	closed
包容	bāoróng	adj./v.	inclusive; tolerant; to tolerate

得代表现代中国的应该是现代化的机场、港口 和四通八达 的高速 铁路和公路，而不应该再是困 在长城里的一条龙了。

港口	gǎngkǒu	n.	port; harbor
四通八达	sìtōng bādá	idm.	(of roads) to extend in all directions; (of a place) be accessible from all sides
高速	gāosù	adj.	high-speed (modifier)
困	kùn	v.	to trap; to strand

I. 词语搭配 *Collocation*

1. 传说＋中＋的 noun

   legendary (personage, etc.)

2. 张+开+嘴巴/眼睛

   to open one's mouth/eyes

3. 头上+长+头发　or　脸上+长+胡子

   hair/facial hair growing out

4. 把 A 绣在＋B 上

   to embroider A on B

5. A 瞪着 B　　　　　　A stares at B

   ……瞪着＋大眼睛　　　to stare (usually in anger)

6. ……误导 sb.　　　… to mislead sb.

   sb.被……误导　　sb. is misled by …

7. A 欺负 B　　　A bullies B

   B 被 / 受 A 欺负　　B is bullied by A

8. 凶猛的动物（老虎/狮子 etc.）

   ferocious animal

9. 形象＋很 / 不+好

   the image (is) good/bad

10. 历史+上

    in history

11. 防御+敌人（的攻击）

    to guard against assault from external enemies

12. 封闭的社会 / 环境

    a closed society/closed environment

13. 四通八达的铁路/公路

    railways/highways that radiate in all directions

14. ……困在 place 里

be stranded/trapped in a certain place

II. 句型结构 *Sentence Pattern and Structure*

1. …people…用 A 来代表 B　　　　use A to represent/stand for B

   A 代表 B　　　　　　　　　　　A represents B

   中国人常常用龙来代表中国。

   城墙代表封闭，四通八达的高速铁路代表开放。

2. Verb 着 object

   Zhe 着 indicates a state or continued action, for example, "the dragon, with its bulging eyes, and with its mouth wide open, on which grows barbel, and flames sometimes shoots out, bares its fangs and brandishes its claws, is extremely terrifying in appearance."

   龙眼睛突出，张着嘴巴，嘴巴上长着胡子，有时还喷着火，张牙舞爪，样子可怕极了。

   有雾霾的时候，很多人都戴着口罩。

3. A（with authority）不许 B+ V.P.　　A does not allow B to do sth.

   B 不许+V.P.　　　　　　　　　　B is not allowed to do sth.

   在古代中国，皇帝不许老百姓把龙绣在衣服上。

   龙在古代中国是皇帝象征，一般老百姓是不许随便把龙绣在衣服上的。

4. A 给 B 的印象＋很好 / 不好　　A gave B a good/bad impression.

   A 给 B 的印象是…clause…　　　The (first) impression that A gave B was that…/B's first impression of A was that…

   中国游客给西方人的印象不太好，因为他们常常不排队。

   中国给外国人的印象是经济发展得很快，但环境却越来越差。

5. …statement…, Sth. 足够（subj.）+V.P.

… is enough (for Subj.) to do sth; to have sufficient…to do sth.

要是有人欺负熊猫，它的"中国功夫"足够自卫。

今天买了很多东西，足够我们吃一个星期。

6. Specific noun 是（scope…）最 adj.的 general noun 之一

…is one of the most adj. in…

长城是人类历史上最伟大的建筑之一。

美国是世界上人口最多的国家之一。

7. 长达＋num.＋公里／米（meter）的 noun

高达＋num.＋米的 noun

重达＋num.＋公斤／磅的 noun

This noun phrase is used to describe somebody or something with a significant length, height, or weight.

古代中国人在群山之间建了一道长达一万多里的城墙。

故宫的外面建了一座高达十几米的门楼，那就是天安门。

颐和园里放着一头重达两千多公斤的铁牛。

8. 虽然……，但是……毕竟…point out an undeniable fact…

This structure, meaning "after all," is used to point out an undeniable fact, emphasizing that this fact needs to be considered.

虽然长城是人类建筑史上的奇迹,中国人应该感到骄傲,但是城墙毕竟代表封闭:城墙一方面使外面的敌人进不来,但另一方面也让里面的中国人出不去。

虽然他做错了,但是他毕竟只是一个孩子。你不能因为他打破了个杯子就要打他。

9. ……，一方面……，但另一方面也……

On one hand…, but on the other hand…

城墙一方面使外面的敌人进不来，但另一方面也让里面的中国人出不去。

去外国留学一方面能让你更好地了解当地的文化，但另一方面也会给你的生活带来不小的挑战。

10. …是…noun1…，而不再是…noun2…了

This structure emphasizes the current state, through a contrast between the past and the present.

我觉得代表现代中国的应该是现代化的机场、港口和四通八达的高速铁路，而不应该再是困在长城里的一条龙了。

中国现在已经是个强大的国家，而不再是一个贫穷落后的半殖民地了。

III. 词语辨析 *Synonym Differentiation*

1. A（with authority）不许 B +V.P.　　　A does not allow B to do sth

　　B 不许+ V.P.　　　　　　B is not allowed to do sth; B must not do sth.

以前，皇帝不许老百姓随便把龙绣在衣服上。

以前，老百姓不许随便把龙绣在衣服上。

A（with authority）不让 B + V.P.　A does not let B do sth.

以前，皇帝不让老百姓随便把龙绣在衣服上。

A（with authority）让 B + V.P.　　　A let B do sth.

不上课的时候，父母会让我晚一点儿回家。

龍與熊貓

中國人常喜歡用龍來代表中國。

龍是一種傳說中的動物，看起來有點兒像長了四條腿的蟒蛇，眼睛突出，張著嘴巴，嘴巴上長著鬍子，有時還噴著火，張牙舞爪，樣子可怕極了。可是，中國人很喜歡龍，常說他們是"龍的傳人"。龍在古代中國也是皇帝的象徵，一般老百姓是不許隨便把龍繡在衣服上的。

如果中國給外國人的印象就像一條龍，瞪著大眼睛，張牙舞爪，我覺得那是不幸的，也是一種誤導。我希望中國給人的印象更像熊貓——可愛，溫和，但並不軟弱，就像電影《功夫熊貓》裡的熊貓。要是有人欺負他，他的"中國功夫"足夠自衛。熊貓不是寵物，但他是大家的朋友，不傷害別人。他不像老虎、獅子，兇猛而且帶著攻擊性。

除了龍以外，中國形象的另一個代表大概是長城。長城是人類歷史上最偉大的建築之一，為了防禦北方的敵人，古代中國人在群山之間建了一道長達万里的城牆，這是人類建築史上的奇跡。中國人應該感到自豪。可是，城牆畢竟代表封閉，城牆一方面使外面的敵人進不來，但另一方面也讓裡頭的中國人出不去。

我希望現代的中國是一個開放的中國，一個包容的中國。所以，我覺得代表現代中國的應該是現代化的機場、港口和四通八達的高速鐵路，而不应該再是困在長城裏的一條龍了。

课后习题
第 2 课

一、词语搭配 (Please pair the term in the left column with the most appropriate term in the right column. Then use the completed phrases to complete the sentences. You can change the order of the words and add more information if needed.)

(C) 凶猛的　　　　A 环境
(A) 封闭的　　　　B 大眼睛
(E) 四通八达的　　C 动物
(D) 张开　　　　　D 嘴巴
(B) 瞪着　　　　　E 铁路

1. 普通人不能养狮子、老虎,因为_____C_____。
2. 他为什么_____B_____? 是不是生气了?
3. 这个国家现在有_____E_____,去哪儿都很方便。
4. 这个国家的人民生活在_____A_____,完全不了解外面的世界。
5. 你说话得_____D_____,要不然,别人根本听不清楚你说什么。

二、选择填空 (Complete the sentences by choosing the most appropriate term.)

1. 不许　A　　不让　B
   在家里,父母从来__B__他自己洗衣服、洗碗,什么事都帮他做。
   这瓶酒你__A__喝,这是给你爸爸买的。

三、完成句子 (Complete the sentence or dialogue with the given item in parentheses.)

1. 长城是人类建筑史上的奇迹,我觉得__中国人用长城来代表他们__。(用 A 来代表 B)
2. A:为什么故宫（The Forbidden City）里有那么多龙呢?

B：因为龙代表皇帝 _____ 。（A 代表 B）

3. 我看不清楚他的脸，因为他 戴着口罩 _____ 。（V 着 O）

4. A：你昨天晚上怎么没来喝酒啊？

B：因为女友不许我出去 _____ 。（A 不许 B V.P.）

5. 这是图书馆，你不许喊出来 _____ 。（不许 V.P.）

6. A：听说你去过北京，你觉得那个地方怎么样？

B：北京给我的印象是很好 _____ 。（A 给 B 的印象是…）

7. A：我一个月给你五千块钱，够不够？

B：够，够，够，五千块钱足够交租 _____ 。（足够+V.P. …）

8. A：你觉得美国政府应不应该每年把那么钱花在军队上？

B：美国的军事预算足够多维持战备状态 _____ 。（足够+V.P. …）

9. A：为什么有那么多人去参观长城？

B：因为长城是世界奇观之一 _____ 。（…之一）

10. A：为什么在美国很多人都想当律师？

B：因为律师是最赚钱的工作之一 _____ 。（…之一）

11. A：熊猫真可爱，我想养一只熊猫。

B：虽然熊猫很可爱，但是他们毕竟是野生动物 _____ 。（虽然…，但是…毕竟…）

12. A：美国经济这么发达，我想美国应该没有穷人了吧。

B：虽然美国很发达，但是贫富毕竟很不平等 _____ 。（虽然 …，但是…毕竟…）

13. 在这个地方开工厂，_____ 。（一方面…，但另一方面也…）

14. 汽车越来越多，一方面方便的，另增加排放 。（一方面…，但另一方面也…）

15. 现在的中国已经 是很有钱而不再是贫困的 。（…是 n.1，而不再是 n.2 了）

四、回答问题 (Answer the questions.)

1. 中国人对"龙"的态度是什么？

2. 西方人对"龙"的印象跟中国人一样吗？为什么有这样的不同？

3. 作者为什么觉得代表中国的动物应该是"熊猫"，而不是"龙"？你同意吗？你觉得龙和熊猫哪一个更能代表中国？

28

4. 长城是什么样的建筑？作者对长城的看法是什么？他的看法有没有道理？

5. 作者认为最能代表"现代中国"的是什么？你同意他的看法吗？

6. 你觉得什么可以代表你的国家？为什么？

第 3 课

软实力

软实力是最近 20 年来汉语中的一个新词。

如果军事力量是硬实力，那么文化力量就是软实力。美国不但在硬实力上，是世界上最强大的国家，在软实力上，美国的电影、电视剧、音乐、饮食、服装，甚至于运动都引领着世界的时尚。

对一般中国老百姓来说，他们对美国的硬实力并没有直接的感受，但是美国的软实力却在日常生活中影响着千千万万的中国人。穿牛仔裤、运

软实力	ruǎn shílì	n.	soft power
军事	jūnshì	n.	military
力量	lìliàng	n.	(physical) strength, ability, power
硬实力	yìng shílì	n.	hard power (military and economic power)
强大	qiángdà	adj.	powerful; strong
电视剧	diànshì jù	n.	TV show/TV series
饮食	yǐnshí	n.	cuisine; food and drink
服装	fúzhuāng	n.	clothing; costume
引领	yǐnlǐng	v.	to lead (e.g. the trend)
时尚	shíshàng	n./adj.	fashion; fashionable
直接	zhíjiē	adj.	direct
感受	gǎnshòu	n.	experience, feeling
日常生活	rìcháng shēnghuó	n.	daily life
千千万万	qiānqiān wànwàn	idm.	thousands upon thousands
牛仔裤	niúzǎi kù	n.	jeans

动鞋，吃麦当劳的汉堡包，喝可口可乐，听美国音乐，看美国电影，已经成了中国人城市生活的一部分。换句话说，中国人在不知不觉中不但接受了美国人的生活方式，而且认同了美国人的价值观。这样看来，美国的软实力可能比硬实力更有影响力。飞机和大炮只能征服土地，而电影、音乐和饮食却可以征服人心。

中国政府对这样的发展是有些顾虑的，但是也想不出什么有效的对策来防止无处不在的西化。有人建议，应该提倡传统中国文化来应对美国

换句话说	huànjùhuàshuō	interj.	in other words
不知不觉	bùzhībùjué	adv.	unconsciously
认同	rèntóng	v.	to identify with (values/cultures/ideas)
价值观	jiàzhí guān	n.	values
影响力	yǐngxiǎnglì	n.	(of a person or country) influence; clout
大炮	dàpào	n.	cannon; artillery
征服	zhēngfú	v.	to conquer; to subdue
土地	tǔdì	n.	land; territory
人心	rénxīn	n.	the will of the people; public feeling
顾虑	gùlǜ	n.	concern
有效	yǒuxiào	adj.	effective
对策	duìcè	n.	the way to deal with a situation
防止	fángzhǐ	v.	to prevent
无处不在	wúchù búzài	idm.	be everywhere; ubiquitous
西化	xīhuà	v./n.	to westernize; Westernization
建议	jiànyì	v.	to suggest; to propose
提倡	tíchàng	v.	to advocate; to promote
应对	yìngduì	v.	to respond (to a change)

软实力的影响，比方说，把清明节、端午节 等传统节日 定为法定假日。

　　近几年来，在中国，从建筑到服装，我们都可以看到一定的复古 倾向。中国人一说到中国文化，说的往往都是中国的旧传统。像书法、茶道、剪纸、功夫、中国结 等等。这些中国人最常介绍给外国人看的所谓"中国文化"，其实，在中国人的日常生活中并不占 重要的地位，甚至正在慢慢地消失。要外国人接受连中国人自己都不感兴趣 的"中国文化"，这是一件很困难的事。

清明节	Qīngmíng jié	n.	Qingming Festival (Tomb Sweeping Day) in early April (lunar month)
端午节	Duānwǔ jié	n.	the Dragon Boat Festival (the fifth day of the fifth lunar month)
节日	jiérì	n.	festival
定为	dìngwéi	v.	to establish as; to recognize as
法定假日	fǎdìng jiàrì	n.	official holidays
复古	fùgǔ	v.-o.	(lit.) to revert to or restore old/ancient ways
倾向	qīngxiàng	n.	tendency; inclination
书法	shūfǎ	n.	calligraphy
茶道	chádào	n.	tea ceremony
剪纸	jiǎnzhǐ	n.	papercutting (traditional Chinese folk art form)
中国结	zhōngguó jié	n.	Chinese knots (traditional Chinese folk art form)
介绍	jièshào	v./n.	to introduce; introduction
占	zhàn	v.	to take up; to occupy
消失	xiāoshī	v.	to disappear
感兴趣	gǎnxìngqu	v.-o.	be interested in…

中国政府在世界各地成立孔子学院，也是希望把中国的语言和文化介绍给外国人。中国的旅游、饮食、文学、艺术和杂技都是软实力最好的资源。我希望美国人也能用比较开放的态度来欣赏中国文化。

世界各地	shìjiè gèdì	idm.	all parts of the world; all over the world;
成立	chénglì	v.	to establish (an organization)
孔子学院	Kǒngzǐ Xuéyuàn	n.	Confucius Institute, established overseas by the PRC government to promote Chinese language and culture.
旅游	lǚyóu	n./v.	traveling; tourism
文学	wénxué	n.	literature
艺术	yìshù	n.	art
杂技	zájì	n.	acrobatics
资源	zīyuán	n.	resources
欣赏	xīnshǎng	v.	to appreciate or enjoy (art/literature/acrobatics)

I. 词语搭配 *Collocation*

1. 力量/实力+强大

   one's power/strength is great

2. 饮食+习惯/文化

   culinary habits/culture

3. 引领+时尚

   to lead the trend

4. sb. 对……有／没有＋直接/强烈+的感受

   sb. has/doesn't have direct feelings/strong feelings toward…

5. 认同+价值观/文化/观念

   to identify with a certain value/culture/idea

6. Sb. 对…有些顾虑

   sb. is concerned about...

7. 想得出／想不出＋对策／办法

   able/unable to figure out a countermeasure/solution

8. 应对＋……的影响／变化

   to respond to/to cope with the influence of … /the change

9. ……的影响／竞争／西化＋无处不在

   influence/competition/westernization is ubiquitous

10. ……在……中占重要的地位

    to occupy an important position in…

11. Sb.对…（不）感兴趣　　　　sb. is interested/not interested in…

    Sb.（不）感兴趣的 noun　　sth. that interests/does not interest sb.

12. 成立+organization（孔子学院/公司/组织 etc.）

    to set up/establish (e.g. the Confucius Institute, a company, etc.)

13. A 把……介绍给 B

    A introduces…to B

14. 欣赏+art（艺术/文学/杂技 etc.）

to appreciate or enjoy art/literature/acrobatics

II. 句型结构 *Sentence Pattern and Structure*

1. （最近/过去）+time duration 来

   In the past…years/months/days (up to the present moment)

   软实力是最近 20 年来汉语中的一个新词。

   过去两个月来，学生的中文水平提高了不少。

2. …Statement…，A，B 甚至于 C (extreme example) 都……

   Shènzhìyú 甚至于, meaning "even (to the extent that)" introduces a more extreme

   example in order to support the foregoing statement.

   美国的软实力非常强大，美国的电影、音乐、饮食、服装，甚至于电视剧和运
   动都引领着世界的时尚。

   苹果手机很受欢迎，小孩子，年轻人甚至于老人都喜欢用。

3. A 已经成了 B（不可缺少）的一部分

   A has already become a part of B

   穿牛仔裤、运动鞋，吃麦当劳的汉堡包，喝可口可乐，听美国音乐，看美国电
   影，已经成了中国城市生活的一部分。

   佛教来自印度，但现在已经成了中国文化的一部分。

4. ……，换句话说，……

   Huàn jù huà shuō 换句话说 is a discourse connector. This pattern, meaning "in

   other words," is often used to introduce a statement that repeats what has been said

   before in a different and usually simpler or more exact way.

   穿牛仔裤、运动鞋，吃麦当劳的汉堡包，喝可口可乐，听美国音乐，看美国电
   影，已经成了中国城市生活的一部分。换句话说，中国人在不知不觉中不但接
   受了美国人的生活方式，而且认同了美国人的价值观。

现在人们用电脑打字，用电子邮件跟人联系，连考试都用电脑。换句话说，用手写字的能力在现代社会变得越来越不重要了。

5. ……在不知不觉中/不知不觉就……

This pattern is used to describe something happened (usually in the form of verb + resultative complement) unknowingly or before people realized it has happened.

中国人在不知不觉中不但接受了美国人的生活方式，而且认同了美国人的价值观。

一年前，他和小王成了同事。他们在工作中一起奋斗，一起面对困难，后来，他不知不觉就爱上了小王。

6. ……，这样看来，……

Zhèyàng kànlái 这样看来 is a discourse connector. This structure, roughly meaning "so", often indicates a sudden realization and is followed with an inference based upon the facts previously mentioned.

中国人在不知不觉中不但接受了美国人的生活方式，而且认同了美国人的价值观。这样看来，美国的软实力可能比硬实力更有影响力。

现在女人也可以工作了，但是女老板还是很少。这样看来，男女平等还没有真正实现。

7. A 只能……，而 B 却可以……

This structure contrasts the limitations and restrictions of A to the superiority of B.

飞机和大炮只能征服土地，而电影、音乐和饮食却可以征服人心。

学数学、化学只能帮你找个工作，而学外语却可以改变你的生活。

8. Sb.一说到……，说的往往都是……，但是/其实，……

"When speaking of… what is said tends to be… but in fact…"

This pattern is often used to correct stereotypical impressions.

中国人一说到中国文化，说的往往都是中国的旧传统。其实，这些传统在中国正在慢慢地消失。

美国人一说到言论自由，说的往往都是一个人有没有批评政府的权利。但是，言论自由也包括不说的自由。

9. Sb. 所谓的 "noun/nominalization of V.P."，其实……

The so-called…is in fact…

This pattern is often used to "demystify" technical or fancy terms.

这些中国人最常介绍给外国人看的所谓"中国文化"，其实，在中国人的日常生活中并不占重要的地位，甚至正在慢慢地消失。

虽然中国人从小就开始学英文，但是他们所谓的"学英文"，其实往往只是在记生词，并不能真正提高语言能力。

III. 词语辨析 *Synonym Differentiation*

1. 力量：(physical) strength, ability, power

实力：actual strength (i.e. economic/military capacity), often the strength of one side in a competition (figuratively)

一个人的力量是有限的，我们需要更多人的帮助。

文化的力量是很强大的，它可以在不知不觉中影响别人。

在这场比赛中，这位中国运动员是最有实力的。

美国的经济实力比任何一个国家都强。

2. 感受：to experience (with one's thoughts and feelings affected); experience

感觉：to feel through the sense organs, to be aware of something physically; feeling

在世界各地，人们都可以感受到美国文化的影响。

今天下雨了，所以我感觉有点儿冷。喝了碗汤以后，我感觉暖和多了。

軟實力

軟實力是最近 20 年來漢語中的一個新詞。

如果軍事力量是硬實力，那麼文化力量就是軟實力。美國不但在硬實力上，是世界上最強大的國家，在軟實力上，美國的電影、電視劇、音樂、飲食、服裝，甚至於運動都引領著世界的時尚。

對一般中國老百姓來說，他們對美國的硬實力並沒有直接的感受，但是美國的軟實力卻在日常生活中影響著千千萬萬的中國人。穿牛仔褲、運動鞋，吃麥當勞的漢堡包，喝可口可樂，聽美國音樂，看美國電影，已經成了中國人城市生活的一部分。換句話說，中國人在不知不覺中不但接受了美國人的生活方式，而且認同了美國人的價值觀。這樣看來，美國的軟實力可能比硬實力更有影響力。飛機和大炮只能征服土地，而電影、音樂和飲食卻可以征服人心。

中國政府對這樣的發展是有些顧慮的，但是也想不出什麼有效的對策來防止無處不在的西化。有人建議，應該提倡傳統中國文化來應對美國軟實力的影響，比方說，把清明節、端午節等傳統節日定為法定假日。

近幾年來，在中國，從建築到服裝，我們都可以看到一定的復古傾向。中國人一說到中國文化，說的往往都是中國的舊傳統。像書法、茶道、剪紙、功夫、中國結等等。這些中國人最常介紹給外國人看的所謂“中國文化”，其實，在中國人的日常生活中並不占重要的地位，甚至正在慢慢地消失。要外國人接受連中國人自己都不感興趣的“中國文化”，這是一件很困難的事。

中國政府在世界各地成立孔子學院，也是希望把中國的語言和文化介紹給外國人。中國的旅遊、飲食、文學、藝術和雜技都是軟實力最好的資源。我希望美國人也能用比較開放的態度來欣賞中國文化。

课后习题

第 3 课

一、词语搭配 (Please pair the term in the left column with the most appropriate term in the right column. Then use the completed phrases to complete the sentences. You can change the order of the words and add more information if needed.)

(B) 引领　　　A 变化

(C) 认同　　　B 时尚

(A) 应对　　　C 价值观

(E) 成立　　　D 艺术

(D) 欣赏　　　E 公司

1. 越来越多外国公司把工厂搬到了东南亚（Southeast Asia），中国政府得_____ A _____。

2. 我希望三十岁以前可以 _____ E _____，自己当老板。

3. 有人说现代艺术很难理解，你知道怎么_____ D _____吗 ？

4. 无论做什么工作都是有价值的，_____ C _____。

5. 在美国，纽约是"时尚之都"（fashion capital），可以说纽约人_____ B _____。

二、选择填空 (Complete the sentences by choosing the most appropriate term.)

1. 力量　　　实力

你为什么不参加这次比赛？你是最有____B____的，赢的机会很大。

中国人常说"人多____A____大"，意思是人越多，做事情越容易。

2. 感受　　　感觉

电影已经看完了，说说你的____A____吧。

喝了那瓶酒以后，我____B____不太舒服。

三、完成句子 (Complete the sentence or dialogue with the given item in parentheses.)

1. A：改革开放已经 40 年了，中国有什么改变？
   B：过去40年来,中国发展进步地很多_____。(最近 / 过去 time duration 来)

2. A：中国的军事力量强大不强大？
   B：中国的军事力量强大,甚至于_____。(…甚至于…都)

3. 在中国手机不但可以用来跟别人联系，而且可以打的，买东西，交新朋友，手机已经成了个人的常键镜_____。(A 已经成了 B 不可缺少的一部分。)

4. 经济水平的提高并不一定就能 换句话说气变成_____。(换句话说)

5. 跟军事力量不同，一个国家的文化 在不知不觉中 传播_____。(在不知不觉中)

6. 他昨天晚上没睡觉，上课的时候 不知不觉就睡着了_____。(不知不觉就 V.P. 了)

7. 龙张牙舞爪，让人害怕，但熊猫温和又不软弱，这样看来你不要低估温顺的人_____。(这样看来)

8. 有重要活动的时候，北京的雾霾，往往可以在短时间之内，突然变成蓝天白云 这样看来,政府能永久修复它_____。(这样看来)

9. 到中国以后，你不能只住在大城市里，也应该去农村走走！城市只能压力你,农村却可以放松你_____。(A 只能…，B 却可以…)

10. 父母不能只重视孩子的成绩，更应该重视孩子的兴趣。成绩只能让你上大学,兴趣却可以让你过好生活_____。(A 只能…，B 却可以…)

11. A：美国人对中国文化有什么印象？
    B：美国人一说到中国文化,说的往往都是专制的,但是中国文化有很丰富的艺术_____。(sb.一说到…，说的往往都是…，但是…)

12. 很多中国学生学习英文只是为了考试，所以说，他们所谓的流畅其实针对考试标准_____。(sb.所谓的…，其实…)

13. 有的留学生到了美国不上课，常常跑出去旅行，这样人们所谓的留学其实是假期_____。(sb.所谓的…，其实…)

四、回答问题 (Answer the questions.)

1. 什么是"软实力"？

2. 世界上哪个国家的"软实力"最强大？请举例说明。

3. 为什么说美国是全世界"软实力"最强的国家？软实力的强大需要什么？

4. "硬实力"和"软实力"有什么关系？你觉得哪一个的影响更大？为什么？

5. 有人认为，美国文化对别国的影响其实是一种"文化侵略"，你同意这个看法吗？

6. 什么是"西化"？面对"西化"的问题，中国政府有什么对策？

7. 中国政府用提倡传统文化来加强软实力，你认为这是个有效的办法吗？

8. 如果中国想增强/提升（tíshēng, to enhance）软实力，应该去哪里找资源？

第 4 课

山寨产品

到中国来旅游、学习和工作的外国人不能不知道"山寨产品"这个词。

"山寨产品"就是仿冒的产品。在中国一不小心就会买到假货，假货看起来和真品几乎一模一样，有时甚至连专家都分辨不出来。在市场上，从衣服、鞋子到手机、电脑，从巧克力糖到名牌手提包都有山寨产品。山寨产品，大多"价廉"而"物不美"，如果你花了高价，买了劣质的山寨

山寨产品	shānzhài chǎnpǐn	n.	knockoff products
仿冒	fǎngmào	v.	to counterfeit
产品	chǎnpǐn	n.	product
假货	jiǎhuò	n.	fakes; counterfeit goods
真品	zhēnpǐn	n.	genuine articles/products
几乎	jīhū	adv.	almost
一模一样	yìmú yíyàng	idm.	be exactly the same; exactly alike
专家	zhuānjiā	n.	expert
分辨	fēnbiàn	v.	to distinguish; to differentiate
市场	shìchǎng	n.	market
糖	táng	n.	candy
名牌	míngpái	adj.	brand name (modifier)
手提包	shǒutí bāo	n.	handbag
物美价廉	wùměi jiàlián	idm.	(of a commodity) inexpensive and high quality; good value for money
高价	gāojià	n.	a high price
劣质	lièzhì	adj.	of poor or low quality; inferior (modifier)

产品，你就上当了。

　　山寨产品在市场上泛滥的现象，一方面反映了有些中国商人不守法；另一方面，也反映了"知识产权"在中国还是一个新观念。很多中国人还没认识到：别人的设计和包装，是不能随便仿冒的，就像学生写报告不能抄袭别人的文章，是一样的道理。

　　因为中国市场上伪劣产品太多，中国人到了外国，喜欢抢购各种各样的商品，从皮鞋、手表到名牌手提包，从化妆品到家用电器，都想买回

泛滥	fànlàn	v.	(lit.) to overflow; to spread unchecked
现象	xiànxiang	n.	phenomenon
反映	fǎnyìng	v.	to reflect; to mirror
商人	shāngrén	n.	merchant; businessman
守法	shǒufǎ	v.-o.	to abide by the law
知识产权	zhīshi chǎnquán	n.	intellectual property rights
设计	shèjì	n./v.	design; to design
包装	bāozhuāng	n.	packaging
抄袭	chāoxí	v.	to plagiarize; to copy
文章	wénzhāng	n.	essay; article
道理	dàolǐ	n.	reason; sense; principle; hows and whys
伪劣产品	wěiliè chǎnpǐn	n.	fake and inferior products
抢购	qiǎnggòu	v.	to rush to purchase (anticipating scarcity)
商品	shāngpǐn	n.	commodity; merchandise
皮鞋	píxié	n.	leather shoes
手表	shǒubiǎo	n.	wrist watch
化妆品	huàzhuāng pǐn	n.	cosmetics; makeup product
家用电器	jiāyòng diànqì	n.	household electronics

43

中国。最让外国人惊讶的是中国人到许多国家大量购买当地生产的奶粉。如果出不了国，他们就会到香港购买进口奶粉。结果，大陆游客把香港的奶粉都买光了，香港政府不得不下令限制大陆游客购买奶粉。这些现象让许多外国人困惑，为什么中国人这么喜欢买外国货？

　　我来了中国以后才了解到：外国货在中国很贵。中国政府对名牌奢侈品征收重税。结果，在美国一双一百美元左右的皮鞋，在北京很可能需要花三四百美元才能买到。这也就难怪中国人到了外国就大量购买外国货了。其实，许多中国人在海外抢购的商品，有的还是在中国制造的呢！

惊讶	jīngyà	v.	to feel surprised
大量	dàliàng	adj./adv.	a large amount of; in great quantities; in volume
购买	gòumǎi	v.	to purchase
当地	dāngdì	n.	local area
生产	shēngchǎn	v.	to produce (milk powder/rice/food…)
奶粉	nǎifěn	n.	milk powder
进口	jìnkǒu	v./adj.	to import; imported
大陆	dàlù	n.	Mainland China
下令	xiàlìng	v.-o.	to give an order; to command
限制	xiànzhì	v.	to restrict; to limit
困惑	kùnhuò	v.	to feel perplexed; to be puzzled
外国货	wàiguóhuò	n.	foreign goods
了解	liǎojiě	v.	to know (a fact); to find out about
奢侈品	shēchǐ pǐn	n.	luxuries
征收	zhēngshōu	v.-o.	to levy (a tax)
重税	zhòng shuì	n.	a heavy tax
难怪	nánguài	adv.	(it's) no wonder/not surprising (that)
制造	zhìzào	v.	to manufacture

　　至于中国人在海外大量购买奶粉，据说是因为中国生产的奶粉有的是伪劣产品。许多婴儿喝了之后生病，影响发育，甚至还有因此死亡的，所以中国家长都不敢给孩子喝中国奶粉。这些现象都值得中国政府注意。

　　中国的食品安全是个比较严重的问题，要解决这个问题，需要有比较健全的检查制度和执法严格的监督机构。

至于	zhìyú	conj.	as for; as to
婴儿	yīng'ér	n.	infant
影响	yǐngxiǎng	v.	to affect; to impair
发育	fāyù	n./v.	(of a child) development; growth; to grow
死亡	sǐwáng	v./n.	to die; death
敢	gǎn	aux.	to dare
食品	shípǐn	n.	food
健全	jiànquán	adj.	a sound and perfect (system)
执法	zhífǎ	v.-o.	to enforce the law
严格	yángé	adv./adj.	strictly
监督	jiāndū	v.	to supervise
机构	jīgòu	n.	organization; institution

I. 词语搭配 *Collocation*

1. 仿冒别人的产品 / 设计 / 包装

   to counterfeit other people's products/design/packaging

2. A 和 B 一模一样

   A and B are exactly the same

3. A 和 B 的不同，sb.分辨不出来

   Sb. is unable to distinguish the differences between A and B

4. A 上 B 的当　　A is duped (into doing sth.) by B

   A 上当了　　　A is duped

5. 山寨产品/假货/色情暴力电影+泛滥

   Knockoff goods/fakes/movies of sex and violence spread unchecked.

6. 限制+……的自由/发展/数量

   to restrict/limit the freedom of…/the development of…/the amount of…

7. ……让 sb.很惊讶

   sb. is surprised by…

8. 政府+对……征收重税

   Government levies a heavy tax on…

9. 影响+发育/健康/学习/生活

   to affect the development (of children)/one's health/study/life

10. 健全的制度

    a sound and perfect system

11. 严格+执法/监督/检查

    strictly enforce the law/supervise/examine

II. 句型结构 *Sentence Pattern and Structure*

1. ……一不小心就会……

   This structure, literally meaning "a little slip in concentration will cause/lead to…," is often used (in a prediction) to stress that it is too easy for something to happen.

中国的假货太多了，在中国一不小心就会买到假货。

在高速公路上开车很危险，一不小心就会撞上别人的车。

2. ……，有时甚至连……都……

"…, sometimes even…" introduces an extreme example to support the previous statement.

假货看起来和真品几乎一模一样，有时甚至连专家都分辨不出来。

GRE 的问题太难了，有时甚至连美国人都不知道怎么做。

3. ……（还没）认识到……

Sb. came to realize that…; negation: sb. has yet to realize that… (note that the verb complement *dào* 到 cannot be omitted).

很多中国人还没认识到：别人的设计和想法，是不能随便仿冒的。

现在的中国人已经认识到保护环境的重要性了。

4. …A…，就像…B…，是一样的道理。

"Just like B, A follows the same principle." This structure is used to explain abstract things (indicated by A) by means of drawing concrete analogies (indicated by B), or to explain a new phenomenon/theory (indicated by A) based on phenomena/theories familiar to the listener (indicated by B).

别人的设计和包装，是不能随便仿冒的，就像学生写报告不能抄袭别人的文章，是一样的道理。

学中文得自己练习说；就像学游泳得到水里自己游，是一样的道理。

5. V 光了

The verb complement *guāng* 光 emphasizes the complete disposal or disappearance of the object and is similar to "(finish, use, etc.) up" in English.

中国游客到了香港，把香港的奶粉都买光了。

他到美国一个月就把钱都花光了。

6. ……让 sb.很困惑/惊讶，为什么……？

This structure is used to first describe a phenomenon that perplexes or puzzles someone, which prompts them to then question the reason of this phenomenon.

这些现象让许多外国人困惑，为什么中国人这么喜欢买外国货？

中国人喝水的习惯让外国人很困惑，为什么中国人在夏天还喝热水？

7. ……以后才了解到：……

It is only after…did sb. get to know the fact that/find out that…

我来了中国以后才了解到，外国货在中国很贵。

在中国的时候我以为美国学生的生活很轻松，到了美国以后我才了解到：美国学生的压力其实也很大，为了准备考试，很多学生每天只睡 3 个小时。

8. ……，难怪……

"(It's) no wonder/not surprising that…," often indicates a sudden realization or understanding behind a puzzling or unusual phenomenon.

在美国一双一百美元左右的皮鞋，在北京很可能需要花三、四百美元才能买到。这也就难怪中国人到了外国就大量采购商品了。

在美国，要上医学院、法学院需要很好的成绩，难怪美国大学生这么重视成绩。

9. A……，至于 B……

Zhìyú 至于 meaning "as for; as to" is often used at the beginning of a second sentence or paragraph to introduce or comment on another aspect of the aforementioned topic.

中国人喜欢在外国抢购名牌奢侈品是因为中国政府对这些商品抽重税，至于抢购奶粉，据说是因为中国生产的奶粉有的是伪劣产品。

中国政府在城市推行"一家一个孩子"政策是因为中国人口太多了，至于在农村让第一个孩子是女孩儿的父母生第二个孩子，据说是因为农村人有重男轻女的观念。

10. ……不敢……   dare not do sth.

……敢不敢……？　　　　　　　Do you dare to do sth?

因为中国制造的奶粉有的是伪劣产品，所以中国家长都不敢给孩子喝中国奶粉。

你晚上敢不敢住在大街上？

11. object 值得（subj.）Verb

The object is worth doing. Note that the object should be put before the verb 值得.

这些现象都值得中国政府注意。

这本书值得（我们）好好看一看。

III. 词语辨析 *Synonym Differentiation*

1. 生产：奶粉/大米/食品　　　　to produce (milk powder/rice/food…)

制造：工业品　　　　　　　　to manufacture

因为土地被污染了，所以农民们生产的大米也有问题。

美国的很多衣服、鞋子、手机都是在中国制造的。

2. V 光了：emphasizing the complete disposal and removal of the object; all gone, nothing left.

V 完了：emphasizing the completion of an action or a task, such as finished one's homework.

他把桌子上的苹果都吃光了，别人一个都没吃。

我已经把今天的作业做完了。

3. 严厉 adj./adv.：(of attitude) stern, severe, for example, 严厉地处罚/批评 to severely punish/severely criticize

严格 adj./adv.: (of method and style) strict, rigorous, for example 严格地检查/监督 to strictly examine/supervise

他上课迟到了，老师严厉地批评了他。

食品安全很重要，政府应该严格监督这些生产食品的公司。

山寨產品

到中國來旅遊,學習和工作的外國人不能不知道"山寨產品"這個詞。

"山寨產品"就是仿冒的產品。在中國一不小心就會買到假貨,假貨看起來和真品幾乎一模一樣,有時甚至連專家都分辨不出來。在市場上,從衣服、鞋子到手機、電腦,從巧克力糖到名牌手提包都有山寨產品。山寨產品,大多"價廉"而"物不美",如果你花了高價,買了劣質的山寨產品,你就上當了。

山寨產品在市場上氾濫的現象,一方面反映了有些中國商人不守法;另一方面,也反映了"知識產權"在中國還是一個新觀念。很多中國人還沒認識到:別人的設計和包裝,是不能隨便仿冒的,就像學生寫報告不能抄襲別人的文章,是一樣的道理。

因為中國市場上偽劣產品太多,中國人到了外國,喜歡搶購各種各樣的商品,從皮鞋、手錶到名牌手提包,從化妝品到家用電器,都想買回中國。最讓外國人驚訝的是中國人到許多國家大量購買當地生產的奶粉。如果出不了國,他們就會到香港購買進口奶粉。結果,大陸遊客把香港的奶粉都買光了,香港政府不得不下令限制大陸遊客購買奶粉。這些現象讓許多外國人困惑,為什麼中國人這麼喜歡買外國貨?

我來了中國以後才瞭解到:外國貨在中國很貴。中國政府對名牌奢侈品徵收重稅。結果,在美國一雙一百美元左右的皮鞋,在北京很可能需要花三四百美元才能買到。這也就難怪中國人到了外國就大量購買外國貨了。其實許多中國人在海外搶購的商品,有的還是在中國製造的呢!

至於中國人在海外大量購買奶粉,據說是因為中國生產的奶粉有的是偽劣產品。許多嬰兒喝了之後生病, 影響發育, 甚至還有因此死亡的, 所以中國家長都不敢給孩子喝中國奶粉。這些現象都值得中國政府注意。

中國的食品安全是個比較嚴重的問題,要解決這個問題,需要有比較健全的檢查制度和執法嚴格的監督機構。

课后习题
第 4 课

一、词语搭配 (Please pair the term in the left column with the most appropriate term in the right column. Then use the completed phrases to complete the sentences. You can change the order of the words and add more information if needed.)

（1）

(A) 仿冒　　　A 设计
(C) 制度　　　B 发育
(B) 影响　　　C 健全

1. 你正在长身体,不能总是不吃饭,这样会____B____的。
2. 要是____C____,贪污腐败的问题很难解决。
3. 这家公司的产品太受欢迎了,所以有些不懂知识产权的商家就开始____A____。

（2）

(B) 限制　　　A 泛滥
(C) 分辨　　　B 数量
(A) 假货　　　C 不同

1. 这两个东西看起来一模一样,我没有办法____C____。
2. 要是____A____,网上市场的发展就会受到限制,因为人们不敢相信网上的商店。
3. 由于交通堵塞的问题越来越严重,政府决定____B____。

二、选择填空 (Complete the sentences by choosing the most appropriate term.)

1. 生产(A)　制造(B)
   据说,东北的黑土地____A____出来的大米,质量是最好的。

"中国 _B_ " 在世界各地都可以看到，这反映了中国在全世界的经济影响力。

2. V 光了　　　V 完了

妈妈给了他一百块钱，他不到半天就都花 _B_ 。他太喜欢乱花钱了。

我借给你的 DVD 已经看 _A_ 吗？我下个星期一想看，请把它们还给我。

3. 严厉　　严格

知道他抄袭同学的作业，老师非常 _A_ 地批评了他。

到了北京机场，机场的人并没有 _B_ 地检查人们的行李。

三、完成句子 (Complete the sentence or dialogue with the given item in parentheses.)

1. 路上都是冰， 一不小心就会 摔倒 。（一不小心就会 V.P.）

2. 这里的冬天太冷了， 一不小心就会管道结冰 。（一不小心就会 V.P.）

3. 哥哥和弟弟长得一模一样， 有时甚至连父母都很难分别 。（有时甚至连…都…）

4. 这条路经常堵车， 有时甚至连步行都更快 。（有时甚至连…都…）

5. A：为什么最近几年学中文的学生越来越多？
   B： 大家认识到中文是很重要 。（认识到）

6. A：我们家孩子每天都想着玩儿，都不知道得学习，怎么办啊？
   B： 他们还没认识到学习很重要 。（还没认识到）

7. A：为什么我们得常常复习学过的东西？
   B： 复习就像 。（…A…，就像…B…，是一样的道理）

8. 这两天由于雾霾很严重，商店里的口罩很快就 卖光了 。（V 光了）

9. A：你学习中文的时候有什么不理解的吗？
   B： 中文让我很困惑 为什么汉字这么难 。（…让 sb. 很困惑，为什么…？）

10. A：你到了中国以后，有什么新发现？
    B： 到中国以后才了解到中国文化 。（…以后才了解到：…）

11. A："中国梦"为什么有强烈的民族主义情绪？
    B：因为 1840 年到 1949 年的一百多年间，中国一直受到帝国主义的侵略。

A：<u>认识这样，难怪中国梦有强烈的民族主义情绪</u>。（…，难怪…）

12. A：在美国，为什么有的学生学习中文，有的选择学习西班牙文（Spanish）？

B：<u>在外国中文很重要，至于在美国，西班牙文很重要</u>（A…，至于 B…）

13. A：为什么政府既得发展经济，也得保护环境？

B：<u>~~中文很重要至于~~</u>　　　　　　　　　　（A…，至于 B…）

14. 中国政府发展经济的政策很有效，<u>做这样很直得</u>（object 值得（subj.）Verb）

做得对

15. A：现在美国政府得注意什么社会问题？

B：<u>收入不平等值得关注</u>　　　　　　　（object 值得（subj.）Verb）

四、回答问题 (Answer the questions.)

1. 什么是"山寨产品"？在中国，山寨产品多不多？容不容易看出来？

2. 在中国，山寨产品为什么这么多？

3. 中国游客到了国外，最喜欢做什么事？

4. 中国游客为什么喜欢买外国货？

5. 中国游客为什么会在香港抢购奶粉？

6. 在中国，食品安全是一个大问题吗？

7. 美国政府是怎么解决食品安全问题的？

第 5 课

"苍蝇" 与 "老虎"

最近几年，中国政府做了一件很得民心 的事，就是"反腐"。报纸上常有"拍 苍蝇，打老虎"的新闻。起先 我不懂反腐和苍蝇、老虎有什么关系，后来我问了中国朋友才知道："苍蝇"代表小贪官，而"老虎"代表大贪官。

过去中国政府也反腐，但是往往只抓 小贪官，而放过 大贪官。这叫做："只拍苍蝇，不打老虎"，结果小贪官受到严厉 的处罚，而大贪官却逍遥法外。贪 了几万块钱的小官被关进监狱，而贪了几亿 的高官，却天天吃喝嫖

苍蝇	cāngying	n.	fly
得民心	dé mínxīn	v.-o.	to win the support of the people
反腐	fǎnfǔ	v.-o.	to fight corruption
拍	pāi	v.	to swat
起先	qǐxiān	conj.	at first; in the beginning
贪官	tānguān	n.	corrupt officials
抓	zhuā	v.	to arrest; to catch
放过	fàngguo	v.-c.	to let sb. off
严厉	yánlì	adj./adv.	severe (punishment/criticism); severely
处罚	chǔfá	n./v.	punishment; to punish
逍遥法外	xiāoyáo fǎwài	idm.	(of criminals) to get off scot-free
贪	tān	v.	to embezzle (a certain amount of money)
监狱	jiānyù	n.	jail
亿	yì	num.	a hundred million
高官	gāoguān	n.	high officials

赌，继续收贿赂、玩女人。老百姓看得很清楚，高官是特权阶级，法律制裁不了他们。大家觉得很不公平，也很气愤！

这次中国政府下了决心：无论官员的地位多高，只要贪污，就得受到法律的制裁。老百姓听了都很高兴。

吃喝嫖赌	chī hē piáo dǔ	idm.	(lit) to go dining, wining, whoring and gambling; to lead a degenerate and decadent life
收	shōu	v.	to accept or take (bribes/gifts/money)
贿赂	huìlù	n./v.	bribes; to bribe
特权	tèquán	n.	privilege; prerogative
阶级	jiējí	n.	(social) class
制裁	zhìcái	v.	to punish (the agent/doer is "法律")
气愤	qìfèn	v.	to feel indignant
决心	juéxīn	n.	determination; resolve
贪污	tānwū	v.	to embezzle

美国也有很多贪官，除了政府反贪 以外，媒体 也起了很大的作用。报纸、电视、网络 天天盯 着官员，只要官员贪污腐化，新闻立刻报道。所以，美国官员最怕新闻记者。

中国的情况有些不同，中国的媒体基本上都是"党的喉舌"，"喉"是"喉咙"，"舌"是"舌头"，都是说话的器官。所谓"党的喉舌"，就是共产党的宣传工具，是不能随便批评政府的。在这样的情况下，媒体不但起不了监督政府的作用，有时还得为政府掩饰错误。我觉得中国腐败 的问题之所以这么严重，和媒体没有新闻自由是分不开的。

开放新闻自由，在我看来，才是反腐最有效的办法！

反贪	fǎn tān	v.-o.	to fight embezzlement
媒体	méitǐ	n.	media
网络	wǎngluò	n.	Internet
盯	dīng	v.	to fix one's eyes on; keep a close watch on
官员	guānyuán	n.	official
贪污腐化	tānwū fǔhuà	v.	to embezzle and be corrupt
立刻	lìkè	adv.	immediately
报道	bàodào	v.	to report; to cover (news)
记者	jìzhě	n.	reporter; journalist
舌头	shétou	n.	tongue
器官	qìguān	n.	organ
宣传	xuānchuán	v.	to propagate; to publicize
工具	gōngjù	n.	tool
掩饰	yǎnshì	v.	to cover up (one's errors/mistakes)
错误	cuòwu	n.	error; mistake
腐败	fǔbài	n/adj.	corruption; corrupt

I. 词语搭配 *Collocation*

1. 政府做得民心的事/政府的政策很得民心

   Government renders services that won over the support of the people

   Government policies won over the support of the people

2. 受到严厉的处罚/制裁/批评

   to be severely punished/sanctioned/criticized

3. 把 criminals/offenders 抓起来

   to arrest (criminals/offenders)

4. criminals/offenders 逍遥法外

   (of criminals and offenders) to get off scot-free

5. 贪+a certain amount of money

   to embezzle (a certain amount of money)

6. Sb.被关进监狱　　　　sb. was sent to jail

   把 sb.关进监狱　　　　to send sb. to jail

7. Sb. （天天）吃喝嫖赌

   Sb. goes dining, wining, whoring and gambling every day, that is, to lead a dissipated life.

8. 收+贿赂/礼物/钱

   to accept or take bribes/gifts/money

9. ……让 sb.很气愤

   sth. makes sb. indignant.

10. 受到法律的制裁

    be punished according to law

11. 下+决心

    to make up one's mind (to do sth.)

12. 起+（很大的）作用

    to play a significant role in

57

13. A 盯着 B

   A keeps a close watch on B

14. （为 sb.）掩饰错误

   to cover up one's faults/mistakes

15. 开放+新闻自由/言论自由

   to lift the ban/restriction on the freedom of the press/freedom of speech

II. 句型结构 *Sentence Pattern and Structure*

1. 起先/开始的时候……，后来……。

   "At first…, later…" is often used to describe a change in a narration of past events.

   起先我不懂反腐和苍蝇老虎有什么关系，后来我问了中国朋友才知道："苍蝇"代表小贪官，而"老虎"代表大贪官。

   我的朋友是去年到北京的。起先，他很不喜欢北京。后来，他交了几个北京朋友，对北京的看法也慢慢改变了。

2. A……，而 B 却……

   This pattern, similar to "whereas" in English, contrasts A and B and stresses that B is contrary to what was expected.

   小贪官受到严厉的处罚，而大贪官却逍遥法外。

   贪了几万块钱的小官被关进监狱里，而贪了几亿的高官，却天天吃喝嫖赌，继续收贿赂，玩女人。

3. V 不了 （起不了作用、解决不了、理解不了、完成不了，做不了 etc.）

   了(liǎo) is a verb complement in this structure, which as a whole, indicates that an action is unable to be completed.

   高官是特权阶级，法律制裁不了他们。

   在没有言论自由的国家里，媒体对政府起不了监督作用。

4. 无论…（有）多 adj.…，都……

No matter how …, …

无论天气多糟糕，学生都会来上课。

无论作业有多难，我都会尽力做完。

无论…（有）多 adj.…，只要……，就……

No matter how…, as long as…

In these two structures, "有" can be omitted.

无论官员的地位多高，只要贪污了，就会受到法律制裁。

在一个法治社会，无论是谁，只要犯了法，就会受到制裁。

5. 所谓的"a specific term"，就是…definition/explanation…

This pattern is often used to define, explain, or sometimes, to "demystify" a technical or fancy term.

所谓"党的喉舌"也就是共产党的宣传工具，是不能随便批评政府的。

所谓的"独生子女政策"，就是政府规定一家只能生一个孩子。

6. 在……的情况下，……   under certain circumstances…

所谓"党的喉舌"也就是共产党的宣传工具，是不能随便批评政府的。在这样的情况下，媒体不但起不了监督政府的作用，有时还得为政府掩饰错误。

大城市的交通越来越拥挤，在这样的情况下，政府不得不开始限制居民买车。

7. …A…之所以……，和 B 是分不开的

(lit) The reason why A…, is inseparable from B. In other words, A is inseparably related/tied to B.

我觉得中国腐败的问题之所以会这么严重，和媒体没有新闻自由是分不开的。

中国人的生活水平之所以能提高，和改革开放是分不开的。

8. …measures…是…a certain goal…最有效的办法

This pattern is used to say that a certain method is the most effective way to achieve a certain goal.

开放新闻自由，在我看来，才是反腐最有效的办法！

多跟中国人聊天是提高中文水平最有效的办法。

III. 词语辨析 *Synonym Differentiation*

1. 处罚：(an organization/unit/policeman) punishes sb.

   制裁：to be punished (the agent/doer is "法律")

   要是你随便停车，警察可以按照规定处罚你。

   政府下了决心，无论官员的地位多高，只要贪污，就得受到法律制裁。

2. V 不到：the verb complement 到 emphasizes that the object of the action is "out of reach", or "unattainable"

   V 不了：了 as a verb complement emphasizes that the action cannot be successfully completed due to constraining conditions.

   《花花公子》（*Playboy*）在中国是被禁的，在中国的书店你买不到这种杂志。

   今天书店不开门，你买不了书了。

   我的电脑坏了，做不了作业。

"蒼蠅"與"老虎"

最近幾年, 中國政府做了一件很得民心的事, 就是"反腐"。報紙上常有"拍蒼蠅, 打老虎"的新聞。起先我不懂反腐和蒼蠅、老虎有什麼關係, 後來我問了中國朋友才知道:"蒼蠅"代表小貪官, 而"老虎"代表大貪官。

過去中國政府也反腐, 但是往往只抓小貪官, 而放過大貪官。這叫做:"只拍蒼蠅, 不打老虎", 結果小貪官受到嚴厲的處罰, 而大貪官卻逍遙法外。貪了幾萬塊錢的小官被關進監獄, 而貪了幾億的高官, 卻天天吃喝嫖賭, 繼續收賄賂, 玩女人。老百姓看得很清楚, 高官是特權階級, 法律制裁不了他們。大家覺得很不公平, 也很氣憤!

這次中國政府下了決心:無論官員的地位多高, 只要貪污, 就得受到法律制裁。老百姓聽了都很高興。

美國也有很多貪官, 除了政府反貪以外, 媒體也起了很大的作用。報紙、電視、網絡天天盯著官員, 只要官員貪污腐化, 新聞立刻報導。所以, 美國官員最怕新聞記者。

中國的情況有些不同, 中國的媒體基本上都是"黨的喉舌", "喉"是"喉嚨", "舌"是"舌頭", 都是說話的器官。所謂"黨的喉舌", 就是共產黨的宣傳工具, 是不能隨便批評政府的。在這樣的情況下, 媒體不但起不了監督政府的作用, 有時還得為政府掩飾錯誤。我覺得中國腐敗的問題之所以這麼嚴重, 和媒體沒有新聞自由是分不開的。

開放新聞自由, 在我看來, 才是反腐最有效的辦法!

课后习题

第 5 课

一、词语搭配 (Please pair the term in the left column with the most appropriate term in the right column. Then use the completed phrases to complete the sentences. You can change the order of the words and add more information if needed.)

（1）

（　　）得　　　　　A 决心
（　　）下　　　　　B 民心
（　　）监督　　　　C 言论自由
（　　）开放　　　　D 政府

1. 要是政府的力量太强大了，有谁可以＿＿＿＿＿＿＿＿＿＿＿＿＿＿＿＿＿＿＿呢？
2. 一个政府好不好，得看政府做的事＿＿＿＿＿＿＿＿＿＿＿＿＿＿＿＿＿＿＿＿。
3. 为了去中国工作，他＿＿＿＿＿＿＿＿＿＿＿＿＿＿＿＿＿＿＿＿＿＿＿＿＿＿。
4. 朝鲜(North Korea)不＿＿＿＿＿＿＿，人们可能会因为不同意政府的看法而被抓起来。

（2）

（　　）掩饰　　　　A 作用
（　　）制裁　　　　B 错误
（　　）起　　　　　C 贿赂
（　　）收　　　　　D 严厉

1. 在有的地方，要是领导做错了，你不但不能说出来，反而＿＿＿＿＿＿＿＿＿＿。
2. 那个学校的领导＿＿＿＿＿＿＿＿＿＿＿＿＿＿＿＿＿＿＿＿＿，被抓起来了。
3. 为了解决环境污染，科学家提出了一些办法，＿＿＿＿＿＿＿＿＿＿＿＿＿＿＿。
4. 这个国家的法律对贪官＿＿＿＿＿＿＿＿＿＿＿＿＿，所以贪污腐化不那么严重。

二、选择填空 (Complete the sentences by choosing the most appropriate term.)

1. 处罚　　制裁

他开车的时候没有看红灯，所以被交通警察_____了。

在美国，官员收贿赂，一定会受到法律的_____。

2. 吃不到　　吃不了

这个地方没有中国饭馆，所以_____中国菜。

今天我牙疼，_____饭，只能喝汤。

3. 看不到　　看不了

家里的电视机坏了，今天晚上_____电视了。

坐在我前面的同学个子太高，我完全_____黑板上的字。

三、完成句子 (Complete the sentence or dialogue with the given item in parentheses.)

1. A：你听到"中国梦"这个词是不是马上就知道它的意思了呢？

B：_____。(起先…，后来…)

2. 在一个社会里，如果"关系"很重要，那可能不太好，因为可能_____

_____。(A…，而 B 却…)

3. A：麦当劳在落后的国家为什么这么受欢迎？在美国，大部分的美国人都不想吃。

B：_____。(A…，而 B 却…)

4. 那个老师说话用的词都太难了，学生们_____。(V 不了)

5. 听说红绿灯在纽约_____，行人常常不看红绿灯。(V 不了)

6. A：中文很难，我劝你不要学了！

B：可是以后中文会很有用，_____。(无论…有多 adj.，都…)

7. A：我知道你不喜欢他，可是他很有钱，你再好好想想。

B：不用想了。_____(无论…多 adj.，…都…)

8. A：有的官员只是贪了一点儿钱，他们不应该受到处罚。

B: _____(无论...有多 adj.,只要...就...)

9. A: 老公,我想买个 LV 的包,可是太贵了。

B: _____(无论...多 adj.,只要...就...)

10. A: 什么是"美国梦"?

B: _____。(所谓的...,就是...)

11. A: 雾霾严重的时候,可以出去运动吗?

B: _____。(在...的情况下)

12. A: "中国梦"里为什么有强烈的民族主义情绪?

B: _____。(在...的情况下)

13. A: 美国的影响力为什么这么大?

B: _____。(A 之所以...,和 B 是分不开的)

14. A: 中国的经济为什么发展得这么快?

B: _____。(A 之所以...,和 B 是分不开的)

15. A: 空气污染这么严重,应该怎么解决?

B: _____。(...是...最有效的办法)

四、回答问题 (Answer the questions.)

1. "拍苍蝇,打老虎"是什么意思?中国老百姓对这件事有什么看法?

2. 以前,中国政府反腐吗?现在的反腐跟以前有什么不同?

3. 美国媒体怎么看中国的反腐?你同意他们的看法吗?

4. 美国有没有贪官?美国怎么防止贪污腐败问题?

5. 你认为什么是反腐最有效的办法?

6. 美国的媒体和中国的媒体有什么不同?

7. 川普总统(President Trump)和媒体的关系一直比较紧张,你觉得这是好事儿还是坏事儿?

第 6 课

关系、人情、法治

　　有些专家认为：中国缺乏新闻自由是造成贪腐的原因之一。另一个原因是中国人有"拉关系，走后门"的传统。所谓"拉关系，走后门"，就是不按照法律的程序来办事，而是通过送礼、请客这些不正当的手段来和政府官员打交道。

　　"天下没有免费的午餐"，一个官员如果收了别人的礼物，吃了别人的饭，就得帮人办事，给人机会。腐败往往就是这么开始的。另一方面，中国有句老话："拿人手短，吃人嘴软"，有些事本来是非法的，但因为收了贿赂，贪官在处理这些问题的时候就"睁一只眼，闭一只眼"，假装看不

人情	rénqíng	n.	a favor done for someone
缺乏	quēfá	v.	to lack; be deficient in; be short of
贪腐	tānfǔ	n.	embezzlement and corruption
按照	ànzhào	prep.	according to; in accordance with
程序	chéngxù	n.	procedure
办事	bànshì	v.-o.	(lit.) to handle affairs; to act
正当	zhèngdàng	adj.	legitimate; (of behavior, etc.) correct, proper
手段	shǒuduàn	n.	(illegal) measures, mean or dirty tactics
打交道	dǎ jiāodào	v.-o.	to come into contact with; have dealings with
午餐	wǔcān	n.	lunch
老话	lǎohuà	n.	old saying; adage
非法	fēifǎ	adj.	illegal
处理	chǔlǐ	v.	to handle (a problem); to deal with

见。中国人的许多买卖 交易 也都是在饭桌上谈成的。请客、吃饭，对这些人来说，绝不是一件轻松 愉快 的事，而是有点儿像在运动场上比赛，甚至像在战场上打仗！

　　另外，中国人也很重视 人情。中国人的人情往来常常表现在送礼这件事上。新朋友初次见面 的时候往往要带一份"见面礼"，而送礼又得讲究"礼尚往来"，结果，人和人的关系就变得越来越复杂了。这样的习惯和政府官员的贪污腐化不能说完全没有关系。

睁	zhēng	v.	to open (one's eyes)
闭	bì	v.	to close (one's eyes)
假装	jiǎzhuāng	v.	to pretend; to feign
买卖	mǎimài	n.	(lit.) buy and sell; business
交易	jiāoyì	n.	deal; trade
轻松	qīngsōng	adj.	relaxed; at ease
愉快	yúkuài	adj.	happy; joyful; cheerful
战场	zhànchǎng	n.	battlefield
打仗	dǎzhàng	v.	to go to war
重视	zhòngshì	v.	to take sth. seriously; to attach importance to; to value
初次见面	chūcì jiànmiàn	phr.	to meet for the first time
份	fèn	m.w.	classifier for gifts, newspaper, magazine, reports, contracts, food, etc.
见面礼	jiànmiàn lǐ	n.	a present given to sb. upon first meeting
讲究	jiǎngjiū	v.	to be particular about (food and clothing/manners/ hygiene)
礼尚往来	lǐshàngwǎnglái	idm.	(lit.) courtesy/friendly politeness demands reciprocity

　　一个外国人到了中国，懂得中国人所谓的"人情"和"关系"是很重要的。这两个词在英文里都没有适当的翻译，所以理解起来很不容易。人情和关系是分不开的，在中国工作、生活过的人大概都知道：在中国想办成一件事，往往需要靠关系。所以，我们常常听到："没有关系是办不成事的"。

　　人情和关系是法治最大的障碍，所有法律的规定都可以因为人情和关系而大打折扣。法律的精神是"法律面前，人人平等"。但是人情和关系却恰恰相反，有了关系就有了特权，有了特权就有了例外。在中国，法律对有特权的人往往是起不了作用的。

复杂	fùzá	adj.	complicated; complex
懂得	dǒngdé	v.	to understand
适当	shìdàng	adj.	suitable; appropriate; proper (in degree)
翻译	fānyì	n./v.	translation; to translate
法治	fǎzhì	n.	the rule of law; govern by law (opp. Govern by men; the rule of men 人治)
障碍	zhàng'ài	n.	obstacle
规定	guīdìng	n.	regulation; stipulation
大打折扣	dàdǎ zhékòu	idm.	(figurative) to fall short of a requirement or promise. 打折扣: to give a discount
精神	jīngshén	n.	spirit; essence
恰恰	qiàqià	adv.	exactly; precisely
相反	xiāngfǎn	adj.	opposite; on the contrary (conj.)
例外	lìwài	n.	exception

　　有些人说，中国人缺乏法治观念，因此，中国很难变成法治国家。其实，中国自古就有主张用法律来治理国家的"法家"。古代中国人对法律的理解和现代西方的法律观念有一点儿不同。法律，在古代中国人看来，只是治理国家的一个工具。法律，是由皇帝来制定，由官员来执行，需要遵守法律的基本上只有老百姓。"法律面前，人人平等"是二十世纪以后，中国人才接触到的新观念。

观念	guānniàn	n.	concept; notion
主张	zhǔzhāng	v.	to advocate; to stand for
治理	zhìlǐ	v.	to govern
法家	Fǎjiā		Legalists (a school of thought in ancient China)
工具	gōngjù	n.	tool
制定	zhìdìng	v.	to make/draw up (the law); to lay down (rules); to formulate (a policy)
执行	zhíxíng	v.	to carry out (a task); to enforce; to execute (an order)
遵守	zūnshǒu	v.	to abide by; to follow
基本上	jīběn shang	adv.	basically; mainly
世纪	shìjì	n.	century
接触	jiēchù	v.	to come into contact with; to get in touch with

I. 词语搭配 *Collocation*

1. 缺乏＋自由／经验／法制观念

   to lack freedom/experience/awareness of the law

2. 拉关系、走后门

   (lit.) to seek contact with sb. (for one's own benefit), and to get in through the back door, meaning to secure advantages through personal connections and unofficial channels.

3. 按照＋程序／规定＋办事

   to act (lit. to handle affairs) in accordance with procedure/rules and regulations

4. 不正当的手段

   illegal means of (doing sth.)

5. A 和 B 打交道

   A has dealings with/comes into contact with B

6. 天下没有免费的午餐

   There is no free lunch (in this world).

7. 拿人手短，吃人嘴软

   (lit) "the hand that receives doesn't reach; the mouth that has been fed is soft." This phrase is often used to warn people against accepting a bribe.

8. 处理＋事情／问题

   to handle or take care of matters/problems

9. (authority) 对… (a problem) …睁(一)只眼，闭(一)只眼

   pretend not to see; to purposely overlook (irregularities); to turn a blind eye to

10. 讲究＋吃穿／礼节／卫生

    be particular about food and clothing/manners/hygiene

11. 治理＋国家

    to govern a country

12. 制定＋法律／规则

    to make or draw up the law/ to lay down rules

69

13. 执行＋法律／规定

to enforce the law/regulations

14. 遵守＋法律／规定／交通规则

to abide by the law/regulations/traffic rules

II. 句型结构 *Sentence Pattern and Structure*

1. ……按照……规定/法律/程序+V.P.

To do sth. according to rules and regulations/the law/procedure

所谓拉关系，走后门，就是不按照法律的程序来办事。

学生得按照学校的规定选课、上课。

2. ……如果……，就……，…unhealthy tendencies…往往就是这么开始的。

If…then…, it is how… (unhealthy tendencies) …usually starts.

This structure is often used to describe how an unhealthy tendency starts and serves as a reminder/warning to nip something in the bud before it becomes even more serious.

一个官员如果收了别人的礼物，吃了别人请的饭，就很难公正地处理事情。腐败往往就是这么开始的。

过马路的时候，如果有一个人不遵守规则，其他人可能就会跟着这样做，交通的混乱往往就是这么开始的。

3. 假装＋V.P.　pretend to do sth.; to make pretense of…

假装成 sb.　　pretend to be someone

因为收了贿赂，贪官在处理这些问题的时候就"睁一只眼，闭一只眼"，假装看不见。

她让她的一个好朋友假装成男朋友，跟自己的父母见面。

4. V＋成

Chéng 成 is verb complement in this structure, meaning the successful completion of the action. V+得/不+成：able/unable to accomplish;

中国人的许多买卖、交易也是在饭桌上谈成的。

夏天的时候，学生们都想去北京，可是要是父母不肯出钱，他们就去不成了。

在中国，想办成一件事，往往需要靠关系。

5. 绝不＋V.P.　never; absolutely/definitely not

请客、吃饭，对这些人来说，绝不是一件轻松愉快的事。

我们绝不能让整天吃喝嫖赌的贪官逍遥法外。

6. A 和 B 不能说+完全没有/没有一点儿+关系

This structure is a double negative sentence. It literally means that "one can hardly say that A and B are completely unrelated." In other words, A has something to do with B.

这样的习惯和政府官员的贪污腐化不能说完全没有关系。

中国的环境污染问题和政府过分重视 GDP 的做法不能说完全没有关系。

7. ……sb. 说的话 / 规定 / 作用 / 效果 / 价值 / 意义……大打折扣

The phrase "打折扣" means to give a big discount, while its figurative meaning is the effect, value, or significance of sth. falls short of a requirement or promise.

人情和关系是法治最大的障碍，所有法律规定的作用都可以因为人情和关系而大打折扣。

吃这种药的时候，不能喝酒。喝了酒，药效就会大打折扣。

8. A……，但 B 却恰恰相反

B is just the opposite of A; A…, on the contrary, B…

法律的精神是"法律面前，人人平等"，但是人情和关系却恰恰相反。

在美国，汽车会让行人，但在中国，情况却恰恰相反。

9. ……自古就……

Ever since ancient times…, …

有些人说中国缺乏法治观念，其实，中国自古就有主张用法律来治理国家的"法家"。

中国的知识分子自古就有参与政治的强烈愿望，这并不是最近几年才出现的新情况。

10. Object 由 doer 来＋verb (处理、解决、制定、执行, etc.)

Yóu 由 in this pattern means "by." The doer is usually someone who is in charge of or responsible for handling the object. Thus, the "verb" in this structure should be a non-state verb, showing that the subj. has a capacity, or in a condition or state of acting or exerting power.

法律，在古代中国人看来，只是治理国家的一个工具。这个工具是由皇帝来制定，由官员来执行，需要遵守法律的基本上只有老百姓。

在中国，先生的收入往往是由太太来处理。

在理想的情况下，国家元首应该是由全体国民选出来的。但实际上，选举的过程会受到很多因素的影响，并不见得总是公平、公正的。

11. Subj. 基本上…

This structure, meaning "basically; for the most part" is used to say that something is generally true or correct.

法律，在古代中国人看来，只是治理国家的一个工具。这个工具是由皇帝来制定，由官员来执行，需要遵守法律的基本上只有老百姓。

八十年代出生的孩子，基本上都是独生子女。

III. 词语辨析 *Synonym Differentiation*

1. 手段：(illegal) measures, mean or dirty tactics
   办法：method

他常常用不正当的手段来跟别人竞争，所以很多人都很不喜欢他。

学中文最有效的办法就是跟中国人聊天。

2. 买卖：(lit.) buy and sell; business (it is usually commercial)

交易：deal, trade (may just be an arrangement for mutual advantage, not necessarily commercial)

他们夫妻是做小买卖的，赚不了很多钱。

我们做了一笔交易：他帮我做作业，我帮他做饭。

3. 懂得：意义、道理、方法　　to know how (得: to obtain)

理解：原因、意义、道理　　to understand why

一个外国人到了中国，懂得 / 理解中国人所谓的"人情"和"关系"是很重要的。

要想成功，除了个人能力以外，你还得懂得怎么跟别人打交道。

我真的不能理解，为什么有的人愿意跟自己不爱的人结婚。

4. 渐渐：gradually (changing in small amounts)

慢慢：slowly (changing or moving in a slow way)

天渐渐 / 慢慢地变黑了。

路上有冰，你得慢慢地走。

人情、關係、法治

　　有些專家認為：中國缺乏新聞自由是造成貪腐的原因之一。另一個原因是中國人有"拉關係，走後門"的傳統。所謂"拉關係，走後門"，就是不按照法律的程序來辦事，而是通過送禮、請客這些不正當的手段來和政府官員打交道。

　　"天下沒有免費的午餐"，一個官員如果收了別人的禮物，吃了別人的飯，就得幫人辦事，給人機會。腐敗往往就是這麼開始的。另一方面，中國有句老話："拿人手短，吃人嘴軟"，有些事本來是非法的事，但因為收了賄賂，貪官在處理這些問題的時候就"睜一隻眼，閉一隻眼"，假裝看不見。中國人的許多買賣交易也是在飯桌上談成的。請客、吃飯，對這些人來說，絕不是一件輕鬆愉快的事，而是有點兒像在運動場上比賽，甚至像在戰場上打仗！

　　另外，中國人也很重視人情。中國人的人情往來常常表現在送禮這件事上。新朋友初次見面的時候往往要帶一份"見面禮"，而送禮又得講究"禮尚往來"，結果，人和人的關係就變得越來越複雜。這樣的習慣和政府官員的貪污腐化不能說完全沒有關係。

　　一個外國人到了中國，懂得中國人所謂的"人情"和"關係"是很重要的。這兩個詞在英文裏都沒有適當的翻譯，所以理解起來很不容易。人情和關係是分不開的，在中國工作、生活過的人大概都知道關係在中國社會裏很重要。在中國想辦成一件事，往往需要靠關係。所以，我們常常聽到："沒有關係是辦不成事的"。

　　人情和關係是法治最大的障礙，所有法律的規定都可以因為人情和關係而大打折扣。法律的精神是"法律面前，人人平等"。但是人情和關係卻恰恰相反，有了關係就有了特權，有了特權就有了例外。在中國，法律對有特權的人往往是起不了作用的。

　　有些人說，中國人缺乏法治觀念，因此，中國很難變成法治國家。其實，中國自古就有主張用法律來治理國家的"法家"。古代中國人對法律的理解和現代西方的法律觀念，有一點不同。法律，在古代中國人看來，只是治理國家的一個工具。這個工具是由皇帝來制定，由官員來執行，需要遵守法律的基本上只有老百姓。"法律面前，人人平等"是二十世紀以後，中國人才接觸到的新觀念。

课后习题

第 6 课

一、词语搭配 (Please pair the term in the left column with the most appropriate term in the right column. Then use the completed phrases to complete the sentences. You can change the order of the words and add more information if needed.)

(1)

(D) 制定 A 问题

(D) 按照 B 规定办事

(C) 讲究 C 吃穿

(A) 处理 D 比赛规则

1. 他家很有钱,所以他_____C_____,对食物和衣服都有很高的要求。

2. 你到了我们这里,就得_____D_____,不能想干什么就干什么。

3. 公司的领导也不是那么容易当的,每天都_____。

4. _____的人不应该参加比赛,要不然对别人不公平。

(2)

(B) 治理 A 交通规则

(C) 缺乏 B 国家

(D) 执行 C 经验

(A) 遵守 D 规定

1. 他参加工作还不到一个月,是个_____C_____的年轻人。

2. 我们不应该选他当总统,一个不诚实的人怎么能_____B_____?

3. 在这个地方,没有人_____A_____,红灯根本不起作用。

4. 领导要求我们严格_____D_____,不能"睁一只眼闭一只眼"。

76

二、选择填空 (Complete the sentences by choosing the most appropriate term.)

1. 手段 办法

有的人用不正当的_____跟别人竞争，真没有道德。

我得在一个小时之内记住 50 个生词，你有没有好_____？

2. 买卖 交易

他怎么会愿意把机会给你，你们是不是有什么_____？

他父亲是做小_____的，不是什么大老板。

3. 懂得 理解

很多外国人都不太_____中国人为什么那么爱喝热水。

你得_____怎么独立学习，不能什么都等老师教你。

4. 渐渐 慢慢

你_____吃，不急，我们还有一个小时才开始上课。

你长大以后，你会发现你_____忘了小时候的事情。

三、完成句子 (Complete the sentence or dialogue with the given item in parentheses.)

1. A：学生们怎么决定自己的专业？

   B：_____。（按照）

2. A：以前政府怎么给大学毕业生分配工作？

   B：_____。（按照）

3. A：学生的发音已经不错了，你别对他们太严格了。

   B：那不行！_____。（如果...就...，...往往就是这么开始的）

4. A：小王要我跟他去看电影，可是我不想去，怎么办？

   B：_____。（假装）

5. A：在中国，只想说中文，不想跟中国人练习英文，怎么办？

B：_____。（假装成）

6. 我们想去看电影，可是电影票都卖完了，所以_____。（没 V-成）

7. A：你不是要去逛街吗？怎么回来了？

B：别提了，_____。（没 V-成）

8. 做生意一定得诚实，_____。（绝不）

9. A：中国的环境问题跟贪污问题有没有关系？

B：_____。（A 和 B 不能说完全没有关系）

10. A：我觉得我们在中国有的时候说英文也没事，还是可以学中文的 。

B：不行，_____。（大打折扣）

11. 吃了这种药以后不能喝酒，要不然_____。（大打折扣）

12. A：中国人喝水的习惯和美国人有什么不同？

B：_____。（A…，但 B 却恰恰相反）

13. A：在中国，行人得让汽车，要不然，可能会被汽车撞。

B：_____。（A…，但 B 却恰恰相反）

14. A：中国人对关系的重视是最近才开始的吗？

B：_____。（自古就…）

15. A：在你们家，有重要的事，谁做决定？

B：_____。（…由…来 V）

16. A：听说他们抓了一个小偷，然后把小偷打了一顿。

B：他们怎么能这样呢？_____。（…由…来 V）

17. 中国的经济发展得很快，在中国农村，人们_____。（基本上）

四、回答问题 (Answer the questions.)

1. 在中国，造成腐败的原因是什么？

2. 为什么有人说"在中国，请客、吃饭绝不是一件轻松愉快的事"？

3. 中国人为什么要送礼？中国人送礼讲究什么？

4. 美国人在什么情况下会送礼？美国人完全不讲究"礼尚往来"吗？

5. 有人说，中国人"重人情，讲关系"，但"人情"、"关系"在美国社会却没有什么作用。你同意这种看法吗？请举例说明？

6. 中国古代有法律吗？中国古人对法律的理解和现代西方社会有什么不同？

7. "人情"、"关系"会不会影响中国成为一个法治国家？

8. "人情"、"关系"对社会只有负面（不好）的影响吗？有没有正面（好）的影响？

第 7 课

我的"中国梦"

　　近几年在中国，人们最关注 的一个话题 是"中国梦"。在街上也能看到许多以中国梦为主题 的标语、广告 和漫画 。

　　当然，说到"中国梦"不能不让我想起美国人常说的"美国梦"。我想，"中国梦"和"美国梦"有个基本 的不同："美国梦"强调 的是个人的成功，是一个人，尤其是移民 到美国的外国人，在美国奋斗 成功的过程 。许多一无所有

中国梦	Zhōngguó mèng	n.	Chinese Dream, proposed by China's President Xi Jinping
关注	guānzhù	v.	to pay close attention to
话题	huàtí	n.	topic
主题	zhǔtí	n.	theme; subject
标语	biāoyǔ	n.	slogan
广告	guǎnggào	n.	advertisement
漫画	mànhuà	n.	comic; cartoon
基本	jīběn	adj.	fundamental; basic
强调	qiángdiào	v.	to stress
个人	gèrén	n./adj.	individual
移民	yímín	n./v.	immigrant; to immigrate
奋斗	fèndòu	v.	to strive, fight for; to struggle hard (for success)
过程	guòchéng	n.	course; process

Written by Chih-p'ing Chou
Prepared by Jincheng Liu & Xin Zou

的外国人移民到了美国以后，先读书，然后找个稳定的工作，结婚，生孩子，买汽车，买房子，家里再养条狗，养只猫，最后成为美国公民。这基本上就实现了美国人所谓的"美国梦"。"美国梦"往往是一个人从一无所有到无所不有的过程，代表的是个人的努力可以带来成功，不需要靠关系，走后门。个人的才能和努力才是成功最主要的因素。

　　"中国梦"，据我的观察，除了个人的成功、汽车、房子这些东西以外，更重要的是从国家的角度来说明中国人期盼着中国要从一个落后的发展中国家转变成一个先进的发达国家，从一个贫穷的农业国家转变成一个

一无所有	yīwúsuǒyǒu	idm.	to not have a single thing to one's name
读书	dúshū	v.-o.	to attend school; to study
稳定	wěndìng	adj.	stable
养	yǎng	v.	to raise (a child/a pet/livestock)
公民	gōngmín	n.	citizen
实现	shíxiàn	v.	to realize (one's ideal/dream/a plan)
无所不有	wúsuǒbùyǒu	idm.	to have everything; all-inclusive; all-embracing
才能	cáinéng	n.	capability; ability; talent
因素	yīnsù	n.	factor; element
观察	guānchá	n./v.	observation; to observe
角度	jiǎodù	n.	perspective; point of view; angle
说明	shuōmíng	v.	to show; to illustrate
期盼	qīpàn	v./n.	yearn for; yearning
落后	luòhòu	adj.	backward; behind the times
转变	zhuǎnbiàn	v.	to transform; to shift
先进	xiānjìn	adj.	advanced
贫穷	pínqióng	adj.	poor; impoverished
农业	nóngyè	adj./n.	agricultural; agriculture

富裕 的工业化 国家，从一个受帝国主义 侵略 的半殖民地 转变成一个独立
自由的主权 国家。这是千千万万中国人的"强国梦"，这里头有很强烈 的民
族主义 情绪，国家越来越强大，这是中国人感到 最自豪最骄傲 的地方。

　　"美国梦"当然多少也有民族主义的情绪，但绝对 没有"中国梦"这么强
烈，也没有中国人感受 得这么迫切。因为美国从来没有被外国打败 过，占

富裕	fùyù	adj.	rich; wealthy
工业化	gōngyè huà	n.	industrialization
帝国主义	dìguó zhǔyì	n.	imperialism
侵略	qīnlüè	v.	to invade
半殖民地	bàn zhímíndì	n.	semi-colony, a Marxist term, referring to a country which is officially an independent nation, but is, in reality, dominated by another imperialist country
独立	dúlì	adj.	independent
主权	zhǔquán	n.	sovereign; sovereignty
强国梦	qiángguó mèng	n.	the dream to be a strong nation
强烈	qiángliè	adj.	strong; intense
民族主义	mínzú zhǔyì	n.	nationalism
情绪	qíngxù	n.	feelings; sentiment
感到	gǎndào	v.-c.	to feel; to sense
骄傲	jiāo'ào	adj.	be proud (of sb.); to take pride in; arrogant
地方	dìfang	n.	part; aspect; place
绝对	juéduì	adv.	absolutely; definitely
感受	gǎnshòu	v.	to experience
迫切	pòqiè	adj.	urgent; pressing
打败	dǎbài	v.	to defeat

领过，而且一战以后，美国始终是世界上最强大的国家。美国在军事上的霸权，更是没有第二个国家可以提出挑战的，所以美国人的民族主义情绪没有中国人那么强烈，这是可以理解的。对中国人来说，航空母舰、远程轰炸机、洲际弹道导弹是中国梦里面很重要的一部分。对一般美国人来说，在他们的"美国梦"里大概不会想到这些武器。因为这些武器美国早就已经有了，而且比任何国家拥有的都多。

　　我到了中国以后，最让我感到不方便和不习惯的是我不能看脸书，不

占领	zhànlǐng	v.	to capture; to occupy
一战	yī zhàn	n.	World War I (1914-1918)
始终	shǐzhōng	adv.	from the beginning to the end (i.e. up to the speaking moment)
军事	jūnshì	n.	military
霸权	bàquán	n.	hegemony
提出	tíchū	v.	to lodge (a challenge); to put forward
挑战	tiǎozhàn	n./v.	challenge
理解	lǐjiě	v.	to understand; to comprehend
航空母舰	hángkōng mǔjiàn	n.	aircraft carrier
远程	yuǎnchéng	adj.	long-range; long-distance
轰炸机	hōngzhàjī	n.	bomber (aircraft)
洲际弹道导弹	zhōujì dàndào dǎodàn	n.	intercontinental ballistic missile
一般	yìbān	adj.	average (people); ordinary
武器	wǔqì	n.	weapon
拥有	yōngyǒu	v.	to possess/command (weapon/land/people)
脸书	liǎnshū	n.	Facebook

能通过谷歌 找我要的东西，不能在网上看《纽约时报》，看不到蓝天白云，呼吸 不到新鲜 空气，所以对一个美国学生来说，我的"中国梦"很简单，既不需要航空母舰、弹道导弹，也不需要汽车、房子。我的"中国梦"只是我可以通过脸书和朋友联系，不必"翻墙"就可以看到《纽约时报》，出门不必戴口罩，打开自来水 就能喝，吃水果不必担心农药 。这些看起来很简单的愿望，在今天的中国还是一个"梦"。

谷歌	gǔgē	n.	Google
纽约时报	Niǔyuē Shíbào	n.	The New York Times
呼吸	hūxī	v.	to breathe
新鲜	xīnxiān	adj.	fresh
联系	liánxì	v.	to contact
翻墙	fānqiáng	v.-o.	(lit.) to climb over the wall; to breach the Great Firewall of China (by using VPN)
自来水	zìláishuǐ	n.	running water; tap water
农药	nóngyào	n.	pesticide
愿望	yuànwàng	n.	wish (often related to personal life)

I. 词语搭配 *Collocation*

1. 关注+话题/新闻/sth.的发展

   to follow a topic/the news/the development of sth.

2. Sb. (从 a country) 移民+到 (了) ＋ a foreign country

   to emigrate/emigrated (from a country) to another country

3. Sb. 一无所有

   Sb. 是一无所有的（穷）人

   Sb. doesn't have a thing to his name

4. 稳定的生活/工作/社会

   a stable life/job/society

5. 养+猫/狗/孩子

   to raise cats/dogs/children

6. 实现+理想/目标

   to realize one's ideals/goals

7. 靠关系，走后门

   to rely on personal connections and to secure advantages through influence (*zǒu hòumén*, literally means "to get in through the back door")

8. 先进的国家/设备/经验/方法/观念

   advanced country/equipment/experience/methods/concept

9. A 受 B 的侵略

   A is invaded by B

10. 强烈的情绪/愿望

    strong sentiments/desire

11. A 为 B（感到）骄傲

    A feels proud of B

12. 迫切的要求/需要/愿望

    an urgent request/need/desire

13. A 向 B (the authority/the superior) 提出挑战

A challenges B (usu. the authority or the stronger one) (to do sth.)

14. 拥有+大量的+武器/土地/人口/资源

to possess/command (usually a large amount of) weapons/land/people/resources

15. A 跟 B 联系

A gets in touch with B

II. 句型结构 *Sentence Pattern and Structure*

1. 以……为主题/中心/基础/目的

To treat/consider…as the theme/center/foundation/goal

这几年在街上能看到许多以中国梦为主题的标语，广告和漫画。

在我看来，婚姻应该以爱情为基础，但是爱情不必以结婚为目的。

2. 看/说+到……，就让 sb.想起……

It reminds sb. of sth. upon seeing…/hearing of…

说到"中国梦"，就让我想起美国人常说的"美国梦"。

看到这张照片，就让我想起了我在中国的留学生活。

3. ……，尤其是……，……

This pattern, meaning "especially, in particular," is often used parenthetically to point out something that deserves special attention.

"美国梦"强调的是一个人,尤其是移民美国的外国人,在美国奋斗成功的过程。

我很喜欢吃水果，尤其是苹果，我每天都吃。

4. 先……，然后……，再……，最后……

This pattern is often used to describe a sequential order.

外国移民到了美国，先读书，然后找个稳定的工作，结婚，生孩子，买汽车，买房子，家里再养条狗，养只猫，最后成为美国公民。

回到家以后，我打算先洗个澡，然后吃晚饭，再喝一杯咖啡，最后做作业。

5. A...不...，B 才......

This structure, meaning "A is not…, rather it is B that/who…; it is not A but rather B that…" negates one thing, in order to emphasize the legitimacy of the other. Take the first sentence for example, "In the US, connections or 'backdoor' influence are not the determining factors to one's success. Rather, it is one's ability and effort that contribute to one's success."

在美国，关系、后门不是决定你成功的因素，个人的才能和努力才是成功最主要的因素。

一个人说了什么并不重要，他做了什么才是最重要的。

6. ……从 A 转变+成 B

"A changes/transformed into B; to shift from A to B" In this structure, *chéng* 成 is a resultative verb complement, which is followed by the result of the action.

中国从一个贫穷落后的农业国家转变成一个工业化国家，从一个受帝国主义欺凌的半殖民地转变成一个独立自主的主权国家。

改革开放以后，中国的经济制度从计划经济转变成了市场经济。

7. 虽然……，但……多少也有+一点儿/一些……+abstract noun

Here *duōshǎo* 多少 means "somewhat; more or less; to some degree," often used to make a statement or description less forceful or definite.

"美国梦"强调个人的成功，而"中国梦"强调国家的强大。虽然"美国梦"强调的是个人成功的过程，但多少也有一些民族主义的情绪。

虽然父母不能帮孩子做决定，但是父母的看法对孩子多少也有一点儿影响。

8. Subj. 始终 + 是/在 doing sth. /坚持/没有/不能/无法……

This pattern is often used to emphasize that the subject remains the same or is consistent from the beginning up to the present moment.

一战以后，美国始终是世界上最强大的国家。

虽然战争早已结束了，但是战争造成的影响却始终无法消除。

87

9. A 没有 B 这么/那么 positive adj.（高、大、好, etc.）

The structure, meaning "A is not as adj. as B" is used to make a comparison (note that this structure indicates that B is better in quality, larger in quantity or higher in degree).

美国人的民族主义情绪没有中国人这么强烈。

中国拥有的武器没有美国那么多。

10. ……，这是可以理解/接受的。　　It is understandable/acceptable that…

美国从来没有被外国打败过，所以美国人的民族主义情绪就没有中国人那么强烈，这是可以理解的。

年轻人还没结婚就住在一起，在城里人看来，这是可以接受的。可是在农村人看来，这是不可以接受的。

11. ……A 早就已经……了，而且比任何…都……

The pattern, meaning "not only has the Subj. already…long ago, but it is more…than anything/anyone else," can be used to point out that A has an advantage over others not only in terms of time but also in other degrees.

中国拥有的武器，美国早就已经有了，而且比任何国家拥有的都多。

这些知识，他早就已经学会了，而且比任何人掌握得都好。

12. ……通过 an intermediary/a method + achieve a goal

To achieve a goal through a medium of…/by means of…

到了中国以后，最让我感到不方便和不习惯的是我不能看脸书，不能通过谷歌找到我要的东西，不能通过脸书和朋友联系。

在网络时代，你可以通过各种各样的方法学中文。

13. …既 negative statement …，也 negative statement …，…只 affirmative statement…

The subject is/does not…nor is/does it…, all the subject is/does is only…The structure, by consecutively make two negations, stresses the importance of the third clause.

我的 "中国梦" 很简单，既不需要航空母舰，弹道导弹，也不需要汽车、房子，我的 "中国梦" 只是一些最简单、最基本的要求。

雾霾严重的时候，打开窗户，你看到的既不是绿水，也不是白云，只有灰蒙蒙的天。

III. 词语辨析 *Synonym Differentiation*

1. 骄傲：to feel proud or take pride (in sb./sth.); arrogant

   自豪：to feel proud (of one's identity, country, etc.)

   他考上了北京大学，他的父母和老师都为他骄傲。

   虽然你的成绩不错，但是你不能骄傲，还得继续努力学习。

   中国的强大让每个中国人感到自豪。

2. 愿望： wish (often related to personal life)

   理想： ideal; aspiration (career related)

   你今年的生日愿望是什么？

   我的理想是当医生，帮助需要帮助的病人。

3. 不能 V.P.： "不能" stresses that the subject is not allowed to do something.

   V 不 Complement： this pattern stresses that it is impossible for the action to happen due to lack of some condition. "V 不到" stresses that the object is unavailable or inaccessible.

   在中国，我不能看脸书，不能通过谷歌找我要的东西，不能在网上看《纽约时报》，看不到蓝天白云，呼吸不到新鲜空气。

   我们现在在上课，你不能进来。

   现在门锁着，我进不来。

我的 "中國夢"

近幾年在中國，人們最關注的一個話題是 "中國夢"。在街上也能看到許多以中國夢為主題的標語、廣告和漫畫。

當然，說到"中國夢"不能不讓我想起美國人常說的"美國夢"。我想，"中國夢"和"美國夢"有個基本的不同："美國夢"強調的是個人的成功,是一個人,尤其是移民到美國的外國人,在美國奮鬥成功的過程。許多一無所有的外國人移民到了美國以後,先讀書,然後找個穩定的工作,結婚,生孩子,買汽車,買房子,家裡再養條狗,養隻貓,最後成為美國公民。這基本上就實現了美國人所謂的"美國夢"。"美國夢"往往是一個人從一無所有到無所不有的過程,代表的是個人的努力可以帶來成功,不需要靠關係,走後門。個人的才能和努力才是成功最主要的因素。

"中國夢"，據我的觀察, 除了個人的成功、汽車、房子這些東西以外,更重要的是從國家的角度來說明中國人期盼著中國要從一個落後的發展中國家轉變成一個先進的發達國家,從一個貧窮的農業國家轉變成一個富裕的工業化國家,從一個受帝國主義侵略的半殖民地轉變成一個獨立自由的主權國家。這是千千萬萬中國人的"強國夢"。這裡頭有很強烈的民族主義情緒, 國家越來越發達, 這是中國人感到最自豪最驕傲的地方。

"美國夢"當然多少也有民族主義的情緒,但絕對沒有"中國夢"這麼強烈,也沒有中國人感受得這麼迫切。因為美國從來沒有被外國打敗過,佔領過,而且一戰以後,美國始終是世界上最強大的國家。美國在軍事上的霸權,更是沒有第二個國家可以提出挑戰的,所以美國人的民族主義情緒沒有中國人那麼強烈,這是可以理解的。對中國人來說,航空母艦、遠程轟炸機、洲際彈道導彈是中國夢裡面很重要的一部分。對一般美國人來說,在他們的"美國夢"裡大概不會想到這些武器。因為這些武器美國早就已經有了,而且比任何國家擁有的都多。

我到了中國以後,最讓我感到不方便和不習慣的是我不能看臉書,不能通過谷歌找我要的東西,不能在網上看《紐約時報》,看不到藍天白雲,呼吸不到新鮮空氣,所以對一個美國學生來說,我的"中國夢"很簡單,既不需要航空母艦、彈道導彈,也不需要汽車、房子。我的"中國夢"只是我可以通過臉書和朋友聯繫,不必"翻牆"就可以看到《紐約時

90

報》,出門不必戴口罩,打開自來水就能喝,吃水果不必擔心農藥。這些看起來很簡單的願望,在今天的中國還是一個"夢"。

课后习题

第 7 课

一、词语搭配 (Please pair the term in the left column with the most appropriate term in the right column. Then use the completed phrases to complete the sentences. You can change the order of the words and add more information if needed.)

（1）

(C) 关注　　　　A 工作
(A) 稳定的　　　B 武器
(B) 拥有　　　　C 话题
(D) 强烈的　　　D 情绪

1. 因为以前受到帝国主义的侵略，"中国梦"里有 D _____。
2. 美国有枪的问题是因为 B _____。
3. 为了让家人过上好日子，A _____。
4. 北京的空气污染是近几年 C _____。

（2）

(D) 先进的　　　A 挑战
(B) 迫切的　　　B 要求
(A) 提出　　　　C 理想
(C) 实现　　　　D 经验

1. 我们到外国来参观是为了学习 D _____，不是为了旅游。
2. 大学生应该努力学习，这样以后才能 C _____。
3. 解决空气污染，改善空气质量，这是老百姓 B _____。
4. 有人认为，中国建造航空母舰是在向美国 A _____。

二、选择填空 (Complete the sentences by choosing the most appropriate term.)

1. 骄傲   自豪

中国人认为，成功了也不能_____，要继续努力。

美国是世界上最自由的国家，作为美国人，我感到很_____。

2. 愿望   理想

长大以后，我想当医生，这是我的_____。

我有一个小小的_____，我希望我生日的时候爸爸能回家。

3. 不能进去   进不去

老师们在里面开会，你现在_____。

教室的门锁着，我_____。

不能吃   吃不完

你今天点了太多东西了，我们根本_____。

这个蛋糕你现在_____，你哥哥还没吃呢。

三、完成句子 (Complete the sentence or dialogue with the given item in parentheses.)

1. A：你们学校常常举行什么样的活动？

   B：_____。(…以…为主题)

2. A： 听说以前的中国人谈恋爱都是为了结婚，现在的年轻人呢？

   B：_____。(…以…为目的)

3. 看到我桌子上摆着的照片，_____。(就让我想起…)

4. 父母常常劝孩子不要去国外工作，_____。(尤其是…)

5. A：你在这么有名的学校当老师，收入一定很高！

   B：_____。(A…不 / 没…，B 才…)

6. A："美国梦"是不是以国家强大为目的的"强国梦"？

B: _____。(A...不 / 没...，B 才...)

7. A：没去过中国的人对中国一点儿都不了解。

　　B: 这不一定。_____。(多少也有一点儿 / 一些 abstract noun)

8. A：你们国家这么注意保护环境，应该没有污染问题吧？

　　B: _____。(多少也有一点儿 / 一些 abstract noun)

9. 从 1978 年改革开放到现在，中国政府_____。

　　　　　　　　　　　　　　　　　　(始终是/在+doing sth./坚持/没有/无法...)

10. 虽然中国现在也拥有航空母舰了，但是_____。

　　　　　　　　　　　　　　　　　　　　　(A 没有 B 这么 / 那么...)。

11. A：我发现在纽约有 "共享单车"，真方便。不知道北京有没有？

　　B: _____。(A 早就已经...了，而且比...都...)

12. 五岁的孩子：我会写字了，你会吗？

　　七岁的孩子：_____。(A 早就已经...了，而且比...)

13. A：你在中国的时候怎么跟美国的朋友联系？

　　B: _____。(通过)

14. 穷人对食物的要求不高，_____。(既不...，也不...，...只...)

15. 穷人对房子的要求也不高，_____。(既不...，也不...，...只...)

四、回答问题 (Answer the questions.)

1. 什么是 "中国梦"？"中国梦" 和 "美国梦" 有什么不同？

2. "美国梦" 为什么更强调个人的成功？这跟美国的历史、社会有没有关系？

3. "中国梦" 为什么有强烈的民族主义情绪？

4. 作者对中国政府发展军事有什么看法？你认为一个强大的国家需不需要有强大的军事力量？

5. 作者认为，"中国梦" 应该强调什么？为什么？

6. "民族主义" (nationalism) 和 "爱国主义" (patriotism) 一样吗？有什么不同？

7. 你以前听说过 "中国梦" 吗？你们国家的媒体对中国政府提出的 "中国梦" 有什么看法？

第 8 课

"宁要大城一张床，不要小城一套房"

A：中国学生   B：美国学生

A：我的一个好朋友马上就要毕业了。他正在考虑，到底是留在北京，还是回老家的小县城工作。

B：我听说，现在中国流行 一句话："宁要大城一张床，不要小城一套房。"意思是，很多年轻人宁可在大城市吃苦奋斗，也不要到小城市过没有激情 的生活。在我看来，这样的决定是对的。要是我是你的朋友，我会选择留在北京。

A：我觉得，你可能不太了解中国的情况。现在在中国的大城市里工作，生活会过得非常辛苦。首先，在大城市里，工作的竞争非常激烈。要

考虑	kǎolǜ	v.	to consider; to think over
县城	xiànchéng	n.	town
流行	liúxíng	v./adj.	to be popular or prevalent
套	tào	m.w	(for an apartment or suite.)
吃苦	chīkǔ	v.	to bear hardships; to suffer a great deal
奋斗	fèndòu	v.	to strive, to make a vigorous fight; to struggle hard (for success)
激情	jīqíng	n.	(lit.) intense emotion; passion; enthusiasm
辛苦	xīnkǔ	adj./adv.	(of life) hard; toilsome; laborious
激烈	jīliè	adj.	fierce (competition)

是一个人不拼命工作，他很可能会被解雇。其次，大城市里的生活费用非常高。每个月光房租就得好几千，再扣掉吃饭，坐车，应酬请客的钱，剩下的就不多了，根本攒不下什么钱。你再看看现在北京、上海、广州的房价，一个普通人工作几十年，恐怕也买不起一套小房子。据说，现在很多北京、上海、广州的毕业生都因为受不了大城市巨大的生活压力而离开了这些一线城市。

B：到小城市工作，情况就会好得多吗？

A：那当然了。到小城市工作，生活会过得很轻松。一方面，小地方的工作压力不大，年轻人会有稳定的工作，稳定的收入，稳定的人际关系，另一方面，小城市的房价、生活费用也都比大城市低得多，用不了几年，

拼命	pīnmìng	adv.	to exert the utmost strength; to give it one's all
解雇	jiěgù	v.	to fire
费用	fèiyòng	n.	expenses; cost
房租	fángzū	n.	rent
扣掉	kòudiào	v.	to deduct…from…
应酬	yìngchóu	v./n.	to (begrudgingly) attend social events (to conform to social norms)
剩下	shèngxià	v.-c.	to be left (over); remain
攒钱	zǎnqián	v.-o.	to save up money
房价	fángjià	n.	price of a house
普通人	pǔtōng rén	n.	ordinary person; average people
巨大	jùdà	adj.	huge; tremendous
一线城市	yīxiàn chéngshì		first-tier cities (e.g. Beijing, Shanghai, Guangzhou, and Shenzhen)
人际关系	rénjì guānxi	n.	interpersonal relations

96

就能买上房子，开上车子，结婚生子了。这样的生活不是比在大城市里的生活幸福得多吗？

　　B：但并不是每个人都追求安稳的生活。到小城市工作虽然可以很快就有房有车，但这种悠闲的生活不能给人带来激情，会让人觉得没有什么成就感。在小城市，年轻人没有什么机会发挥自己的能力，用自己学到的知识来获得更大的发展。相反，大城市的机会就多多了，像苹果、麦当劳这些国际大公司都在北京、上海设立办事处。如果能进入这样的大公司，年轻人不但会有很高的收入，而且能积累丰富的工作经验，还可以开始建立一些人脉。有了这些经验和人脉，以后就能找到更好的工作。对我来说，这两个选择代表两种生活态度。选择大城市是选择奋斗，而选择小城市是选择安稳。我不想刚毕业就过"退休"的生活。

幸福	xìngfú	adj./n.	happy; happiness
追求	zhuīqiú	v.	to pursue; to seek
安稳	ānwěn	adj.	secure and peaceful
悠闲	yōuxián	adj.	leisurely and carefree
成就感	chéngjiù gǎn	n.	a sense of fulfillment; a sense of achievement
发挥	fāhuī	v.	to give full play to (one's ability)
获得	huòdé	v.	to gain (opportunity; experience, etc.)
设立	shèlì	v.	to establish; to set up
办事处	bànshì chù	n.	office; agency
积累	jīlěi	v.	to accumulate
建立	jiànlì	v.	to establish (connections; an institute)
人脉	rénmài	n.	connections; social network
退休	tuìxiū	v.	to retire

97

A：不可否认，中国最好的资源都集中在大城市里，像北京、上海广州、深圳这些一线城市，到处都是机会。可是在这些一线城市很难拿到户口。你听说过"北漂"吗？

B：什么是"北漂"？

A："北漂"就是在北京工作的外地人。他们没有北京的户口，又买不起房子，生活很不稳定，就像漂在水上的树叶一样。"北漂"们没有户口，即使他们有钱，也买不了房子，买不了汽车，他们的孩子也上不了公立学校。如果"北漂"的收入够高，他们的孩子还可以上国际学校。但要是他们的收入不够高，那孩子上学就是个大问题了。

B：户口的问题可以以后慢慢解决，二十多岁的大学毕业生，不能年纪轻轻就放弃奋斗和理想。而且，我相信大城市丰富的文化、娱乐活动更吸

否认	fǒurèn	v.	to deny
集中	jízhōng	v.	to concentrate
深圳	Shēnzhèn	n.	Shenzhen, a major city and financial center in South China, located immediately north of Hong Kong
户口	hùkǒu	n.	registered permanent residence
外地人	wàidì rén	n.	non-local people; people from out of town (Local people: 本地人；当地人)
漂	piāo	v.	to float (on the water); to drift (down the stream)
树叶	shùyè	n.	leaves (of a tree)
公立	gōnglì	adj.	public (school, hospital, etc.)
放弃	fàngqì	v.	to give up; to abandon
理想	lǐxiǎng	n.	ideal; aspiration (career related)

引 年轻人。平时 年轻人工作可能非常忙碌，但到了周末，可以看看电影、演出，泡泡酒吧、咖啡馆什么的。

A：但你也别忘了大城市的污染、交通问题。再说，现在中国的城乡差距 这么大，主要就是因为小城市严重缺乏人才。要是大学毕业生都留在大城市里，那贫富差距会继续拉大。大学生是社会的精英，是不是应该为社会的发展做一点贡献 呢？

B：你别说 我自私，但我觉得缩小 城乡差距是政府的责任，不是大学毕业生的。中国政府得先想办法给小城市投入 资金，发展小城市的经济，创造 更多更好的工作机会，才能吸引优秀 的人才到小城市工作。

娱乐	yúlè	n.	entertainment
吸引	xīyǐn	v.	to attract
平时	píngshí	t.w.	ordinarily; in regular times
忙碌	mánglù	adj.	busy (formal)
差距	chājù	n.	gap; disparity
人才	réncái	n.	talented person; talent; human resources
拉大	lādà	v.	(of gap) to widen
精英	jīngyīng	n.	elite
贡献	gòngxiàn	n./v.	contribution; to contribute
说	shuō	v.	to criticize; to blame
自私	zìsī	adj.	selfish
缩小	suōxiǎo	v.	to narrow (a gap); reduce (in width, size, scope)
投入	tóurù	v.	to invest; to input
资金	zījīn	n.	fund; capital
创造	chuàngzào	v.	to create
优秀	yōuxiù	adj.	outstanding; excellent; splendid

I. 词语搭配 *Collocation*

1. Sb. 留在 place　　to stay/remain at

2. ……在 (a certain place) 很流行

   (of a style of clothing, song, argument, etc.) is very popular/prevalent in (a certain place)

   (A certain place) 流行＋一句话：……

   …is a saying that is prevalent in (a certain place)

3. 生活过得很＋辛苦 / 轻松 / 幸福

   to lead a… (difficult/easy/happy) …life

4. 竞争＋激烈

   fierce competition

5. A 解雇 B　　A fires B

   B 被 A 解雇　　B is fired by A

6. 费用＋高 / 低

   a large/small expense

7. 攒下＋一些/很多＋钱

   to save up a little/a lot of money (*xià* 下 is a resultative complement)

8. 追求+……的生活/目标/理想

   to pursue/seek a certain kind of life/goal/ ideal

9. 发挥＋能力

   to give full play to one's ability/to bring one's ability into full play

10. 积累+经验/知识

    to accumulate experience/knowledge

11. 丰富的经验/知识/资源

    a wealth of experience/knowledge/resources

12. 建立+人脉

    to establish one's connections/social network

13. 生活 / 工作＋忙碌

busily occupied (with life/work)

14. 泡＋酒吧 / 网吧 / 咖啡馆

to kill time/dally in the bar/internet café/café

15. 差距＋大 / 小

a large/small gap

16. 缺乏＋人才 / 资源 / 了解 / 沟通 / 交流

to lack human resources/natural resources /basic understanding /mutual

understanding/communication

17. A 为 B（one's country/society）做贡献

A makes a contribution to B

18. 缩小/拉大＋差距

to narrow/widen the gap

19. （在……方面）投入＋资金 / 时间

to invest money/time in…

20. 创造＋机会/环境

to create opportunities/a certain environment

II. 句型结构 *Sentence Pattern and Structure*

1. ……宁可 A，也不 B.

"The subject would rather do A than do B," is used when one has to pick the lesser of
the two evils (usually indicated by A)
为什么人们宁可要大城市里的一张床，也不要小城市里的一套房呢？
看看世界历史，你会发现，有的人是宁可牺牲生命，也不要失去自由的。

2. …statement…，首先……，其次……

"…, first of all,…, secondly…," is often used to arrange sentences in a logic order.
住在大城市里，生活会过得非常辛苦。首先，在大城市里，工作的竞争非常激烈，

101

你得拼命工作。其次，大城市里的生活费用非常高，你攒不下什么钱。

3. ...statement 很高 / 多 / 贵 / ...，光...example...就得＋number phrase

In this structure, the clause after *guāng* 光 emphasizes a single example that supports the previous statement.

大城市里的生活费用非常高。每个月光租房子就得好几千。

这个星期的作业很多，光中文课的作业就得做五六个小时。

4. Verb 不 Complement 什么 Object

e.g. 找不到什么好工作   I cannot find many good jobs

没有什么 object

e.g. 没有什么朋友   have few friends/do not have many friends

不是什么 object

e.g. 不是什么问题   not a big problem/no big deal

In the structures above, *shénme* 什么 denotes "not many or not much." (Note that it is different from "not any." For example, to say 我没有什么朋友 (I do not have many friends) is not same as 我没有朋友 (I do not have any friends.)

住在大城市里攒不下什么钱，可是，在小城市找不到什么好工作。

在小城市，年轻人没有什么机会发挥自己的能力。

虽然在大公司工资高，但是没有时间享受生活，这不是什么好事。

5. ......，恐怕......

This structure, meaning "I am afraid that...," expresses one's concern or regret over an unwanted situation (note that the "I am" part is usually omitted in Chinese).

现在北京、上海、广州的房价太高了，恐怕一个普通人工作几十年也买不起一套小房子。

现在经济形势不太好，找工作恐怕也不容易。

6. Verb 不 + 起

Qĭ 起 is a verb complement, indicating the subject can't afford to do sth."

北京、上海、广州的房价太高了，普通人买不起。

北京的文化活动不少，但是价格也不低，穷学生往往看不起现场演出，只好躲在屋里看电影。

7. ……，一方面……，另一方面，…也…

This structure indicates that two actions or situations coexist and supplement each other. Both of them are used to support the previous statement.

到小城市工作，生活会过得很轻松。一方面，小地方的工作压力不大，另一方面，小城市的房价、生活费用也比大城市低得多。

在中国学习中文，一方面可以有更多机会练习，另一方面也可以更好地了解中国。

8. ……用不了 + time duration 就能……了

This structure can be used to make an optimistic prediction, meaning that "in less than a certain period of time, the subject will be able to do sth. that he/she is unable to do at the moment."

到小城市工作，用不了几年就能买上房子，开上车子，结婚生子了。

许多"北漂"相信，只要肯吃苦，够努力，用不了几年就能在北京稳定下来了。

9. Verb 上 Object

Shang 上 is used as a verb complement, indicating the attainment of the object. This structure, often related to one's financial ability, denotes the improvement of one's life.

在银行工作几年以后，他就买上了房子，开上了好车。

以前，这里的人们只能喝河水，后来村里有了电，人们也喝上了自来水了。

10. ……，相反，……

"…on the contrary/quite the contrary…" is used to form a contrast with the previous

103

statement, or to simply state that the opposite of what was said before is true.

在小城市，年轻人没有什么机会发挥自己的能力，用自己学到的知识来获得更大的发展。相反，大城市的机会就多多了，年轻人可以进入大公司，积累丰富的工作经验，还可以开始建立一些人脉。

他上个星期没通过考试，但他并没有失去希望，相反，他投入了更多时间去学习。

11. ……刚…action 1…就…action 2…

This structure means that action 2 took place immediately or shortly after action 1 and indicates that action 2 happened earlier than expected.

我不想刚毕业就过"退休"的生活。

因为他父母有钱有势，所以他刚毕业就找到了工作，还买了房子。

12. 不可否认，……

It is undeniable that…

不可否认，中国最好的资源都集中在大城市里。

虽然高考制度存在一定的问题，但不可否认，这个制度也提供了公平竞争的机会。

13. ……集中在…… (里 / 上 / …)

(Attention, efforts, strength, resources, etc.) be concentrated in one place or aspect.

中国最好的资源、机会都集中在大城市里。

他的注意力都集中在学习上，根本不考虑别的事。

14. 像 A、B、（C、D）这些…general noun…   such as

像北京、上海、广州、深圳这些一线城市，到处都是机会。

像长城、故宫这些景点，一年到头都人山人海。

15. 即使 A……，也……

即使 A……，B 也……   even if

"北漂"们没有户口，即使他们有钱，也买不了房子，买不了汽车。

选择做"北漂"是个艰难的决定,即使年轻人自己愿意,他们的家人也未必愿意。

16. ……年纪轻轻就……　　at a young age

This pattern is often used to emphasize that the age and one's behavior or accomplishment, do not match.

二十多岁的大学毕业生,不能年纪轻轻就放弃奋斗和理想。

他年纪轻轻就当上了公司的 CEO,以后一定会有更大的成就。

III. 词语辨析 *Synonym Differentiation*

1. 拼命: to exert the utmost strength with all one's might (the subject is usually animate)

   努力:to make great efforts; to try hard

   在银行工作的压力非常大,年轻人得拼命工作才能成功。

   政府应该努力解决老百姓的问题。

2. 创造: to create + positive object (to cause something new to happen, e.g. opportunities 机会/a certain environment 环境)

   造成:to cause + negative object. (e.g. a problem)

   政府应该努力为年轻人创造更好的工作机会和工作环境。

   车辆过多容易造成交通堵塞的问题。

3. 稳定:stable (emphasis on state)

   安稳:to feel secure and peaceful (emphasis on feeling)

   在小城市,工作,收入,人际关系都比较稳定。

   他的生活很悠闲,所以他晚上睡觉睡得很安稳。

4. 恐怕:(I am) afraid that…

   可怕:fearful; scary

   他很可怕,恐怕没有人会喜欢他。

105

"寧要大城一張床，不要小城一套房"

　　A：中國學生　　　　B：美國學生

　　A：我的一個好朋友馬上就要畢業了。他正在考慮，到底是留在北京還是回老家的小縣城工作。

　　B：我聽說現在中國流行一句話："寧要大城一張床，不要小城一套房"，意思是，很多年輕人寧可在大城市吃苦奮鬥，也不要到小城市過沒有激情的生活。在我看來，這樣的決定是對的。要是我是你的朋友，我會選擇留在北京。

　　A：我覺得，你可能不太瞭解中國的情況。現在在中國的大城市裏工作，生活會過得非常辛苦。首先，在大城市裏，工作的競爭非常激烈。要是一個人不拼命工作，他很可能會被解雇。其次，大城市裏的生活費用非常高，每個月光租房子就得好幾千，再扣掉吃飯，坐車，應酬請客的錢，剩下的就不多了，根本攢不下什麼錢。你再看看現在北京的房價，一個普通人工作幾十年，恐怕也買不起一套小房子。據說，現在很多北京、上海、廣州的畢業生都因為受不了大城市巨大的生活壓力而離開了這些一線城市。

　　B：到小城市工作，情況就會好得多嗎？

　　A：那當然了。到小城市工作，生活會過得很輕鬆。一方面，小地方的工作壓力不大，年輕人會有穩定的工作，穩定的收入，穩定的人際關係；另一方面，小城市的房價，生活費用也都比大城市低得多。用不了幾年，就能買上房子，開上車子，結婚生子了。這樣的生活不是比在大城市裏的生活幸福得多嗎？

　　B：但並不是每個人都追求安穩的生活。到小城市工作雖然可以很快就有房有車，但這種悠閑的生活不能給人帶來激情，會讓人覺得沒有什麼成就感。在小城市，年輕人沒有什麼機會發揮自己的能力，用自己學到的知識來獲得更大的發展。相反，大城市的機會就多多了，像蘋果，麥當勞這些國際大公司都在北京、上海設立辦事處。如果能進入這樣的大公司，年輕人不但會有很高的收入，而且能積累豐富的工作經驗，還可以建立一些人脈。有了這些經驗和人脈，以後就能找到更好的工作。對我來說，這兩個選擇

106

代表兩種生活態度。選擇大城市是選擇奮鬥，而選擇小城市是選擇安穩。我自己不想剛畢業就過"退休"的生活。

A：不可否認，中國最好的資源都集中在大城市裏，像北京、上海、廣州、深圳這些一線城市，到處都是機會。可是在這些一線城市很難拿到戶口。你聽說過"北漂"嗎？

B：什麼是"北漂"？

A："北漂"就是在北京工作的外地人。他們沒有北京的戶口，又買不起房子，生活很不穩定，就像漂在水上的樹葉一樣。"北漂"們沒有戶口，即使他們有錢，也買不了房子，買不了汽車，他們的孩子也上不了公立學校。如果"北漂"的收入夠高，他們的孩子還可以上國際學校。但要是他們的收入不夠高，那孩子上學就是個大問題了。

B：戶口的問題可以以後慢慢解決，二十多歲的大學畢業生，不能年紀輕輕就放棄奮鬥和理想。而且，我相信大城市豐富的文化、娛樂活動更吸引年輕人。平時年輕人工作可能非常忙碌，但到了周末，可以看看電影、演出，泡泡酒吧、咖啡館什麼的。

A：但你也別忘了大城市的污染、交通問題。再說，現在中國的城鄉差距這麼大，主要就是因為小城市嚴重缺乏人才。要是大學畢業生都留在大城市裏，那小城市怎麼發展呢？這也會讓貧富差距越來越大。大學生是社會的精英，是不是應該為社會的發展做一點貢獻呢？

B：你別說我自私，但我覺得縮小城鄉差距是政府的責任，不是大學畢業生的。政府得先想辦法給小城市投入資金，發展小城市的經濟，創造更多更好的工作機會，才能吸引優秀的人才。

课后习题

第 8 课

一、词语搭配 (Please pair the term in the left column with the most appropriate term in the right column. Then use the completed phrases to complete the sentences. You can change the order of the words and add more information if needed.)

(1)

(B) 忙碌的   A 竞争
(D) 丰富的   B 生活
(A) 激烈的   C 说法
(C) 流行   D 资源

1. 他一个星期得工作 60 个小时，这种_____B_____让他觉得很辛苦。

2. 在中国，公立学校因为有政府的资金投入，能为学生提供更_____D_____。

3. 在中国_____C_____，"美国的大选（presidential election）是有钱人的游戏。"

4. 中国的人才都集中在大城市里，因此，_____A_____。

(2)

(D) 解雇   A 经验
(C) 建立   B 目标
(B) 追求   C 人脉
(A) 积累   D 工人

1. 中国要在 2050 年实现"中国梦"，这是中国政府现在_____B_____。

2. 因为经济越来越差，很多公司不得不_____D_____。

3. 他上大学的时候教过很多学生，在这方面_____A_____。

4. 在中国，不少人认为吃饭、喝酒是_____C_____的好办法。

（3）

（ C ）缩小　　A 时间
（ B ）发挥　　B 能力
（ D ）创造　　C 差距
（ A ）投入　　D 环境

1. 教育孩子不轻松，父母得送孩子上学，给孩子做饭，陪孩子看书，换句话说，父母需要____A____。
2. 我们应该多给年轻人一些机会，让他们去_____B_____，为社会做贡献。
3. 现在有钱人越来越有钱，穷人越来越穷，政府应该____C____。
4. 要想发展农村，政府就应该为农村____D____。

二、选择填空 (Complete the sentences by choosing the most appropriate term.)

1. 拼命(A)　　努力(B)
   他的女朋友爱上了别人，跟他分手了。他最近天天泡酒吧，_B_喝酒。
   政府应该_A_让人们过上幸福的生活，这样才能获得人们的支持。

2. 创造(A)　　造成(B)
   社会的精英都集中在大城市里，这_B_了城乡差距的拉大。
   学校应该为学生_A_一个轻松的学习环境。

3. 稳定(A)　　安稳(B)
   他跟太太结婚十年了，婚姻一直都很_A_。
   最近他的日子过得不太_B_，不是工作有问题，就是家里有问题。

4. 恐怕(A)　　可怕(B)
   要是你总是一有困难就放弃理想，_A_你很难获得成功。
   吃苦其实并不_B_，不吃苦怎么能得到幸福的生活呢。

三、完成句子 (Complete the sentence or dialogue with the given item in parentheses.)

1. A：我想买个名牌包，但真的太贵，假的质量又不好，如果你是我，你会怎么做？

    B：＿＿＿＿＿＿＿＿＿＿＿＿＿＿＿＿＿＿＿＿＿＿。(…宁可 A，也不 B)

2. A：大城市生活压力大，可是小城市没什么工作机会，你毕业后想去大城市还是小城市工作？

    B：＿＿＿＿＿＿＿＿＿＿＿＿＿＿＿＿＿＿＿＿。(…宁可 A，也不 B)

3. A：怎么样才能缩小城乡差距？

    B：＿＿＿＿＿＿＿＿＿＿＿＿＿＿＿＿＿＿＿＿。(首先…，其次…)

4. 学外语得花很多时间，＿＿＿＿＿＿＿＿＿＿＿＿＿＿＿＿＿＿＿。

    (光…example…就得＋number phrase)

5. 出国旅行得花很多钱，＿＿＿＿＿＿＿＿＿＿＿＿＿＿＿＿＿＿＿。

    (光…example…就得＋number phrase)

6. A：听说你找到了一个好工作，现在已经是有钱人了。

    B：怎么可能？我刚开始工作，＿＿＿＿＿＿＿＿＿＿＿＿。(没 V 什么 Object)

7. A：学校附近的百货商场是不是可以买到很多好东西？

    B：那个商场太小了，＿＿＿＿＿＿＿＿＿。(Verb 不 Complement 什么 Object)

8. A：你的朋友找到工作了吗？

    B：他没什么工作经验，＿＿＿＿＿＿＿＿＿＿＿＿＿＿＿＿＿。(恐怕)

9. 在中国宝马汽车(BMW)很贵，＿＿＿＿＿＿＿＿＿＿＿＿＿＿。(V 不起)

10. 了解中国的人情、关系很重要，＿＿＿＿＿＿＿＿＿＿＿＿＿＿＿＿。

    (一方面……，另一方面，…也…)

11. 他学东西特别快，＿＿＿＿＿＿＿＿＿。(用不了＋time duration 就能…了)

12. 他跑得很快，＿＿＿＿＿＿＿＿＿。(用不了＋time duration 就能…了)

13. A：改革开放以后，中国人的生活有什么改变？

    B：＿＿＿＿＿＿＿＿＿＿＿＿＿＿＿＿＿。(Verb 上 Object)

14. A：在大城市生活和在小城市生活有什么不同？

    B：＿＿＿＿＿＿＿＿＿＿＿＿＿＿＿＿＿＿＿。(相反)

15. 他太能吃了，＿＿＿＿＿＿＿＿＿＿＿＿＿＿＿＿＿。(刚 VP1 就 VP2)

16. 他这个星期的作业太多了，_____。（刚 VP1 就 VP2）

17. A：美国不能总是批评别的国家，美国自己也有很多问题。

　　B：_____，但是我们不能因此就不讨论这些问题了。（不可否认）

18. A：他怎么连他太太的生日都忘了？

　　B：_____。（…集中在…上 / 里）

19. A：在美国，上私立大学得花很多钱吗？

　　B：_____。（像 A、B、（C、D）这些…general noun…）

20. A：山寨产品很便宜，你别买真货了，太贵了。

　　B：_____。（即使 Subject 1……，Subject 2 也……）

21. A：你为什么不帮他呢？是没有时间吗？

　　B：我不喜欢他！_____。（即使 Subject 1……，也……）

22. A：为什么有那么多人觉得 Mark Zuckerberg 很厉害？

　　B：_____。（年纪轻轻就…）

四、回答问题 (Answer the questions.)

1. 你毕业以后想在大城市生活，还是在小城市生活？为什么？

2. 在大城市和小城工作、生活的好处是什么？坏处呢？

3. 作者认为，选择大城市和小城市代表不同的两种生活态度，你同意吗？为什么？

4. 在中国，大城市和小城市的差距大不大？这跟中国的发展方式有没有关系？

5. 在中国，小城市发展面临的最大问题是什么？应该怎么解决？

6. 在你们国家，城乡差距大不大？为什么？

第9课

老乡

　　在中国人的朋友关系里，有一种关系叫"老乡"或"同乡"，意思是说我们是从同一个地方来的。这个地方可以大到一个省，小到一个县或一个村。地方越小，往往表示关系就越近。这种同乡或老乡的关系在美国不是那么重要。

　　在中国两个陌生人见面，双方问完了姓名，往往接下来就问："您是哪儿人啊？"

　　"我是成都人。"

　　"我也是四川人。"

　　"啊！我们是同乡啊！"

老乡	lǎoxiāng	n.	fellow-townsman/villager
同乡	tóngxiāng	n.	(lit.) a person from the same village, town or province (can be used synonymously with 老乡)
省	shěng	n.	province
县	xiàn	n.	county
村	cūn	n.	village
双方	shuāngfāng	pron.	both sides; the two parties involved
接下来	jiēxiàlai	interj.	next; then
成都	Chéngdū	n.	the capital of Sichuan Province
四川	Sìchuān	n.	a province in the southwest of China

这时往往就改用方言交谈，感觉特别亲切。

汉语里问"你是哪儿人？"问的并不是"你现在住在哪儿？"而是你的"籍贯"，也就是你父母，甚至是你的祖父母是从哪儿来的。"籍贯"在中国人身份认同上的重要性，仅次于名字，有时和名字是分不开的。

这种因为同乡而发展出来的关系叫做"乡谊"。中国人特别重视乡谊，我想这和家乡观念是分不开的，所以在中国文学里，"思乡"是许多文学作品的主题。

唐朝有个诗人叫李白，他的《静夜思》是每个中国人都会背诵的：

改用	gǎiyòng	v.	to use (sth. else) instead; to switch to
方言	fāngyán	n.	dialect
交谈	jiāotán	v.	to converse; have a conversation (formal)
亲切	qīnqiè	adj.	warm; (a thing) feels near and dear to sb.
籍贯	jíguàn	n.	the place of one's origin
祖父母	zǔfùmǔ	n.	grandfather and grandmother
身份	shēnfèn	n.	identity
认同	rèntóng	v.	to identify with
重要性	zhòngyàoxìng	n.	importance
仅次于	jǐncìyú	v.	(the importance/grade/status or standing/level of...) is second only to...; be only inferior to
乡谊	xiāngyí	n.	fellow-villager's mutual affection; friendship between people from the same native place.
家乡	jiāxiāng	n.	hometown
思乡	sīxiāng	v-o.	to be homesick
作品	zuòpǐn	n.	works of (literature or art)
唐朝	Táng cháo	n.	The Tang Dynasty (618-907)

chuáng qián míng yuè guāng
床　前　明　月　光，　　　　　　Moonlight in front of my bed--

yí shì dì shàng shuāng
疑　是　地　上　霜。　　　　　　I took it for frost on the ground.

jǔ tóu wàng míng yuè
举　头　望　明　月，　　　　　　I lift my eyes to watch the bright moon,

dī tóu sī gù xiāng
低　头　思　故　乡。　　　　　　lower them and dream of home.

[trans. by Burton Watson (1925-2017)]

这首诗就是"思乡"最好的代表作。

有的中国人一离开家乡就会生病，这叫做"水土不服"。"水土不服"就是不适应外地的生活，对外地的水和泥土都不习惯。一个感到"水土不服"的人只要一回到家乡，他的病就好了。所以有的中国人在离开家乡的

诗人	shīrén	n.	poet
静夜思	Jìngyè sī	n.	"Thoughts on a Tranquil Night," a poem title.
背诵	bèisòng	v.	to recite; to repeat from memory
首	shǒu	m.w.	(for songs or poems)
诗	shī	n.	poem; verse
代表作	dàibiǎozuò	n.	representative works; masterpiece
水土不服	shuǐtǔ bùfú	v.	to be unaccustomed to the environment and climate of a new place; not acclimatized.
适应	shìyìng	v.	to acclimatize; to adapt to
泥土	nítǔ	n.	earth; soil

时候，要在行李里带一包故乡的土，据说这样做能避免到了外地发生水土不服的问题。这多么形象地说明了中国人对故乡土地的依恋！

中国人对乡土的依恋特别表现在方言和饮食习惯上。美国人语言和饮食的地方色彩远没有中国人那么强烈。纽约汉堡包、牛排和烤鸡的做法，跟芝加哥、旧金山的基本上是一样的。说英文的时候，纽约人的发音和旧金山人也没有什么不同。中国的情况是很不一样的：每个省不但有自己的方言，也有自己的饮食习惯。北方人的主食是面，而南方人是米饭；北方人喜欢吃水饺，而南方人喜欢吃馄饨；四川人和湖南人喜欢吃辣，而江苏人、浙江人喜欢在菜里加糖。北京烤鸭到了南京成了板鸭和咸水鸭。每个地方都有当地的特色小吃。所以在中国竟没有一种像麦当劳这样全中国人都能接受的中国食物，麦当劳在中国打破了中国人在饮食上的地域性，这是很值得研究的。当然，麦当劳受欢迎只能反映当代中国的城市文化，而不能反映农村的情况。

行李	xínglǐ	n.	luggage
故乡	gùxiāng	n.	hometown
避免	bìmiǎn	v.	to avoid
形象	xíngxiàng	adv.	vividly
依恋	yīliàn	v.	to feel attached to
色彩	sècǎi	n.	color
主食	zhǔshí	n.	staple food; principal food
馄饨	húndùn	n.	wonton
板鸭	bǎnyā	n.	pressed/dried salted duck
咸水鸭	xiánshuǐ yā	n.	brine duck
地域性	dìyù xìng	n.	local or regional peculiarity
当代	dāngdài	n.	the contemporary era; the present age

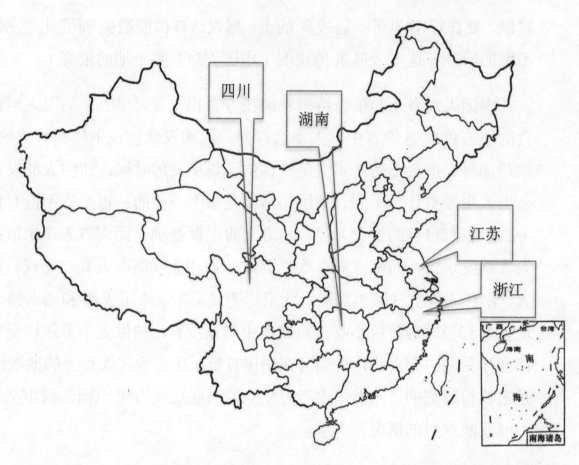

　　家乡观念让一个人爱护他的家乡，这对家乡的发展是有帮助的；但是，家乡观念过分强烈的时候，也让人形成"小圈子"，妨碍他和外地人的交往；或者因为过分依恋家乡的一切，使一个人离不开家乡，而老死在一个小地方。

爱护	àihù	v.	to cherish and take care of
圈子	quānzi	n.	circle; clique
妨碍	fáng'ài	v.	to hamper (one's relationship with others/…); to impede one's study/work
交往	jiāowǎng	v./n.	to be in contact with; to associate with
一切	yíqiè	pron.	everything; all
老死	lǎosǐ	v.	to die (of old age)

家乡观念和交通落后是联系在一起的。交通越不发达的地方，家乡观念越重。大都市里的人因为经常和其他地方的人接触，他们的家乡观念就没有农村人那么重。随着高速铁路、公路和航空的快速发展，我相信中国人的家乡观念也会跟着改变的。

Note:

李白　　Lǐ Bái (701-762) was a Chinese poet who lived during the Tang dynasty. Li Bai is often regarded, along with Du Fu, as one of the two greatest poets in China's literary history.

联系	liánxì	v.	to connect; to link; to relate
大都市	dà dūshì	n.	metropolis
接触	jiēchù	v.	come into contact with
航空	hángkōng	n.	aviation
快速	kuàisù	adv.	fast; rapidly

I. 词语搭配 *Collocation*

1. 跟 sb. 交谈

   to have a conversation with sb.

2. 感觉很亲切

   (a thing/a place that) feels near and dear to sb.

3. 适应+外地的生活/新生活/新环境

   adapt to+ life away from home/new life/new environment

4. 依恋+家乡/故乡/父母

   to feel attached to and be reluctant to leave one's hometown/parent

5. 特色+菜/小吃

   special dish/food (specialty)

6. 爱护+孩子/家乡/眼睛/动物

   to take good care of/to treasure children/one's hometown/eyes/animal

7. 形成+小圈子

   to form a small circle/clique

8. 妨碍……的交往/进步/发展/学习/工作

   to hamper one's relationship with others/the progress of…/the development of…; to impede study/work

9. 快速+发展/提高/增加

   rapidly develop/improve/increase

10. 家乡观念+很重

    A strong sense of/deep-rooted provincialism

    法制观念+很强

    A strong awareness of the legal system

II. 句型结构 *Sentence Pattern and Structure*

1. 同一+measure word +noun

   The same (place/time/person/thing, etc.). "同一+measure word +noun" involves only one place/time/person/thing that connects to more than one subject. For example, 我们从同一个地方来 means that "we come from the same place (only one place)." However, "一样" also indicates that there are two or more things sharing a quality or characteristic. For example, 这个地方和那个地方一样 means "this place and that place are the same (two places)."

在中国人的朋友关系里，有一种关系叫"老乡"或"同乡"，意思是说我们是从同一个地方来的。

上大学的时候，我们两个就住同一个宿舍，所以关系一直很好。

2. A 越……，B（就）越……

"The more A…, the more B…" is used to describe a correlation between A and B.

地方越小，往往表示关系就越近。

交通越不发达的地方，家乡观念就越重。

3. V 了 O，接下来就……

After…is finished, the very next thing was/will be…

中国人第一次见面的时候，双方问完了姓名，往往接下来就问："您是哪儿人啊？"

中国人说"成家立业"，意思是说，一个人结了婚，接下来就应该追求事业上的发展。

4. ……不是……，而是……

This structure, meaning "(the subj.) is not…but…" is often used to correct a misunderstanding or presumption.

汉语里问"你是哪儿人"，问的并不是"你现在住在哪儿"，而是你的"籍贯"。

随地吐痰这类的事情，不是道德问题，而是经济问题。经济发展了，这些坏习惯自然也就改掉了。

5. A 的重要性/成绩/地位/水平+仅次于 B

The importance/grade/status or standing/level of A is second only to B.

"籍贯"在中国人身份认同上的重要性仅次于名字。

在海外的中国城里，广东话的重要性仅次于英文，因为那里的人或者他们的祖先大都是从广东来的。

6. …concrete example…形象地+说明/反映/表现…abstract concept…

　　…vividly illustrates/reflects/shows or manifests

一个感到"水土不服"的人只要一回到家乡，他的病就好了，……这多么形象地说明了中国人对故乡土地的依恋。

他的作品形象地反映了那个时代的特点。

7. …abstract concept…表现在…concrete example…上

　　　…is manifested in…

中国人对乡土的依恋特别表现在方言和饮食习惯上。

中国人的热情往往表现在饭桌上。在饭桌上，他们特别喜欢劝酒劝菜。

8. A 远没有 B（那么）positive adj.

A is far less (adj.) than B

indicates that A is no match for B; A is far inferior to B.

美国人的语言和饮食虽然也有地方色彩，但远没有中国人那么强烈。

中国各地的发展还不平衡，农村地区远没有城市发达。

9. ……对 V.P./……的发展/进步/提高+有帮助

… is helpful to …V.P./the development of…/progress of…/improvement of…

家乡观念让一个人爱护他的家乡，这对家乡的发展是有帮助的。

投资教育对整个国家的发展是有帮助的。

10. 过分+disyllabic adjective/爱护/强调/注意/重视/依恋

excessively; over- (too much or too great)

家乡观念过分强烈的时候，也让人形成"小圈子"，妨碍他和外地人的交往；或者因为过分依恋家乡的一切，使一个人离不开家乡，而老死在一个小地方。

11. A 和 B 是联系在一起的，A 越……，B 越……

A and B are related/linked together, the more A…, the more B…

家乡观念和交通落后是联系在一起的。交通越不发达的地方，家乡观念越重。

经济发展的情况和保护环境的意识是联系在一起的。经济越发达，保护环境的意识越强。

12. 随着 A 的发展/提高/增加/……，B 也跟着+发展/提高/增加/……

Along with the development/improvement/increase of A, B will also develop/improve/increase

随着高速铁路，公路和航空的快速发展，我相信中国人的家乡观念也会跟着改变的。

随着经济的发展，老百姓的生活水平也跟着提高了。

13. …会…的

This structure can be used as a prediction that something will happen in the future.

随着高速铁路，公路和航空的快速发展，我相信中国人的家乡观念也会跟着改变的。

你穿这么少，出去会感冒的。

III. 词语辨析 *Synonym Differentiation*

1. 爱护：to take good care of, to treasure, to cherish

   保护：to protect (sb./sth from being hurt/polluted/damaged)

   家乡观念让一个人爱护他的家乡，这对家乡的发展是有帮助的。

   发展经济和保护环境是一样重要的。

老鄉

　　在中國人的朋友關係裏，有一種關係叫"老鄉"或"同鄉"，意思是說我們是從同一個地方來的。這個地方可以大到一個省，小到一個縣或一個村。地方越小，往往表示關係就越近。這種同鄉或老鄉的關係在美國不是那麼重要。

　　在中國兩個陌生人見面，雙方問完了姓名，往往接下來就問："您是哪兒人啊？"

　　"我是成都人。"

　　"我也是四川人。"

　　"啊！我們是同鄉啊！"

　　這時往往就改用方言交談，感覺特別親切。

　　漢語裏問"你是哪兒人？"問的並不是"你現在住在哪兒？"而是你的"籍貫"，也就是你父母，甚至是你的祖父母是從哪兒來的。"籍貫"在中國人身份認同上的重要性，僅次於名字，有時和名字是分不開的。

　　這種因為同鄉而發展出來的關係叫做"鄉誼"。中國人特別重視鄉誼，我想和家鄉觀念是分不開的，所以在中國文學裏，思鄉是許多文學作品的主題。

　　唐朝有個詩人叫李白，他的《靜夜思》是每個中國人都會背誦的：

牀前明月光，
疑是地上霜。
舉頭望明月，
低頭思故鄉。

　　這首詩就是"思鄉"最好的代表作。

　　有的中國人一離開家鄉就會生病，這叫做"水土不服"。"水土不服"就是不適應外地的生活，對外地的水和泥土都不習慣。一個感到"水土不服"的人只要一回到家鄉，他的病就好了。所以有的中國人在離開家鄉的時候，要在行李裏帶一包故鄉的土，據說這樣做能避免到了外地發生水土不服的問題。這多麼形象地說明了中國人對故鄉土地的依戀！

　　中國人對鄉土的依戀特別表現在方言和飲食習慣上。美國人語言和飲食的地方色彩遠沒有中國人那麼強烈。紐約漢堡包、牛排和烤雞的做法，跟芝加哥、舊金山的基本上是一樣的。說英文的時候，紐約人的發音和舊金山人也沒有什麼不同。中國的情況是很不一樣的：每個省不但有自己的方言，也有自己的飲食習慣。北方人的主食是面，而南方人是米飯；北方人喜歡吃水餃，而南方人喜歡吃餛飩；四川人和湖南人喜歡吃辣，而江蘇人、浙江人喜歡在菜裏加糖。北京烤鴨到了南京成了板鴨和鹹水鴨。每個地方都有當地的特色小吃。所以在中國竟沒有一種像麥當勞這樣全中國人都能接受的中國食物，麥當勞在中國打破了中國人在飲食上的地域性，這是很值得研究的。當然，麥當勞受歡迎只能反映當代中國的城市文化，而不能反映農村的情況。

　　家鄉觀念讓一個人愛護他的家鄉，這對家鄉的發展是有幫助的；但是，家鄉觀念過分強烈的時候，也讓人形成"小圈子"，妨礙他和外地人的交往；或者因為過分依戀家鄉的一切，使一個人離不開家鄉，而老死在一個小地方。

　　家鄉觀念和交通落後是聯繫在一起的。交通越不發達的地方，家鄉觀念越重。大都市裏的人因為經常和其他地方的人接觸，他們的家鄉觀念就沒有農村人那麼重。隨著高速鐵路、公路和航空的快速發展，我相信中國人的家鄉觀念也會跟著改變的。

课后习题
第9课

一、词语搭配 (Please pair the term in the left column with the most appropriate term in the right column. Then use the completed phrases to complete the sentences. You can change the order of the words and add more information if needed.)

(1)

(B) 形象地　　A 发展
(A) 快速地　　B 说明
(C) 过分地　　C 爱护

1. 要想_____A_____,就必须有发达的交通。
2. 很多中国父母_____C_____,什么事都帮孩子考虑,结果,孩子很难真正独立。
3. "睁一只眼,闭一只眼"_____B_____"假装看不见一些问题"的表现。

(2)

(B) 适应　　A 父母
(C) 妨碍　　B 新生活
(A) 依恋　　C 交往

1. 有的孩子为什么不能独立,就是因为过分_____A_____,什么时候都离不开父母。
2. 他们是同屋,可是却很少说话,因为文化的不同_____C_____。
3. 进入大学以后,有的学生不能很快地_____B_____,结果,影响了他们的学习。

(3)

(B) 形成　　A 眼睛
(A) 爱护　　B 小圈子
(　) 感觉　　C 亲切

1. 父母常常告诉孩子，要_____A_____，不要在很黑的地方看书。

2. 我们在交朋友的时候常常会____B____，因为我们总是喜欢跟自己差不多的人。

3. 到了国外，当你看到从自己国家来的人，往往会有一种____C_____。

二、选择填空 (Complete the sentences by choosing the most appropriate term.)

1. 爱护　　保护

    你自己一个人在国外，遇到危险的时候，你一定要知道怎么__B__自己。

    我们应该____A__公物（public property），不要在教室里的桌子上乱写乱画。

2. 特色　　特点

    北京烤鸭是北京的____A__菜，很多中国人，甚至是外国人都喜欢这道菜。

    跟中文、英文不同，日文把动词放在一个句子的最后，这是日文的____B__。

三、完成句子 (Complete the sentence or dialogue with the given item in parentheses.)

1. A："同屋"或者"室友"是什么意思？

    B：_____。（同一+measure word +noun）

2. A：在很多地方，为什么"关系"很重要？

    B：_____。（A 越…，B（就）越…）

3. A：没有新闻自由和贪污腐化有关系吗？

    B：_____。（A 越…，B（就）越…）

4. 中国人常说"吃人嘴软，拿人手短"，意思是_____。（V 了 O，接下来就…）

5. 在中国，男女朋友双方的父母见了面，_____。（接下来就…）

6. A：中国北方人的主食是米饭吗？

    B：_____。（不是…，而是…）

7. 中国的经济实力已经很强大，现在_____。（仅次于）

8. 在美国，西班牙语（Spanish）很重要，_____。（仅次于）

9. "走后门"这个词_____。（形象地+说明）

10. A：大家都说中国人爱面子，是真的吗？

　　B：是真的，＿＿＿＿＿＿＿＿＿＿＿＿＿＿＿＿＿。（abstract 表现在 concrete 上）

11. 中国的强大表现在＿＿＿＿＿＿＿＿＿＿＿＿＿＿＿＿。（abstract 表现在 concrete 上）

12. A：中国和美国差不多一样大，人口呢？

　　B：＿＿＿＿＿＿＿＿＿＿＿＿＿＿＿＿＿。（A 远没有 B（那么）positive adj.）

13. A：中国的方言差别很大，美国也有方言的差别吗？

　　B：＿＿＿＿＿＿＿＿＿＿＿＿＿＿＿＿＿。（A 远没有 B（那么）positive adj.）

14. A：老师为什么要求我们每天看中文电视？

　　B：＿＿＿＿＿＿＿＿＿＿＿＿＿＿＿。（对 V.P./...的发展/进步/提高+有帮助）

15. 政府对小城市投入资金，＿＿＿＿＿＿。（对 V.P./...的发展/进步/提高+有帮助）

16. A："虎妈"的教育方式有很大的问题，＿＿＿＿＿＿＿＿（过分+强调/重视）

17. A：为什么教育落后的地方往往也是经济不发达的地方？

　　B：＿＿＿＿＿＿＿＿＿＿＿＿＿＿＿＿＿＿＿＿＿。

　　　　　　　　　　　（A 和 B 是联系在一起的，A 越...，B 越...）

18. A：对一个国家来说，经济发展和文化的影响力有什么关系？

　　B：＿＿＿＿＿＿＿＿＿＿＿＿＿＿＿＿＿＿＿＿＿。

　　　　　　　（随着 A 的发展/提高/增加/...，B 也跟着+发展/提高/增加/...）

19. A：交通的发展对一个地区有什么影响？

　　B：＿＿＿＿＿＿＿＿＿＿＿＿＿＿＿＿＿＿＿＿＿。

　　　　　　　（随着 A 的发展/提高/增加/...，B 也跟着+发展/提高/增加/...）

20. 你得注意休息，要不然＿＿＿＿＿＿＿＿＿＿＿＿＿＿＿。（...会...的）

四、回答问题　(Answer the questions.)

1. "老乡" 是一种什么样的关系？这种关系在美国有没有？

2. 对中国人来说，"家乡"为什么很重要？

3. 中国对家乡的依恋表现在什么地方？

4. 中国文学中有很多"思乡"的作品。美国文学中有没有这样的作品？请介绍一个。

5. 中国的饮食有很强的地域性，请举例说明。在美国有没有类似的情况？为什么？

6. 家乡观念的好处和坏处是什么？

7. 你觉得中国人的家乡观念会不会消失？家乡观念可能会被哪些观念取代？

第 10 课

高铁

　　"高铁"就是"高速铁路"的简称。最近十几年来，中国在高铁的建设上真可以说是突飞猛进。高铁的平均时速在 300 公里左右。以前从上海到北京坐火车大概需要一天的时间，现在乘高铁只需五六个小时就到了，比以前快了三四倍。与此同时，中国的高速公路也四通八达，使原本非常偏僻的地方也能快速方便地和外界来往。

　　公共交通上的大改进改变了中国人的生活内容和方式，也改变了中国

简称	jiǎnchēng	n.	abbreviation
建设	jiànshè	v./n.	to construct; construction
突飞猛进	tūfēi měngjìn	idm.	to make a sudden stride in progress; to advance by leaps and bounds
平均	píngjūn	adj./adv.	average; equally
时速	shísù	n.	speed (per hour)
乘	chéng	v.	to travel by (train, bus or air)
倍	bèi	n.	times; -fold
偏僻	piānpì	adj.	remote
外界	wàijiè	n.	the external or outside world
来往	láiwǎng	v.	to have contact or dealings with sb.
改进	gǎijìn	v./n.	to improve; improvement
内容	nèiróng	n.	content
方式	fāngshì	n.	way; manner; style

人对空间、距离的看法。原来北京人觉得去趟上海是件大事，轻易不出这样的远门。现在不同了，坐上早上 6 点的班车，10 点半就到了上海，还赶得上中午的会议。晚饭以后，坐 7、8 点的高铁回北京，午夜以后也就能回到家了。这样的行程在有高铁以前是不能想象的，但现在有不少人经常这样往返。

　　这次从北京到上海，高铁给我的印象好极了，从火车站到火车上的设备都非常现代化，服务也很周到。我最喜欢的是看沿途的风景，中国的北

空间	kōngjiān	n.	room; space
趟	tàng	mw.	(for trips)
轻易	qīngyì	adv.	easily
班车	bānchē	n.	scheduled train/bus
赶上	gǎnshàng	v.-c.	to catch up with
会议	huìyì	n.	meeting; conference
午夜	wǔyè	n.	midnight
行程	xíngchéng	n.	itinerary
想象	xiǎngxiàng	v./n.	to imagine; imagination
往返	wǎngfǎn	v.	to shuttle; to take a roundtrip
设备	shèbèi	n.	equipment
周到	zhōudào	adj.	thoughtful; considerate
沿途	yántú	adj.	on the way; throughout a journey
风景	fēngjǐng	n.	scenery (usually a view of natural features); landscape

方大多是平原或高原。火车一过长江，绿色的稻田和河流、湖泊就明显增加了，怪不得中国人总说"江南"好。长江以南，不但天气比较暖和，物产也比较丰富，所以"江南"也叫"鱼米之乡"。

平原	píngyuán	n.	plain
高原	gāoyuán	n.	plateau
长江	Cháng Jiāng	n.	the Yangtze River
稻田	dàotián	n.	rice field
河流	héliú	n.	rivers (collective noun)
湖泊	húpō	n.	lakes (collective noun)
明显	míngxiǎn	adj./adv.	obvious; obviously
怪不得	guàibude	adv.	no wonder
江南	Jiāngnán	n.	south of the Yangtze River
物产	wùchǎn	n.	products; produce
鱼米之乡	yúmǐzhīxiāng	idm.	a region where the cultivation of rice and the breeding of fish flourish

在古代中国，政治中心往往在北方，而经济中心在南方。现在还是这样，北京是中国的政治中心，而上海是中国的经济中心。

中国是个有几千年历史，十几亿人口的大国，最粗略的区分办法是把中国划分为南方和北方。南北的划分是所有中国人都能接受的。淮河是大家公认的南北分界线。淮河以北是北方，淮河以南是南方。

南方人和北方人在语言上，生活习惯上，甚至于性情和长相上都有一定的不同。北方话比较接近普通话，南方话中影响最大的是上海话和广东话。我虽然学了几年中文，可是完全听不懂中国的南方方言，中国人自己也说"天不怕，地不怕，就怕广东人说普通话！"这句话当然有些夸张，但也能说明广东话和普通话在发音上的距离是很大的。其实，现在能说标准普通话的南方人并不比北方人少。

粗略	cūlüè	adj.	rough
区分	qūfēn	v.	differentiate; distinguish
划分	huàfēn	v.	divide
淮河	Huáihé	n.	The Huai river is located about midway between the Yellow River and Yangtze River. The Huai River is generally regarded as the geographical dividing line between Northern and Southern China.
公认	gōngrèn	v.	generally acknowledged; universally accepted
分界线	fēnjiè xiàn	n.	line of demarcation; boundary
长相	zhǎngxiàng	n.	looks; appearance
接近	jiējìn	v.	to be similar to (quality, interests, opinions)
标准	biāozhǔn	adj.	standard

一般中国人都认为北方人比南方人高大一些，而在性情上，北方人比较爽朗，而南方人比较温和，尤其是女人，一般的看法是南方女人比较温柔，北方女人比较直率。这些不同，在坐高铁的时候都能有直接的观察和感受。

我喜欢坐高铁的另一个原因是：高铁比飞机准点得多，飞机常常因为天气等原因晚点，而且一晚点就是好几个钟头。除非遇到大风雪或大暴雨，要不然高铁都能准点开车，准点到达目的地。

因为航空、铁路、公共交通非常方便，使原本"安土重迁"的中国人成了最喜欢旅游的人。每年出国旅游的中国人据说在全世界排第一位，中国成了旅游大国，不但去中国旅游的外国人多，出国旅游的中国人更多。

性情	xìngqíng	n.	disposition; temperament
爽朗	shuǎnglǎng	adj.	hearty; frank and open
温柔	wēnróu	adj.	gentle; sweet
直率	zhíshuài	adj.	frank; candid; straightforward
准点	zhǔndiǎn	adj./adv.	punctual; on time
晚点	wǎndiǎn	v.	to be late (for trains/flights); to be behind schedule
钟头	zhōngtóu	n.	hour
暴雨	bàoyǔ	n.	downpour
到达	dàodá	v.	to arrive
目的地	mùdì dì	n.	destination
安土重迁	āntǔ zhòngqiān	idm.	be attached to one's native land and unwilling to leave it
排	pái	v.	to rank… (a particular position) …in...

　　近几年来，中国交通建设的大发展，使许多原本偏远的地方都开发成了旅游景点。这一方面带动了当地的经济发展，提高了人民生活的水平，也缩小了城乡的差距，但是，另一方面，游客的大量增加造成了环境污染；原本清新美丽的自然景观，多出了许多非常俗气的装饰和贩卖劣质纪念品的小商店。

　　中国政府一方面要发展经济，一方面也得保护环境。政府不可以为了发展经济而污染环境；也不可以为了保护环境而不发展经济。怎么样在这两者之间取得平衡，这对中国政府和人民来说，都是很大的挑战。

偏远	piānyuǎn	adj.	remote (modifier)
开发	kāifā	v.	to start up and develop
景点	jǐngdiǎn	n.	scenery spot; place of interest; attraction
带动	dàidòng	v.	to bring along or to give an impetus to (economic growth/consumption)
清新	qīngxīn	adj.	pure and fresh
美丽	měilì	adj.	beautiful; pretty
景观	jǐngguān	n.	landscape; (natural/tourist) sight
俗气	súqì	adj.	vulgar; tacky; gaudy
装饰	zhuāngshì	n.	ornament
贩卖	fànmài	v.	to peddle
劣质	lièzhì	adj.	of poor quality (modifier)
纪念品	jìniàn pǐn	n.	souvenir
两者	liǎng zhě	pron.	both sides, both parties
取得	qǔdé	v.	to obtain; to gain
平衡	pínghéng	v./n.	to balance; balance

I. 词语搭配 *Collocation*

1. ……发展/建设/语言水平+突飞猛进

   The development of…/the construction of…/language proficiency advanced by leaps and bounds

2. 改进+制度/设备/方法　　to improve a system/equipment/method

   在……上的改进　　　　　an improvement on/over…

3. 出+远门

   to go on a long journey

4. 赶不上+activity/火车/飞机

   unable to catch the train/flight; unable to be on time for an activity

5. 服务/考虑+周到

   to offer attentive service; be very thoughtful

6. 物产+丰富

   rich in natural resources

7. 把……划分为 A 和 B

   divide…into A and B

8. 到达+目的地

   to arrive at the destination

9. 在……排第 n 位

   to rank… (a particular position) …in...

10. 开发+旅游景点

    to start up/develop tourist attractions

11. 带动+经济发展/消费

    to bring along/to give an impetus to economic growth/consumption

12. 在 A 和 B 之间取得/达到平衡

    to strike a balance between A and B

II. 句型结构 *Sentence Pattern and Structure*

1. ......可以说是......

    One may well say…/it may be said that…

    最近十几年来，中国在高铁的建设上真可以说是突飞猛进。

    纽约可以说是美国的经济和文化中心。

2. amount + 左右

    about, or so (used after a number)

    高铁的平均时速在 300 公里左右。

    完成这个考试需要 3 个小时左右。

3. 五六个小时、三四倍

    five or six hours/three to four times, in Chinese, you can use two consecutive numbers (usually from 1 to 9) to give an approximation. But note that "One or two people" should be translated as "一两个人" instead of "一二个人".

    现在乘高铁只需五、六个小时就到了，比以前快了三四倍。

    在北京，我们一个班只有四五个学生。

4. ......，与此同时，......　　　　　　　　…, meanwhile, …

    最近十几年来，中国在高铁的建设上真可以说是突飞猛进。与此同时，中国的高速公路也四通八达，使原本非常偏僻的地方也能与外界来往。

    过去十年，中国的城市快速发展，与此同时，农村也有了很大的进步。

5. Subj. 轻易+不+vp　　　　　　　Sb. hardly ever does sth.

    原来北京人觉得去趟上海是件大事，轻易不出这样的远门。

    我轻易不去市场买东西，因为我不会讲价，很容易上当。

6. ......在...certain time...以前/certain place 是不能想象的。

It would have been unimaginable before a certain time/in a certain place.

早上从北京去上海，晚上就能回北京，这样的行程在有高铁以前是不能想象的。

有大房子住，有汽车开，这样的生活，在二十年前的中国是不能想象的。

7. ……一……就……

This pattern is used to either mean 1) "as soon as"; or 2) "once; every time…, one would…," to describe a repeated, habitual action.

火车一过长江，绿色的稻田和河流、湖泊就明显增加了。

我一喝冰水就拉肚子。

8. …explanation…，怪不得，…unusual phenomenon…

This structure, meaning "no wonder; …that explains why…" is often used to explain an unusual phenomenon that the speaker has finally come to understand.

火车一过长江，绿色的稻田和河流、湖泊就明显增加了。怪不得中国人总说"江南"好。

中国人都相信喝冰水会拉肚子，怪不得他们总是喜欢喝热水。

9. ……是大家/全国/全世界……+公认的 title/term

……is widely/nationally/worldly recognized as……

淮河是大家公认的南北分界线。

美国是全世界公认的"超级大国"。

10. place 以+南/北/东/西

To the south/north/east/west of a place

淮河是大家公认的南北分界线。淮河以北是北方，淮河以南是南方。

"柏林墙"（The Berlin Wall）把德国划分为两个部分，柏林墙以东是东德，柏林墙以西是西德。

11. …常常 verb…，而且一 verb 就是+time duration

This structure denotes that the subject often does something and once the action starts, it will last for a long time. Note that this pattern often implies the excessiveness of the action.

飞机常常因为天气等原因晚点，而且一晚点就是好几个钟头。

这条路常常堵车，而且一堵就是好几个小时。

12. 除非……，要不然……

Chúfēi 除非, when used correlatively with *yàoburán* 要不然，means "unless/only in the case that…, otherwise, the subject will/will not…"

除非遇到大风雪或大暴雨，要不然高铁都能准点开车，准点到达目的地。

过去，女人在经济上依靠男人。除非没有办法，要不然女人是不会离婚的。

III. 词语辨析 *Synonym Differentiation*

1. 改善+生活/关系/情况/环境　　to improve one's life/relations (between two countries)/the situation/the environment of…

改进+设备/制度/方法　　　　to improve equipment/system/method

要改善自己的生活，就得努力工作。

这个工厂的设备非常落后，迫切需要改进。

2. 趟　a measure word often used to refer to a specific trip (usually a round trip) or action.

For example: Last week, I made a trip to Hong Kong. 上个星期，我去了一趟香港。

次　a measure word, meaning occurrence, or time (e.g. once, twice, three times, etc.)

For example: I've been to Hong Kong three times. 我去过三次香港。

Compare:

Please see your teacher in her office (make a trip/visit to your teacher's office) when you have a chance.

你有空的时候请去一趟老师的办公室.

I want to visit my teacher just once, for I've never been there before.

我想去一次老师的办公室，因为我从来没去过。

3. 温和：mild (tone, weather); gentle (disposition), it could refer to both male and female

温柔：gentle (usually refers to women)

南方人性情比较温和，南方女人比较温柔。

这里的气候温和，冬天不冷，夏天不热。

4. 漂亮：good-looking; pretty (usually physical attractiveness)

美丽：beautiful (hometown, mind, it is often used in literary language)

你的笔真漂亮！

有的人长得不漂亮，可是他们有一个颗美丽的心灵，什么时候都愿意帮助别人。

高鐵

"高鐵"就是"高速鐵路"的簡稱。最近十幾年來，中國在高鐵的建設上真可以說突飛猛進。高鐵的平均時速在 300 公里左右。以前從上海到北京坐火車大概需要一天的時間，現在乘高鐵只需五六個小時就到了，比以前快了三四倍。與此同時，中國的高速公路也四通八達，使原本非常偏僻的地方也能快速方便地和外界來往。

公共交通上的大改進改變了中國人的生活內容和方式，也改變了中國人對空間、距離的看法。原來北京人覺得去趟上海是件大事，輕易不出這樣的遠門。現在不同了，坐上早上 6 點的班車，10 點半就到了上海，還趕得上中午的會議。晚飯以後，坐7、8 點的高鐵回北京，午夜以後也就能回到家了。這樣的行程在有高鐵之前是不能想像的，但現在有不少人經常這樣往返。

這次從北京到上海，高鐵給我的印象好極了，從火車站到火車上的設備都非常現代化，服務也很周到。我最喜歡的是看沿途的風景，中國的北方大多是平原和高原。火車一過長江，綠色的稻田和河流、湖泊就明顯增加了，怪不得中國人總說"江南"好。長江以南，不但天氣比較暖和，物產也比較豐富，所以江南也叫"魚米之鄉"。在中國古代，政治中心往往在北方，而經濟中心在南方。現在還是這樣，北京是中國的政治中心，而上海是中國的經濟中心。

中國是個有幾千年歷史，十幾億人口的大國，最粗略的區分辦法是把中國劃分為南方和北方。南北的劃分是所有中國人都能接受的。淮河是大家公認的南北分界線。淮河以北是北方，淮河以南是南方。

南方人和北方人在語言上，生活習慣上，甚至於性情和長相上都有一定的不同。北方話比較接近普通話，南方話中影響最大的是上海話和廣東話。我雖然學了幾年中文，可是完全聽不懂中國的南方方言，中國人自己也說"天不怕，地不怕，就怕廣東人說普通話！"這句話當然有些誇張，但也能說明廣東話和普通話在發音上的距離是很大的。其實，現在能說標準普通話的南方人並不比北方人少。

一般中國人都認為北方人比南方人高大一些,而在性情上,北方人比較爽朗,而南方人比較溫和，尤其是女人，一般的看法是南方女人比較溫柔，北方女人比較直率。這些不同，在坐高鐵的時候都能有直接的觀察和感受。

我喜歡坐高鐵的另一個原因是：高鐵比飛機準點得多，飛機常常因為天氣等原因晚點，而且一晚點就是好幾個鐘頭。除非遇到大風雪或大暴雨，要不然高鐵都能準點開車，準點到達目的地。

因為航空、鐵路、公共交通非常方便，使原本"安土重遷"的中國人成了最喜歡旅遊的人。每年出國旅遊的中國人據說在全世界排第一位，中國成了旅遊大國，不但去中國旅遊的外國人多，出國旅遊的中國人更多。

近幾年來，中國交通建設的大發展，使許多原本偏遠的地方都開發成了旅遊景點。這一方面帶動了當地的經濟發展，提高了當地人的生活水平，也縮小了城鄉之間的差距，但是，另一方面，遊客的大量增加造成了環境污染；原本清新美麗的自然景觀，多出了許多非常俗氣的裝飾和販賣劣質紀念品的小商店。

中國政府一方面要發展經濟，一方面也得保護環境；政府不可以為了發展經濟而污染環境；也不可以為了保護環境而不發展經濟。怎麼樣在這兩者之間取得平衡，這對中國政府和人民來說，都是很大的挑戰。

课后习题
第 10 课

一、词语搭配 (Please pair the term in the left column with the most appropriate term in the right column. Then use the completed phrases to complete the sentences. You can change the order of the words and add more information if needed.)

（1）

(C) 物产　　A 周到
(A) 服务　　B 平衡
(B) 取得　　C 丰富

1. 我们既要重视孩子的兴趣,也不能忽视孩子的成绩,所以＿＿＿＿＿B＿＿＿＿＿。
2. 中国的江南地区＿＿＿＿＿C＿＿＿＿＿,中国人把这个地区叫做"鱼米之乡"。
3. 中国的高铁＿＿＿A＿＿＿,你有什么问题,高铁上的工作人员都会努力帮助你。

（2）

(B) 开发　　A 发展
(A) 带动　　B 旅游景点
(C) 改进　　C 制度

1. 这里有美丽的自然风景,我们应该＿＿＿＿＿B＿＿＿＿＿,吸引游客来参观 。
2. 政府在这个地区开发了很多旅游景点是为了＿＿＿A＿＿＿。
3. 目前中国的经济制度还是有很多问题,＿＿＿＿C＿＿＿＿。

二、选择填空 (Complete the sentences by choosing the most appropriate term.)

1. 改善　　改进
　　A　　B
   我们努力工作是为了＿A＿我们的生活，让我们的家人过更好的日子。

你们的工作方法太有问题了，要是你们不能＿＿＿＿，就不要在这里工作了。

2. 趟　　次

那个城市他一＿＿＿＿都没去过，所以他对那个地方一点儿都不了解。

下个星期，我得去一＿＿＿＿上海，我的好朋友结婚，我得去参加她的婚礼。

3. 温和　　温柔

他是一个性情＿＿＿＿的人，我从来没见他生过气。

她的父母从小就教育她：女孩子说话要＿＿＿＿，不能太大声，更不能大喊大叫。

4. 漂亮　　美丽

你今天穿的衣服真＿＿＿＿，在哪儿买的？我也想买一件。

无论有多么困难，他也要回到那个地方，因为那里有他＿＿＿＿的家乡。

三、完成句子 (Complete the sentence or dialogue with the given item in parentheses.)

1. A：美国的经济中心在哪儿？

   B：＿＿＿＿＿＿＿＿＿＿＿＿＿＿＿＿＿＿＿＿＿＿＿＿＿＿。（可以说是）

2. A：你每个星期花多少时间学习中文？

   B：＿＿＿＿＿＿＿＿＿＿＿＿＿＿＿＿＿＿＿＿＿＿。（amount + 左右）

3. 过去三十年来，中国的经济快速发展，＿＿＿＿＿＿＿＿＿＿＿。（与此同时）

4. A：中国人很喜欢问别人一个月赚多少钱，美国人也一样吗？

   B：＿＿＿＿＿＿＿＿＿＿＿＿＿＿＿＿＿＿＿＿＿。（轻易+不+vp）

5. 这个地方很危险，晚上的时候，＿＿＿＿＿＿＿＿＿＿＿。（轻易+不+vp）

6. 现在几乎每个大学生都有电脑，＿＿＿＿＿＿＿。（在...以前/place 是不能想象的）

7. 很多广东人说普通话都说得不标准，＿＿＿＿＿＿＿＿＿＿。（一...就...）

8. A：中国人为什么说"天不怕，地不怕，就怕广东人说普通话"？

   B：广东话跟普通话有很大的不同，所以广东人说普通话都说不好。

   A：＿＿＿＿＿＿＿＿＿＿＿＿＿＿＿＿＿＿＿＿＿＿＿＿。（怪不得）

9. A：世界上哪些城市可以算是"时尚之都"？

　　 B：_____（公认的 title）

10. A：中国有哪个建筑可以说是"建筑奇迹"？

　　 B：_____（公认的 title）

11. A：中国的南方和北方是怎么划分的？

　　 B：_____。(place 以+南/北/东/西）

12. A：北京的堵车问题很严重，美国的大城市也堵车吗？

　　 B：_____。

　　　　　　　　　　　（常常 verb…，而且一 verb 就是+time duration）

13. A：你跟谁最谈得来？

　　 B：_____。

　　　　　　　　　　　（常常 verb…，而且一 verb 就是+time duration）

14. A：周末我应该开车还是坐火车去纽约呢？

　　 B：_____。（除非…，要不然…）

15. A：你怎么样才愿意告诉我你的电话号码？

　　 B：_____。（除非…，要不然…）

四、回答问题 (Answer the questions.)

1. 高铁给中国人的生活、工作带来了什么改变？
2. 交通上的改进会怎么影响人们对空间和距离的看法？
3. 中国的北方和南方有什么不同？在你的国家呢？
4. 跟其他交通工具相比，高铁有什么优点？
5. 交通建设有什么好处？会带来什么问题？
6. 你觉得美国应不应该建设高铁？为什么？

第 11 课

中国人在改变

　　许多人谈到近年来中国的进步，大多用都市或高铁的建设作为例子，这是大家都看得到的具体 改变：破落 陈旧 的四合院、小胡同少了，几十层 高的摩天大楼 越来越多了；二十世纪六七十年代满街的自行车早已被汽车取代了。这些改变，有些人认为是进步；也有不少人，尤其是外国人，认为是对环境、历史和古迹的破坏。不过，我相信，多数 开汽车住高楼的中国人都是欢迎 这些改变的，他们并不怀念 挤在四合院里，过着没有自来水、抽水马桶 和空调的日子。

具体	jùtǐ	adj.	concrete; specific
破落	pòluò	adj.	dilapidated
陈旧	chénjiù	adj.	outdated; obsolete
四合院	sìhéyuàn	n.	a compound with houses around a square courtyard
胡同	hútong	n.	lane; alley
层	céng	m.w.	story; floor
摩天大楼	mótiān dàlóu	n.	skyscraper
破坏	pòhuài	v.	to destroy; to do great damage to
多数	duōshù	n.	the majority
欢迎	huānyíng	v.	to welcome
怀念	huáiniàn	v.	to remember fondly; to reminisce
自来水	zìlái shuǐ	n.	running water; tap water
抽水马桶	chōushuǐ mǎtǒng	n.	flush toilet

　　除了这些看得到的改变以外，还有一些变化，在我看来，更能说明中国的进步。十几年前，在公共场合抽烟是很平常的事，饭馆儿里，电影院里，虽然都贴着"请勿吸烟"的牌子，但是吸烟的人却比比皆是，火车上，公交车上，甚至在电梯里都有人吸烟！那个时候，在中国几乎没有不吸二手烟的自由。最近几年，这种情况至少在大都市里有了显著的改善。一方面政府加大了禁烟的力度，另一方面，老百姓也变得越来越自觉，在公共场合违规吸烟的人越来越少了。

　　外国人最怕在中国过马路，因为在中国，汽车是不让行人的，而开车的人又不很遵守交通规则，闯红灯是天天都发生的事。上个月，我去

公共	gōnggòng	adj.	public; common
场合	chǎnghé	n.	occasion; situation
平常	píngcháng	adj.	ordinary; common
贴	tiē	v.	to put up (a poster, notice, etc.)
请勿吸烟	qǐng wù xīyān	phr.	No smoking
牌子	páizi	n.	plate, sign
比比皆是	bǐbǐ jiēshì	adj.	can be found everywhere; all around
电梯	diàntī	n.	lift; elevator
二手烟	èrshǒu yān	n.	second-hand smoke
显著	xiǎnzhù	adj.	notable; remarkable
加大	jiādà	v.	to enlarge; to augment; to increase
禁烟	jìnyān	v.-o.	to ban smoking (in public areas)
力度	lìdù	n.	strength; force
自觉	zìjué	adj.	consciously; on one's own initiative
违规	wéiguī	v.-o.	to violate regulations; to break the rules
规则	guīzé	n.	regulation; rule

了一趟杭州，居然 发现汽车等行人先过街，这样的改变正悄悄 地在全中国发生。

　　中国人最受外国人批评的生活习惯是不排队和随地吐痰。"争先恐后"这四个字最能形容 中国人的群众心理，只要人一多，大家就没了秩序，人挤人成了具有 中国特色的景观 。无论是在食堂 买饭，还是在车站买票，成群 的人挤在一个窗口 抢饭、抢票是常常发生的事。现在因为科技的发达，车票、机票大多在网上订购，大大地缓解 了在车站抢购车票的问题，中国人也因此慢慢地养成 了排队的习惯。最近我在北京

闯红灯	chuǎng hóngdēng	v.o.	to run a red light
居然	jūrán	adv.	unexpectedly; surprisingly
悄悄	qiāoqiāo	adv.	secretly
随地吐痰	suídì tǔtán	phr.	to spit indiscriminately
争先恐后	zhēngxiān kǒnghòu	idm.	(lit.) strive to be the first and fear being left behind; vie for
形容	xíngróng	v.	to describe
群众心理	qúnzhòng xīnlǐ	n.	mentality of the masses
秩序	zhìxù	n.	order
具有	jùyǒu	v.	to possess or have (sth. immaterial)
景观	jǐngguān	n.	landscape; scene
食堂	shítáng	n.	canteen
成群	chéngqún	adj.	in groups; in great numbers
窗口	chuāngkǒu	n.	window
抢	qiǎng	v.	to scramble for; to vie for; to snatch
订购	dìnggòu	v.	to order (goods); to place an order for
缓解	huǎnjiě	v.	to alleviate; to ease
养成	yǎngchéng	v.	to cultivate the habit of

搭地铁、公交,居然看到中国人也排起队来了,这才是中国进步的证明。这比中国有了航空母舰更值得中国人骄傲!

　　随地吐痰还是许多中国人改不掉的坏习惯,我打的的时候,最怕司机摇下窗子,向外 pa 的吐口痰,我真怕那口痰吹到我脸上。中国人随地吐痰可能和空气污染有关系,空气太脏了,总觉得喉咙里有痰,等到空气污染有了改善,咳嗽吐痰的人也会减少的。

　　许多人把不排队和随地吐痰看成是个道德问题,其实,与其把这些毛病看成道德问题,不如把这些看成经济或者科技和医学的问题。经济发达了,科技和医学进步了,不排队和随地吐痰的人也会渐渐地减少的。

　　上海人是中国人里优越感最强的人,100 多年来,上海一直是中国的经济中心,也是中国西化最早的城市,因此,在上海人的眼里,除了上海人,其他地方的中国人都是"乡下人"。上海人在一起,一定得说上海话,这才能显示他们"与众不同"。但是,最近我看到电视报道:

搭	dā	v.	to take (a subway, ship, car, public transportation etc.)
打的	dǎdī	v.-o.	to take a taxi
摇	yáo	v.	to roll (up/down the car window)
口	kǒu	m.w.	a mouthful of (food, water, etc.)
吹	chuī	v.	to blow
毛病	máobìng	n.	defect; shortcoming; bad habit
医学	yīxué	n.	medical science
优越感	yōuyuègǎn	n.	sense of superiority
乡下人	xiāngxià rén	n.	country folk; hick
显示	xiǎnshì	v.	to show; to display; to demonstrate

许多上海的小学生已经不会说上海话了，大家都说普通话。100 多年来，先进的中国知识分子都主张推行 普通话，现在连上海人都说普通话了。中国终于 有了统一 的语言。普通话的胜利，在我看来，比高铁的建设更有意义！我的中国梦是上海人不说上海话了，广东人不说广东话了，台湾人不说闽南话 了，中国人都说普通话！就像美国人都说英文。

与众不同	yǔzhòngbùtóng	idm.	different "with" (from) the others; unconventional
推行	tuīxíng	v.	to promote (system, ideas); to carry into effect (new laws, practices)
终于	zhōngyú	adv.	at (long) last; in the end; finally
统一	tǒngyī	adj.	unified; unitary
胜利	shènglì	n.	victory; triumph
闽南话	Mǐnnán huà	n.	Southern Fujian dialect

I. 词语搭配 Collocation

1. 破落的＋村子 / 建筑 / 胡同 / 四合院儿

   dilapidated village/architecture/alley/*siheyuanr*

2. 怀念+过去的日子 / 生活

   to reminisce over past days/old life

3. 平常的+事 / 东西 / 现象

   ordinary matters/things/phenomena

4. ……有+显著的进步 / 改善 / 提高

   to have significant progress/improvement/increase

5. 加大…禁烟 / 投资 / 建设 / 发展 / …的力度

   to redouble the effort/strength of …smoking bans/investment/development

6. 具有……的特色 / 特点 / 作用

   to have/possess the characteristic of/function of……

7. 缓解……的问题 / 压力 / 紧张关系

   to alleviate the problem of…/stress/tension

8. 搭+地铁 / 公交 / 火车 / 飞机

   to take subway/public transportation/train/airplane

9. 改掉……坏习惯

   to rid oneself of the bad habit of…

10. 优越感+很强

    a strong sense of superiority

11. 与众不同的特点 / 想法 / 意见

    extraordinary features/ideas/opinions

12. 推行＋普通话 / 政策

    to promote *Putonghua* (common speech of the Chinese language)/to carry into effect a policy

II. 句型结构 *Sentence Pattern and Structure*

1. 用 A 作为 B

   to use A as B

   许多人谈到近年来中国的进步，大多用都市或高铁的建设作为例子。

   在汽车出现以前，人们主要用马车作为交通工具。

2. 满一：满大街／满屋子／满城／满树／满地／满桌子

   ……is filled/covered with……

   二十世纪六、七十年代满街的自行车早已被汽车取代了。

   你家真乱！满屋子都是没洗的脏衣服。

3. …a lot of people…挤在+ place + localizer

   to be pressed together into a confined place

   挤在+一起　　to press close together

   我相信，多数开汽车、住高楼的中国人都是欢迎这些改变的，他们并不怀念挤在四合院里，过着没有自来水、抽水马桶和空调的日子。

   那么多人挤在一起，发生什么事了？

4. 虽然……，但是……比比皆是

   "Although…, …. can be found everywhere," is used to show the ubiquity of happenings that usually are not supposed to happen.

   饭馆儿里，电影院里，虽然都张贴着"请勿吸烟"的牌子，但是吸烟的人却比比皆是。

   虽然学历对找工作有帮助，但是找不到工作的大学生也比比皆是。

5. A，B，甚至于 C ……

A, B, and even (to the extent that) C...; what goes after "甚至于" is usually an extreme example that lends support to the speaker's argument.

十几年前，在公共场合抽烟是很平常的事，......火车上，公交车上，甚至于电梯里都有人吸烟。

苹果公司的产品很受欢迎，年轻人，中年人，甚至于老年人都喜欢用。

6. 争先恐后(地)+VP

strive to be the first and fear being left behind; vie with

改革开放以后，外国公司争先恐后地到中国来投资。

上课的时候，学生争先恐后地回答老师的问题。

7. 只要......一......，就......

At the first sign of..., ...; used to express an outcome that will occur at the first sign of something.

"争先恐后"这四个字最能形容中国人的群众心理，只要人一多，大家就没了秩序的观念。

只要一有重要的活动，北京的雾霾就会消失。

8. sb. 养成......的习惯

......让 sb. 养成......的习惯

to cultivate the habit of......

现在因为科技的发达，车票、机票大多在网上订购，大大地缓解了在车站抢购车票的问题，中国人也因此慢慢地养成了排队的习惯。

科技的发达让中国人养成了排队的习惯。

9. Subj. 与其...A...，不如...B...

Rather than doing A, it is better to do B, or, it is better for the subject to do B than to do A. This structure is often used to promote a new proposal (B), which is, in the speaker's opinion, better than the previously proposed one (A).

许多人把不排队和随地吐痰看成是个道德问题，其实，与其把这些毛病看成道德问题，不如把这些看成经济或者科技和医学的问题。

要想真正了解中国，与其去参观旅游景点，不如去小公园走走，因为在那儿你才能观察到普通中国人的生活。

10. 把 A 看 / 当+成 B

to regard/take A as B (suggestion)

我们不应该把中国人不排队的毛病看成经济的问题，其实，我们可以把它看成经济问题。

你可以把这里当成你的家，有什么问题就告诉我们。

11. 在 sb. 眼里，……是……

in the eyes of sb. (a personal opinion, not necessarily true)

在上海人的眼里，除了上海人，其他地方的中国人都是"乡下人"。

在父母的眼里，自己的孩子是最可爱的。

III. 词语辨析 Synonym Differentiation

1. 多数：多数的 noun　　the majority of...

　　大多：大多+VP　　　　mostly

在这个学校，多数的学生都骑自行车来上课。

在这个学校，学生大多骑自行车来上课。

2. 在 sb.看来：it is often used to express one's opinion

在 sb 眼里 (动词一般是"是")：it is often used to pass a judgment based on one's personal standard or by one's own definition.

在上海人眼里，其他地方的人都是"乡下人"。

在我看来，老师不应该随便批评学生。

中國人在改變

許多人談到近年來中國的進步，大多用都市或高鐵的建設作為例子，這是大家都看得到的具體改變：破落陳舊的四合院、小胡同少了，幾十層高的摩天大樓越來越多了；20世紀六七十年代滿街的自行車早已被汽車取代了。這些改變，有些人認為是進步，也有不少人，尤其是外國人，認為是對環境、歷史和古跡的破壞。不過，我相信，多數開汽車住高樓的中國人都是歡迎這些改變的，他們並不懷念擠在四合院裏，過著沒有自來水、抽水馬桶和空調的日子。

除了這些看得到的改變以外，還有一些變化，在我看來，更能說明中國的進步。十幾年前，在公共場合抽煙是很平常的事，飯館兒裏，電影院裏，雖然都貼著"請勿吸煙"的牌子，但是吸煙的人卻比比皆是，火車上，公交車上，甚至於電梯裏都有人吸煙！那個時候，在中國幾乎沒有不吸二手煙的自由。最近幾年，這種情況至少在大都市裡有了顯著的改善。一方面政府加大了禁煙的力度，另一方面，老百姓也變得越來越自覺，在公共場合違規吸煙的人越來越少了。

外國人最怕在中國過馬路，因為在中國，汽車是不讓行人的，而開車的人又不很遵守交通規則，闖紅燈是天天都發生的事。上個月，我去了一趟杭州，居然發現汽車等行人先過街，這樣的改變正悄悄地在全中國發生。

中國人最受外國人批評的生活習慣是不排隊和隨地吐痰。"爭先恐後"這四個字最能形容中國人的群眾心理，只要人一多，大家就失掉了秩序的觀念，人擠人成了具有中國特色的景觀。無論是在食堂買飯，還是在車站買票，成群的人擠在一個窗口搶飯、搶票是常常發生的事。現在因為科技的發達，車票、機票大多在網上訂購，大大地緩解了在車站搶購車票的問題，中國人也因此慢慢地養成了排隊的習慣。最近我在北京搭地鐵、公交，居然看到中國人也排起隊來了，這才是中國進步的證明。這比中國有了航空母艦更值得中國人驕傲！

隨地吐痰還是許多中國人改不了的壞習慣，我打的的時候，最怕司機搖下窗子，向外 pa 的吐口痰，我真怕那口痰吹到我臉上。中國人隨地吐痰可能和空氣污染有關係，空氣太髒了，總覺得喉嚨裏有痰，等到空氣污染有了改善，咳嗽吐痰的人也會減少的。

許多人把不排隊和隨地吐痰看成是個道德問題，其實，與其把這些毛病看成道德問題，不如把這些看成經濟或者科技和醫學的問題。經濟發達了，科技和醫學進步了，不排隊和隨地吐痰的人也會漸漸地減少的。

上海人是中國人裏優越感最強的人，100 多年來，上海一直是中國的經濟中心，也是中國西化最早的城市，因此，在上海人的眼裏，除了上海人，其他地方的中國人都是"鄉下人"。上海人在一起，一定得說上海話，這才能顯示他們"與眾不同"。但是，最近 我看到電視報道：許多上海的小學生已經不會說上海話了，大家都說普通話。100 多年來，先進的中國知識分子都主張推行普通話，現在連上海人都說普通話了。中國終於有了統一的語言。普通話的勝利，在我看來，比高鐵的建設更有意義！我的中國夢是上海人不說上海話了，廣東人不說廣東話了，臺灣人不說閩南話了，中國人都說普通話！就像美國人都說英文。

课后习题

第 11 课

一、词语搭配 (Please pair the term in the left column with the most appropriate term in the right column. Then use the completed phrases to complete the sentences. You can change the order of the words and add more information if needed.)

（1）

(C) 具有　　　　A 普通话

(D) 搭　　　　　B 坏习惯

(B) 改掉　　　　C 作用

(A) 推行　　　　D 地铁

1. 中国的方言太多,为了让说不同方言的人能沟通,_____A_____。
2. 在大城市里,堵车问题很严重,所以很多人选择_____D_____。
3. 随地吐痰是一个很不文明的行为,中国人应该_____B_____。
4. 女人们喜欢用化妆品是因为她们相信_____C_____。

（2）

(C) 想法　　　　A 提高

(A) 显著的　　　B 日子

(D) 破落的　　　C 与众不同

(B) 怀念　　　　D 村子

1. 改革开放以后,中国人的生活水平有了_____A_____。
2. 在偏远的地区,你能看到的不是繁荣的城市,而是_____D_____。
3. 改革开放以前,很多人吃不饱,穿不暖,我相信没有人会_____B_____。
4. 由于_____C_____,多数的人不能理解他的想法,觉得他很奇怪。

（3）

（　A　）强烈的　　　A　优越感
（　D　）缓解　　　　B　力度
（　B　）加大　　　　C　很平常
（　C　）现象　　　　D　压力

1. 由于美国是世界上最强大的国家，有的美国人＿＿＿A＿＿＿＿＿＿＿＿＿。
2. 为了发展小城市的经济，创造更多的工作机会，政府需要＿＿B＿＿＿＿＿＿＿。
3. 以前，成群的人挤在一个窗口争先恐后地抢票，这种＿＿＿C＿＿＿＿＿＿＿。
4. 中国政府推行"一家一个孩子"的政策是为了＿＿＿D＿＿＿＿＿＿＿＿。

二、选择填空 (Complete the sentences by choosing the most appropriate term.)

1. 多数　　大多

食堂的饭菜好吃而且便宜，因此，学生们＿B＿在学校的食堂里吃饭。

在北京，＿A＿破落陈旧的四合院、小胡同被摩天大楼取代，但这到底是不是一种进步，不同人有不同的看法。

2. 在美国人看来　　　在美国人眼里

＿B＿＿，中国大学不应该只看一次考试的成绩就决定是否接受一个学生。

＿A＿＿，个人自由是最重要的，所以美国人比较尊重个人的意见和选择。

三、完成句子 (Complete the sentence or dialogue with the given item in parentheses.)

1. A：参加这次会议的人来自世界各地，你们用什么语言交流？

B：＿＿＿＿＿＿＿＿＿＿＿＿＿＿＿＿＿＿＿＿＿＿＿。（用 A 作为 B）

2. 微信（WeChat）在中国很受欢迎，＿＿＿＿＿＿＿＿＿＿。（用 A 作为 B）

3. A：北京哪里可以找到饭馆？

B：＿＿＿＿＿＿＿＿＿＿＿＿＿＿＿＿＿＿＿。（满+大街/屋子/…）

4. 我不太喜欢坐电梯,因为＿＿＿＿＿＿＿＿＿＿＿＿＿。(挤在…里/挤在一起)

5. A:现在医学很发达,不管是在现代化的城市还是偏远的农村,所有人都应该

相信医学,你觉得呢?

B:＿＿＿＿＿＿＿＿＿＿＿＿＿＿＿＿＿。(虽然…,但是…比比皆是)

6. 在纽约,虽然街上都有红绿灯,但是＿＿＿＿＿＿＿＿＿＿。(比比皆是)

7. 在中国,使用微信的人非常多,＿＿＿＿＿＿＿＿＿＿。(A, B, 甚至于 C)

8. 微信的功能(function)也很多,＿＿＿＿＿＿＿＿＿。(A, B, 甚至于 C)

9. 这个地区要停水三天,所以＿＿＿＿＿＿＿＿＿＿。(争先恐后+vp)

10. 在高速公路上,很多人开车开得太快了,可是＿＿＿＿＿。(只要…一…就…)

11. 在飞机上一定不可以吸烟,＿＿＿＿＿＿＿＿＿。(只要…一…就…)

12. 妈妈每天晚上都和孩子一起看一个小时的书,＿＿＿＿＿。(养成…的习惯)

13. 他从小就＿＿＿＿＿＿＿,所以他的房间一直都是干干净净的。(养成…的习惯)

14. A:这些破落陈旧的四合院,留着没什么用,拆了又挺可惜的,应该怎么办呢?

B:＿＿＿＿＿＿＿＿＿＿＿＿＿＿＿＿(Subj. 与其…A…,不如…B…)

15. A:我想更进一步了解中国,所以我要再一次北京上海等大城市,你觉得呢?

B:＿＿＿＿＿＿＿＿＿＿＿＿＿＿＿＿(Subj. 与其…A…,不如…B…)

16. A:中国人不排队,真没有道德!

B:我倒不这么看。＿＿＿＿＿＿＿＿＿＿＿＿。(把 A 看 / 当+成 B)

17. 学校是学生生活、学习的地方,学生们应该＿＿＿＿＿＿(把 A 看 / 当+成 B)

18. ＿＿＿＿＿＿＿,不管自己的孩子是什么样子,他都是最可爱的。(在 sb. 眼里)

19. A:为什么那么多西方人反对中国政府的"一家一个孩子"的政策?

B:＿＿＿＿＿＿＿＿＿＿＿＿＿＿＿＿(在 sb. 眼里,…是…)

四、回答问题 (Answer the questions.)

1. 中国近年来有哪些改变?所有的改变都是进步吗?

2. 有的西方人认为,中国人在改善生活的同时也破坏了环境和历史。如果你是

中国人,你会怎么选择?

3.　在中国，吸烟是一个大问题吗？请你举例说明。

4.　中国人过去为什么不习惯排队？这个情况现在有改善吗？

5.　不排队、随地吐痰，这些问题是道德问题、经济问题还是文化问题？

6.　中国人都说普通话了，这是好事吗？

第 12 课

从 "写字" 到 "打字"

　　笔记本电脑和智能手机的快速普及，已经使 "提笔写字" 这个几千年来人类书写的技能面临空前的考验。"写字"（不只是写汉字，写英文和其他文字也都包括在内），对绝大多数人来说，已经被 "打字" 取代了。今天 "写汉字" 几乎已经只是少数书法家的艺术活动，而不再是人与人之间沟通的技能了。

打字	dǎzì	v.-o.	to type
笔记本电脑	bǐjìběn diànnǎo	n.	laptop
智能手机	zhìnéng shǒujī	n.	smart phone
普及	pǔjí	v.	to popularize; to make widely available
提笔写字	tíbǐ xiězì	idm.	to take up a pen and write
书写	shūxiě	v.	to write (formal)
技能	jìnéng	n.	skill
空前	kōngqián	adj.	unprecedented
考验	kǎoyàn	n./v.	test; ordeal; to put to the test
文字	wénzì	n.	writing system; characters
绝大多数	juédàduōshù	pron.	the overwhelming majority
取代	qǔdài	v.	to replace
少数	shǎoshù	pron.	minority
书法家	shūfǎjiā	n.	calligrapher
沟通	gōutōng	v./n.	to communicate; communication

Written by Chih-p'ing Chou
Prepared by Jincheng Liu & Xin Zou

　　我经常问我的中国朋友："最近你们用笔写过字吗？"他们几乎没有例外的都说："都什么年代了，还有谁用笔写字啊？我已经想不起来上次用笔写东西是什么时候了。有了电脑、手机，还有谁用笔写字啊？"中国人都不写字了，可是学汉语的外国学生，却还得天天写汉字，否则考试就会通不过。这有点儿滑稽，也有点儿讽刺。

　　因为科技的发达，"识字"和"写字"的距离几乎已经不存在了。任何一个能用电脑输入汉字的人，只要能"认识"那个汉字——从同音字中选出对的汉字来——也就能"打"出这个字来，这也就完成了所谓"书写"的任务。

　　因为工具的改变，使原本用笔书写的技能成了手指和键盘的配合。在地铁里，我们看到小学生、初中生埋头用两个手指，飞快地摁着手机，我

年代	niándài	n.	a decade; era
否则	fǒuzé	conj.	otherwise; or else
通过	tōngguò	v.	to pass (an exam)
滑稽	huájī	adj.	funny-looking; comical
讽刺	fěngcì	adj./v.	ironic; to satirize/ridicule
科技	kējì	n.	science and technology
识字	shízì	v.-o.	(lit.) to learn to read; to recognize characters; to become literate
距离	jùlí	n.	distance
存在	cúnzài	v.	to exist
输入	shūrù	v.	to input
同音词	tóngyīn cí	n.	homonym
任务	rènwù	n.	task
原本	yuánběn	adj.	original

们必须承认：他们正在 "写" 信。虽然这种 "写" 法和传统的写字完全不一样，但是他们在 "写" 信却是谁都不能否认的。

我相信，以后提笔忘字的人一定会越来越多。但只要一打开手机、电脑，忘记的字就都能打出来了。从这个角度来看，我们所说的汉字书写能力，与其从字形入手，不如从语音入手。换句话说，书写工具的改变使 "发对音" 成了 "写对字" 的先决条件。

手指	shǒuzhǐ	n.	finger
键盘	jiànpán	n.	keyboard
配合	pèihé	v./n.	to cooperate; cooperation
初中生	chūzhōngshēng	n.	junior high school students
埋头	máitóu	v.	(lit.) to bury one's head in; to immerse oneself in (work or study)
飞快	fēikuài	adv.	very fast; at lightning speed; (cannot be modified by 很)
摁	èn	v.	to press
承认	chéngrèn	v.	to admit
提笔忘字	tíbǐ wàngzì	idm.	(lit.) to forget how to write words by hand; to have writer's block
字形	zìxíng	n.	structure and form of a Chinese character
入手	rùshǒu	v.	从⋯入手; to start with; to begin with
语音	yǔyīn	n.	pronunciation
先决条件	xiānjué tiáojiàn	n.	prerequisite

　　所以，汉字书写能力的培养必须先从发音准确入手。部首字形的分析，笔画顺序和手写汉字的重复练习，在对外汉语教学中应占多少分量，是值得老师们重新考虑的。

准确	zhǔnquè	adj./adv.	accurate; accurately
部首	bùshǒu	n.	Chinese radicals
笔画	bǐhuà	n.	stroke
顺序	shùnxù	n.	order; sequence
重复	chóngfù	v.	to repeat
对外汉语教学	duìwài hànyǔ jiàoxué	n.	Teaching Chinese as a Second Language
分量	fènliàng	n.	(to carry) weight; significance
重新	chóngxīn	adv.	all over again

I. 词语搭配 *Collocation*

1. 电脑/手机/教育/观念(的)+普及

    to make computers/cell-phones/education/a concept widely available

2. 空前的考验/发展/影响/进步/繁荣

    an unprecedented challenge/development/influence/progress/prosperity

3. A 取代 B　　　　A replaces B

    B 被 A 取代　　　B is replaced by A

4. 想不起来

    unable to recall

5. 通过+考试

    to pass an exam

6. 完成+任务/工作/计划

    to complete a task/a job/a plan

7. ……存在+……问题/现象

    the problem/phenomenon of…exists/is present in…

8. 埋头+看书/学习/做作业/工作/做研究

    to bury one's head in reading/studying/doing one's homework/doing one's job/doing the research (埋头 denotes that one is fully concentrating on something, undistracted by external influences)

9. ……占很大的分量/只占很小的分量

    …to carry a lot of/a little weight

II. 句型结构 *Sentence Pattern and Structure*

1. …general…，不只是 A，B（和 C）也包括在内，……。

    This structure, meaning that "not only A, but also including B and C," denotes that a situation or a theory is not only applicable to B, it also holds true for B (and C).

    "写字"（不只是写汉字，写英文和其他文字也都包括在内），对绝大多数人来说，已经被 "打字" 取代了。

用汉字的地方，不只是中国大陆，香港和台湾也包括在内，都应该用简体字。

2. ……几乎+只……

……几乎+negation form（不/没/Verb 不 complement）……

In this structure, *jīhū* 几乎 is an adverb meaning "almost, nearly," and it is often a slight exaggeration that the speaker uses in order to make his point.

今天 "写汉字" 几乎已经只是少数书法家的艺术活动。

因为科技的发达，"识字" 和 "写字" 的距离，几乎已经不存在了。

现在的年轻人几乎都写不出漂亮的字了。

3. ……不再……了

不再…了, meaning "the subject no longer…," is used to say that something that was once true or possible is not now true or possible any more, or to describe the end of an action or a phenomenon.

今天的 "写汉字" 不再是人与人之间沟通的技能了。

改革开放以后，中国人不再担心 "温饱" 问题了。

4. 都什么年代了，还有谁……啊? Did you forget what year it is? Who still…?

This structure is a rhetorical question, stressing that an idea or behavior is out of date or behind the times.

都什么年代了，还有谁用笔写字啊?

都什么年代了，还有谁只想生儿子，不想生女儿啊?

5. …得/应该 suggestion…，否则，…bad consequence 会…

This structure means "one has to or should do something; otherwise……" and is often used as a warning.

学汉语的外国学生得天天写汉字，否则，考试就会通不过。

你应该多吃青菜少吃肉，否则，你会越来越胖。

6. V 出 O 来

Chūlái 出来 is a directional complement meaning "out (from somewhere)" and by extension, could be used to describe that the object is turning from invisible to visible. Note that the object, if there is one, is often inserted between 出 and 来. For example, 想出办法来 to figure out a solution, 写出文章来 to write (out) an essay, 打出字来 to type (out) characters, or 检查出问题来 to find out problems.

只要你会拼音（pinyin），就能打出汉字来。

他中文学得很好，一个小时就能写出一篇 500 字的文章来。

7. 任何……的 noun，只要……，就……

Anyone who…or anything that…, as long as…, (the subject) will… This structure is used in conditionals, emphasizing that it is easy to achieve a certain goal.

任何一个能用电脑输入汉字的人，只要能"认识"那个汉字，也就能"打"出这个字来。

任何生活在美国的外国人，只要会说英文，就能找到工作。

任何你想要的东西，只要买得到，我都愿意买给你。

8. 虽然……，但是……却是谁都不能否认的。

"Although…, it is undeniable /incontestable that…" is used to emphasize that although the subject still has some problems, one should still look at the positive side.

虽然这种"写"法和传统的写字完全不一样，但是他们在"写"信却是谁都不能否认的。

虽然中国现在还有不少问题，但是过去三十年的进步却是谁都不能否认的。

9. ……，从这个角度来看，……

"From this perspective or in this regard," is used to explain the reason why the speaker came up with a certain suggestion or formed a certain opinion.

我相信，以后提笔忘字的人一定会越来越多。但只要一打开手机、电脑，所忘的字就都认出来了。从这个角度来看，我们所说的汉字书写能力，与其从字形入手，不如从语音入手。

美国大公司把工厂设在中国，给中国人提供了很多就业机会，从这个角度来看，吸引外国公司来中国投资是一个很好的决定。

10. …to achieve a goal…必须从…first step…入手

"[To achieve a certain goal], one must start with…/ one must begin with [first step]"

This structure is used to stress the first step one should take in order to achieve a goal.

汉字书写能力的培养必须先从发音准确入手。

要保护环境必须从减少浪费入手。

III. 词语辨析 *Synonym Differentiation*

1. 对 sb.来说：this structure, meaning "for sb…, …" is used to emphasize the experience of the person to whom a statement pertains. Note that this structure is used to give one's comments or thoughts on something that they have personally experienced.

    在 sb.看来：it is used to express one's comments on something, often as an outsider, and is not necessarily based on one's experience.

    对中国高中生来说，高考制度是公平的。

    在美国学生看来，高考都考一样的问题，这对中国农村的学生不太公平。

2. 考试：*n.* examination; can be a test organized by a school or institution to show a person's progress, knowledge, or ability.

    考验：*n./v.* test, trial, to put to test (the quality, value, or belief of sb). The subject may be a person, an organization but may also be an abstract difficulty or challenge.

    明天早上我有一个数学考试，我晚上得准备。

    新年的时候，几乎所有中国人都要回家。这对中国的铁路是一个很大的考验。

你的太太让你跟那个女人一起去上海，其实是在考验你，她想看看你会不会发生婚外关系。

3. 又：to describe something that happened again in the past

再：to say something will happen again in the future

重新："re-" (e.g. reconsider 重新考虑，redo 重新做一次，reread 重新读一次, etc.); to start all over again, usually because it was unsatisfactorily done before. It can be used in conjunction with 又 and 再.

这个饭馆的菜太好吃了。上个星期他去了一次，昨天又去了一次，明天他想再去一次。

我的作业不见了，今天晚上我得再做一次。

我的作业做得不好，老师让我（再）重新做一次。

我第一次看这篇文章的时候，没看懂。所以我昨天（又）重新看了一次。

從 "寫字" 到 "打字"

　　筆記本電腦和智能手機的快速普及，已經使 "提筆寫字" 這個幾千年來人類書寫的技能面臨空前的考驗。"寫字"（不只是寫漢字，寫英文和其他文字也都包括在內），對絕大多數人來說，已經被 "打字" 取代了。今天 "寫漢字" 幾乎已經只是少數書法家的藝術活動，而不再是人與人之間溝通的技能了。

　　我經常問我的中國朋友: "最近你們用筆寫過字嗎？" 他們幾乎沒有例外的都說: "都什麼年代了，還有誰用筆寫字啊？我已經想不起來上次用筆寫東西是什麼時候了。有了電腦、手機，還有誰用筆寫字啊？" 中國人都不寫字了，可是學漢語的外國學生，卻還得天天寫漢字，否則考試就會通不過。這有點兒滑稽，也有點兒諷刺。

　　因為科技的發達，"識字" 和 "寫字" 的距離幾乎已經不存在了。任何一個能用電腦輸入漢字的人，只要能 "認識" 那個漢字——從同音字中選出對的漢字來——也就能 "打" 出這個字來，這也就完成了所謂 "書寫" 的任務。

　　因為工具的改變，使原本用筆書寫的技能成了手指和鍵盤的配合。在地鐵裡，我們看到小學生、初中生埋頭用兩個手指，飛快地摁著手機，我們必須承認: 他們正在 "寫" 信。雖然這種 "寫" 法和傳統的寫字完全不一樣，但是他們在 "寫" 信卻是誰都不能否認的。

　　我相信，以後提筆忘字的人一定會越來越多。但只要一打開手機、電腦，忘記的字就都能打出來了。從這個角度來看，我們所說的漢字書寫能力，與其從字形入手，不如從語音入手。換句話說，書寫工具的改變使 "發對音" 成了 "寫對字" 的先決條件。

　　所以，漢字書寫能力的培養必須先從發音準確入手。部首字形的分析，筆劃順序和手寫漢字的重複練習，在對外漢語教學中應占多少分量，是值得老師們重新考慮的。

课后习题

第 12 课

一、词语搭配 (Please pair the term in the left column with the most appropriate term in the right column. Then use the completed phrases to complete the sentences. You can change the order of the words and add more information if needed.)

（1）

（ B ）通过　　A 做研究

（ C ）完成　　B 考试

（ A ）埋头　　C 任务

1. 老板要求我在三个小时之内做好下个星期的会议安排,可是＿＿＿ C ＿＿＿。

2. 他是一名大学教授,每天只知道＿＿＿ A ＿＿＿,生活上的事情他完全不关心。

3. 这个考试对他来说很重要,要是＿＿＿ B ＿＿＿,他就不能毕业。

（2）

（ A ）普及　　A 教育

（ C ）存在　　B 发展

（ B ）空前　　C 问题

1. 一个国家的发展进步离不开人民教育水平的提高,因此＿＿ A ＿＿。

2. 2000 年以后,中国的网络科技得到了＿＿＿ B ＿＿＿。

3. 虽然中国人的生活水平提高了,可是在生活习惯上＿＿＿ C ＿＿＿。

二、选择填空 (Complete the sentences by choosing the most appropriate term.)

1. 对美国学生来说　　在美国学生看来

＿ A ＿,写汉字比看懂汉字难,所以他们更希望能用电脑打字,不用手写字。

_____B____,中国的高考制度不好,因为中国学生能不能上大学只看一次考试的成绩。

2. 考试^A　　考验^B

他这个星期有一个交通规则___A___,通过了以后他就可以在这个地方开车了。

怎么让学生觉得写汉字是一个有意思的事情,这对每一个中文老师来说都是一个

不小的___B___。

3. 又^A　　再^B　　重新^C

虽然你写得没错,可是这个字比较难,你最好___A___写几遍,这样才能记住。

我的作业做得不好,老师让我___C___做一遍。

这个字我上个星期写了五遍,昨天___B___写了五遍,总算记住了。

三、完成句子 (Complete the sentence or dialogue with the given item in parentheses.)

1. A:中国人所说的"西方国家"只包括欧洲国家吗?

   B:_____。(不只是 A,B 也包括在内,...)

2. A:要是我只说一个字,比方说,"yī",中国人知道我说的是哪个字吗?

   B:中文里的同音词太多了,_____。(几乎+...不/没...)

3. 在雾霾严重的时候,_____。(几乎+...不/没...)

4. 智能手机也可以照相,自从我有了智能手机以后,_____。(不再...了)

5. A:你知道哪里可以买到 BP 机(pager)吗?

   B:_____。(都什么年代了,还有谁...啊?)

6. A:学外语的时候,最重要的是什么?

   B:_____。(得...,否则...会...)

7. A:跟中国人打交道,得注意什么?

   B:_____。(得...,否则...会...)

8. 考口语考试的时候,他紧张得_____。(V(不)出 O 来)

9. 要想解决记不住汉字的问题,最好_____。(V 出 O 来)

10. A:为什么"美国梦"可以吸引那么多人?

B：_____。（任何…，只要…就… ）

11. A：在有些地方，丈夫不允许妻子工作，他们要求妻子在家照顾家人。

B：真不敢相信！_____。（任何…的 Noun，只要…就… ）

12. A：中国人还随地吐痰，太不文明了，改革开放这么多年了，一点儿进步都没有。

B：_____。（虽然…，但是…却是谁都不能否认的）

13. A：改革开放以来，中国社会的进步大不大？

B：_____（…从这个角度来看…）

14. A：中国是不是一个世界强国？

B：_____（…从这个角度来看…）

15. A：怎么才能学好中文？

B：_____（…必须从…入手）

16. A：怎么才能让人们改掉生活上的坏习惯？

B：_____（…必须从…入手）

四、回答问题 (Answer the questions.)

1. 笔记本电脑和智能手机的普及对书写技能有什么影响？

2. "识字"等于会"写字"吗？现在，"识字"和"写字"的距离越来越大，还是越来越小？为什么？

3. 你觉得书写工具的改变会不会影响书写系统？这是好事儿还是坏事？

4. 现在的中国学生有没有必要练习写汉字？学中文的外国学生呢？

5. 在现代社会，"提笔忘字"的现象越来越普遍，你担心不担心这个问题？

6. 你觉得应不应该用拼音取代汉字？拼音会不会取代汉字？

第 13 课

网上世界与共享单车

　　一个刚到中国的外国人，要想在当代 中国的大都市里生活，就必须尽快 地进入中国的"网上世界"；否则 你就被排挤 在整个系统 之外，对日常生活造成许多不便。

　　网上世界在几年前还被认为是个"虚拟"的世界，现在这个虚拟的世界和真实 的世界已经完全结合 在一起了。这几年，中国在英特网上的技术 发展非常快，上"淘宝"买东西已经成了许多人生活的常态。几年

单车	dānchē	n.	bicycle
当代	dāngdài	adj.	contemporary
尽快	jǐnkuài	adv.	as quickly as possible
否则	fǒuzé	conj.	otherwise
排挤	páijǐ	v.	to push aside; to exclude
系统	xìtǒng	n.	system
不便	búbiàn	n.	inconvenience
虚拟	xūnǐ	adj.	virtual
真实	zhēnshí	adj.	true; real
结合	jiéhé	v.	to combine; to unite
英特网	Yīngtèwǎng	n.	Internet
技术	jìshù	n.	technology
常态	chángtài	n.	the norm; a normal part of life 生活常态

前，还有不少人担心网上购物，容易上当受骗，买到假货；现在，由于科技的不断进步和服务质量的提升，这样的顾虑已经越来越少了。

网上市场的快速发展也就意味着传统商店生意的萎缩，从书店、超市到百货商场没有不受到影响的。网上超市既不需要实体的店面，也不需要售货员和收银员，大大地降低了经营的成本，传统商店在这方面是无法和网上市场竞争的。

上当受骗	shàngdàng shòupiàn	idm.	to be duped and swindled
科技	kējì	n.	science and technology
不断	búduàn	adv.	continuously; uninterruptedly
提升	tíshēng	v.	to improve (quality)
意味	yìwèi	v.	to mean; to signify
生意	shēngyì	n.	business
萎缩	wěisuō	v.	(of a market, economy, etc.) to shrink, sag
实体	shítǐ	n.	physical (brick and mortar, opp. online retailer)
店面	diànmiàn	n.	shop front; sales floor (part of the store where sales are conducted)
售货员	shòuhuò yuán	n.	shop assistant
收银员	shōu yíng yuán	n.	cashier
经营	jīngyíng	v.	to run (a business)
成本	chéngběn	n.	cost
无法	wúfǎ	v.	unable

　　网上购物快速的发展一方面造成了传统商店生意的萧条，但另一方面，也带动了许多新型的行业，其中发展最快的就是快递业务的兴起。

　　中国的快递真做到了价廉而且高效，国内的包裹当天或第二天送到是很平常的。价廉而且高效的快递缩短了网上超市和实体商店之间的距离，一个人在手机上下了单，你要的东西在几小时甚至几分钟之内，就有专人送到你手上，这样的服务在美国是不多的。最好的例子就是餐点的外卖，有不少人一日三餐全靠外卖，连麦当劳也有外卖的服务。外卖从手机下单，到餐点送达，一般都在一小时以内。

萧条	xiāotiáo	adj.	(of business) very dull; (of general conditions) depressed
新型	xīnxíng	adj.	new type; new pattern (modifier)
行业	hángyè	n.	trade; profession; industry
其中	qízhōng	p.w.	among which
快递	kuàidì	n.	express delivery
业务	yèwù	n.	business
兴起	xīngqǐ	v.	to rise; to spring up
高效	gāoxiào	adj.	highly efficient
包裹	bāoguǒ	n.	parcel
当天	dāngtiān	n.	the same day
下单	xiàdān	v.	to place an order online
专人	zhuānrén	n.	person specially assigned to a task or job
餐点	cāndiǎn	n.	meal and refreshments
外卖	wàimài	n.	take-out
送达	sòngdá	v.	to deliver

在中国，最近 10 年来，现金交易正在快速地消失。

一般人都以"微信"或"支付宝"来支付所有的费用，从卖水果的小摊到国营的大企业都接受电子付款，这对中国人的日常生活起着革命性的改变。

一般中国人从来没使用过支票，支票是单位才使用的支付方式，个人都是用现金来交易的。就这一点来说，中国的改变是"跳跃式"的——许多中国人"跳"过了"支票"或"信用卡"这一阶段，而直接进入到了电子付款。当然，电子付款之所以可行，电脑和手机的普及是先决条件。

现金	xiànjīn	n.	cash
消失	xiāoshī	v.	to disappear
支付	zhīfù	v.	to pay (money)
小摊	xiǎotān	n.	vendor's stall
国营	guóyíng	adj.	state-run
企业	qǐyè	n.	enterprise; business
电子	diànzǐ	adj.	electronic
付款	fùkuǎn	v.-o.	to pay a sum of money
革命性	gémìng xìng	adj.	revolutionary
使用	shǐyòng	v.	to use
支票	zhīpiào	n.	check
跳跃式	tiàoyuè shì	adj.	(to develop) by leaps and bounds
信用卡	xìnyòng kǎ	n.	credit card
阶段	jiēduàn	n.	stage

　　网上购物不但改变了中国人的消费习惯，也改变了中国人对东西使用和拥有的观念，共享单车的出现是这一改变最好的说明。以前单车是每个中国家庭必不可少的交通工具，要用单车，就得买单车。有了共享单车之后，骑一次，租一次。单车是租的，而不是买的；单车是拿来用的，而不必拥有。换句话说，人和东西的关系从永久的变成暂时的，甚至于只是"一次性"的。

　　这种转变有时也体现在人与人的关系上，目前流行的两个词："约炮"和"炮友"正在悄悄地取代原来的"约会"和"男/女朋友"。这就是男女关系由永久转变成暂时，由"拥有"转变成"使用"的最好说明。

　　"约炮"和"炮友"这两个词，当然不高雅。你绝不会在父母的面前介绍说，"他/她是我的炮友"。但在十八九岁的年轻人之间，这两个

消费	xiāofèi	v.	to consume
必不可少	bìbùkěshǎo	adj.	absolutely necessary; indispensable
交通工具	jiāotōng gōngjù	n.	means of transportation
租	zū	v.	to rent
永久	yǒngjiǔ	adj.	permanent
暂时	zànshí	adj.	temporary
一次性	yícì xìng	adj.	one-time; disposable (goods)
体现	tǐxiàn	v.	to embody
约炮	yuēpào	v.	(slang) to hook up for a one night stand; booty call
炮友	pàoyǒu	n.	(slang) friend with benefits
由	yóu	prep.	from
高雅	gāoyǎ	adj.	elegant; refined; tasteful

词已经被广泛 接受了。许多人担心，这种新词的出现说明这一代年轻人对男女性关系 越来越随便 的态度；可是，我倒觉得这种新词的出现，也可以说明年轻人对虚伪 的一种鄙视。

有些事，只能做，不能说，说出来，大家都觉得尴尬；可是做的时候，却觉得理所当然。

你同意这个说法吗？

广泛	guǎngfàn	adj.	widespread; wide ranging
性关系	xìng guānxi	n.	sexual relationship
随便	suíbiàn	adv.	casual; random
虚伪	xūwěi	adj.	hypocritical
鄙视	bǐshì	v.	to despise; to look down upon
尴尬	gān'gà	adj.	embarrassing; awkward
理所当然	lǐsuǒdāngrán	idm.	It is only right and proper

I. 词语搭配 Collocation

1. 不断+进步／提高／发展／增加

   to make continuous progress/to improve/develop/increase continuously

2. 提升+服务质量／实力／水平／能力

   to improve quality of service/one's actual strength/level of (performance, proficiency, etc.)/ability

3. 生意／规模／市场／需求／大脑+萎缩

   business/scale/market/(market) demand/brain shrinks

4. 经济／生意+萧条

   economy/business slump

5. 服务／工作+高效

   highly efficient service/job

6. 送到 sb.手上

   to deliver the goods to sb.

7. 支付+费用

   to pay for …

8. ……被广泛接受／……对……产生了广泛的影响

   …to be widely accepted…; to exert wide influence on…

II. 句型结构 *Sentence Pattern and Structure*

1. 要想……，就必须……；否则…就…

   If one wants to…, he/she must…; otherwise…

   This pattern introduces the essential condition for the realization of the subject matter.

   一个刚到中国的外国人，要想在当代中国的大都市里生活，就必须尽快地进入中国的"网上世界"；否则你就被排挤在整个系统之外，对日常生活造成许多不便。

   要想学好一门语言，就必须常常听，常常说；否则很快就会忘记。

2. ……几年前还……，现在已经……了

A few years ago, it was only/merely…, now it has already……

This pattern is often used to describe dramatic changes that have happened in the past few years.

网上世界在几年前还被认为是个"虚拟"的世界，现在这个虚拟的世界和真实的世界已经完全结合在一起了。

几年前，还有不少人担心网上购物，容易上当受骗，买到假货；现在，由于科技的不断进步和服务质量的提升，这样的顾虑已经越来越少了。

3. A 意味着 B

A implies B……

网上市场的快速发展也就意味着传统商店生意的萎缩。

你男朋友忘了你的生日不意味着他不喜欢你了，可能他最近真的太忙了。

4. Subj. 没有不……的 (without exception)

This pattern is a double negation; it suggests that there is no exception to the situation described before.

网上市场的快速发展也就意味着传统商店生意的萎缩，从书店、超市到百货商场没有不受到影响的。

这里的学生没有不想自己开公司的，他们都希望以后能自己当老板。

5. ……，其中，…… among which

网上购物快速的发展一方面造成了传统商店生意的萧条，但另一方面，也带动了许多新型的行业，其中发展最快的就是快递业务的兴起。

改革开放使中国在很多方面都有巨大的进步，其中，经济方面的进步是最明显的。

6. ……以 tool + 来 VP

to do sth. with the help of…/by means of…

一般人都以"微信"或"支付宝"来支付所有的费用。

以科技力量来提升服务质量是这个公司成功的重要原因。

7. ……对+社会 / 日常生活 / 教育 / …起着/了革命性的改变

 to bring revolutionary change to the society/daily life/education

一般人都以"微信"或"支付宝"来支付所有的费用，从卖水果的小摊到国营的大企业都接受电子付款，这对中国人的日常生活起着革命性的改变。

两百年前，电的出现对经济的发展起了革命性的改变。

8. A 之所以可行，B 是先决条件

B is a prerequisite for A

电子付款之所以可行，电脑和手机的普及是先决条件。

民主（democracy）之所以可行，教育（的普及/水平的提高）是先决条件。

9. A 是 B 最好的说明

A is the best example of B

网上购物不但改变了中国人的消费习惯，也改变了中国人对东西使用和拥有的观念，共享单车的出现是这一改变最好的说明。

手机成了人们必不可少的东西，这是科技影响生活最好的说明。

10. V1 一 m.w.，V2 一 m.w.

骑一次，租一次：pay as you go; no down payment and pay for each rental

吃一个，拿一个：to take according to what you actually need

以前单车是每个中国家庭必不可少的交通工具，要用单车，就得买单车。有了共享单车之后，骑一次，租一次。

吃一个，拿一个，别一次拿太多，那会造成浪费。

11. abstract concept 体现在 specific example（noun/Noun Phrase）上

(abstract concept) is embodied in (specific example)

这种转变（从永久变成暂时）有时也体现在人与人的关系上。

一个社会的开放主要体现在对不同看法的包容上。

公平不只体现在结果上，也体现在过程上。

12. ……由 A 转变成 B   A changes into B

目前流行的两个词："约炮"和"炮友"正在悄悄地取代原来的"约会"和"男/女朋友"。这就是男女关系由永久转变成暂时，由"拥有"转变成"使用"的最好说明。

中国由一个贫穷落后的农业国家转变成一个工业化国家，由一个受帝国主义欺凌的半殖民地转变成一个独立自主的主权国家。

13. (Situation A,) sb.觉得不可接受 / 尴尬，可是 (situation B) 却觉得理所当然

While sb. considers (situation A) as unacceptable/embarrassing, they consider
(situation B) to be totally right and proper/they take (situation B) for granted.

有些事，只能做，不能说，说出来，大家都觉得尴尬；可是做的时候，却觉得理所当然。

在传统社会，丈夫死了妻子再嫁，很多人觉得不可接受；可是妻子死了，丈夫再娶，大家却觉得理所当然。

III. 词语辨析 Synonym Differentiation

1. 业务：noun   business affairs; professional work
   服务：noun / verb   service; to serve
   你们公司有什么业务？
   只要你买我们的产品，我们一定给您提供最好的服务。我们很高兴能为您服务。

2. 支付：transitive verb
   付款：v.+obj.

While 支付 and 付款 both mean to "pay", the former is a transitive verb while and latter is a verb plus object.

请问您怎么支付这笔费用？信用卡还是现金？

请问您怎么付款？信用卡还是现金？

3. 尴尬：embarrassing; embarrassed; awkward

不好意思： to feel embarrassed; to feel sorry (apologetic)

他买了在中国生产的产品来送给中国朋友，这让他很尴尬／不好意思。

他跟现在的女朋友在饭馆里吃饭，没想到，以前的女朋友也来这家饭馆，真是尴尬。

真是不好意思，浪费你那么多时间。

網上世界與共享單車

　　一個剛到中國的外國人，要想在當代中國的大都市裡生活，就必須盡快地進入中國的"網上世界"；否則你就被排擠在整個系統之外，對日常生活造成許多不便。

　　網上世界在幾年前還被認為是個"虛擬"的世界，現在這個虛擬的世界和真實的世界已經完全結合在一起了。這幾年，中國在英特網上的技術發展非常快，上"淘寶"買東西已經成了許多人生活的常態。幾年前，還有不少人擔心網上購物，容易上當受騙，買到假貨；現在，由於科技的不斷進步和服務質量的提升，這樣的顧慮已經越來越少了。

　　網上市場的快速發展也就意味著傳統商店生意的萎縮，從書店、超市到百貨商場沒有不受到影響的。網上超市既不需要實體的店面，也不需要售貨員和收銀員，大大地降低了經營的成本，傳統商店在這方面是無法和網上市場競爭的。

　　網上購物快速的發展一方面造成了傳統商店生意的蕭條，但另一方面，也帶動了許多新型的行業，其中發展最快的就是快遞業務的興起。

　　中國的快遞真做到了價廉而且高效，國內的包裹當天或第二天送到是很平常的。價廉而且高效的快遞縮短了網上超市和實體商店之間的距離，一個人在手機上下了單，你要的東西在幾小時甚至幾分鐘之內，就有專人送到你手上，這樣服務在美國是不多的。最好的例子就是餐點的外賣，有不少人一日三餐全靠外賣，連麥當勞也有外賣的服務。外賣從手機下單，到餐點送達，一般都在一小時以內。

　　在中國，最近 10 年來，現金交易正在快速地消失。

　　一般人都以"微信"或"支付寶"來支付所有的費用，從賣水果的小攤到國營的大企業都接受電子付款，這對中國人的日常生活起著革命性的改變。

　　一般中國人從來沒使用過支票，支票是單位才使用的支付方式，個人都是用現金來交易的。就這一點來說，中國的改變是"跳躍式"的——許多中國人"跳"過了

"支票"或"信用卡"這一階段，而直接進入到了電子付款。當然，電子付款之所以可行，電腦和手機的普及是先決條件。

網上購物不但改變了中國人的消費習慣，也改變了中國人對東西使用和擁有的觀念，共享單車的出現是這一改變最好的說明。以前單車是每個中國家庭必不可少的交通工具，要用單車，就得買單車。有了共享單車之後，騎一次，租一次。單車是租的，而不是買的；單車是拿來用的，而不必擁有。換句話說，人和東西的關係從永久的變成暫時的，甚至於只是"一次性"的。

這種轉變有時也體現在人與人的關係上，目前流行的兩個詞："約炮"和"炮友"正在悄悄地取代原來的"約會"和"男/女朋友"。這就是男女關係由永久轉變成暫時，由"擁有"轉變成"使用"的最好說明。

"約炮"和"炮友"這兩個詞，當然不高雅。你絕不會在父母的面前介紹說，"他/她是我的炮友"。但在十八九歲的年輕人之間，這兩個詞已經被廣泛接受了。許多人擔心，這種新詞的出現說明這一代年輕人對男女性關係越來越隨便的態度；可是，我倒覺得這種新詞的出現，也可以說明年輕人對虛偽的一種鄙視。

有些事，只能做，不能說，說出來，大家都覺得尷尬；可是做的時候，卻覺得理所當然。

你同意這個說法嗎？

课后习题

第 13 课

一、词语搭配 (Please pair the term in the left column with the most appropriate term in the right column. Then use the completed phrases to complete the sentences. You can change the order of the words and add more information if needed.)

(1)

(C) 服务   A 费用

(A) 支付   B 进步

(B) 不断   C 高效

1. 在中国，餐点外卖的___C___，下单后半个小时之内，东西就能送到你的手上。

2. 我相信，随着_____B_____，人们的一些落后观念也会渐渐地被新观念取代。

3. 坐 Uber 的时候不用给司机现金，___A_____。

(2)

(C) 经济   A 影响

(A) 广泛   B 萧条

(D) 提升   C 实力

1. _____B_____的表现是市场需求大大减少，商业和制造业都没有以前的繁荣。

2. 每一个国家都一直在努力地_____AC_____，因为经济的影响力比军事的更大。

3. 西方文化对全世界_____A_____。

二、选择填空 (Complete the sentences by choosing the most appropriate term.)

1. 提高   提升

怎么样才能快速__D__自己的汉语水平？这是很多学中文的学生常常问的问题。

他在工作上非常努力，两年后，他被__A__为经理。

2. 业务   服务

我们公司的主要__A__是帮我们的客户做各种各样的市场调查。

这家饭馆的饭菜虽然好吃，可是__b__太不周到了，我不想再来了。

3. 支付   付款

先生，您已经在网上__b__了一百块钱，还需要再付 50 块钱。

先生，请您在这里__A__，一共一百块钱，谢谢！

三、完成句子 (Complete the sentence or dialogue with the given item in parentheses.)

1. A：要想让自己的产品受欢迎，必须怎么做？

    B：_____。（要想…，就必须…；否则…就…）

2. A：要想成为一个好的运动员，必须怎么做？

    B：_____。（要想…，就必须…；否则…就…）

3. 中国的变化真大，_____。（…几年前还…，现在已经…了）

4. 我们学校的变化真大，_____。（…几年前还…，现在已经…了）

5. 电脑、智能手机的普及_____。（意味着）

6. 高铁的快速发展_____。（意味着）

7. A：中国人喜欢苹果手机吗？

    B：_____。（…没有不…的）

8. 北京烤鸭是最好吃的中国菜之一，_____。（…没有不…的）

9. A：你们学校有几种外语课？哪一种外语课的学生最多？

    B：_____。（其中）

10. A：中国人到外国常常抢购哪些商品？哪一种商品是最受中国女性欢迎的？

    B：_____。（其中）

11. A：一个国家应该怎么增强自己的软实力？

    B：_____。（以 tool 来 V.P.）

12. A：在过去半个世纪里，什么东西对人类社会的影响最大？

B：＿＿＿＿＿＿＿＿＿＿＿＿＿＿＿＿＿＿＿。（起+着 / 了+革命性的改变）

13. A：有人建议，在学校里应该用打字来代替写字，可行吗？

B：＿＿＿＿＿＿＿＿＿＿＿＿＿＿＿＿。（A 之所以可行，B 是先决条件）

14. A：用法律来治理国家，为什么有的国家可以做到，有的国家做不到？

B：＿＿＿＿＿＿＿＿＿＿＿＿＿＿＿＿。（A 之所以可行，B 是先决条件）

15. A：我们怎么看出中国社会到底有没有进步？

B：＿＿＿＿＿＿＿＿＿＿＿＿＿＿＿＿＿。（A 是 B 最好的说明）

16. 超市总是通过打折（sales）活动来让顾客多买商品，因此顾客常常买了很多却用不完。其实，对顾客来说，最好的办法是＿＿＿＿＿＿＿＿＿＿＿＿＿＿。

（V1 一 m.w.，V2 一 m.w.）

17. A：人人都说美国是一个自由的国家。美国的自由体现在哪儿？

B：＿＿＿＿＿＿＿＿＿＿＿＿＿＿＿＿。（…体现在…上）

18. A：你觉得中国的高考是不是一个公平的考试？

B：＿＿＿＿＿＿＿＿＿＿＿＿＿＿＿＿。（…体现在…上）

19. 改革开放后，中国＿＿＿＿＿＿＿＿＿＿＿＿＿＿＿。（由 A 转变成 B）

20. A：中国政府常常批评西方国家看到中国的发展，心理不平衡，这是什么意思？

B：西方国家有这样一种心理：＿＿＿＿＿＿＿＿＿＿＿＿＿。

（(Situation A) sb.觉得不可接受，可是 (situation B) 却觉得理所当然）

21. 在一个社会里，年轻人往往比较开放，而老年人却大多比较保守，比如说，

＿＿＿＿＿＿＿＿＿＿＿＿＿＿＿＿＿＿＿＿＿＿＿。

（…Situation… sb.1 觉得不可接受，可是 sb.2 却觉得理所当然）

四、回答问题 (Answer the questions.)

1. 你觉得网络世界是一个"虚拟"世界还是一个真实的世界？为什么？
2. 网上市场的发展对传统商店有什么影响？你觉得传统商店以后会消失吗？
3. 中国的快递业务怎么样？为什么中国的快递行业发展得这么快？
4. 网上市场的发展需要哪些条件？举例说说，美国的网上市场发达不发达？

5. 电子支付对中国人的生活有什么影响？

6. 为什么电子支付在美国远没有中国那么普及？应该鼓励美国人使用电子支付吗？

7. 你觉得"共享单车"是不是一个好主意？可能会引起什么问题？

8. 除了单车，你认为还有哪些东西可以"共享"，可以"使用"而不"拥有"？哪些东西最好还是个人使用？

第 14 课
"留学热" 背后的思考

　　现在越来越多的美国大学生利用 暑假到中国来实习、打工；有的甚至毕业后选择到中国来工作一、两年。在这些美国大学生当中，不少人从事 的是教育工作。比方说，到学校或英语培训 机构 去教英文，或者到留学中介 去当留学顾问，指导 学生准备申请材料，建议学生参加哪些课

留学热	liúxué rè	n.	craze of studying abroad
背后	bèihòu	n.	behind; back
思考	sīkǎo	v.	to consider; to contemplate
利用	lìyòng	v.	to utilize; to take advantage of
实习	shíxí	v./n.	(of students or trainees) practice (what has been learnt in class); internship
打工	dǎgōng	v.-o.	to work (physical work; temporary or causal job)
从事	cóngshì	v.	to undertake; to take up (as a profession); to go in for
培训	péixùn	v./n.	to train; training
机构	jīgòu	n.	organization
中介	zhōngjiè	n.	intermediate; agency
顾问	gùwèn	n.	consultant
指导	zhǐdǎo	v.	to guide; to direct

外活动 等等。

　　英语在中国的教育中占很重要的地位，从小学、初中、高中，到大学，英语一直都是必修课，而不是选修课；中考、高考，甚至于考研，英语也都是必考的科目。中国学生学习英文的热情也超乎美国人想象。只要碰到美国人，中国学生就会设法跟他练习几句英文。连普通美国人在中国都很受欢迎，英文外教在中国受欢迎的程度也就可想而知了。至于当留学顾问的工作机会，是最近几年随着留学热潮的兴起才出现的。

　　留学热潮的出现主要是因为中国人普遍认为西方的教育制度比中

课外活动	kèwài huódòng	n.	extracurricular activity
初中	chūzhōng	n.	middle school
必修课	bìxiū kè	n.	required (obligatory) course
选修课	xuǎnxiū kè	n.	optional (selective) course
中考	zhōngkǎo	n.	entrance examination for senior high school
考研	kǎoyán	v.	to take the graduate entrance examination
必考	bìkǎo	adj.	(of an exam) required (subject)
科目	kēmù	n.	subject (in a curriculum)
超乎	chāohū	v.	to exceed; to go beyond;
			超乎想象: beyond imagination 超乎寻常:
			(lit.) be out of the ordinary; extraordinary
外教	wàijiào	n.	foreign teacher
程度	chéngdù	n.	degree; level
可想而知	kěxiǎng érzhī	idm.	one can well imagine
热潮	rècháo	n.	great mass fervor; all the rage
兴起	xīngqǐ	v.	to rise; to spring up

国的好。在中国，洋学历 也比本土 的学历值钱 得多。而且，中国人一向重视教育，尤其是下一代的教育。中国人常说："书中自有黄金屋"，意思是只要学习好，自然就能赚大钱。中国人相信：知识的力量是巨大的，它能创造财富 。收入水平大大提高的中国父母更相信，"不能让孩子输在起跑线上"。只要有可能，中国父母一定会把孩子送到国外去"镀金 "。

于是，最近几年，出国留学出现了低龄化 的倾向。以前，出国的留学生主要是本科毕业生，他们出国是为了读硕士 或者读博士。而现在，越来越多的高中生放弃高考，选择出国读本科。众所周知，中国高考的

洋学历	yáng xuélì	n.	degrees obtained from abroad
本土	běntǔ	adj.	local
值钱	zhíqián	adj.	valuable
一向	yíxiàng	adv.	all along; consistently
财富	cáifù	n.	wealth
输	shū	v.	to lose; to be defeated (opp. 赢 yíng)
起跑线	qǐpǎo xiàn	n.	starting line (for a race); (figurative) level; standard
镀金	dùjīn	v.	to gild; to cover or coat with gold; (fig.) to acquire guild (usually said of students who go abroad to study)
低龄化	dīlíng huà	adj.	skew toward the younger end of the spectrum; tend to be younger
倾向	qīngxiàng	n.	tendency; trend; inclination
本科生	běnkē shēng	n.	undergraduate student
硕士	shuòshì	n.	Master (of Science or Arts)
众所周知	zhòngsuǒzhōuzhī	idm.	as everyone knows; as is known to all

竞争是非常激烈的，每年只有一次机会；而且在高考制度下，整个高中教育都在为高考做准备。这种应试教育对培养学生的分析、创新能力是非常不利的。很多父母觉得自己的孩子不擅长考试，而且将来找工作，公司看的是孩子的综合素质，因此，只要条件允许，中国父母们都会把孩子送到国外去读大学。

还有一些父母在孩子读高中，甚至是读初中的时候就把孩子送出去。这样做值不值得，是中国父母需要仔细考虑的。且不说每年需要负担的高额留学费用，就算他们负担得起，也得看看孩子是不是已经为留学做好了心理准备。太早出国的坏处一方面是孩子不够成熟，适应不了国外的新环境，另一方面是如果不考虑移民，早晚得回国找工作，太早离开

应试	yìngshì	adj.	examination-oriented
培养	péiyǎng	v.	to cultivate; to foster (a certain spirit) in sb.
创新	chuàngxīn	v./n.	to bring forth new ideas; to innovate
擅长	shàncháng	v.	to be good at; to master in
将来	jiānglái	n.	future
综合	zōnghé	adj.	comprehensive; overall
素质	sùzhì	n.	quality (of citizens)
允许	yúnxǔ	v.	to allow; if…condition…allows/permits (在)条件允许(的情况下)
仔细	zǐxì	adv.	attentively; meticulously
高额	gāoé	n.	huge amount
心理	xīnlǐ	n.	mentality; psychology
成熟	chéngshú	adj.	mature; ripe
早晚	zǎowǎn	adv.	sooner or later

中国，回来以后又适应不了国内的环境。

　　盲目追求海外教育背景的另一个表现是，明明能力不够，却还是想方设法地实现"留学梦"。比方说，找留学中介公司帮忙。留学中介会帮助这些学生准备申请材料，甚至是造假，比方说，做假的成绩单，做假的活动证明等等。比较大的留学中介公司在国内外都有一定的关系。他们能找到一些老师来帮这些学生写推荐信，同时也能找到一些比较愿意接受中国学生的美国大学。而一些美国大学，由于缺乏教育经费，也乐意接受中国学生，因为一个国际学生的学费往往是当地学生的三倍。但即使能被国外的大学录取，这些能力不够的学生也很难在国外完成学业。据说，过去几年，每年都有几千名中国学生因为学习表现不佳被美国大学开除。这些造假的学生不但给自己带来了麻烦，也连累了其他申请美

盲目	mángmù	adv.	blindly
想方设法	xiǎngfāng shèfǎ	idm.	to do everything possible; try every means
造假	zàojiǎ	v.	to counterfeit
成绩单	chéngjì dān	n.	transcript; school report
推荐信	tuījiàn xìn	n.	recommendation letter
经费	jīngfèi	n.	funds
乐意	lèyì	v.	be happy to do sth.
录取	lùqǔ	v.	to admit
学业	xuéyè	n.	one's studies; school work
不佳	bùjiā	adj.	(of one's performance, grades, image) not good 表现/成绩/形象 不佳
开除	kāichú	v.	to expel; to dismiss
连累	liánlèi	v.	to implicate; to cause or bring trouble to another

国大学的中国学生。因为他们的行为让美国大学教授对中国学生的印象
变得很差。

　　出国留学有很多好处，但自己是不是适合？是不是做好了准备？这
也许是每一个想出国留学的学生应该先考虑清楚的问题。

适合　　　　　　　shìhé　　　　v.　　　to suit; to fit

195

I. 词语搭配 *Collocation*

1. 超乎 sb 的想象

   beyond one's imagination

2. 从事…教育 / 医疗 / field…工作

   to take up...teaching/medical and health work...as a profession

3. 书中自有黄金屋

   As long as one studies hard, wealth will come his way.

4. 创造+财富

   to build wealth

5. 不能（让孩子）输在起跑线上

   cannot allow (one's child) to lose at the starting line

6. 培养+孩子/兴趣/能力

   to educate and cultivate children/to develop an interest (in sth.)/to develop the ability of...

7. 负担+…（不小/高额的）…费用

   to bear or shoulder expenses

8. 高额+费用

   huge amount of expenses; high cost

9. 为……做好+心理准备

   to be psychologically prepared for...

10. 适应+新环境

    to adapt to a new environment

11. 盲目+追求/相信

    indiscriminately seek sth./to have a blind belief in sth.

12. Sb. 被…(an institute)…录取

    to be admitted (to an institute)

13. 表现/成绩/效果/作用/状况+不佳

bad performance/grade/effect/situation

II. 句型结构 *Sentence Pattern and Structure*

1. 一热 craze：留学热 craze of studying abroad，旅游热 the traveling craze，购房热 property craze

   中国最近几年兴起了留学热。

   购房热是中国最近十年出现的情况，到现在还在持续着。

2. Subj. 利用 (a tool/an opportunity) +V.P.

   Subj. utilizes a tool or takes advantage of an opportunity to do sth.

   现在越来越多的美国大学生利用暑假到中国来实习，打工。

   学校里的资源很丰富，你应该好好利用这些资源来学习。

3. 在……当中　　among...

   在这些美国大学生当中，不少人从事的是教育行业的工作。

   在这些学校当中，很难说哪个是最好的。

4. ……，…situation/consequence…可想而知

   One can well imagine that...

   连普通美国人在中国都很受欢迎，英文外教受欢迎的程度就可想而知了。

   在这家公司里，迟到都会被批评，旷工(不来上班)会有什么样的后果，也就可想而知了。

5. 众所周知，……　　as everyone knows; as is known to all

   众所周知，中国高考的竞争是非常激烈的。

   众所周知，移民为美国的发展做出了巨大的贡献。

6. ……对……是（很）不利/有利的　　be detrimental/beneficial to

A 对 B 是不是有利？

A 对 B 有利还是不利？

这种应试教育对培养学生的分析、创新能力是非常不利的。

发展公共交通对缓解交通问题是有利的。

7. 擅长+V.P.　　be good at; be expert in

很多父母觉得自己的孩子不擅长考试。

这里的学生个个都擅长唱歌、跳舞，多才多艺。

8. ……看的是……　　what Subj. looks for/considers is…

将来找工作，很多大公司看的是孩子的综合素质。

大学录取学生，看的是什么？

9. 且不说 A，就算 A，也得…B…

This pattern is often used to describe the difficulties in achieving a goal. In order to achieve this goal, one needs to fulfil a certain requirement (indicated by A), which is already very difficult. Even if this is not a problem, one still needs to deal with other difficulties (indicated by B).

还有一些父母在孩子读高中，甚至是读初中的时候就把孩子送出去。这样做值不值得，是中国父母需要仔细考虑的。且不说每年需要负担的高额留学费用，就算他们负担得起，也得看看孩子是不是已经为留学做好了心理准备。

你为什么找他帮忙？且不说他愿不愿意，就算他愿意，也得看他到底有没有能力。

10. 早晚+会 V.P. 的/得 V.P.　　sooner or later

如果不考虑移民，早晚得回国找工作，太早离开中国，回来以后又适应不了国内的环境。

你做事总是不小心，早晚会出事的。

11. ……明明……却……　　It is obvious that..., yet...

This pattern emphasizes the absurdity of an obvious mistake.

盲目追求海外教育背景的另一个表现是，明明能力不够，却还是想方设法地实现"留学梦"。

他明明是个中国人，为什么说话的时候却总要夹杂几个英文字？

12. 想方设法　　to do everything possible; try every means

盲目追求海外教育背景的另一个表现是，明明能力不够，却还是想方设法地实现"留学梦"。

肥胖问题已经成了一个社会问题，很多人都在想方设法地减肥。

III. 词语辨析 *Synonym Differentiation*

1. 学业：noun, a person's studies, esp. school or college studies.

   学习：noun / verb　　studies in general

   你不能上一年大学就不上了，你必须得完成你的学业。

   对他来说，学习是一件快乐的事。

   你得多向他学习学习。

2. 乐意：be happy to

   愿意：be willing to

   你有问题随时找我，我很乐意帮你解决问题。

   你愿意跟他做朋友吗？

3. 仔细：pay(ing) attention to every detail, do(ing) things carefully; attentive,

   小心：be cautious (in order to avoid danger or risk)

把考试交给老师以前，你得仔细检查。

如果考试的时候想作弊，你得小心，如果被发现了会被开除的！

小心开车！

4. 一向：consistently; all along (habitual)

一直：continuously

总是：always; invariably (with no exception)

他一向不喜欢学习。

昨天晚上八点到十点，我一直在宿舍学习。

我每次去找他的时候，他总是在学习，没有时间跟我说话。

"留學熱"背後的思考

　　現在越來越多的美國大學生利用暑假到中國來實習、打工；有的甚至畢業後選擇到中國來工作一、兩年。在這些美國大學生當中，不少人從事的是教育工作。比方說，到學校或英語培訓機構去教英文，或者到留學中介去當留學顧問，指導學生準備申請材料，建議學生參加哪些課外活動等等。英語在中國的教育中占很重要的地位，從小學、初中、高中到大學，英語一直都是必修課，而不是選修課；中考、高考，甚至於考研，英語也都是必考的科目。中國學生學習英文的熱情也超乎美國人想象。碰到美國人，中國學生就會設法跟他練習幾句英文。因此，英文外教在中國受歡迎的程度也就可想而知了。至於當留學顧問的工作機會，是最近幾年隨著留學熱潮的興起才出現的。

　　留學熱潮的出現主要是因為中國人普遍認為西方的教育制度比中國的好。在中國，洋學歷也比本土的學歷值錢得多。而且，中國人一向重視教育，尤其是下一代的教育。中國人常說："書中自有黃金屋"，意思是只要學習好，自然就能賺大錢。中國人相信：知識的力量是巨大的，它能創造財富。收入水平大大提高的中國父母更相信，"不能讓孩子輸在起跑線上"。只要有可能，中國父母一定會把孩子送到國外去"鍍金"。

　　於是，最近幾年，出國留學出現了低齡化的傾向。以前，出國的留學生主要是本科生，他們出國是為了讀碩士或者讀博士。而現在，越來越多的高中生放棄高考，選擇出國讀本科。眾所周知，中國高考的競爭是非常激烈的，每年只有一次機會；而且在高考制度下，整個高中教育都在為高考做準備。這種應試教育對培養學生的分析、創新能力是非常不利的。很多父母覺得自己的孩子不擅長考試，而且將來找工作，很多公司看的是孩子的綜合素質，因此，只要條件允許，中國父母們都會把孩子送到國外去讀大學。

　　還有一些父母在孩子讀高中，甚至是讀初中的時候就把孩子送出去。這樣做值不值得，是中國父母需要仔細考慮的。且不說每年需要負擔的高額留學費用，就算他們負擔得起，也得看看孩子是不是已經為留學做好了心理準備。太早出國的壞處一方面是孩子不夠成熟，適應不了國外的新環境，另一方面是如果不考慮移民，早晚得回國找工作，太早離開中國，回來以後又適應不了國內的環境。

盲目追求海外教育背景的另一個表現是，明明能力不夠，卻還是想方設法地實現"留學夢"。比方說，找留學中介公司幫忙。留學中介會幫助這些學生準備申請材料，甚至是造假，比方說，做假的成績單，做假的活動證明等等。比較大的留學中介公司在國內外都有一定的關係。他們能找到一些老師來幫這些學生寫推薦信，同時也能找到一些比較願意接受中國學生的美國大學。而一些美國大學，由於缺乏教育經費，也樂意接受中國學生，因為一個國際學生的學費往往是當地學生的三倍。但即使能被國外的大學錄取，這些能力不夠的學生也很難在國外完成學業。據說，過去幾年，每年都有幾千名中國學生因為學習表現不佳被美國大學開除。這些造假的學生不但給自己帶來了麻煩，也連累了其他申請美國大學的中國學生。因為他們的行為讓美國大學教授對中國學生的印象變得很差。

出國留學有很多好處，但自己是不是適合出國留學？是不是做好了準備？這也許是每一個想出國留學的學生應該先考慮清楚的問題。

课后习题
第 14 课

一、词语搭配 (Please pair the term in the left column with the most appropriate term in the right column. Then use the completed phrases to complete the sentences. You can change the order of words and add more information if needed.)

(1)

(C) 从事　　A 费用
(A) 负担　　B 准备
(B) 做好　　C 工作

1. 你的爷爷这次病得很严重,你得_____B_____,他的时间可能不多了。

2. 你毕业以后想_____C_____,为了这个目标,你做了什么样的准备?

3. 在美国,在孩子十八岁以前,父母有责任_____A_____。

(2)

(D) 创造　　A 想象
(A) 超乎　　B 兴趣
(B) 培养　　C 学生
(C) 录取　　D 财富

1. 一个成功的公司既要_____D_____,也得考虑为社会做出自己的贡献。

2. 在北京,交通拥挤的情况已经_____A_____,这个问题必须解决。

3. 除了重视孩子的成绩以外,父母也应该注意_____B_____。

4. 你们大学每年_____C_____?怎么样才能申请上你们大学?

(3)

(B) 表现   A 费用

(D) 盲目   B 不佳

(A) 高额   C 新环境

(C) 适应   D 追求

1. 虽然 GDP 可以反映经济的发展,可是政府不应该_____D_____。

2. 有些工人因为_____B_____被老板解雇(fire)了。

3. 培养孩子的兴趣常常需要花很多钱,比方说,学钢琴（piano）,父母都得
_____A_____。

4. 到了一个新学校,一定要快一点儿_____C_____,这样才能好好学习。

二、选择填空 (Complete the sentences by choosing the most appropriate term.)

1. 学习   学业

   在你完成__A__以前,你不可以结婚。

   对现代人来说, __B__不只是在学校里的事情,工作了以后还是可以继续。

2. 乐意   愿意

   你参加这些课外活动是自己__B__参加的吗?

   父母帮他找了一份在培训机构的工作,可是他不是很____去那儿工作。

3. 仔细   小心

   请你____看一看这篇文章,如果有什么问题,请告诉我。

   你拿刀的时候一定要____。

4. 一向   一直   总是

   他____喜欢安静,所以他应该不会来参加今天的晚会。

这里的火车太不准时了，___A___ 晚点。

我们上课得___B___上到 12 点才能休息。

三、完成句子 (Complete the sentence or dialogue with the given item in parentheses.)

1. A：暑假你有什么计划？

   B：_____。（利用）

2. A：高中的时候你们有几门必修课？哪一门是你最感兴趣的？

   B：_____。（在…当中）

3. A：中国大学生找工作的竞争激烈吗？

   B：_____。（可想而知）

4. A：非洲（Africa）还很落后吗？

   B：_____。（可想而知）

5. A：为什么每年有那么多中国学生去美国留学？

   B：_____。（众所周知）

6. A：为什么暑假有很多大学生要去实习？

   B：_____。（对…有利/不利）

7. A：很多美国人对中国学生的印象是什么？

   B：_____。（擅长）

8. A：大学录取学生，看的是什么？

   B：_____。（看的是）

9. A：听说在北京买房子很难，为什么？

   B：_____。（且不说 A，就算 A，也得…B…）

10. A：为什么美国政府不解决枪支问题？

    B：_____。（且不说 A，就算 A，也得…B…）

11. 你常常为了看电影晚上不睡觉，_____。（早晚+会 V.P.的/得 V.P.）

12. A：小王说他已经做完作业才出来玩，他真的做完了吗？

    B：_____。（明明…却…）

13. A：脸书的 CEO 为什么开那么普通的车？

B：我也不懂，_____。（明明…却…）

14. 我的朋友很胖，为了健康，_____。（想方设法）

四、回答问题 (Answer the questions.)

1. 为什么中国会出现留学热潮？

2. 为什么出国留学会出现低龄化的倾向？这是不是好事？

3. "留学"对每个人来说都是最好的选择吗？

4. 美国学生喜欢去哪些国家留学？美国学生留学的目的和中国学生一样吗？

第 15 课

外国的月亮是不是比较圆？

A：美国学生　　　B：中国学生

A：昨天我们讨论留学问题的时候，老师说："有的中国人觉得'外国的月亮比较圆'。"月亮不是只有一个吗？外国的月亮怎么会比中国的圆呢？这句话到底是什么意思啊？

B：这句话是讽刺有些中国人崇洋媚外，觉得外国什么东西都是好的，就连在外国看到的月亮都比在中国看到的圆。

A：原来是这样，但这个说法未免太夸张了。

B：这个说法是有些夸张，但中国社会上的确存在崇洋媚外的现象。有的中国人有钱了，买东西就都要买外国商品，从家用电器、名牌服装

月亮	yuèliang	n.	moon
崇洋媚外	chóngyán mèiwài idm.		to revere foreign things and pander to foreign powers; blind worship of foreign goods and ideas
原来	yuánlái	adv.	as it turns out; actually
未免	wèimiǎn	adv.	a bit too…;
的确	díquè	adv.	indeed

到婴儿用品，甚至于连酱油都恨不得买外国生产的。在有些地区，比方说广东和香港，好好的中国话不说，非得在中国话里头夹杂几个英文单词，以此来显示自己的国际化。

A：这种心态是可以理解的。一百多年前，中国很落后，方方面面都不如西方国家，受到帝国主义的侵略。这个情况一直持续了一百多年。结果，中国人渐渐对自己的一切丧失了自信，处处以西方为榜样。

B：你对中国的历史倒挺了解的嘛。以前，到美国的中国人几乎个个都想留在美国，成为美国公民。中国的人才外流问题非常严重。但现在，有不少出国留学的中国人选择回到中国工作。我的一个朋友，两年前从

婴儿用品	yīng'ér yòngpǐn	n.	baby products
酱油	jiàngyóu	n.	soy sauce
恨不得	hènbudé	v.	to be dying to; to wish one could
广东	Guǎngdōng	n.	Guangdong Province
夹杂	jiāzá	v.	be mixed with; be mingled with
国际化	guójì huà	adj.	internationalized
心态	xīntài	n.	psychology; mentality
方方面面	fāngfāng miànmiàn	idm.	all aspects; all sides
持续	chíxù	v.	to continue; to carry on
丧失	sàngshī	v.	to lose (ambition, ability, senses, etc.).
自信	zìxìn	n./adj.	self-confidence; confident
处处	chùchù	adv.	everywhere; in all aspects
榜样	bǎngyàng	n.	model; a good example
人才外流	réncái wàiliú	idm.	brain drain; outflow of talented people

哥伦比亚大学 毕业以后就进入了华尔街 的投资银行工作。她的收入很高，公司也有意 帮她申请绿卡 。我本来以为她会像大多数在美国工作、学习的中国人那样一步步 实现自己的"美国梦"，但她最近却放弃了华尔街的高薪 工作，放弃申请绿卡的机会，回到了上海。

A：她回到上海做什么？

B：她回上海跟几个朋友一起创业，开设 网络约车 服务。

A：是不是就像美国的 Uber？

B：对，网络约车服务虽然是从美国开始的，但它在中国的发展却比美国快得多。在中国，关于网络约车的法律几年前就已制定好，实现了合法化 。在科技方面，中国的发展可以说是突飞猛进。

A：看来，中国的确在科技发展上下了很大的功夫 。是什么吸引你

哥伦比亚大学	Gēlún bǐyà dàxué	n.	Columbia University
华尔街	Huáěr jiē	n.	Wall Street
有意	yǒuyì	v.	to have a mind to; be inclined to
绿卡	lùkǎ	n.	"Green Card," permanent residence permit for foreigners
一步步	yí bùbù	adv.	step by step
高薪	gāoxīn	adj.	high-paying (jobs)
创业	chuàngyè	v.	to start an enterprise
开设	kāishè	v.	to offer (a course in college, a service)
网络约车	wǎngluò yuēchē	n.	online taxi reservation
合法化	héfǎ huà	v.	to legalize; to legitimize
下功夫	xià gōngfu	v.	to put in time and energy

朋友回国发展的？

　　B：我觉得是机会，成功的机会。中国的市场实在太大了，人口多，老百姓的购买力也在增强。只要你的产品和设计有足够的创意，你的投入就一定能获得丰厚的回报。

　　A：是的，我觉得中国人在批评一些人崇洋媚外的时候，也应该好好反思为什么很多中国人更喜欢外国货。中国人买外国货可能是喜欢外国人的生活方式，可能是为了赶时髦，也可能是出于好奇，但说到底，还是因为外国货品质优良，产品设计有新意。中国人要想改变这种情况，

发展	fāzhǎn	n./v.	development; to develop
购买力	gòumǎi lì	n.	purchasing power
增强	zēngqiáng	v.	to increase and strengthen (power, capability, influence, etc.)
创意	chuàngyì	n.	original idea
丰厚	fēnghòu	adj.	generous
回报	huíbào	v.	to repay; reciprocate
反思	fǎnsī	v.	to reflect; rethink
赶时髦	gǎn shímáo	v.o.	to follow the fashion; be in style
出于	chūyú	prep.	out of (e.g. good intention 出于好心); stem from
说到底	shuō dàodǐ	adv.	after all; simply put
优良	yōuliáng	adj.	(of quality, grades) fine
新意	xīnyì	n.	(of a book, product, plan, etc. to have) original and creative ideas

210

还得创造自己的品牌。

　　B：没错。要想设计生产出好的产品，就必须有优秀的人才。现在中国政府已经认识到这一点。如果说改革开放初期中国需要吸引的是外国的资金，那么现在这个阶段，中国迫切需要的是各行各业的高端人才。因此，政府采取了一系列的措施来吸引留学海外的优秀人才回国。比方说，很多大学都有引进海外优秀人才的计划。与在中国本土接受教育的科研人员相比，海外人才拿到的工资和科研经费可能高出好几倍。 另外，政府也鼓励创业，不断简化各种手续，为年轻人创业创造宽松的环境。

　　A；可是在中国，要办事，关系不是很重要的吗？这些从海外回来

品牌	pǐnpái	n.	brand; make
初期	chūqī	n.	initial stage; early days
阶段	jiēduàn	n.	stage; phase
高端	gāoduān	adj.	high-end; upscale; up-market (opp. 低端)
采取	cǎiqǔ	v.	to adopt (measures); to take (steps)
一系列	yí xìliè		a series of
措施	cuòshī	n.	measures
引进	yǐnjìn	v.	to introduce (from elsewhere); to bring in
科研	kēyán	n.	scientific research
人员	rényuán	n.	personnel
不断	búduàn	adv.	continuously
简化	jiǎnhuà	v.	to simplify
手续	shǒuxù	n.	procedure; formality
宽松	kuānsōng	adj.	(of policy) flexible, relaxed

的人又没有什么关系。

B：现在在中国，关系不能说不重要，有关系还是好办事。但是俗话说，"是金子，总会发光的"。只要你有才能，你还是有可能受到重视的。

A：那现在最优秀的人才是不是都选择回到中国呢？

B：虽然这些措施取得了不错的效果，成功地吸引了一大批人才回国，但是现在中国的人才流失仍然很严重。很多留学生在做决定的时候还是有顾虑，会犹豫要不要回国。要想吸引更多优秀人才回国，政府还得努力创造更加宽松自由的学术环境，让他们看到中国的发展与改变，让他们相信，在今天的中国，靠自己的能力也能成功。

俗话	súhuà	n.	common saying; proverb
取得	qǔdé	v.	to gain, acquire, obtain
效果	xiàoguǒ	n.	effect, result
一大批	yí dàpī		large quantities of; a big lot (of goods); a large group (of people)
流失	liúshī	v.	to lose/drain; 资金~: money flows out
犹豫	yóuyù	v.	to hesitate
学术	xuéshù	adj.	academic

I. 词语搭配 *Collocation*

1. sb. 崇洋媚外

   (lit.) to worship everything foreign, and pander to foreign powers

2. 原来是这样

   So that's how it is! / So that's what happened! /Now I see!

3. 丧失+自信/尊严/语言或生育能力

   to lose self-confidence/dignity/the ability to speak or give birth (fertility)

4. 以……为榜样

   to look up to…as a model

5. ……合法化/把……合法化

   to legitimize, legalize

6. 购买力/影响力/软实力+增强

   an increase in purchasing power/influence/soft power

7. 产品/设计+有创意

   The product/design is full of original ideas.

8. 丰厚的回报

   rich and generous payback

9. 品质+优良

   fine quality

10. 高端+人才/技术/产品/设备

    high-end talents or personnel/technology/product/equipment or facilities

11. 引进+人才

    to bring in talents

12. 简化+手续

    to simplify the procedure or formalities

13. 宽松的+环境/政策

    a free and relaxed environment/flexible policies

14. 是金子，总是会发光的

(lit.) the gold will glitter wherever it is; if you are truly talented or capable, you will
be recognized no matter where you go.

15. policy 取得…很好的/显著的…效果

to achieve very good/remarkable results

II. 句型结构 *Sentence Pattern and Structure*

1. ……不是……吗？……怎么……呢？

Isn't it that…, how come…? (a rhetorical question)

月亮不是只有一个吗？外国的月亮怎么会比中国的圆呢？

你不是不喜欢喝咖啡吗？怎么又喝起咖啡来了呢？

2. Interrogative pronouns (谁，什么，哪儿, etc.) 都……，就连……都……

used to emphasize all the things that fall under a certain umbrella/scope

有些中国人崇洋媚外，觉得外国什么东西都是好的，就连在外国看到的月亮
都比在中国看到的圆。

谁都得遵守法律的规定，就连总统都不例外。

3. ……未免+有点儿 negative adj. /太 negative adj. 了

(of something that one finds has gone too far) rather, a bit too

这个说法未免太夸张了。

你的办法未免有点儿太复杂了，有没有简单点儿的？

4. 恨不得+…立刻/马上/现在就/连…都…V.P. （exaggeration）

one only wishes one could; be dying to

有的中国人有钱了，买东西就都要买外国商品，从家用电器，名牌服装到婴
儿用品，甚至于连酱油都恨不得买外国生产的。

214

我实在太想家了，恨不得现在就飞回家去。

5. 好好的 noun 不 v，非得……

好好的: in perfectly good condition

This structure is often used to criticize those who gave up great opportunities or desirable things (at least in the eyes of the speaker) to seek something else indiscriminately.

在有些地区，比方说广东和香港，好好的中国话不说，非得在中国话里头夹杂几个英文单词，以此来显示自己的国际化。

你真是奇怪！好好的学不上，非得去工厂打工。

6. ……，以此来显示/表现/证明……

to show/prove……with this (here "this" refers to what has just been mentioned in the previous sentence)

在有些地区，比方说广东和香港，好好的中国话不说，非得在中国话里头夹杂几个英文单词，以此来显示自己的国际化。

他非常努力地工作，希望以此来证明没有父亲的帮助，他也能成功。

7. 有意+V.P.　（negation: 无意）

to have a mind to; to be inclined to

两年前从哥伦比亚大学毕业以后就进入了华尔街的投资银行工作。她的收入很高，公司也有意帮她申请绿卡。

有意申请工作的人，请把你的申请材料交给我。无意申请工作的人，就不必麻烦了。

8. 在……方面+下了很大的功夫　　to have put a lot of work/effort into…

应该在……方面+多下功夫　　should put more work/effort into…

最近中国政府在打击腐败方面下了很大的功夫。

美国政府应该在国内经济发展方面多下功夫。

9. ……是出于……好奇 / 同情 / 礼貌 / 对…的尊重

out of curiosity/sympathy/courtesy/respect

中国人买外国货可能是喜欢外国人的生活方式，可能是为了追赶时髦，还可能是出于对外国的好奇。

你给他钱，是出于同情吗？

10. ……，说到底，…还是/就是因为…(最根本的原因 the root cause)…

After all, the fundamental reason/the root cause is still, or, is simply…

中国人买外国货可能是喜欢外国人的生活方式，可能是为了追赶时髦，还可能是出于对外国的好奇。但说到底，还是因为外国货质量优良，产品设计有新意。

你不要再找什么借口了，说到底，你不敢去见他，就是因为你怕他。

11. A 比 B 多/高出 num.倍　　　　A is several times more than B

与 B 相比，A 多/高出 num.倍

与 B 相比，A…adj.得多

海外人才的收入比中国本土接受教育的科研人员高出三、四倍。

与在中国本土接受教育的科研人员收入相比，海外人才的工资高出好几倍。

与本地的科研人员相比，海外人才的收入要高得多。

12. Sb. 犹豫+要不要……　　　　hesitate to do sth.

很多人在做决定的时候还是有顾虑，会犹豫要不要回国。

我一直在犹豫要不要去美国留学。

III. 词语辨析 *Synonym Differentiation*

1. 持续：持续 + time duration　to last (from the beginning to the end)

   继续：继续 + verb phrase　　to resume

   我们上个星期的晚会，从开始到结束，一共持续了五个小时。

   我们昨天的会持续了两个小时，但我们要讨论的内容还没讨论完，所以今天我们继续讨论。

2. 榜样：a model (that should be followed)

   例子：an example (to help explain what you are saying or to show that a general statement is true)

   他又聪明又努力，是同学们学习的好榜样。

   开放的市场对经济发展有帮助，深圳的发展就是一个很好的例子。

3. 丧失：丧失+abstract noun

   e.g. to lose ability 丧失能力/senses 丧失理智/confidence 丧失自信

   失去：失去+abstract noun / sb.

   e.g. to lose one's parents　失去父母

   中国人渐渐对自己的一切丧失／失去了自信，处处以西方为榜样。

   他在这次事故（accident）中失去了父母。

外國的月亮是不是比較圓？

A：美國學生　　　　B：中國學生

A：昨天我們討論留學問題的時候，老師說："有的中國人覺得'外國的月亮比較圓'。"月亮不是只有一個嗎？外國的月亮怎麼會比中國的圓呢？這句話到底是什麼意思啊？

B：這句話是諷刺有些中國人崇洋媚外，覺得外國的什麼東西都是好的，就連在外國看到的月亮都比在中國看到的圓。

A：原來是這樣，但這個說法未免太誇張了。

B：這個說法誇張是誇張，但中國社會上的確存在崇洋媚外的現象。有的中國人有錢了，買東西就都要買外國商品，從家用電器、名牌服裝到嬰兒用品，甚至於連醬油都恨不得買外國生產的。在有些地區，比方說廣東和香港，中國話不好好說，非得在中國話裏頭夾雜幾個英文單詞，以此來顯示自己的國際化。

A：這種心態是可以理解的。一百多年前，中國很落後，方方面面都不如西方國家，因此常常受帝國主義的侵略。這個情況一直持續了一百多年。結果，中國人漸漸對自己的一切喪失了自信，處處以西方為榜樣。

B：你對中國的歷史倒挺了解的嘛。以前，到美國的中國人幾乎個個都想留在美國，成為美國公民。中國的人才外流問題非常嚴重。但現在，有不少出國留學的中國人選擇回到中國工作。我的一個朋友，兩年前從哥倫比亞大學畢業以後就進入了華爾街的投資銀行工作。她的收入很高，公司也有意幫她申請綠卡。我本來以為她會像大多數在美國工作、學習的中國人那樣一步步實現自己的"美國夢"，但她最近卻放棄了華爾街的高薪工作，放棄申請綠卡的機會，回到了上海。

A：她回到上海做什麼？

B：她回上海跟幾個朋友一起創業，開設網絡約車服務。

A：是不是就像美國的 Uber？

B：對，網絡約車服務雖然是從美國開始的，但它在中國的發展卻比美國快。在中國，關於網絡約車的法律幾年前就已制定好，實現了合法化。在科技方面，中國的發展可以說是突飛猛進。

A：看來，中國在科技發展上下了很大的功夫。是什麼吸引你朋友回國發展的？

B：我覺得是機會，成功的機會。中國的市場實在太大了，人口多，老百姓的購買力也在增強。只要你的產品和設計有足夠的創意，你的投入就一定能獲得豐厚的回報。

A：是的，我覺得中國人在批評一些人崇洋媚外的時候，也應該好好反思為什麼很多中國人更喜歡外國貨。中國人買外國貨可能是喜歡外國人的生活方式，可能是為了追趕時髦，還可能是出於對外國的好奇，但說到底，還是因為外國貨質量優良，產品設計有新意。中國人要想改變這種情況，還得創造自己的品牌。

B：沒錯。要想設計生產出好的產品，就必須有優秀的人才。現在中國政府已經認識到這一點。如果說改革開放初期中國需要吸引的是外國的資金，那麼現在這個階段，中國迫切需要的是各行各業的高端人才。因此，政府采取了一系列的措施來吸引留學海外的優秀人才回國。比方說，很多大學都有引進海外優秀人才的計劃。與在中國本土接受教育的科研人員相比，海外人才拿到的工資和科研經費可能高出好幾倍。另外，政府也鼓勵創業，不斷簡化各種手續，為年輕人創業創造寬松的環境。

A；可是在中國，要辦事，關係不是很重要的嗎？這些從海外回來的人又沒有什麼關係。

B：現在在中國，關係不能說不重要，有關係還是好辦事。但是俗話說，"是金子，總會發光的"。只要你有才能，你還是有可能受到重視的。

A：那現在最優秀的人才是不是都選擇回到中國呢？

B：雖然這些措施取得了不錯的效果，成功地吸引了一大批人才回國，但是現在中國的人才流失在全世界還是排第一位。很多人在做決定的時候還是有顧慮，一直在猶豫要不要回國。要想吸引更多優秀人才回國，政府還得努力創造更加寬鬆自由的學術環境，讓他們看到中國的發展與改變，讓他們相信，現在在中國靠自己的能力也能成功。

课后习题

第 15 课

一、词语搭配 (Please pair the term in the left column with the most appropriate term in the right column. Then use the completed phrases to complete the sentences. You can change the order of words and add more information if needed.)

(1)

(C) 设计　　A 简化

(D) 影响力　B 人才

(B) 引进　　C 有创意

(A) 手续　　D 增强

1. 大学要想有更好的发展，一方面得努力改善教学条件，另一方面也得＿＿B＿＿。

2. 随着中国经济的发展，＿D＿。中国在很多国际问题的解决上起着重要的作用。

3. 据说，以前要在开公司得办很多手续，但现在＿＿＿＿A＿＿＿＿＿＿。

4. 苹果公司的产品能吸引年轻人是因为＿＿＿＿C＿＿＿＿，比方说苹果手机能分辨不同人的脸，这样的设计不但有用，也让人觉得很有趣。

(2)

(B) 取得　　A 优良

(C) 宽松的　B 效果

(A) 品质　　C 环境

1. 中国吸引外国公司投资的政策＿＿＿＿C＿＿＿＿，很多的国际大公司都在中国设立了办事处。

2. 在美国，人们认为＿＿＿＿＿B＿＿＿＿＿有利于科学研究的进行。

3. 在中国，人们对进口货的印象是＿＿＿＿A＿＿＿＿＿。

(3)

（ C ）高端的　　　　A 自信

（ B ）丰厚的　　　　B 回报

（ A ）丧失　　　　　C 技术

1. 他参加了 4 次高考，都没考上大学，他已经＿＿＿＿ A ＿＿＿＿。

2. Space X 这家大公司拥有大量＿＿＿＿＿ C ＿＿＿＿＿，比方说人工智能（AI）。

3. 为什么外国大公司愿意来中国投资？这是因为＿＿ B ＿＿。

二、选择填空 (Complete the sentences by choosing the most appropriate term.)

1. 持续 A　　继续 B

从 1840 年开始，帝国主义对中国的侵略＿＿ A ＿＿了一百年。

这次你考得很好，希望你＿ B ＿努力，下次考 100 分。

2. 榜样 A　　例子 B

他通过自己的努力实现了自己的理想，真是值得我们学习的好＿＿ A ＿＿。

你有什么＿ B ＿可以说明关系、人情在中国很重要？

3. 丧失 A　　失去 B

在那次车祸（car accident）中，他＿ B ＿了他的爱人和孩子，还有，他的腿受了很严重的伤，结果＿＿ A ＿＿了行动能力。

三、完成句子 (Complete the sentence or dialogue with the given item in parentheses.)

1. Situation：A 去过美国，但只去过纽约。

A：爱荷华（Iowa）在哪儿？

B：＿＿＿＿＿＿＿＿＿＿＿＿＿＿＿＿＿＿＿。（…不是…吗？…怎么…呢？）

2. Situation：A 的眼镜戴在头上，可是他忘了。

A：我的眼镜呢？我找不到了。

B：_____。(…不是…吗？…怎么…呢？)

3. A：在北京、上海等大城市，什么东西可以网购（=从网上购买）？

B：_____。(Interrogative pronouns 都…，就连…都…)

4. 他的哥哥很聪明，_____。(Interrogative pronouns 都…，就连…都…)

5. Situation：A 和 B 一起走路去 B 的家，他们走了半个小时了。

A：我走了半天了，怎么还没到啊？我要累死了。

B：_____。(…未免+太 negative adj.了)

6. A：要是家里的钱不够，很多中国父母会选择让儿子去上学，而不是让女儿去

上学。

B：_____。(…未免+有点儿 negative adj.)

7. A：他的太太为什么那么生气？

B：他的太太发现他跟别的女人发生了关系，_____

_____。(恨不得+立刻就 VP)

8. 他太喜欢他的新 iPad 了，到哪儿都带着它，

_____。(恨不得+连…都…VP)

9. A：妈妈，我不想睡床，我要睡吊床（hammock）。

B：_____。(好好的 noun 不 v，非得…)

10. Situation：在地铁上，有的农民工 (immigrant worker) 没有坐在椅子上，而是

坐在地上。你会问：_____。(好好的 noun 不 v，非得…)

11. A：很多国家的问题明明跟美国没有关系，美国却要帮助这些国家，为什么？

B：_____。(以此来显示/表现/证明)

12. A：为什么有的中国父母选择送孩子去上国际学校？

B._____。(有意+VP)

13. 过去十年，中国的高铁建设突飞猛进，可以说_____。

（在…方面+下了很大的功夫）

14. A：我的孩子成绩很不错，要申请美国的名牌大学，还应该做什么？

B：_____。(应该在…方面+多下功夫)

15. A：学生不能去上课，为什么得给老师发电子邮件？

　　B：＿＿＿＿＿＿＿＿＿＿＿＿＿＿＿＿＿＿＿。（…是出于…）

16. A：人们看到小乞丐（beggar）为什么会给他们钱？

　　B：＿＿＿＿＿＿＿＿＿＿＿＿＿＿＿＿＿＿＿。（…是出于…）

17. A：为什么中国父母要送孩子去美国留学？

　　B：＿＿＿＿＿＿＿＿＿＿＿＿＿＿＿。（…，说到底，…还是/就是因为…）

18. A：在美国，医生的收入高，还是大学老师的收入高？为什么？

　　B：＿＿＿＿＿＿＿＿＿＿＿＿＿。（A 比 B 多/高出 num.倍）

19. A：在现代化的大城市，茶馆多还是咖啡馆多？为什么？

　　B：＿＿＿＿＿＿＿＿＿＿＿＿。（与 B 相比，A…adj.得多）

20. A：＿＿＿＿＿＿＿＿＿＿＿＿＿。（Sb.犹豫+要不要…）

　　B：要是你想跟朋友一起吃饭，你当然应该打电话问问。如果他没有时间，那你就自己吃。这不是什么大事，不用想那么多。

四、回答问题 (Answer the questions.)

1. "外国的月亮比较圆"这句话是什么意思？中国人为什么会这么说？美国有没有类似的说法？

2. 你觉得中国人"崇洋媚外"吗？如果这是真的，为什么会这样？

3. 现在的中国留学生跟以前有什么不同？

4. 改革开放初期，中国的发展最需要什么？现在呢？

5. 怎样才能吸引优秀人才回到中国？请你给中国政府一些好建议。

第 16 课

中国人的节日

中国的节日和美国最大的不同是：美国的节日大多是宗教性的。像圣诞节是庆祝耶稣生日，复活节是纪念耶稣复活。所以庆祝的活动往往都在教堂举行。

中国主要的节日和宗教是没有关系的，宗教在中国文化中所占的地位没有在西方文化中那么重。中国到处都有寺庙，有的是佛教的，有的是道教的，还有的是纪念历史上的名人，像孔子和关公的。中国人对不同宗教

节日	jiérì	n.	festival; holiday
宗教性	zōngjiào xìng	n.	it is often used to modify "节日", meaning religious (holidays).
圣诞节	Shèngdàn jié	n.	Christmas
庆祝	qìngzhù	v.	to celebrate
耶稣	Yēsū	n.	Jesus
复活节	Fùhuó jié	n.	Easter
纪念	jìniàn	v.	to commemorate
复活	fùhuó	v./n.	(lit.) to come back to life; to resurrect; resurrection
教堂	jiàotáng	n.	church
宗教	zōngjiào	n.	religion
寺庙	sìmiào	n.	temple
佛教	Fójiào	n.	Buddhism
道教	Dàojiào	n.	Daoism
名人	míngrén	n.	famous figures; celebrity

的包容是很了不起的。这种包容的态度，在西方是不能想像的！在西方历史上，主要的战争往往和宗教有关系，但是在中国历史上，没有大规模的宗教战争，这是中国文化的特色。

中国人到寺庙去的时候，并不在意寺庙里供奉的是什么神，他们甚至分不清道教和佛教到底有什么不同。他们到寺庙去往往有一定现实的目的，比方说：希望神能帮自己的孩子考上大学，找到工作，希望一家人都平安，子女早点儿成家立业。从这方面来看，中国人是非常实际的。

中国主要的节日反映的是农业社会生活的内容，这些节日都是用农历来计算的。像五月初五的端午节，据说是为了纪念两千多年前一个伟大的

了不起	liǎobuqǐ	adj.	extraordinary; terrific
战争	zhànzhēng	n.	war
大规模	dàguīmó	adj.	large-scale (usu. as a modifier)
在意	zàiyì	v.	to mind; to take to heart
供奉	gòngfèng	v.	to enshrine and worship
神	shén	n.	deity
分不清	fēnbuqīng	v.-c.	cannot distinguish (A from B)
现实	xiànshí	adj.	practical
平安	píng'ān	adj.	safe and sound
成家立业	chéngjiā lìyè	idm.	get married and start one's career
实际	shíjì	adj.	practical; realistic
农历	nónglì	n.	lunar calendar
计算	jìsuàn	v.	to calculate
初五	Chū Wǔ	t.w.	the fifth day of a month (of the Chinese lunar calendar)
端午节	Duānwǔ jié	n.	the Dragon Boat Festival

爱国诗人屈原，可是，对绝大多数的中国人来说，端午节吃粽子是最重要的，至于为什么有这个节日，他们并不是那么关心。八月十五的中秋节，家人会在一起吃月饼。据说这天晚上的月亮特别圆，也特别亮，代表家人团圆。当然最重要的节日是春节，相当于美国人的新年。这个假期往往会持续两个星期。

　　因为中国主要的节日都是用农历来计算的，而国际通用的历法是公历，也叫西元。这对日常生活有很大的影响。中国社会其实是农历和公历同时使用的。这对一个美国学生来说是很新鲜的，当然也有些不习惯。每年春

粽子	zòngzi	n.	a pyramid-shaped sticky rice ball made of glutinous rice and wrapped in bamboo leaves
关心	guānxīn	v.	to care about
中秋节	Zhōngqiū jié	n.	the Mid-Autumn Festival
月饼	yuèbǐng	n.	mooncake
亮	liàng	adj.	bright
团圆	tuányuán	v./n.	(of a family) to reunite; family reunion　跟家人团圆；全家团圆
春节	Chūnjié	n.	the Spring Festival
相当于	xiāngdāngyú	v.	to be equivalent to
假期	jiàqī	n.	holiday
通用	tōngyòng	v.	to be in common use
历法	lìfǎ	n.	calendar; calendric system
公历	gōnglì	n.	Western calendar
西元	xīyuán	n.	the Christian era
新鲜	xīnxian	adj.	new; novel; strange

季学期什么时候开学 得看春节在什么时候。春节从阳历的一月中到二月底都有可能，所以每年放寒假 的时间也就各不相同，很难提前 做计划。在美国大学，每个学期考试和放假 的时间，基本上都差不多，每年最多有一两天的出入，在中国两三个星期的不同是很平常的事。

　　中国人的节假日 受到西方文化很大的影响。大城市里，很多年轻人都庆祝西方的情人节、感恩节 和圣诞节。他们一样送礼物，吃火鸡，高高兴兴地参加朋友的聚会。他们很少问这个节日是中国的还是西方的。只要过得高兴有趣，就达到了庆祝的目的。就这一点来说，中国人在接受外来文化的时候是很开放，很包容的。你能想像美国年轻人在美国庆祝端午节和中秋节吗？

春季	chūnjì	n.	spring (formal)
学期	xuéqī	n.	semester
开学	kāixué	v.	school begins, (a new) term begins
寒假	hánjià	n.	winter break
各不相同	gèbùxiāngtóng	adj.	have nothing in common with each other
提前	tíqián	adv.	in advance; to be earlier than planned or expected
放假	fàngjià	v.-o.	to give sb. a vacation; to have a holiday
出入	chūrù	n.	discrepancy (compared to one's estimation)
节假日	jiéjià rì	n.	holiday
情人节	Qíngrén jié	n.	Valentine's Day
感恩节	Gǎnēn jié	n.	Thanksgiving Day
火鸡	huǒjī	n.	turkey
聚会	jùhuì	n.	gather-together; gathering
达到	dádào	v.	to achieve or attain (a goal)

当然，这也说明中国文化的"软实力"在目前是无法和美国文化相提并论的。

Notes:

屈原　　　Qū Yuán (340?-278 B.C.), a poet and minister of Chu 楚 during the Warring States period of China, was exiled for perceived disloyalty.

孔子　　　Kǒngzǐ, or Confucius (551-479 B.C.), was a thinker, philosopher and educator. He was considered the founder of what was later known as *Rújiā* 儒家 (the Confucian school), arguably the most influential school in premodern China and beyond.

关公　　　Guāngōng, or Lord Guan (160-220 A.D.), was a loyal and courageous general who played a significant role in the establishment of the Shu Han during the Three Kingdoms period and was later worshipped by many Chinese people.

无法	wúfǎ	v.	unable
相提并论	xiāngtí bìnglùn	idm.	[usu. in the negative] to mention in the same breath; to place on a par

I. 词语搭配 *Collocation*

1. 庆祝+holidays（圣诞节/复活节/……）

   to celebrate + holidays (e.g. Christmas/Easter, etc.)

2. A 对 B 很包容

   A is tolerant of B (willing to accept feelings, habits, or beliefs that are different)

3. 大规模的战争

   A large-scale/massive war

4. 分不清 A 和 B（有什么不同）

   unable to distinguish A from B

5. 放…time duration…（暑/寒/春/秋）假

   to have (summer/winter/spring/fall) break

6. 达到……的目的

   to achieve or attain the goal (of…)

II. 句型结构 *Sentence Pattern and Structure*

1. ……有一定的关系/影响/作用/好处 abstract noun

   to have some relation to/ influence/effect on…/some benefit to

   中国人到寺庙去往往有一定现实的目的。

   虽然在这里工作有一定的好处，但坏处也是很明显的。

2. A…positive…，至于 B，…negative…

   Zhìyú 至于 meaning "as for; as to" is often used at the beginning of a second sentence

   or paragraph to introduce or comment on another aspect of the aforementioned topic.

   对几乎所有的中国人来说，端午节吃粽子是最重要的，至于为什么有这个日，

   他们一点儿都不关心。

   我只知道他结婚了，至于他是什么时候结婚的，我就不清楚了。

3. A 的 noun 1 相当于 B 的 noun 2

This structure, meaning "… is equivalent to…," is often used to introduce a new thing or concept (A 的 n1) through an analogy to a more familiar thing or concept (B 的 n2).

在中国，最重要的节日是春节，中国的春节相当于美国人的新年。

中国的"人人网"相当于美国的 Facebook，都是网上的社交（social）工具。

4. …question form…，得看……

"…depends on…" means that the topic of the sentence is determined or decided by something else.

每年春季学期什么时候开学得看春节在什么时候。

明天我们能不能出去玩儿，得看天气怎么样。

5. 每 + m.w. + noun +（的……）各不相同

a plural noun 各不相同

春节从阳历的一月中到二月底都有可能，所以每年寒假的时间也就各不相同。

他们来这里的目的各不相同。

6. 有…amount/很大/一点儿…出入

to have a very big/a small discrepancy (compared to one's estimation or the previous situation)

在美国大学，每个学期考试和放假的时间，基本上都差不多，每年最多有一两天的出入。

我现在的工资，跟我工作以前想象的有很大的出入。

7. ……，就这一点来说，……

Based solely on this…

他们很少问：中国人过美国人的节日有没有意义？只要过得高兴有趣，就达到了庆祝的目的。就这一点来说，中国人在接受外来文化的时候是很开放，很包容的。

在这里，女人的工资和男人一样高，就这一点来说，男女很平等。

8. A（的地位／影响力／实力）无法／不能和 B 相提并论

[usu. in the negative] A cannot be mentioned in the same breath with B, that is, A is far inferior to B.

这也说明中国文化的"软实力"在目前是无法和美国文化相提并论的。

副总统的地位跟总统根本不能相提并论。

III. 词语辨析 *Synonym Differentiation*

1. 关心：to care about; to be concerned about; to pay close attention to

在意：to mind; to take to heart

老师很关心学生。

这个国家的大学生都很关心国家大事。

他很在意别人对他的看法。

2. 达到：达到+目的/水平　　　　　to reach or achieve the goal/level

实现：实现+目的/理想/计划　to realize the goal/dream/plan

对中国人来说，只要过得高兴有趣，就达到了庆祝的目的。

我希望我的理想都能实现。

3. (a person) 过+holidays

(people, a group of people) 庆祝+holidays（圣诞节/复活节/……）

你们在中国过复活节吗？有什么庆祝活动？

4. 现实：adj./n.　the real world: 现实的社会 reality: 社会现实

实际：adj.　　actual（actually 实际上）

有钱不一定什么事都能做，但没钱什么事都做不了，这就是社会现实。

那个明星说他有一米八（180 cm），可他实际身高只有一米七五（175cm）。

中國人的節日

中國的節日和美國最大的不同是：美國的節日大多是宗教性的。像聖誕節是慶祝耶穌生日，復活節是紀念耶穌復活。所以慶祝的活動往往都在教堂舉行。

中國主要的節日和宗教沒有什麼關係，宗教在中國文化中所占的地位沒有在西方文化中那麼重。中國到處都有寺廟，有的是佛教的，有的是道教的，還有的是紀念歷史上的名人的，像孔子和關公。中國人對不同宗教的包容是很了不起的。這種包容的態度，在西方是不能想象的！在西方歷史上，主要的戰爭往往和宗教有關係，但是在中國歷史上，沒有大規模的宗教戰爭，這是中國文化的特色。

中國人到寺廟去的時候，並不在意廟裏供奉的是什麼神，他們甚至分不清道教和佛教到底有什麼不同。他們到寺廟去往往有一定現實的目的，比方說：希望神能幫自己的孩子考上大學，找到工作，希望一家人都平安，子女早點兒成家立業。從這方面來看，中國人是非常實際的。

中國主要的節日反映的是農業社會生活的內容，這些節日都是用農曆來計算的。像五月初五的端午節據說是為了紀念兩千多年前一個偉大的愛國詩人屈原，可是，對絕大多數的中國人來說，端午節吃粽子是最重要的，至於為什麼有這個節日，他們並不是那麼關心。八月十五的中秋節，家人會在一起吃月餅。據說這天晚上的月亮特別圓，也特別亮，代表家人團圓。當然最重要的節日是春節，相當於美國人的新年。這個假期往往會持續兩個星期。

因為中國主要的節日都是用農曆來計算的，而國際通用的曆法是公曆，也叫西元。這對中國人的日常生活有很大的影響。中國社會其實是農曆和公曆同時使用的。這對一個美國學生來說是很新鮮的，當然也有些不習慣。每年春季學期什麼時候開學得看春節在什麼時候。春節從公曆的一月中到二月底都有可能，所以寒假的時間也就每年不同，很難做計劃。在美國大學，每個學期考試和放假的時間，基本上都差不多，每年最多有一兩天的出入，在中國，兩三個星期的不同是很平常的事。

中國人的節假日受到西方文化很大的影響。大城市裏，很多年輕人都慶祝西方的情人節，感恩節和聖誕節。他們一樣送禮物，吃火雞，高高興興地參加朋友的聚會。他們很少問這個節日是中國的還是西方的？只要過得高興有趣，就達到了慶祝的目的。就這一點來說，中國人在接受外來文化的時候是很開放，很包容的。你能想象美國年輕人在美國慶祝端午節和中秋節嗎？

　　當然，這也說明中國文化的"軟實力"在目前是無法和美國文化相提並論的。

课后习题

第16课

一、词语搭配 (Please pair the term in the left column with the most appropriate term in the right column. Then use the completed phrases to complete the sentences. You can change the order of words and add more information if needed.)

(1)

（ D ）现实的　　　　A 团圆
（ A ）家人　　　　　B 目的
（ D ）庆祝　　　　　C 战争
（ C ）大规模的　　　D 感恩节

1. 美国人怎么_____D_____？除了吃火鸡以外，还有什么？
2. 春节的时候中国人一定会想办法回家是因为_____A_____。
3. 大多数人上大学都有_____B_____，那就是毕业以后找份好工作。
4. 希望我们的世界不会发生_____C_____，要不然，人类可能会失去生活的家园。

(2)

（ D ）新鲜的　　　　A 名人
（ C ）包容的　　　　B 目的
（ A ）纪念　　　　　C 态度
（ B ）达到　　　　　D 事情

1. 你这次出国旅行怎么样？有没有什么_____D_____，快跟我们说说。
2. 人们_____A_____是为了让后代了解他们对社会做过什么贡献。
3. 虽然很多中国人没有宗教信仰，但是他们对不同的宗教都有一种_____C_____。
4. 有的人为了_____B_____，什么坏事都做，这种人真坏！

二、选择填空 (Complete the sentences by choosing the most appropriate term.)

1. 关心 (A) 　　在意 (B)

你有空应该多____(B)一下你的父母，他们已经老了，需要孩子的照顾。

他刚才说的那些难听的话你别太__A__，他只是有点儿生气，明天就没事了。

2. 现实 (A) 　　实际 (B)

你要看清楚社会____(A)，不能活在自己的想象里。

____(B)上，中国人是可以有宗教信仰的。

3. 达到 　　实现

你的中文已经_____能看懂中文报纸的水平了吗？

年轻人应该努力_____自己的理想，不能只想着享受生活。

三、完成句子 (Complete the sentence or dialogue with the given item in parentheses.)

1. A：不会说中文就到中国留学是不是不太好？

　　B：_____。（有一定的 abstract noun ）

2. A：美国的软实力那么强大，美国的文化会受其他文化的影响吗？

　　B：_____。（有一定的 abstract noun ）

3. A：端午节和中秋节都是为了纪念名人的节日吗？

　　B：_____。（A...positive...，至于 B，...negative...）

4. A：西方人过圣诞节都是因为宗教的原因吗？

　　B：_____。（A...positive...，至于 B，...negative...）

5. A：你知道优酷（www.youku.com）吗？

　　B：_____。（A 的 n1 相当于 B 的 n2）

6. A：你今年去不去美国留学？

　　B：_____。（...question form...，得看...）

7. A：你毕业以后会去哪里工作？

B：＿＿＿＿＿＿＿＿＿＿＿＿＿＿＿＿＿＿＿＿＿＿。（…question form…，得看…）

8. A：在美国，所有大学的中文课都用一样的中文书吗？

B：＿＿＿＿＿＿＿＿＿＿＿＿＿＿＿＿＿＿＿＿＿＿。（各不相同）

9. A：你考得怎么样？跟你自己估计（estimation）的一样吗？

B：＿＿＿＿＿＿＿＿＿＿＿＿＿＿＿＿＿＿＿＿＿＿。（有…出入）

10. A：你开始计划几天完成任务？到现在为止，实际完成了多少了？

B：＿＿＿＿＿＿＿＿＿＿＿＿＿＿＿＿＿＿＿＿＿＿。（有…出入）

11. A：随着中国的发展，现在美国的软实力还是世界上最强大的？

B：＿＿＿＿＿＿＿＿＿＿＿＿＿＿＿＿＿＿＿＿＿＿。（就这一点来说）

12. A：美国的教育制度好，还是中国的教育制度好？

B：＿＿＿＿＿＿＿＿＿＿＿＿＿＿＿＿＿＿＿＿＿＿。（就这一点来说）

13. A：中国餐馆在美国也很受欢迎，这是不是说明中国的软实力跟美国的一样强大了？

B：＿＿＿＿＿＿＿＿＿＿＿＿＿＿＿＿＿＿＿＿。（A 无法／不能和 B 相提并论）

四、回答问题 (Answer the questions.)

1. 中国的节日和西方的节日有什么不同？

2. 端午节、中秋节、春节是什么样的节日？

3. 中国社会同时使用公历和农历，这对人们的生活有什么影响？

4. 你觉得中国人有没有宗教信仰？中国人对宗教的态度是什么？

5. 宗教对西方人有什么影响？好的影响多，还是坏的影响多？

第 17 课

传统节日成为法定节日的意义

　　2008 年，中国政府把传统节日"清明节"、"端午节"和"中秋节"定为法定节假日，各放一天假。同时，取消"五一"七天长假，改为放假一天。

　　"五一"是"国际劳动节"，"十一"是中国的"国庆节"。这两个节日是两个政治性节日，本来都只放一天假。2000 年，中国政府把这两个假日改为三天，同时移动前后两个周末，把这两个假日都变成了七天长假。中国政府采取这个新措施是为了拉动内需，刺激消费。改革开放二十多年，人民

节假日	jiéjiàrì	n.	holidays and vacations
各	gè	pron.	each
取消	qǔxiāo	v.	to cancel; to abolish
长假	chángjià	n.	long vacation
改为	gǎiwéi	v.	to change into
劳动	láodòng	v./n.	to do physical work; to labor; work; labor
移动	yídòng	v.	to move
采取	cǎiqǔ	v.	to take or carry out (new measures)
措施	cuòshī	n.	step; measure
拉动	lādòng	v.	to promote; to boost
内需	nèixū	n.	domestic demand
刺激	cìjī	v./n.	to stimulate; stimulus
消费	xiāofèi	v./n.	to consume; consumption

的生活水平不断提高，消费能力也日益增强。在此之前，中国人的长假只有春节。但按照传统，春节期间中国人都要回家团聚，一般不会出门旅行。其他假期，时间太短，不利于长途旅行。有了"五一"和"十一"两个长假，外出旅行的人数大幅增加。"五一"和"十一"期间，各大城市旅游景区人山人海的景象就是最好的证明。然而，这也造成了景区垃圾过多、环境破坏的问题，不利于景区的保护。另外，由于出行人数过多，铁路、航空系统也面临巨大压力。每到这两个节假日，火车站、飞机场都人山人海。因此，每年都有人建议取消"五一"和"十一"两个长假。

日益	rìyì	adv.	day by day
增强	zēngqiáng	v.	increase and strengthen (power, capability influence, etc.)
在此之前	zàicǐzhīqián	phr.	before this (referring to an aforementioned specific point in time)
团聚	tuánjù	v.	(of a family) to reunite
不利于	búlìyú	v.	to be adverse to; to be detrimental to
长途	chángtú	adj.	long-distance
大幅	dàfú	adv.	by a big margin; substantially
景区	jǐngqū	n.	attractions; scenic area
人山人海	rénshānrénhǎi	idm.	huge crowds of people in the open air
景象	jǐngxiàng	n.	scene; phenomenon
证明	zhèngmíng	v./n.	to prove; proof
然而	rán'ér	conj.	however
破坏	pòhuài	v.	to destroy (environment/traditional cultures); to sabotage
出行	chūxíng	v./n.	to travel; travel
系统	xìtǒng	n.	system

　　2008 年，中国政府采纳了这个建议，取消"五一"长假，同时把"清明节"、"端午节"和"中秋节"定为法定节假日。为了缓解交通系统的压力，政府也开始提倡带薪假期。这些新规定反映了中国社会阶段性的变化。

　　上个世纪六十年代文化大革命期间，中国传统文化受到巨大的破坏，大量文物被毁坏，传统价值观念受到挑战，甚至传统的习俗都被抛弃了。比方说，春节不放假了，亲友见面不能说"恭喜发财"，而得说"祝您今年见到毛主席！"

　　改革开放以后，中国社会在经济、文化各方面受到西方很大的影响。中国人在生活方式上也快速西化。由于中国的传统节日没有宗教性，而是反映农业社会生活的内容，所以生活方式改变了，这些节日也就失去了原

采纳	cǎinà	v.	(of authority) to accept (opinions, suggestions)
缓解	huǎnjiě	v.	to relieve
带薪假期	dàixīnjiàqī	n.	paid vacation
阶段性	jiēduànxìng	adj.	staged (used as a modifier)
文化大革命	Wénhuà dà gémìng	n.	The Cultural Revolution (1966-1976)
文物	wénwù	n.	cultural and historical relics
毁坏	huǐhuài	v.	to destroy; to damage
习俗	xísú	n.	custom; convention
抛弃	pāoqì	v.	to abandon
亲友	qīnyǒu	n.	family and friends
恭喜发财	gōngxǐfācái	idm.	Have a happy and prosperous New Year!
祝	zhù	v.	"Wish you…" (followed by good wishes and blessings)

来特定的意义。越来越多时髦的年轻人过起了西洋节日，比方说，"感恩节"、"圣诞节"等等。但对他们来说，这些节日也只是另一个"购物节"。

进入新世纪以后，中国经济继续发展，老百姓生活大大改善，同时，中国在国际社会的地位也快速提高，在世界政治、经济领域都有举足轻重的影响。因此，中国政府也希望中国文化在世界上能有一定的影响力。作为传统节日，"清明节"、"端午节"和"中秋节"自然是中国文化的最佳代表。通过把三大传统节日定为法定假日，政府一方面想给老百姓提供更多与家人团聚的机会，另一方面也想引起老百姓对传统文化的重视。

中国的知识分子好像也感受到了这个改变。一些大学生开始提倡在重要节日穿传统服装，学习传统礼仪等等。尽管有人批评这种行为是作秀，

特定	tèdìng	adj.	particular; given
时髦	shímáo	adj.	fashionable
西洋	xīyáng	adj.	Western
购物节	gòuwùjié	n.	shopping festival; retail holiday
领域	lǐngyù	n.	field
举足轻重	jǔzúqīngzhòng	idm.	to play a decisive role; to exert an overwhelming influence on…
自然	zìrán	adv.	naturally
最佳	zuìjiā	adj.	best (used as a modifier)
引起	yǐnqǐ	v.	to lead to; to bring (emphasis on); to elicit (discussion/interest)
重视	zhòngshì	v.	to value; to take sth. seriously; to think highly of
礼仪	lǐyí	n.	etiquette
尽管	jǐn guǎn	conj.	although

但也有不少人支持，认为是中国文化复兴的一种象征。

作秀	zuòxiù	v.	(lit.) to put on a show; to grandstand
复兴	fùxīng	v.	to revitalize; to revive
象征	xiàngzhēng	v./n.	to symbolize; symbol

I. 词语搭配 *Collocation*

1. 采取＋新措施

   to take on or carry out new measures

2. 刺激＋消费

   to stimulate consumption

3. authority 采纳＋建议

   (authorities) to accept a suggestion

4. 缓解＋压力/紧张关系

   to relieve stress/the tension (between two countries)

5. 破坏＋环境/传统文化

   to destroy environment/traditional cultures

6. 抛弃＋传统/习俗/观念/价值观

   to abandon tradition/custom/old conception/value system

7. 大幅＋提高/发展/增加/减少/降低

   to improve/develop/increase/decrease/reduce by a big margin or substantially

II. 句型结构 *Sentence Pattern and Structure*

1. A、B（、C）各＋V.P.

   The subject (plural) each…

   2008 年，中国政府把传统节日"清明节"、"端午节"和"中秋节"定为法定节假日，各放一天假。

   2000 年，中国政府规定，"五一"和"十一"各放一个星期假。

2. 把 A 改为 B

   Wéi 为 is a verb complement in this structure, which literally means "to become." Thus, this structure means to change A (usually something old) into B (something new).

   "五一"和"十一"本来只放一天假，2000 年，中国政府把本来一天的假改为三天。

   以前，北京不叫"北京"，而是叫"北平"。1949 年，政府决定把"北平"改为"北京"。

3. Object 日益+提高/增强/进步/disyllabic adj.

(of the object) to rise or improve/increase/make progress day by day

改革开放二十多年来，人民的生活水平不断提高，消费能力也日益增强。

最近几年，虽然城市经济日益发展，但是环境问题却日益严重。

4. ……，在此之前，……

…, before this (referring to a aforementioned specific point in time)…

2000 年，中国政府把这两个假日改为三天，同时移动前后两个周末，把这两个假日都变成了七天长假。在此之前，中国人的长假只有春节。

下个星期，我会带你去见这个公司的老板，在此之前，你得想好，你为什么要来这个公司。

5. 按照……传统/规定/法律，…content…

According to the tradition/regulations/the law of…, …

按照传统，春节期间中国人都要回家团聚，一般不会出门旅行。

按照学校的规定，每个学生借书的时间不能超过一个月。

6. ……不利于+V.P./……的发展/提高/进步

…is detrimental to the development/increase/advancement of…

其他假期，时间太短，不利于人们出行。

美国大学的环境其实并不利于学生学习外语，因为他们每天还有很多别的课。

7. A 是 B 最好的证明

A is the best proof of B/that B is true

有了"五一"和"十一"两个长假，外出旅行的人大幅增加。"五一"和"十一"期间，各大城市旅游景区人山人海的场景就是最好的证明。

出国旅游的中国人越来越多，这是中国人生活水平提高最好的证明。

8. V 起 O

This structure denotes that the subject "(often unexpectedly) start to do sth."

越来越多时髦的年轻人过起了西洋节日，比方说，"感恩节"、"圣诞节"等等。

上课的时候，有一个学生突然唱起了歌。

9. A 对 B 有举足轻重的影响

A exerts an overwhelming influence over B

中国在国际社会的地位也快速提高，在世界政治、经济领域都有举足轻重的影响。

中国政府的对外政策对亚洲有举足轻重的影响。

10. ……，…自然…

Zìrán 自然, meaning "naturally, of course," is used to say that something is expected or normal.

作为传承几千年的传统节日，"清明节"、"端午节"和"中秋节"自然是中国文化的最佳代表。

你每天坚持说中文，你的中文水平自然就会提高。

11. ……引起 sb. (对 issue) 的重视 / 注意 / 讨论 / 兴趣

…to direct someone's attention (to an issue); to arouse debate on/interest in ...

通过把三大传统节日定为法定假日，政府一方面想给老百姓提供更多与家人团聚的机会，另一方面也想引起老百姓对传统文化的重视。

最近的新闻引起了美国人对欧洲移民问题的兴趣。

12. 尽管……，但……

This structure means "even though…, (but)…" is used to introduce a different fact or opinion despite the aforementioned fact (after "尽管").

尽管有人批评这种行为是作秀，但也有不少人支持，认为是中国文化复兴的一种象征。

尽管最近几年美国的经济遇到不少问题，但美国还是世界上最强大的国家。

III. 词语辨析 *Synonym Differentiation*

1. 增加：增加+数量/机会

   to increase the amount of…/opportunities

   增强：增强+能力/…的意识/…感

   to increase in degree/to increase one's ability/the awareness of/the sense of…

   最近几年，这个地方的人口数量增加得很快。

   怎么才能增强自己的专业能力？这是现在的年轻人应该考虑的。

2. 破坏：破坏+环境 / 传统文化

   to cause damage to the environment/traditional culture

   毁坏：文物/机器/设备/名誉/形象

   to destroy historical relic/machine/facilities; to damage one's reputation/image

   文革期间，传统文化受到严重的破坏，大量的文物被毁坏。

傳統節日成為法定節日的意義

　　2008 年，中國政府把傳統節日"清明節"、"端午節"和"中秋節"定為法定節假日，各放一天假。同時，取消"五一"七天長假，改為放假一天。

　　"五一"是"國際勞動節"，"十一"是中國的"國慶日"。這兩個節日是兩個政治性節日，本來都只放一天假。2000 年，中國政府把這兩個假日改為三天，同時移動前後兩個週末，把這兩個假日都變成了七天長假。中國政府採取這個新措施是為了拉動內需，刺激消費。改革開放二十多年來，人民的生活水平不斷提高，消費能力也日益增強。在此之前，中國人的長假只有春節。但按照傳統，春節期間中國人都要回家團聚，一般不會出門旅行。其他假期，時間太短，不利於長途旅行。有了"五一"和"十一"兩個長假，外出旅行的人大幅增加。"五一"和"十一"期間，各大城市旅遊景區人山人海的景象就是最好的證明。然而，這也造成了景區垃圾過多，環境破壞的問題，不利於景區的保護。另外，由於出行人數過多，鐵路、航空系統也面臨巨大壓力。每到這兩個節假日，火車站，飛機場都人山人海。因此，每年都有人建議取消"五一"和"十一"兩個長假。

　　2008 年，中國政府採納了這個建議，取消"五一"長假，同時把"清明節"、"端午節"和"中秋節"定為法定節假日。為了緩解交通系統的壓力，政府也開始提倡帶薪假期。這些新規定反映了中國社會階段性的變化。

　　上個世紀六十年代文化大革命期間，中國傳統文化受到巨大的破壞，大量文物被毀壞，傳統價值觀念受到挑戰，甚至傳統的習俗都被拋棄了。比方說，春節不放假了，親友見面不能說"恭喜發財"，而得說"祝您今年見到毛主席！"

　　改革開放以後，中國社會在經濟、文化各方面受到西方很大的影響。中國人在生活方式上也快速西化。由於中國的傳統節日沒有宗教性，而是反映農業社會生活的內容，所以生活方式改變了，這些節日也就失去了原來特定的意義。越來越多時髦的年輕人過起了西洋節日，比方說，"感恩節"、"耶誕節"等等。但對他們來說，這些節日也只是另一個"購物節"。

　　進入新世紀以後，中國經濟繼續發展，老百姓生活大大改善，同時，中國在國際社會的地位也快速提高，在世界政治、經濟領域都有舉足輕重的影響。因此，中國政府也希望中國文化在世界上能有一定的影響力。作為傳統節日，"清明節"、"端午節"和"中秋節"自然是中國文化的最佳代表。通過把三大傳統節日定為法定假日，政府一方面想給老百姓提供更多與家人團聚的機會，另一方面也想引起老百姓對傳統文化的重視。

　　中國的知識份子好像也感受到了這個改變。一些大學生開始提倡在重要節日穿傳統服裝，學習傳統禮儀等等。儘管有人批評這種行為是作秀，但也有不少人支持，認為是中國文化復興的一種象徵。

课后习题

第 17 课

一、词语搭配 (Please pair the term in the left column with the most appropriate term in the right column. Then use the completed phrases to complete the sentences. You can change the order of words and add more information if needed.)

(1)

(　) 日益　　　A 观念

(　) 采取　　　B 压力

(　) 缓解　　　C 措施

(　) 抛弃　　　D 增强

1. 大学生就业的竞争日益激烈,政府应该创造更多就业机会来_____。

2. 山寨产品的问题越来越严重,政府有必要_____。

3. 随着老百姓收入的增加,_____。

4. "重男轻女"的观念使很多女孩儿失去上学的机会,_____。

(2)

(　) 破坏　　　A 提高

(　) 大幅　　　B 消费

(　) 刺激　　　C 建议

(　) 采纳　　　D 传统

1. 有的人不喜欢现代化,因为他们认为_____。

2. 节假日期间,很多商店都会通过降低商品价格来_____。

3. 由于生产成本提高了很多,苹果公司不得不_____。

4. 领导做决定的时候,应该适当地_____。

二、选择填空 (Complete the sentences by choosing the most appropriate term.)

1. 增加　　增强

   学好一门外语可以_____大学生的就业机会。

   怎么样_____国家的影响力？用什么手段最好？这是政府应该考虑的。

2. 毁坏　　破坏

   那场火灾_____了很多的古代建筑，真是可惜。

   由于严重的工业污染，当地的环境受到了严重的_____。

三、完成句子 (Complete the sentence or dialogue with the given item in parentheses.)

1. Situation：小王和小张去书店，小王买了五本书，小张也买了五本书。你可以说：

   _____。（A、B（、C）各+vp）

2. A：中国古代建筑的大门一般是什么样的？

   B：_____。（A、B（、C）各+vp）

3. A：什么？老师要求我们每天早上 7:30 来上课？太早了！

   B：我也觉得太早了，我希望_____。（把 A 改为 B）

4. 开始老师让学生写 200 字的小作文，可是后来觉得太容易了，所以就

   _____。（把 A 改为 B）

5. 最近几年,随着经济的发展,_____。（日益）

6. A：这个学期的期末考试是什么时候？学校规定，学生什么时候才可以离开学校？

　　B：＿＿＿＿＿＿＿＿＿＿＿＿＿＿＿＿＿＿＿＿＿＿。（在此之前）

7. A：中国什么时候才允许外国公司进入中国？

　　B：＿＿＿＿＿＿＿＿＿＿＿＿＿＿＿＿＿＿＿＿＿＿。（在此之前）

8. A：美国人怎么庆祝感恩节？

　　B：＿＿＿＿＿＿＿＿＿＿＿＿＿＿＿＿＿＿＿＿。（按照…传统）

9. A：在你们大学，图书馆的书一般可以借多长时间？

　　B：＿＿＿＿＿＿＿＿＿＿＿＿＿＿＿＿＿＿＿＿。（按照…规定）

10. A：中文老师为什么不喜欢学生上课的时候说英文？

　　B：＿＿＿＿＿＿＿＿＿＿＿＿＿＿＿。（…不利于＋V.P./…的提高/进步）

11. 很多人认为，新闻不自由＿＿＿＿＿＿＿＿＿＿＿＿＿＿。（…不利于＋V.P.）

12. A：人人都说中国人的生活水平大幅提高了，从哪些事情可以看出来？

　　B：＿＿＿＿＿＿＿＿＿＿＿＿＿＿＿。（A是B最好的证明）

13. 早上天气还很好，可是下午＿＿＿＿＿＿＿＿＿＿。（V起O（来））

14. 我记得你说过你不喜欢喝咖啡，你今天怎么＿＿＿＿＿＿？（V起O（来））

15. 美国的经济和军事实力是世界上最强大的,所以＿＿＿＿＿＿＿＿＿＿＿。

　　　　　　　　　　　　　　　　　　　　　（A 对 B 有举足轻重的影响）

16. A：美国总统访问中国的时候，为什么要大公司的CEO跟他一起去？

　　B：＿＿＿＿＿＿＿＿＿＿＿＿＿。（A 对 B 有举足轻重的影响）

17. A：我刚到这个公司，怎么才能交到新朋友？

　　B：＿＿＿＿＿＿＿＿＿＿＿＿＿＿＿＿＿＿。（自然）

18. A：孔子学院为什么要向外国人介绍中国的书法？

　　B：＿＿＿＿＿＿＿＿＿＿＿＿＿＿＿＿＿＿＿＿。（自然）

19. A：孔子学院应不应该向外国人介绍中国的书法？

　　B：＿＿＿＿＿＿＿＿＿＿＿＿＿＿＿。（引起 sb. (对 issue) 的重视 / 兴趣）

20. A：你为什么不去中国上大学呢？

　　B：＿＿＿＿＿＿＿＿＿＿＿＿＿＿＿＿＿＿。（尽管…，但…）

四、回答问题　(Answer the questions.)

1. "五一"和"十一"是什么样的节日？这两个节日对中国人有什么意义？

2. 中国政府为什么选择在"五一"、"十一"这两个节日放"七天长假"？有什么好处和坏处？

3. 中国政府还把什么节日定为了法定节假日？为什么这样做？

4. 中国年轻人过西洋节日，这是好事还是坏事？你有什么看法？

5. 提倡传统对增强国家影响力和民族自信心有没有帮助？

6. 在你的国家，有哪些传统节日或者宗教节日成为了法定假日？请你介绍一个。

第 18 课
北京 798 艺术区

近 30 年来，中国人的改变是多方面的，除了饮食习惯、生活方式以外，在时尚的追求上也有了新的喜好；尤其是有钱人，在有了豪宅、名车之后，就想收藏些名贵的艺术品来装饰他的家和办公室。因此，中国艺术品市场近几年来蓬勃发展；社会上多了许多从事艺术创作的职业画家、书法家、雕刻家和音乐的演奏者。北京 798 艺术区的兴起就是这个改变最好的证明。

艺术区	yìshù qū	n.	art zone or art district
喜好	xǐhào	n.	what sb. likes or loves
豪宅	háozhái	n.	mansion
名车	míngchē	n.	luxury car
收藏	·shōucáng	v./n.	to collect; collection
名贵	míngguì	adj.	famous and precious
艺术品	yìshù pǐn	n.	work of art
装饰	zhuāngshì	v./n.	to decorate
蓬勃发展	péngbó fāzhǎn	V.P.	to flourish; to boom in development
创作	chuàngzuò	v.	to create (work of art)
职业	zhíyè	att.	professional
雕刻	diāokè	v.	to carve; to engrave; 雕刻家: sculptor
演奏	yǎnzòu	v.	to give an instrumental performance

　　我来中国之前就听说过，北京有个艺术家聚集的 798 艺术区，今天，我从学校用"滴滴出行"叫了一部车，用"支付宝"付了车费。在北京生活，只要有个手机，从叫车，订餐到购物，付款都可以用手机来处理，几乎可以不用现金了，真方便！

　　新中国成立（1949）不久，政府在 798 这个地区建了不少工厂，用来发展中国工业。但几十年下来，厂房年久失修，破旧不堪，国营企业

聚集	jùjí	v.	to gather; assemble
滴滴出行	Dīdī Chūxíng		See Notes at the end of this text.
部	bù	m.w.	m.w. for cars
支付宝	Zhīfùbǎo		See Notes at the end of this text.
订餐	dìngcān	v.o.	to order food
购物	gòuwù	v.o.	to go shopping
付款	fùkuǎn	v.o.	to pay (a sum of money)
现金	xiànjīn	n.	cash
成立	chénglì	v.	to found; establish
厂房	chǎngfáng	n.	factory building
年久失修	niánjiǔ shīxiū	idm.	(of a building) worn down by years without repair
破旧不堪	pòjiùbùkān	adj.	(of a house) unbearably or extremely broken down; dilapidated
国营	guóyíng	adj.	state-run

在改革开放中，有的改为民营，这些厂房就废弃不用了。2000 年前后，有几个北京的艺术家就利用这些旧厂房，改造成了他们的画室，并举办画展。这样一传十，十传百，十几年下来，聚集到这个地区来的艺术家就越来越多了。现在不但有画家还有雕刻家、摄影师和从事传统工艺美术品创作的工匠和小贩。有一家专卖中国传统油纸雨伞的小店，店里

企业	qǐyè	n.	enterprise
民营	mínyíng	adj.	privately run; run by private citizens (as opposed to state-run companies)
废弃	fèiqì	adj.	abandoned
旧	jiù	adj.	used; worn; old
改造	gǎizào	v.	to transform; to remodel
画室	huàshì	n.	studio
举办	jǔbàn	v.	to run or hold (an event)
画展	huàzhǎn	n.	exhibition of paintings
传	chuán	v.	to pass on (orally)
摄影	shèyǐng	n.	photography; 摄影师: photographer
工艺	gōngyì	n.	craftsmanship; technical skill
美术	měishù	n.	the fine arts
工匠	gōngjiàng	n.	artisan; craftsman
小贩	xiǎofàn	n.	small peddler
专	zhuān	adv.	exclusively; (of a shop) specialized in
油纸	yóuzhǐ	n.	oilpaper

的每一把雨伞都有艺术家独特的创作。我以前只知道中国人的扇子很讲究，扇子上又有书法又有画，没想到连雨伞也可以做为艺术品。

去 798 参观的外国人也很多，他们惊喜地发现，在交通堵塞，雾霾严重，生活紧张的北京城里，居然还有这么一片属于艺术家的小天地。在这里，他们画画，摄影，雕刻，制作工艺品，通过艺术的手法来表现自己，来赚取自己的生活费。我很羡慕他们，也很佩服他们。

艺术创作是表达思想的另一种方式，在一个言论自由不能完全开放的社会里，艺术创作也往往会受到一定的限制。在 798 我倒没有看到太

独特	dútè	adj.	unique; distinctive
扇子	shànzi	n.	fan
惊喜	jīngxǐ	adv./v.	(pleasantly) surprised
堵塞	dǔsè	v.	to stop up; to block up
居然	jūrán	adv.	unexpectedly; to one's surprise
片	piàn	m.w.	m.w. for stretches of land or scenery
属于	shǔyú	v.	belong to
天地	tiāndì	n.	(lit.) heaven and earth; a little world in itself
制作	zhìzuò	v.	to create; manufacture
手法	shǒufǎ	n.	technique
赚取	zhuànqǔ	v.	to make a profit
羡慕	xiànmu	v.	to admire (a person); to envy (one's luck, honor, wealth, etc.)
佩服	pèifú	v.	to admire from the heart; to admit superiority (to a person)
表达	biǎodá	v.	to express

多政治宣传，这或许 也是 798 能在短时间之内，能把艺术家都聚集到一起的原因之一。今天，我在 798 度过了一个轻松愉快的下午，看了许多免费的展览，在小咖啡店里和陌生人谈了不少有趣的话题。

今年夏天在北京学习中文，我也趁着这个机会去看了几次话剧、歌剧和京剧 的演出。虽然我没全都听懂，但我发现北京人很喜欢这样的文娱活动，几乎每次演出都是客满。而票价 往往差不多是一个老师一天的收入。这不但说明北京人的消费能力很强，他们的文化水平也很高。

古代中国有个政治家 说过一句很深刻 的话："仓廪实而知礼节，衣食足而知荣辱"。这句话的意思是经济发展以后，老百姓的文化水平会随着

宣传	xuānchuán	v.	to propagate; to publicize
或许	huòxǔ	adv.	perhaps; maybe
度过	dùguò	v.	to spend time
展览	zhǎnlǎn	n.	exhibition
趁	chèn	v.	to take advantage
话剧	huàjù	n.	modern drama; stage play
歌剧	gējù	n.	opera
京剧	Jīngjù	n.	Beijing opera
演出	yǎnchū	n.	performance
文娱活动	wényú huódòng	n.	recreational activities
客满	kèmǎn	n.	(of a theater, cinema, etc.) to have a full house
票价	piàojià	n.	ticket price
政治家	zhèngzhì jiā	n.	statesman
深刻	shēnkè	adj.	deep; profound

经济条件的改善而提高，而他们的行为 举止 也会变得更文明，更讲礼节。换句话说，经济是文化和教育的基础。过去 30 年来，中国在经济上的发展受到全世界的肯定，但老百姓在日常生活上还有一些引起别人批评的地方，像随地吐痰，开车不遵守交通规则，随便停放 车辆 等等。但是我相信随着经济更进一步的发展，中国老百姓的文明程度也一定会有更进一步的提高。

Notes:

滴滴打车　　　Dīdī Chūxíng, founded in 2012, is a major Chinese ride-sharing company offering a range of mobile tech-based transportation services. Some consider it as the Chinese equivalent of Uber.

支付宝　　　Zhīfùbǎo, or Alipay, is a third-party mobile and online payment platform established in 2004 by the Alibaba Group. Some consider it as the Chinese equivalent of PayPal.

行为	xíngwéi	n.	behavior
举止	jǔzhǐ	n.	manner; bearing
文明	wénmíng	adj.	civilized
礼节	lǐjié	n.	protocol; etiquette
基础	jīchǔ	n.	foundation
肯定	kěndìng	n.	(to give or receive) recognition
停放	tíngfàng	v.	to park (a vehicle)
车辆	chēliàng	n.	(collective noun) cars; vehicles

仓廪实而知礼节，衣食足而知荣辱。

Cānglǐn shí ér zhī lǐjié, yīshí zú ér zhī róngrǔ.

(lit.) When the granaries are full, people will then respect rites and obligations; when food and clothing are sufficient, people will then know honor and shame.

I. 词语搭配 *Collocation*

1. 收藏+艺术品／古书／古董

   to collect works of art/ancient books/antiques

2. ……行业市场／学科／艺术／事业／经济+蓬勃发展

   The ……industry/market/field/art/career/economy flourishes

3. 叫+车／外卖　　to hail a taxi/to order take-out

4. 破旧／拥挤／混乱／痛苦+不堪

   unbearably or extremely broken down/crowded/chaotic/painful

5. 给 sb. 一个惊喜　to give sb. a (pleasant) surprise

   惊喜地发现　be astonished to find…

6. 举办+画展／活动／比赛

   To hold an exhibition of paintings/an activity/a competition

7. 表达+思想／意见／情绪

   to express one's thoughts/opinions/feelings

8. 度过…(轻松/愉快)…的一个下午／一天…

   to have/enjoy a… (relaxing/happy) …afternoon/day…

9. 深刻的思想／意义

   deep thoughts/profound meaning

10. 讲+礼节／卫生

    to pay attention to or be particular about + etiquette /hygiene

II. 句型结构 *Sentence Pattern and Structure*

1. 在…time point/event…之后/之前　before…/after…

   有钱人在有了豪宅、名车之后，就想收藏些名贵的艺术品来装饰他的家和办公室。

   在 2000 年之前，只有春节放七天长假。

2. ...event...不久，...（就）...

Shortly/soon after...

新中国成立（1949）不久，政府在 798 这个地区建了不少工厂，用来发展中国工业。

他刚离开家不久，警察就来家里找他了。

3. ...action/status...，Time duration 下来，...result (a significant change)

This pattern is often used to emphasize that the action in the first clause will lead to a significant result after a certain period of time.

新中国成立（1949）不久，政府在 798 这个地区建了不少工厂，用来发展中国工业。但几十年下来，厂房年久失修，破旧不堪。

暑假他去北京学中文，两个月下来，中文进步了不少。

4. Time point / holiday 前后　　Around the time of...

2000 年前后，有几个北京的艺术家就利用这些旧厂房，改造成了他们的画室，并举办画展。

在美国，圣诞节前后，是最多人旅行的时候。

5. ......，并... ...　　　　furthermore

2000 年前后，有几个北京的艺术家就利用这些旧厂房，改造成了他们的画室，并举办画展。

皇帝让这些人得到了自由，并给了他们土地。

6. ......，这样/后来 一传十，十传百，......

This fixed expression is often used to stress a piece of news/information, or a good reputation, spread quickly from mouth to mouth.

2000 年前后，有几个北京的艺术家就利用这些旧厂房，改造成了他们的画室，并举办画展。这样一传十，十传百，十几年下来，聚集到这个地区来的艺术家就越来越多了。

开始，只有哈佛(Harvard)大学里的几个学生用"脸书"(Facebook)，可是他们很快就把这个网站推荐给了朋友，朋友又推荐给了他们的朋友，这样一传十，十传百，Facebook 成了最常用的社交媒体(social media)。

7.　专+V.P.

be specific to; devoted to a specific use

有一家专卖中国传统油纸雨伞的小店，店里的每一把雨伞都有艺术家独特的创作。

这家商店专卖苹果电脑。

8.　……，Subj. 趁这个机会 V.P.

…, Subj. takes the opportunity to do sth.

今年夏天在北京学习中文，我也趁着这个机会去看了几次话剧、歌剧和京剧的演出。

下个星期我要去你们学校参加比赛，我正好趁这个机会去看看你。

9.　A 是 B 的基础

A is the foundation of B

经济是文化和教育的基础。

有的人认为，爱情是婚姻的基础，但有的人却认为，金钱才是婚姻的基础。

10. …的表现/发展/进步/…+受到（了）sb. /…+的肯定

One's performance/development/progress received recognition from…

过去 30 年来，中国在经济上的发展受到全世界的肯定，但老百姓在日常生活上还有一些引起别人批评的地方。

他的表现受到了老师们的肯定。

11. 随着 A 的进一步+发展/增加/提高，B 也会+越来越 adj.

随着 A 的进一步+发展/增加/提高，B 也会有进一步的发展/增加/提高……

This pattern, meaning "along with A's…, B also…," is often used to describe a correlation between A and B.

我相信随着经济更进一步的发展，中国老百姓的文明程度也一定会有更进一步的提高。

随着科技水平的进一步提高，人们的生活也会越来越方便。

III. 词语辨析 *Synonym Differentiation*

1. 举办：由 organizer 举办/是 organizer 举办的

举行：在 place 举行

这次会议是由北京大学举办的。

这次会议是在北京大学举行的。

2. 趁（着）：*prep.* (precede a verb)　to take the advantage/opportunity *to do sth.*

趁着+…的时候/机会+ **verb**

利用：*verb*　to exploit; to use

利用+time/opportunity 机会/resources/connections 关系

老师带我们来参观这个学校，我趁这个机会在他们的图书馆找了点儿材料。

学校里有很多资源，你可以好好利用。

北京 798 藝術區

近 30 年來，中國人的改變是多方面的，除了飲食習慣、生活方式以外，在時尚的追求上也有了新的喜好。尤其是有錢人，在有了豪宅名車之後，就想收藏些名貴的藝術品來裝飾他的家和辦公室。因此，中國藝術品市場近幾年來蓬勃發展；社會上多了許多從事藝術創作的職業畫家、書法家、雕刻家和音樂的演奏者。北京 798 藝術區的興起就是這個改變最好的證明。

我來中國之前就聽說過，北京有個藝術家聚集的 798 藝術區，今天，我從學校用"滴滴出行"叫了一部車，用"支付寶"付了車費。在北京生活，只要有個手機，從叫車，訂餐到購物，付款都可以用手機來處理，幾乎可以不用現金了，真方便！

新中國成立（1949）不久，政府在 798 這個地區建了不少工廠，用來發展中國工業。幾十年下來，廠房年久失修，破舊不堪，國營企業在改革開放中，有的改為民營，這些廠房就廢棄不用了。2000 年前後，有幾個北京的藝術家就利用這些舊廠房，改造成了他們的畫室，並舉辦畫展。這樣一傳十，十傳百，十幾年下來，聚集到這個地區來的藝術家就越來越多了。現在不但有畫家還有雕刻家，攝影師和從事傳統工藝美術品創作的工匠和小販。有一家專賣中國傳統油紙雨傘的小店，店裏的每一把雨傘都有藝術家獨特的創作。我以前只知道中國人的扇子很講究，扇子上又有書法又有畫，沒想到連雨傘也可以做為藝術品。

去 798 參觀的外國人也很多，他們驚喜地發現，在交通堵塞，霧霾嚴重，生活緊張的北京城裏，居然還有這麼一片屬於藝術家的小天地。在這裏，他們畫畫，攝影，雕刻，製作工藝品，通過藝術的手法來表現自己，來賺取自己的生活費。我很羨慕他們，也很佩服他們。

藝術創作是表達思想的另一種方式，在一個言論自由不能完全開放的社會裏，藝術創作也往往會受到一定的限制。在 798 我倒沒有看到太多政治宣傳，這或許也是 798 能在短時間之內，能把藝術家都聚集到一起的原因之一。今天，我在 798 度過了一個輕鬆愉快的下午，看了許多免費的展覽，在小咖啡店裏和陌生人談了不少有趣的話題。

今年夏天，我也趁著在北京學習中文的機會去看了幾次話劇、歌劇和京劇的演出。雖然我沒全都聽懂，但我發現北京人很喜歡這樣的文娛活動，幾乎每次演出都是客滿。而票價往往差不多是一個老師一天的收入。這不但說明北京人的消費能力很強，他們的文化水平也很高。

古代中國有個政治家說過一句很深刻的話：“倉廩實而知禮節，衣食足而知榮辱”。這句話的意思是經濟發展以後，老百姓的文化水平會隨著經濟條件的改善而提高，而他們的行為舉止也會變得更文明，更講禮節。換句話說，經濟是文化和教育的基礎。過去 30 年來，中國在經濟上的發展受到全世界的肯定，但老百姓在日常生活上還有一些引起別人批評的地方，像隨地吐痰，開車不遵守交通規則，隨便停放車輛等等。但是我相信隨著經濟更進一步的發展，中國老百姓的文明程度也一定會有更進一步的提高。

课后习题

第 18 课

一、词语搭配 (Please pair the term in the left column with the most appropriate term in the right column. Then use the completed phrases to complete the sentences. You can change the order of the words and add more information if needed.)

(1)

(　) 叫　　　　　　A 蓬勃发展

(　) 讲　　　　　　B 卫生

(　) ……行业　　　C 外卖

1. 我今天很忙,没时间出去吃饭,所以我用"饿了吗"这个 APP＿＿＿＿＿＿＿＿。

2. 父母常常教育孩子要＿＿＿＿＿＿＿＿＿＿,吃饭以前,上厕所以后都要洗手。

3. 最近几年,＿＿＿＿＿＿＿＿＿＿＿＿＿＿＿＿＿。现在你要买东西,只要在手机上下单,就有专人送到你手上。

(2)

(　) 地铁　　　A 活动

(　) 收藏　　　B 拥挤不堪

(　) 举办　　　C 古董

1. 每天下午 5 点到 7 点,北京的＿＿＿＿＿＿＿＿,因为这是人们下班回家的时间。

2. 那个有钱的商人非常喜欢历史,所以他＿＿＿＿＿＿＿＿＿＿＿＿＿＿＿＿。

3. 为了让学生更了解中国画,＿＿＿＿＿＿＿＿＿＿＿＿＿＿＿＿＿＿。

二、选择填空 (Complete the sentences by choosing the most appropriate term.)

1. 举行　　举办

这次的"话剧艺术节"是由国家话剧院＿＿＿＿的。

2008 年的奥运会是在北京＿＿＿＿的。

2. 趁着　　利用

暑假没有课，要是想好好做你自己的研究，你应该好好＿＿＿＿这段时间。

你应该＿＿＿＿暑假不上课的时候好好做你自己的研究。

三、完成句子 (Complete the sentence or dialogue with the given item in parentheses.)

1. A：在美国，孩子一般什么时候开始独立生活？

B：＿＿＿＿＿＿＿＿＿＿＿＿＿＿＿＿＿＿＿＿＿＿。（在…time point/event…之后/之前）

2. A：你什么找到工作的？你毕业前一个月还说你没找到工作。

B：＿＿＿＿＿＿＿＿＿＿＿＿＿＿＿＿＿＿＿＿＿。（…event…不久，…（就）…）

3. A：你在大学学了多长时间的中文了？进步大不大？

B：＿＿＿＿＿＿＿＿＿＿＿＿＿＿＿＿＿＿＿。（Time duration 下来）

4. 我想减肥，朋友建议我游泳。我已经游了两个月了。＿＿＿＿＿＿＿＿＿＿＿

＿＿＿＿＿＿＿＿＿＿＿＿＿＿＿＿＿＿＿＿。（Time duration 下来）

5. A：在中国，什么时候交通最拥挤？

B：＿＿＿＿＿＿＿＿＿＿＿＿＿＿＿＿＿＿＿。（Time point / holiday 前后）

6. A：听说你的好朋友生病住院了，你去看他了吗？

B：＿＿＿＿＿＿＿＿＿＿＿＿＿＿＿＿＿＿＿＿。（V.P.1，并 V.P.2）

7. A：那个司机不遵守交通规则，警察批评他了吗？

B：＿＿＿＿＿＿＿＿＿＿＿＿＿＿＿＿＿＿＿＿。（V.P.1，并 V.P.2）

8. 现在脸书、微信都有传递信息的作用。很多信息都是从一个人的脸书、微信

上传出来，＿＿＿＿＿＿＿＿＿＿＿＿＿＿＿＿。（这样一传十，十传百，…）

9. A：苹果公司是什么样的公司？

　　B：＿＿＿＿＿＿＿＿＿＿＿＿＿＿＿＿＿＿＿＿＿＿＿。（专+V.P.）

10. 有的电影院不放最新的电影,相反,＿＿＿＿＿＿＿＿＿＿＿＿＿＿。（专+V.P.）

11. A：听说你周末要去上海,你去上海做什么？

　　B：＿＿＿＿＿＿＿＿＿＿＿＿＿＿＿＿＿＿＿＿。（Subj.趁这个机会 V.P.）

12. 我今天下午要跟中文老师谈话,＿＿＿＿＿＿＿＿＿＿。（Subj.趁这个机会 V.P.）

13. A：为什么我们的中文老师那么强调要练好发音？

　　B：＿＿＿＿＿＿＿＿＿＿＿＿＿＿＿＿＿＿＿＿＿。（A 是 B 的基础）

14. A：为什么很多中国人都坚持没有钱就不结婚？

　　B：＿＿＿＿＿＿＿＿＿＿＿＿＿＿＿＿＿＿＿＿＿。（A 是 B 的基础）

15. A：听说他的成绩从 B 提高到了 A,进步真大啊！

　　B：是啊,＿＿＿＿＿＿＿＿＿＿＿＿＿＿＿＿＿＿。（受到...的肯定）

16. A：你觉得北京的文化演出会越来越受欢迎吗？

　　B：＿＿＿＿＿＿＿＿＿＿＿＿＿＿＿＿＿＿＿＿＿＿＿＿＿＿＿。

　　　　　（随着 A 的进一步+发展/增加/提高,B 也会+越来越 adj.）

17. A：你觉得中国的影响力会进一步增强吗？

　　B：＿＿＿＿＿＿＿＿＿＿＿＿＿＿＿＿＿＿＿＿＿＿＿＿＿＿＿。

　　　　　（随着 A 的进一步+发展/增加/提高,B 也会有进一步的发展/增加/提高......）

四、回答问题 (Answer the questions.)

1. 近几年中国的艺术市场发展得怎么样？有什么例子可以证明？

2. 请说说 798 艺术区的历史。

3. 在 798 艺术区,游客可以做什么？

4. "仓廪实而知礼节,衣食足而知荣辱" 这句话是什么意思？你觉得这句话有道理吗？请举例说明。

5. 经济和文化、教育的关系是什么样的？经济水平提高了,老百姓的文化水平一定也会跟着提高吗？

第 19 课

顺口溜儿和北京人的幽默

北京人有很多顺口溜儿。顺口溜儿有点儿像诗，可是又不是诗。顺口溜儿也有点儿像美国人的说唱，可是也不完全一样。顺口溜儿用简单的几句话来概括社会上的许多现象和问题，是中国人发表意见的特殊形式。因为顺口溜儿有深刻的含义，又经常是押韵的，所以不容易忘记。我听得懂的顺口溜儿不多，但是只要听懂了，就忘不了。

顺口溜儿	shùnkǒuliūér	n.	jingle; doggerel
说唱	shuōchàng	n.	rap (music style)
概括	gàikuò	v.	to summarize
发表	fābiǎo	v.	to express; to put forward
特殊	tèshū	adj.	special
形式	xíngshì	n.	form
深刻	shēnkè	adj.	profound
含义	hányì	n.	connotation
押韵	yāyùn	v-o.	to rhyme

Written by Chih-p'ing Chou
Prepared by Jincheng Liu & Xin Zou

　　最近中国政府在打击 腐败方面下了很大的功夫。贪官（绝大多数都是男的）的行为 往往表现在贪财 和好色 两点上。贪财就是收取 金钱 和礼物；好色是和很多女人发生性关系，这也叫"通奸 "。社会上流行着两句顺口溜儿来说一个贪官："薪水 基本 不用，老婆基本 不碰 "。看来，贪官的老婆并不"性福 "！哦，哦，我是说"幸福"。简简单单的两句话，把一个又贪财又好色的贪官形象 生动 地描写 出来了。

　　1949 年以后，有一段时间，共产党的干部 相信"为人民服务"是一个官员应有的工作态度，但是贪官一多，就成了"人民为贪官服务"了！老百姓又

打击	dǎjī	v.	to take strong measures against; to crack down on (corruption, crimes)
行为	xíngwéi	n.	behavior
贪财	tāncái	adj.	avaricious; greedy
好色	hàosè	adj.	lustful; lecherous; lascivious
收取	shōuqǔ	v.	to take (bribes)
金钱	jīnqián	n.	money (collective noun)
通奸	tōngjiān	v.-o.	to commit adultery
薪水	xīnshuǐ	n.	wage
基本	jīběn	adv.	basically
碰	pèng	v.	to touch
性福	xìngfú		a play on words on "幸福", which means "to feel content sexually".
形象	xíngxiàng	adj./adv.	vivid; vividly
生动	shēngdòng	adj./adv.	lively; vividly
描写	miáoxiě	v.	to describe
段	duàn	m.w.	measure word (for passage, paragraph, time, etc.)
干部	gànbu	n.	cadres; government officials

编了一段顺口溜儿：以前咱们的干部是"老婆兼秘书"；现在的干部是"秘书兼老婆"。以前的干部，"老婆一个，孩子一堆，"现在的干部，"老婆一堆，孩子一个。"

描述社会风气的顺口溜儿也很有趣。从前在中国，婚前和婚外的性关系是严格禁止的。现在可不同了："男的不坏，女的不爱"。"男人有钱就变坏，女人变坏才有钱"。像这样的说法，在美国，很有可能被认为是性别歧视。而在中国这方面是比较宽松的。许多人说，中国缺乏言论自由，其实，在中国，你只要不批评政府，言论的限制是很少的。

编	biān	v.	to make up (jokes, jingles, etc.)
兼	jiān	v.	to hold two or more posts or to play two roles at the same time; and (connecting two titles)
秘书	mìshu	n.	secretary
堆	duī	m.w.	pile
描述	miáoshù	v.	to describe and narrate
风气	fēngqì	n.	ethos; the general mood (of a society)
禁止	jìnzhǐ	v.	to forbid
性别	xìngbié	n.	gender
歧视	qíshì	v./n.	to discriminate; discrimination

271

多年前，中国人常常讨论资本主义 和社会主义 有什么不同。有人说"资本主义，大家有饭吃"，而"社会主义，有饭大家吃"。多么简单的两句话，就说明了资本主义注重 的是生产，而社会主义注重 的是分配 。

当然，真正 改变中国社会面貌 的一句话是 1978 年邓小平说的："不管黑猫白猫，只要会抓 老鼠 的就是好猫！"到了今天，还有不少人引用 这句话，但多少有点儿变味儿 。"不管做什么，只要能赚钱，就是好事！"目的真的可以使手段变得正当吗？为了达到目的，真的可以不择手段 吗？

中国人真是一个幽默的民族！

多年前	duōnián qián	t.w.	many years ago
资本主义	zīběn zhǔyì	n.	capitalism
社会主义	shèhuì zhǔyì	n.	socialism
注重	zhùzhòng	v.	to lay emphasis on
分配	fēnpèi	v.	to allocate
真正	zhēnzhèng	adv./adj.	truly; authentic
面貌	miànmào	n.	appearance (of things); look; aspect
抓	zhuā	v.	to catch
老鼠	lǎoshǔ	n.	mouse; rat
引用	yǐnyòng	v.	to cite
变味儿	biànwèir	v.	to get distorted
不择手段	bùzéshǒuduàn	idm.	by hook or crook (derogatory term)

　　上面所说的这些顺口溜儿，在中国不至于冒犯别人，但在美国可能就不太合适了。尤其是关于男女关系的顺口溜，在中国的尺度比美国要宽松得多。美国把许多事情看成是"政治正确"的问题，像男女、种族、堕胎、枪支控制、宗教信仰等等。为了保持所谓的"政治正确"，大家都避免谈这些话题。在我看来，"政治正确"已经影响到了言论自由。我们应该争取"政治不正确"的言论自由。

冒犯	màofàn	v.	to offend (superiors, gods, taboos); to incur (displeasure)
尤其	yóuqí	adv.	in particular; especially
尺度	chǐdù	n.	(lit.) measurement; limitation or tolerance (of free speech, etc.)
许多	xǔduō	attr.	many; a great deal of
政治正确	zhèngzhì zhèngquè	n.	political correctness—conforming to a belief that language and practices which could offend political sensibilities (e.g. sex, race, religion, etc.) should be avoided.
种族	zhǒngzú	n.	race
堕胎	duòtāi	n./v.	abortion; to induce abortion
枪支控制	qiāngzhī kòngzhì	N.P.	gun control
信仰	xìnyǎng	n.	creed; belief; conviction
避免	bìmiǎn	v.	to avoid
争取	zhēngqǔ	v.	to strive for; to fight for

Notes:

薪水基本不用，老婆基本不碰。

Xīnshuǐ jīběn búyòng, lǎopó jīběn búpèng.

(lit.) Salary basically not spent; wife basically not touched (intimately)

男人有钱就变坏，女人变坏才有钱。

Nánrén yǒuqián jiù biànhuài, nǚrén biànhuài cái yǒuqián.

Here, 变坏 means to "go bad", which often implies engaging in improper sexual relations. The sentence literally means, "men go bad once they become rich; women will only become rich if they go bad."

邓小平 (1904-1997)

Dèng Xiǎopíng was a Chinese politician and reformist, who led China's economic reform, more often known as "Reform and Opening-Up" (改革开放 gǎigé kāifàng). Deng was best known as a pragmatist who focused on the problems of the day, unencumbered by history or ideology. His most famous aphorism was an old proverb from his native Sichuan: "It doesn't matter whether a cat is black or white, as long as it catches mice." (不管黑猫白猫，只要会抓老鼠的就是好猫)

I. 词语搭配 *Collocation*

1. 用几句话来概括……

   to sum sth. up in a few sentences

2. 发表+意见/看法

   to express one's opinion/view

3. Sb.（in power）（向 sb.）收取+金钱/礼物

   Someone (in power) collects (i.e. to ask for and get) money or gifts (from sb.)

4. 把……的形象生动地描写出来

   to vividly depict/portray the image of…in words

5. ……是 sb.应有的+态度/责任感/贡献/作用

   …is the attitude/sense of responsibility/contribution/role befitting to sb.

6. 编+段子/笑话/故事

   to write/compose a short comedic piece online/joke/story

7. 严格+禁止/遵守/要求

   to strictly forbid/follow/to have stringent requirement for

8. 严肃的态度

   a serious attitude

9. 为了达到目的不择手段　　（不择手段 is a derogatory term.）

   to achieve a certain level unscrupulously/ without principles

10. 尺度+宽松　relaxed requirements/regulations

    放宽(fàngkuān)/收紧(shōujǐn)…的尺度　to relax/tighten the regulation of…

11. 争取+自由/机会/时间

    to strive/fight for freedom/opportunities; to race or work against time

II. 句型结构 *Sentence Pattern and Structure*

1. 因为…reason 1…，…又 reason 2…，所以……

   Because…, in addition/on top of that…, therefore…

   因为顺口溜儿有深刻的含义，又经常是押韵的，所以不容易忘记。

因为这家饭馆的饭菜很好吃，离学校又近，所以很多学生都来这里吃饭。

2. ……绝大多数都……

The overwhelming majority of…are…

贪官绝大多数都是男人。

女权主义者绝大多数都是知识分子。

3. ……表现在…noun…上

……表现在…V.P.这一点上/V.P.这种行为上……

…sth. general…is manifested/revealed in…something concrete…

贪官（绝大多数都是男人）的行为往往表现在贪财和好色两点上。

中国人的热情常常表现在饭桌上，他们总是喜欢劝酒劝菜。

4. 不管……，只要……，就……

This structure stresses that the second criterion (after 只要) is the only criterion against which the value or effect of sth. will be assessed.

不管黑猫白猫，只要会抓老鼠的就是好猫。

不管你要什么东西，只要买得到的，我就一定买给你。

5. ……到了今天还……

Even to this day, Subj. still…

This structure indicates that the speaker feels very surprised, even shocked, to find that the situation remains unchanged over a long period of time.

邓小平有一句话，不管黑猫白猫，只要会抓老鼠的就是好猫。到了今天，还有不少人引用这句话。

到了今天，还有不少中国父母有重男轻女的观念。

6. （虽然）……，但……多少有点儿 undesirable verb/adj.

"多少" in this structure means "more or less, somewhat" and is often followed by an adj. or verb that is undesirable.

到了今天，还有不少人引用这句话，但多少有点儿变味儿。

虽然我知道不是每个学生都会喜欢这个安排，但看到学生的批评还是让我多少有点儿难过。

7.　……所+V+的（N）　　　　that which (N. Verbs); that which (Verbed by N.)

Note that this pattern is a Noun Phrase.

"that which/what was mentioned above" 上面所说的(这些话)

"what one sees and hears" 所见所闻

上面所说的这些顺口溜，在中国不至于冒犯别人，但在美国可能就不太合适了。

有时候，你所看到的、所听到的不一定就是真的。

8.　……（虽然……，但还）不至于……

Although…, it is unlikely to go as far as to…/it is not as bad as…

上面所说的这些顺口溜，（虽然不一定合适或礼貌，但）在中国还不至于冒犯别人。

他的成绩（虽然不好，但）不至于不及格（fail to pass examinations）。

9.　Statement，尤其+是 example/psych. verb……

Statement，（而其中）example 尤其……

上面所说的这些顺口溜儿,在中国不至于冒犯别人,但在美国可能就不太合适了，尤其是关于男女关系的。

有些人很喜欢上面所说的这些顺口溜儿，尤其爱听关于男女关系的。

上面所说的这些顺口溜儿，在美国可能不合适，（而其中）关于男女关系的尤其不合适/可能冒犯别人。

III. 词语辨析 *Synonym Differentiation*

1. 第二天：the next day (in narrating a story)

    明天：tomorrow

    上个星期一，他来找你。我告诉他你不在家，可是他第二天又来找了你一次。

    明天你想去哪里？我跟你一起去。

2. 尤其：*adv.* in particular, especially; used to indicate something that deserves special mention. Thus, 尤其 usually appears in the second clause of a sentence to introduce an example to support the previous statement.

    特别：*adv.* (for a particular purpose or person) specially

    　　　　adj. special, unique

    学生们每天都很忙，尤其/特别是星期五，又得上课，又得考试。

    为了欢迎新同学，老师们特别准备了一场晚会。

    你的这支笔很特别，在哪儿买的？我也想买一支。

3. 许多：许多+noun (often used as a modifier before a noun)

    很多：很多+noun / noun +很多 (nominal modifier & predicate)

    在美国，许多人/很多人都喜欢对国家大事发表自己的意见。

    在美国，喜欢对国家大事发表自己意见的人很多。

順口溜兒和北京人的幽默

北京人有很多順口溜兒。順口溜兒有點兒像詩，可是又不是詩。順口溜兒也有點兒像美國人的說唱，可是也不完全一樣。順口溜兒用簡單的幾句話來概括社會上許多現象和問題，是中國人發表意見的特殊形式。因為順口溜兒有深刻的含義，又經常是押韻的，所以不容易忘記。我聽得懂的順口溜兒不多，但是只要聽懂了，就忘不了。

最近中國政府在打擊腐敗方面下了很大的功夫。貪官（絕大多數都是男人）的行為往往表現在貪財和好色兩點上。貪財就是收取金錢和禮物；好色是和很多女人發生性關係，這也叫"通奸"。社會上流行著兩句順口溜說一個貪官："工資基本不用，老婆基本不碰"。看來，貪官的老婆並不"性"福，哦，哦，我是說"幸福"。簡簡單單的兩句話，把一個又貪財又好色的貪官形象生動地描寫出來了。

1949 年以後，有一段時間，共產黨的幹部相信"為人民服務"是一個官員應有的工作態度，但是貪官一多，就成了"人民為貪官服務"了！老百姓又編了一段順口溜：以前咱們的幹部是"老婆兼秘書"；現在幹部是"秘書兼老婆"。以前的幹部，"老婆一個，孩子一堆，"現在的幹部，"老婆一堆，孩子一個。"

描述社會風氣的順口溜兒也很有趣。從前，在中國婚前和婚外的性關係是嚴格禁止的。現在可不同了："男的不壞，女的不愛"。"男人有錢就變壞，女人變壞才有錢"。像這樣的說法，在美國，很有可能被認為是性別歧視，而在中國這方面是比較寬鬆的。許多人說，中國缺乏言論自由，其實，在中國，你只要不批評政府，言論的限制是很少的。

多年前，中國人常常討論資本主義和社會主義有什麼不同。有人說"資本主義是'大家有飯吃'"，而"社會主義是'有飯大家吃'"。多麼簡單的兩句話，就說明了資本主義注重的是生產，而社會主義注重的是分配。

當然，真正改變中國社會面貌的一句話是 1978 年鄧小平說的："不管黑貓白貓，只要會抓老鼠的就是好貓！"到了今天，還有不少人引用這句話，但多少有點兒變味兒。"不管做什麼，只要能賺錢，就是好事！"目的真的可以使手段變得正當嗎？為了達到目的，真的可以不擇手段嗎？

中國人真是一個幽默的民族！

上面所說的這些順口溜兒。在中國不至於冒犯別人。但在美國可能就不太合適了，尤其是關於男女關係的笑話，在中國的尺度比美國寬鬆得多。美國把許多事情看成是"政治正確"的問題，像男女、種族、墮胎、槍枝控制、宗教信仰等等。為了保持所謂"政治正確"，大家都避免談論這些問題。在我看來，"政治正確"已經影響到了言論自由。我們應該爭取"政治不正確"的言論自由。

课后习题
第 19 课

一、词语搭配 (Please pair the term in the left column with the most appropriate term in the right column. Then use the completed phrases to complete the sentences. You can change the order of words and add more information if needed.)

（1）

（　　）发表　　　A 严肃
（　　）争取　　　B 看法
（　　）态度　　　C 机会

1. 政府官员在开会的时候_____,不可以随便开玩笑。

2. 你在面试的时候要好好表现,为自己_____。

3. 现在年轻人上网的时候很喜欢_____。

（2）

（　　）严格　　　A 责任感
（　　）应有的　　B 礼物
（　　）收取　　　C 遵守

1. 老百姓有困难了,政府应该努力帮助他们解决困难,这是_____。

2. 开车的时候,司机_____,要不然,很容易出车祸。

3. 那个官员_____,这件事被发现以后,他受到了严厉的处罚。

二、选择填空 (Complete the sentences by choosing the most appropriate term.)

1. 明天　　第二天
上个星期一我去了北京,不过,_____因为学校有事我就回来了。

今天我没做完工作，_____还得继续做。

2. 尤其　　特别

这是我们为您_____准备的礼物。

你们准备的礼物太_____了，_____是这支笔，能同时写出七种颜色的字。

3. 许多　　很多

在汉语里，_____词儿都是两个字的，这是汉语的一个特点。语言学家把这个现象叫做"双音化"。

周末的时候，来这个公园休息的人_____，老年人尤其多。

三、完成句子　(Complete the sentence or dialogue with the given item in parentheses.)

1. A：现在中国人为什么都喜欢坐高铁旅行？

   B：_____。（因为 reason 1，又 reason 2，所以…）

2. A：为什么很多年轻人宁可在大城市吃苦奋斗，也不去小城市享受安稳的生活？

   B：_____。（因为 reason 1，又 reason 2，所以…）

3. A：在发达国家，有没有污染非常严重的地方？

   B：_____。（绝大多数都+V.P.）

4. 美国拥有大量的枪支，老百姓很容易就能买到枪。但在中国，

   _____。（绝大多数都+V.P.）

5. A：一个国家有没有言论自由，可以从什么地方看出来？

   B：_____。（…abstract…表现在…concrete…上）

6. A：你觉得美国是一个男女平等的社会吗？

   B：_____。（…abstract…表现在…concrete…上）

7. A：在一个民主国家，政府会限制老百姓的宗教信仰吗？

   B：_____。（不管…，只要…，就…）

8. A：邓小平说："不管黑猫白猫，只要会抓老鼠的，就是好猫。"这句话什么意思？

   B：_____。（不管…，只要…，就…）

9.　在中国农村,很多人家里还挂着毛主席的照片,没想到＿＿＿＿＿＿。(到了今天还...)

10. A：中国很安全,为什么你妈妈还要求你一个星期给她打一个电话?

　　B：＿＿＿＿＿＿＿＿＿＿＿＿＿。(虽然...,但...多少有点儿 undesirable verb/adj.)

11. A：你花了一个星期准备考试,应该很有信心了吧?

　　B：＿＿＿＿＿＿＿＿＿＿＿＿＿。(虽然...,但...多少有点儿 undesirable verb/adj.)

12. A：我觉得言论自由就是想说什么,就说什么

　　B：我不同意,＿＿＿＿＿＿＿＿＿＿＿＿＿＿＿＿。(...所+V+的(N))

13. A：我听说小李不是一个好学生,他是不是常常打同学?

　　B：＿＿＿＿＿＿＿＿＿＿＿＿＿＿＿＿＿＿。(...(虽然...,但)不至于...)

14. A：最近中国和美国关系比较紧张,会不会打仗 (dǎzhàng, go to war) 啊?

　　B：＿＿＿＿＿＿＿＿＿＿＿＿＿＿＿＿。(...(虽然...,但)不至于...)

15. A：北京的旅游景点什么时候人比较多?

　　B：＿＿＿＿＿＿＿＿＿＿＿＿＿＿＿＿＿。(...,...尤其...)

16. A：美国人喜欢用苹果手机吗?

　　B：＿＿＿＿＿＿＿＿＿＿＿＿＿＿＿＿＿。(...,...尤其...)

四、回答问题 (Answer the questions.)

1.　什么是"顺口溜儿"? 顺口溜儿有什么特点?

2.　"薪水基本不用,老婆基本不动",这句顺口溜儿描写的是什么现象? 反映了什么态度?

3.　你对描写贪官的顺口溜儿有什么看法? 这能不能说明中国人有言论自由?

4.　你怎么理解"资本主义,大家有饭吃;社会主义,有饭大家吃"这句话? 你觉得哪一种说法对人更有吸引力?

5.　只要目的正当,就可以不择手段吗? 请用例子来说明你的看法。

6.　课文里的顺口溜儿在美国能不能讲? 为什么?

7.　请用一两个例子说明什么是"政治正确"? "政治正确"会不会影响言论自由?

8.　作者认为,我们应该争取"言论不正确"的自由。请用一两个例子说明作者的意思。你同意作者的看法吗?

第 20 课

正能量

　　最近几年，"正能量"是在中国的媒体、网络上常常出现的一个词儿。所谓的"正能量"，就是积极 向上、正面 乐观 的动力 和情感。现在媒体把所有给人力量，让人感动的事情都贴上"正能量"的标签。比方说，国庆节期间，海外留学生与国旗 合影，写下祝福 祖国 的话；大学生拾金

正能量	zhèng néngliàng	n.	positive energy
积极	jījí	adj.	active; positive; enthusiastic
正面	zhèngmiàn	adj.	positive (opp. negative 负面)
乐观	lèguān	adj.	optimistic
动力	dònglì	n.	motive; driving force
情感	qínggǎn	n.	emotion
感动	gǎndòng	v.	to move or touch (sb. emotionally)
贴标签	tiē biāoqiān	v.o.	to label sth. as…; to stereotype
国旗	guóqí	n.	national flag
合影	héyǐng	v.	to take (joint/group) photo with…
祝福	zhùfú	v.	to wish sb. well; to invoke a blessing
祖国	zǔguó	n.	homeland; motherland

不昧，把在公交车上捡到的钱包还给失主；环卫工人收养被遗弃的婴儿等等。

　　但前不久，央视的一条"正能量"微博报道却受到了人们的质疑。今年夏天，武汉发生水灾，很多地方都被淹了。武汉政府出动军队救灾。央视的微博这样描述士兵救灾的情形："在大雨里，他们不穿雨衣；

拾金不昧	shíjīn búmèi	idm.	(lit) one does not pocket the money he/she finds but returns it to its owner.
捡	jiǎn	v.	to pick up (someone else' lost article)
失主	shīzhǔ	n.	owner of lost property
环卫工人	huánwèi gōngrén	n.	sanitation worker
收养	shōuyǎng	v.	to adopt (a child/pet)
遗弃	yíqì	v.	to abandon
央视	Yāngshì	abbr.	China Central Television (CCTV)
质疑	zhìyí	v.	to call in question; to raise doubt
武汉	Wǔhàn	n.	the capital of Hubei 湖北 province
水灾	shuǐzāi	n.	flood
淹	yān	v.	to flood; submerge
出动	chūdòng	v.	to dispatch or send out (troops)
军队	jūnduì	n.	troops
救灾	jiùzāi	v.	to provide disaster relief
士兵	shìbīng	n.	soldiers
情形	qíngxíng	n.	situation

为了运沙袋，他们浑身是泥，里外湿透；六十斤的沙袋，每个人扛三百个；雨水加馒头，就是他们的食物……"。很多人看到这条微博的反应是："政府每年投入那么多军费，为什么救灾设备还这么差？让救灾的士兵吃雨水馒头，怎么可以这样对待我们的英雄……"最后，在网友激烈的批评下，央视删掉了这条"正能量"微博。

媒体、网络传播所谓的"正能量"本来是很有意义的事情，这些积极、正面的例子，为人们树立了良好的榜样，让人们保持乐观的生活态度，对社会充满信心与希望。但如果过分强调"正能量"，新闻报道可能就容易变成一种"煽情"的宣传。这种"煽情"不但不能让人们相信新

雨衣	yǔyī	n.	raincoat
运	yùn	v.	to transport
沙袋	shādài	n.	sandbag
浑身	húnshēn	adv.	whole body; from head to foot
湿透	shītòu	v.c.	wet through; drenched
斤	jīn	m.w.	a traditional unit of weight, equivalent to 0.5 kilograms
扛	káng	v.	to shoulder; to carry on the shoulder
军费	jūnfèi	n.	military expending
对待	duìdài	v.	to treat
英雄	yīngxióng	n.	hero
网友	wǎngyǒu	n.	fellow netizen
删掉	shāndiào	v.	to delete
传播	chuánbō	v.	to disseminate; to propagate
树立	shùlì	v.	to set (an example)
良好	liánghǎo	adj.	(of one's performance, habit, etc.) good
煽情	shānqíng	v.	to arouse emotions and sentiment

闻的真实性，反而会让人们质疑媒体的客观性。

　　媒体、网络的作用不仅仅是传播"正能量"，还需要曝光社会的黑暗面，监督政府贪污腐化。比方说，之前网友通过新闻里的照片对比发现，一个政府官员在不同场合戴着不同款式的名牌手表。这些名贵的手表，像他这样的政府官员是根本负担不起的。网友们纷纷质疑这个官员收入的合法性。在舆论的压力下，政府对这位官员进行调查，最终发现了他的贪污腐化行为。这是一个"网络反腐"的成功案例，但这样的案例还只是少数。

　　媒体、网络的另一个作用，应该是鼓励人们参与公共事务讨论。很多中国人还不习惯公开讨论公共事务，他们总觉得自己一个人的力量太小，不可能有什么影响，或者认为这种事情都是政府的事情，跟自己没有什么关系。在西方国家，大多数人都有积极参与公共事务讨论的意识，

真实性	zhēnshí xìng	n.	authenticity; veracity
客观性	kèguān xìng	n.	objectivity
曝光	bàoguāng	v.	to expose (scandals, etc.)
黑暗面	hēi'àn miàn	n.	the dark side
之前	zhīqián	n.	before; prior to…
对比	duìbǐ	v.	to compare (side by side)
款式	kuǎnshì	n.	design; style
纷纷	fēnfēn	adv.	(of comments, falling objects, etc.) numerous and in succession
舆论	yúlùn	n.	public opinion; media
最终	zuìzhōng	conj.	finally; in the end
案例	ànlì	n.	case
参与	cānyù	v.	to participate; to be involved in
公共事务	gōnggòng shìwù	n.	public affairs

大到总统选举，小到社区建设，很多人都愿意发表自己的意见。在这个方面，中国人应该好好向西方人学习。

在科技发达的现代社会，媒体、网络的作用是很大的。它不应该只报道正面的新闻，而不报道负面的新闻。开放包容的网络、媒体，不但能为人们提供有用的信息，更能促进社会的发展与进步。开放新闻自由，对中国的进步是有巨大的帮助的。

| 负面 | fùmiàn | adj. | negative (effect) |
| 促进 | cùjìn | v. | to boost; to stimulate (the development of…) |

I. 词语搭配 *Collocation*

1. 与……合影

   to take a joint or group photo

2. Sb.拾金不昧，把……还给失主。

   Sb. does not pocket the money he/she has found, but instead, return…to its owner.

3. 遗弃+婴儿/孩子/妻儿

   to abandon an infant/one's children/wife and children (family)

4. ……受到 sb. 的质疑

   to be questioned and challenged by sb.

5. 出动+军队/警察

   to dispatch or send out troops/the police

6. 浑身是+水/血/泥/土

   (the entire body is) covered with water/blood/mud/dust

7. 激烈的批评/辩论

   fierce and sharp criticism; heated debate

8. 树立+榜样

   to set a (glowing) example

9. 保持+…积极/乐观…的态度

   to keep…a positive/an optimistic attitude

10. 对……充满信心/希望

    …to feel fully confident/hopeful about…

11. 质疑+……的合法性/公正性/合理性/客观性

    question or challenge the legitimacy/justness/reasonableness/objectivity of…

12. 曝光+丑闻/黑暗面/问题/贪污腐化

    to expose a scandal/dark secret/problem/government corruption

13. 参与+……的讨论/准备/制定/组织

    to participate in the discussion/preparation/making/organization of…

14. 促进+……的发展/进步/提高

to boost the development/advancement/improvement of…

II. 句型结构 *Sentence Pattern and Structure*

1. 把 sth. 贴上……的标签

   sth. 被贴上……的标签

   (lit.) to attach a label to sth., usually unthinking and unsophisticated comment or criticism, stereotype.

   现在媒体把所有给人力量，让人感动的事情都贴上"正能量"的标签。

   现在很多活动都被贴上"文化交流"的标签，因此，有人开玩笑说"文化是个筐（kuāng, basket），什么都能装。"

2. 在…A…的批评/教育/帮助/…下，B…(changed/improved)…

   Under/with the criticism/education/help of A, B…

   最后，在网友激烈的批评下，央视删掉了这条"正能量"微博。

   在老师的帮助下，我的中文进步得很快。

3. ……不但不 / 没……，反而……

   Subj. didn't or can't achieve a goal as the subj. hoped or was supposed to, on the contrary, (the opposite/worse consequence) …

   这种"煽情"不但不能让人们相信新闻的真实性，反而会让人们质疑媒体的客观性。

   你上次的办法不但没帮上什么忙，反而让问题更严重了。

4. Subj.……不仅仅……，还……

   Subj.…not only…, but also…

   媒体、网络的作用不仅仅是传播"正能量"，还需要曝光社会的黑暗面，监督政府贪污腐化。

他不仅仅是我们的老师，还是我们的朋友。

5. 纷纷+V.P.

(of comments, falling objects, etc.) numerous and in succession (usually unorganized and unplanned)

这些名贵的手表，像他这样的政府官员是根本负担不起的。网友们纷纷质疑这个官员收入的合法性。

政府决定成立艺术博物馆，喜欢艺术的人对这个决定纷纷表示支持。

6. 在……的压力/影响/环境……下

under the pressure/influence/circumstance of…

在舆论的压力下，政府对这位官员进行调查，最终发现了他的贪污腐化行为。

中国人在恶劣的环境下也可以自己取乐。

7. ……对 object 进行+disyllabic verb (调查/分析/研究/……)

to carry out or conduct an investigation/analysis/research…

The structure "对……进行……" moves the object of a sentence in front of the verb and carries a very formal tone. For example, one may regard this sentence——"政府对这个官员进行了调查" as a result of "fronting" the object "官员" in "政府调查了这个官员".

在舆论的压力下，政府对这位官员进行调查，最终发现了他的贪污腐化行为。

警察必须对不遵守交通规则的人进行处罚。

8. 鼓励 sb. +V.P.　　　　to encourage sb. to do sth.

不鼓励 sb. +V.P.　　　　do not encourage sb. to do sth.

媒体、网络的另一个作用，应该是鼓励人们参与公共事务讨论。

作为老师，我不鼓励你们住在学校外面。住在外面不太安全。

9. …statement…，大到……，小到……，…都…

This pattern is often used to delimit the scope and range of sth. (from…to…), and stresses that the foregoing rule (in the previous clause) is applicable to all within.

在西方国家，大多数人都有积极参与公共事务讨论的意识，大到总统选举，小到社区建设，很多人都愿意发表自己的意见。

中国人说的"老乡"，意思是来自同一个地方的人，这个地方可以大到一个省，小到一个村，都是可以算是老乡。

III. 词语辨析 *Synonym Differentiation*

1. 参与：参与+…event…的安排 / 计划 / 组织 / 讨论

   to be involved in…

   参加：参加+活动 / 比赛 / 组织

   to take part in (an activity)/a contest/to join (a group/organization)

   虽然他没有参加比赛，可是他参与了这次比赛的组织。

2. 遗弃：遗弃+孩子 / 妻儿 / 婴儿

   to abandon, forsake and leave sb. behind

   抛弃：抛弃+孩子 / 妻儿 / 传统

   　　　抛弃+旧观念 (to rid sb. of the burden of old tradition/thinking)

   他因为遗弃孩子，受到了人们的批评。

   我们应该抛弃旧观念，接受新思想。

正能量

　　最近幾年，"正能量"是在中國的媒體、網絡上常常出現的一個詞兒。所謂的"正能量"，就是積極向上、正面樂觀的動力和情感。現在媒體把所有給人力量，讓人感動的事情都貼上"正能量"的標籤。比方說，國慶節期間，海外留學生與國旗合影，寫下祝福祖國的話；"大學生拾金不昧，把在公交車上撿到的錢包還給失主"；"環衛工人收養被遺棄的嬰兒"等等。

　　但前不久，中央電視臺的一條"正能量"微博報道卻受到了人們的質疑。今年夏天，武漢發生水災，很多地方都被淹了。武漢政府出動軍隊救災。央視的微博這樣描述士兵救災的情形："在大雨裏，他們不穿雨衣；為了運沙袋，他們渾身是泥，裏外濕透；六十斤的沙袋，每個人扛三百個；雨水加饅頭，就是他們的食物……"。很多人看到這條微博的反應是："政府每年投入那麼多軍費，為什麼救災設備還這麼差？讓救災的士兵吃雨水饅頭，怎麼可以這樣對待我們的英雄……"最後，在網友激烈的批評下，央視刪掉了這條"正能量"微博。

　　媒體、網絡傳播所謂的"正能量"本來是很有意義的事情，這些積極、正面的例子，為人們樹立了良好的榜樣，讓人們保持樂觀的生活態度，對社會充滿信心與希望。但如果過分強調"正能量"，新聞報道可能就容易變成一種"煽情"的宣傳。這種"煽情"不但不能讓人們相信新聞的真實性，反而會讓人們質疑媒體的客觀性。

　　媒體、網絡的作用不僅僅是傳播"正能量"，還需要曝光社會的黑暗面，監督政府貪污腐化。比方說，之前網友通過新聞裏的照片對比發現，一個陝西省政府官員在不同場合戴著不同款式的名牌手表。這些手表都非常貴，像他這樣的政府官員是負擔不起的。網友們紛紛質疑這個官員收入的合法性。在輿論的壓力下，政府對這位官員進行調查，最終發現了他的貪污腐化行為。這是一個"網絡反腐"的成功案例，但這樣的案例還只是少數。

　　媒體、網絡的另一個作用，應該是鼓勵人們參與公共事務討論。很多中國人還不習慣公開討論公共事務，他們總覺得自己一個人的力量太小，不可能有什麼影響，或者認為這種事情都是政府的事情，跟自己沒有什麼關係。在西方國家，大多數人都有積極參與公共事務討論的意識，大到總統選舉，小到社區建設，很多人都願意發表自己的意見。在這個方面，中國人應該好好向西方人學習。

在科技發達的現代社會，媒體、網絡的作用是很大的。它不應該只報道正面的新聞，而不報道負面的新聞。開放包容的網絡、媒體，不但能為人們提供有用的信息，更能促進社會的發展與進步。開放新聞自由，對中國的進步是有巨大的幫助的。

课后习题

第 20 课

一、词语搭配 (Please pair the term in the left column with the most appropriate term in the right column. Then use the completed phrases to complete the sentences. You can change the order of words and add more information if needed.)

(1)

（　　　）质疑　　　A 军队

（　　　）出动　　　B 信心

（　　　）充满　　　C 公正性

1. 由于发生了严重的水灾，当地政府不得不_____。

2. 过去三四十年来，中国一直都发展得很好，老百姓_____。

3. 有的新闻单位常常为政府掩饰错误，因此，_____。

(2)

（　　　）保持　　　A 榜样

（　　　）树立　　　B 活动

（　　　）参与　　　C 乐观

1. 他拾金不昧，乐于助人，_____ ____，我们都应该向他学习。

2. 他虽然为这次活动提供了资金，但_____。

3. 在面对困难的时候，人们应该_____。

(3)

(	) 曝光	A	提高
(	) 促进	B	批评
(	) 积极的	C	问题
(	) 激烈的	D	态度

1. 这家工厂大量排放污染物，严重污染了当地的环境，当地电视台_____。

2. 政府希望通过吸引外国公司的投资来_____。

3. 虽然现在情况不是很理想，但是_____。

4. 总统因为不允许难民（refugee）进入美国而受到_____。

二、选择填空 (Complete the sentences by choosing the most appropriate term.)

1. 参与　　参加

他是一个篮球运动员，能去美国 NBA____篮球比赛是他的梦想。

这次演出虽然只有 5 个人____了表演，但是很多人都____了演出的准备和组织。

2. 遗弃　　抛弃

"重男轻女"的传统观念很落后，我们必须____。

那个孩子一出生就有严重的身体问题，所以他出生不久就被父母____了。

三、完成句子 (Complete the sentence or dialogue with the given item in parentheses.)

1. A：很多人认为"言论自由"就是什么话都可以说，不管他们所说的是真的还是假的，对的还是错的。

B：我不同意，_____。（贴上…的标签）

2. A：美国常常批评别国的"人权"问题，比方说中国的独生子女政策。中国对美国的批评有什么看法？

B：_____。（贴上…的标签）

3. A：他不是生病了吗？怎么这么快就好了？

　　B：_____。（在…下）

4. A：他以前说他不喜欢学中文，现在怎么学起中文来了？

　　B：_____。（在…下）

5. A：要帮助穷人，就应该给他们钱，这是最有效的办法。

　　B：我不同意，_____。（…不但不…，反而…）

6. A：你帮他洗了衣服，他有没有谢谢你？

　　B：别提了，_____。（…不但没…，反而…）

7. A：我觉得中国的贪污腐化问题之所以这么严重是因为没有新闻自由。

　　B：我同意，但是_____。（…不仅仅…，还…）

8. A：孩子的行为完全是受父母的影响。

　　B：我不完全同意_____。（…不仅仅…，还…）

9. A：老百姓对政府"拍苍蝇，打老虎"的行动有什么看法？

　　B：_____。（纷纷）

10. 美国总统访问中国是很重要的事，中美两国的新闻媒体都_____。（进行）

11. 小王在学校里打了同学，老师在全班同学面前_____。（进行）

12. A：要是孩子大学生毕业后想自己开公司，父母应该怎么做？

　　B：_____。（鼓励）

13. A：学校可以帮助学生解决哪些问题？

　　B：_____。（大到…，小到…，…都…）

14. A：美国的媒体会报道哪些新闻？

　　B：_____。（大到…，小到…，…都…）

四、回答问题　(Answer the questions.)

1. 什么是"正能量"？请你举几个例子说明。

2. 请你介绍一下央视删掉"正能量"微博的故事。央视为什么要发这条微博，为什么又要删掉？

3. 你觉得媒体、网络的作用应该是传播正能量还是曝光黑暗面？

4. 你觉得美国人参与公共事务积极不积极？请举例说明。

第 21 课
网络暴力与言论自由

A：美国学生　　　B：中国学生

A：你平时上网会看论坛上的帖子吗？

B：会啊，论坛上有很多有趣的事情。我不但看帖子，而且也发帖子。网络给了我们发表意见的空间，从国家大事，到身边的小事，每个人都可以对这些问题发表自己的看法。

A：你最近看到什么有趣的帖子了吗？

B：有一个关于应不应该在网上骂 "小三儿" 的讨论，我觉得挺有意思的。

A："小三儿" 是什么？

B："小三儿" 就是跟已经结婚的男人发生婚外关系的女人。

A：人们有什么看法？

B：很多中国人都觉得 "小三儿" 破坏别人的家庭，非常可恨，谁都

网络暴力	wǎngluò bàolì	n.	cyber bullying; online trolling
言论自由	yánlùn zìyóu	n.	freedom of speech
论坛	lùntán	n.	a forum for discussion
帖子	tiězi	n.	a (forum) post, thread on Internet
骂	mà	v.	to verbally abuse; curse
婚外关系	hūnwài guānxi	n.	extramarital affairs

可以骂。如果对"小三儿"太宽容，那一定会影响社会上的婚姻道德观念。

A：你的话让我想起了一个人。

B：谁？

A：莱温斯基（Monica Lewinsky）。

B：你说的是那个跟美国总统克林顿（Bill Clinton）发生过婚外关系的女人？

A：是的，就是她。最近我看了莱温斯基的演讲，她的演讲让我很感动，也改变了我对她的看法，我觉得她真是一个坚强的女人。

B：我很好奇，她讲了什么？

A：她在加拿大温哥华做了一个关于"网络暴力"的演讲。

B：什么是"网络暴力"？

A：所谓的"网络暴力"包括把一个人的私人谈话、照片、视频放到网络上来羞辱这个人；在网上散布谣言或者还没有得到证实的传闻，破

可恨	kěhèn	adj.	hateful; detestable
宽容	kuānróng	adj.	tolerant; open-minded
演讲	yǎnjiǎng	n./v.	speech; talk; to give a talk
坚强	jiānqiáng	adj.	(of a person's character) strong; tough
加拿大	Jiānádà	n.	Canada
温哥华	Wēngēhuá	n.	Vancouver
私人	sīrén	adj.	private
视频	shìpín	n.	video
羞辱	xiūrǔ	v.	to humiliate

坏一个人的名声；以及在网上不断用恶毒的语言来攻击一个人。

　　B：这真是可怕。可是我觉得，一般只有那些明星、政治人物才会成为"网络暴力"的对象，毕竟，人们只对这些人的丑闻感兴趣。

　　A：你错了！名人固然容易受到这种困扰，可是普通人有时也不可避免会成为受害者。在演讲中，莱温斯基提到了一个因为无法忍受"网络暴力"而自杀的年轻大学生。有一次，这个男大学生和他的男朋友在宿舍里发生关系。他的同屋用网络摄像头偷拍下了整个过程，然后把它放到了网上。很快，这个视频就吸引了无数人的注意。很多陌生人开始在网上羞辱、

散布	sànbù	v.	to spread; to disseminate (rumors)
谣言	yáoyán	n.	rumor
证实	zhèngshí	v./n.	to verify; to confirm (sth. to be true)
传闻	chuánwén	n.	hearsay
名声	míngshēng	n.	reputation
恶毒	èdú	adj.	vicious
明星	míngxīng	n.	star; celebrity
政治人物	zhèngzhì rénwù	n.	political figure
名人	míngrén	n.	celebrity
困扰	kùnrǎo	v.	to bother; to trouble
不可避免	bùkěbìmiǎn	idm.	inevitable
受害者	shòuhàizhě	n.	victim
忍受	rěnshòu	v.	to endure; to put up with
自杀	zìshā	v.	to commit suicide
网络	wǎngluò	n.	Internet
摄像头	shèxiàngtóu	n.	webcam
偷拍	tōupāi	v.	to take a picture of a person without his/her permission or without his/her knowledge.

攻击这个年轻的大学生。最后，这个大学生实在无法忍受这种羞辱，跳河自杀了。

B：这么年轻就死了，真让人难过。他的心理怎么这么脆弱呢？

A：你不要低估"网络暴力"的伤害。羞辱造成的伤害比其他伤害都大，再加上这种困扰让受害者一辈子都无法摆脱。所以，这个年轻人才会选择自杀。

B：这些人为什么要羞辱、攻击这个大学生？

A：可能是因为这些人没有同情心；可能是因为在网上发表言论是匿名的，不用对自己网上的言论负责；也可能是因为他们自己生活不幸福，所以要发泄自己的不满。更可怕的是，有的网站为了赚钱，故意公开别人的隐私，他们用这个办法来增加网站的点击量，点击量越高，他们收的广

生命	shēngmìng	n.	life
脆弱	cuìruò	adj.	(mentally or psychologically) fragile
低估	dīgū	v.	to underestimate
摆脱	bǎituō	v.	to get rid of; to extricate from
同情心	tóngqíng xīn	n.	compassion; sympathy
言论	yánlùn	n.	expression of opinion; speech
匿名	nìmíng	adj.	anonymous
发泄	fāxiè	v.	to vent (one's anger or dissatisfaction)
不满	bùmǎn	adj./n.	dissatisfied; dissatisfaction
网站	wǎngzhàn	n.	website
故意	gùyì	adv.	on purpose
点击量	diǎnjī liàng	n.	(of websites) number of clicks; web traffic
收	shōu	v.	to charge (fees)

302

告费 就越高。

B：这些人真可恨！不过，莱温斯基有什么资格 站出来 呼吁 停止 “网络暴力”？

A：她以前也是受害者啊。那个时候，新闻单位没有经过 她的同意就把她和总统的私事公布在网上，让她受到全世界的嘲笑 和攻击。她和总统的事，除了总统夫人以外，并没有伤害别人。新闻单位没有权利把这个事情公布出来。她和那个自杀的大学生一样，都是 “网络暴力” 的受害者。

B：我不同意。她的情况和那个大学生的情况不能相提并论。她做了不道德的事，受到人们的批评不等于受到 “网络暴力” 的伤害。

A：在网上骂 “小三儿” 这种行为就是一种 “网络暴力”。难道只有等到 “小三儿” 自杀的时候，人们才会认为这是 “网络暴力” 吗？再说，她已经真诚 地道过歉 了，一个人做错了事就一辈子都不能被原谅吗？不管怎么样，她有一句话说得很对：“现在人们过分注意言论自由的权利，而忽视

广告费	guǎnggào fèi	n.	advertising expense
资格	zīgé	n.	qualification; right
站出来	zhàn chūlai	v.-c.	to stand up
呼吁	hūyù	v.	to appeal
停止	tíngzhǐ	v.	to stop
经过	jīngguò	prep.	with (one's permission) 经过 sb.的同意
嘲笑	cháoxiào	v.	to ridicule; to laugh at
等于	děngyú	v.	to be equal to
真诚	zhēnchéng	n.	sincerity
道歉	dàoqiàn	v.	to apologize
原谅	yuánliàng	v.	to forgive

了言论自由背后的责任。" 无论是在美国，还是在中国，网络的发达都给我们带来了言论上的自由，但每个人在享受这份自由的同时也应该对自己说过的话负责。

忽视　　　　hūshì　　　　v.　　　to ignore

I. 词语搭配 *Collocation*

1.	发+帖子	to make a post on an online forum
2.	发表+看法/意见/言论	to express one's views/opinions/remarks
3.	发生+婚外关系/性关系	to have extramarital affairs/sexual relation with sb.
4.	A 对 B 很宽容	A is tolerant of B
5.	散布+谣言	to disseminate rumors
6.	破坏+sb.的名声	to harm/ruin the reputation of sb.
7.	用恶毒的语言来攻击 sb.	to use foul language to verbally attack sb.
8.	吸引+sb.的注意	to attract the attention of sb.
9.	心理+脆弱	psychologically fragile
10.	摆脱+困扰	to extricate oneself from troubles
11.	发泄+不满	to vent one's discontent
12.	……对……负责	be responsible for…

II. 句型结构 *Sentence Pattern and Structure*

1. ……，毕竟，…point out an undeniable fact…

    This term *bìjìng* 毕竟, meaning "after all," is used to point out an undeniable fact, emphasizing a fact that needs to be considered.

    可是我觉得，一般只有那些明星、政客才会成为"网络暴力"的对象，毕竟，人们只对这些人的丑闻感兴趣。

    他看不懂"经济"这个词一点儿都不奇怪，毕竟，他只学了一个月的中文。

2. ……固然……，可是……

    This structure, meaning "it is true/no doubt that…, but…", expresses concession. By granting the first clause as true, it takes a step further to express the speaker's actual viewpoint or another aspect of the matter concerned.

    名人固然容易受到这种困扰，可是普通人也不可避免会成为受害者。

    钱固然是生活中非常重要的东西，可是很多东西是钱买不到的，像健康，爱情。

3. ……不可避免会+ verb phrase (undesirable)

It is inevitable that…

名人固然容易受到这种困扰，可是普通人也不可避免会成为受害者。

汽车太多，不可避免会造成环境污染。

4. ……因为…a short phrase…而 V.P.

"Because of…, the subject did something as a consequence." In this structure, 而 is used to connect an action (the verb phrase after 而) and the reason that lead to this action (after 因为).

在演讲中，莱温斯基提到了一个因为无法忍受"网络暴力"而自杀的年轻大学生。

她因为父母的压力而被迫跟自己不喜欢的人结婚。

5. 有一次，……

One time, …

有一次，这个男大学生和他的男朋友在宿舍里发生关系。他的同屋用网络摄像头偷拍下了整个过程。

有一次，我的手机在教室里被偷了。在警察的帮助下，我最后找回了手机。

6. ……，再加上……，所以……

"…, moreover/in addition…, therefore…." This structure is often used to introduce reasons or causes that lead to a certain result.

羞辱造成的伤害比其他伤害都大,再加上放在网上的那些东西可能会跟着受害者一辈子，让受害者无法摆脱这些困扰。所以，这个年轻人才会选择自杀。

最近他跟同屋的关系比较紧张，再加上他工作上的压力很大，所以他看起来有点儿不太高兴。

7. Sb.有什么资格+V.P.？（rhetorical question）

What right does sb. have to do sth.?

Sb.没有资格+V.P.

Sb. does not have the right or is not in the right position to do sth.

莱温斯基有什么资格站出来呼吁停止"网络暴力"？

美国国内也存在很多问题，美国有什么资格批评别的国家不民主，没人权？

8. Authority/an influential person　呼吁 people…

to appeal for…

莱温斯基有什么资格站出来呼吁停止"网络暴力"？

很多专家都呼吁人们注意保护传统文化。

9. A 没有经过 B 的同意就……

This structure means that A did something without the approval or consent of B and the adverb 就 denotes that what A did was earlier than it was supposed to be.

新闻单位没有经过她的同意就把她和总统的私事公布在网上，让她受到全世界的嘲笑和攻击。

我很生气，他没有经过我的同意就用我的电脑上网。

要……，得经过……的同意。

(If you) want to…, you have to get the approval/consent of…

要看别人的东西，得经过别人的同意。

在学校里，要组织大活动，得经过学校的同意。

10. A 不等于 B

"A is not the same as B" or "A does not mean B"

她做了不道德的事，受到人们的批评不等于受到"网络暴力"的伤害。

学过了不等于学会了，你一定得常常复习。

11. ……过分注意……，而忽视了……

The subject overemphasized… but ignored…

现在人们过分注意言论自由的权利，而忽视了言论自由背后的责任。

很多发展中国家过分注意经济发展，而忽视了环境保护。

12. 不管怎么样，……

anyway, …

不管怎么样，她有一句话说得很对：现在人们过分注意言论自由的权利，而忽视了言论自由背后的责任。

不管怎么样，他是你的爸爸，即使他做错了，你也不能批评他。

III. 词语辨析 *Synonym Differentiation*

1. 虽然：conj.; "Although……" It can be used to express the speaker's opinion or simply to state the fact.

   固然：conj.; "Although it is true/no doubt that…, but…" express the speaker's opinion and should always be placed after the subject.

   虽然他的看法不是完全没有道理，可是他的看法实在太奇怪了。（opinion）

   虽然他昨天生病了，可是还是坚持来上课。（fact）

   他的看法固然不是完全没有道理，可是实在太奇怪了。（opinion）

2. 宽容：tolerant, able to allow or accept mistakes, something that is harmful, unpleasant, etc.

   包容：inclusive, willing to accept feelings, habits, or beliefs that are different from your own

   对坏人的宽容可能会造成更大的问题，他们会觉得做坏事也可以被原谅，所以，做坏事不会有什么大问题。

   北京是一个包容的城市，各种各样的文化在这里和谐共存。

網路暴力與言論自由

A：美國學生　　　B：中國學生

A：你平時上網會看論壇上的帖子嗎？

B：會啊，論壇上有很多有趣的事情。我不但看帖子，而且也發帖子。網絡給了我們發表意見的空間，從國家大事，到身邊的小事，每個人都可以對這些問題發表自己的看法。

A：你最近看到什麼有趣的帖子了嗎？

B：有一個關於應不應該在網上罵"小三兒"的討論，我覺得挺有意思的。

A："小三兒"是什麼？

B："小三兒"就是跟已經結婚的男人發生婚外關係的女人。

A：人們有什麼看法？

B：很多中國人都覺得"小三兒"破壞別人的家庭，非常可恨，誰都可以罵。如果對"小三兒"太寬容，那一定會影響社會上的婚姻道德觀念。

A：你的話讓我想起了一個人。

B：誰？

A：萊溫斯基。

B：你說的是那個跟美國總統克林頓發生過婚外關係的女人？

A：是的，就是她。最近我看了萊溫斯基的演講。她的演講讓我很感動，也改變了我對她的看法，我覺得她真是一個堅強的女人。

B：我很好奇，她講了什麼？

A：她在加拿大溫哥華做了一個關於"網絡暴力"的演講。

B：什麼是"網絡暴力"？

A：所謂的"網絡暴力"包括把一個人的私人談話，照片，視頻放到網絡上來羞辱這個人；在網上散布謠言或者沒有得到證實的傳聞，破壞一個人的名聲；以及在網上不斷用惡毒的語言來攻擊一個人。

B：這真是可怕。可是我覺得，一般只有那些明星、政客才會成為"網絡暴力"的對象，畢竟，人們只對這些人的醜聞感興趣。

A：你錯了！名人固然容易受到這種困擾，可是普通人也不可避免會成為受害者。在演講中，萊溫斯基也提到了一個因為無法忍受"網絡暴力"而自殺的年輕大學生。有一次，這個男大學生和他的男朋友在宿舍裏發生關係。他的同屋用網絡攝像頭偷拍下了整個過程，然後把它放到了網上。很快，這個視頻吸引了無數人的注意。很多陌生人開始在網上羞辱、攻擊這個年輕的大學生。最後，這個大學生實在無法忍受這種羞辱，跳河自殺了。

B：這麼年輕就死了，真讓人難過。他的心理怎麼這麼脆弱呢？

A：你不要低估"網絡暴力"的傷害。羞辱造成的傷害比其他傷害都大，再加上這種困擾讓受害者一輩子都無法擺脫。所以，這個年輕人才會選擇自殺。

B：這些人為什麼要羞辱攻擊這個大學生？

A：可能是因為這些人沒有同情心，喜歡看別人丟臉；也可能是因為在網上發表言論是匿名的，不用對自己網上的言論負責；還可能是因為他們自己生活不幸福，所以要發泄自己的不滿。更可怕的是，有的網站為了賺錢故意公開別人的隱私，他們用這個辦法來增加網站的點擊量，點擊量越高，他們收的廣告費就越高。

B：這些人真可恨！不過，萊溫斯基有什麼資格站出來呼籲停止"網絡暴力"？

A：她以前也是受害者啊。那個時候，新聞單位沒有經過她的同意就把她和總統的私事公布在網上，讓她受到全世界的嘲笑和攻擊。她和總統的事，除了總統夫人以外，並沒有傷害別人。新聞單位沒有權利把這個事情公佈出來。她和那個自殺的大學生一樣，都是"網絡暴力"的受害者。

B：我不同意。她的情況和那個大學生的情況沒有可比性。她也是一個"小三兒"，她做了不道德的事，受到人們的批評不等於受到"網絡暴力"。

A：在網上罵"小三兒"這種行為就是一種"網絡暴力"。難道只有等到"小三兒"忍受不了攻擊選擇自殺的時候，人們才會認為這是"網絡暴力"嗎？再說，萊溫斯基已經真誠地道過歉了，一個人做錯了事就一輩子都不能被原諒嗎？不管怎麼樣，她有一句話說得很對："現在人們過分注意言論自由的權利，而忽視了言論自由背後的責任。"無論是在美國，還是在中國，網絡的發達都給我們帶來了言論上的自由，但每個人在享受這份自由的同時也應該對自己說過的話負責。

课后习题
第21课

一、词语搭配 (Please pair the term in the left column with the most appropriate term in the right column. Then use the completed phrases to complete the sentences. You can change the order of the words and add more information if needed.)

（1）

（　　）摆脱　　　　A 脆弱
（　　）心理　　　　B 不满
（　　）发泄　　　　C 帖子
（　　）发　　　　　D 困扰

1. 他用这么恶毒的语言来攻击别人，完全是为了_____。
2. 有些孩子_____,不能接受任何批评,这种情况需要改变。
3. 在论坛上,人们不但可以看帖子,也可以_____。
4. 这件事情对她的伤害很大,她一辈子都无法_____。

（2）

（　　）发生　　　　A 名声
（　　）发表　　　　B 谣言
（　　）散布　　　　C 意见
（　　）破坏　　　　D 婚外关系

1. 根据美国法律的规定,每个公民都有_____的权利和自由。
2. 最近, 一个男子突然在电影院里大叫"着火了", 造成了很大的混乱。事后, 警察发现他完全是故意_____, 对他进行了严厉的处罚。
3. 川普总统 (President Trump) 否认他和很多女性发生过性关系,他表示媒体报道这些"假新闻"(fake news)只是为了_____。

4.　虽然克林顿（Clinton）_____，不少美国人觉得他仍然是一个好总统。

二、选择填空 (Complete the sentences by choosing the most appropriate term.)

1.　宽容　　包容

美国是一个很_____的国家，欢迎外来的移民和文化，所以又叫做

"大熔炉" (rónglú, melting pot)。

有的国家法律规定很严，而有的国家对违法的人却很_____。

2.　虽然　　固然

_____我不同意你的看法，但是我尊重你发表看法的自由。

A：我觉得言论自由是最重要的权利。

B：言论自由_____很重要，但我认为更重要的是自由背后的责任。

三、完成句子 (Complete the sentence or dialogue with the given item in parentheses.)

1.　A：莱温斯基（Monica Lewinsky）破坏了别人的家庭，真可恨！

B：我不这么看，_____。（毕竟）

2.　A：网络暴力是名人应该担心的问题，和我们普通人没什么关系。

B：_____。(…固然…，可是…)

3.　A：我觉得，找工作的时候，最重要的是看能赚多少钱。

B：_____。(…固然…，可是…)

4.　网络的发展给人们带来了自由，但是_____。（不可避免）

5.　到今天还有一些女性_____(因为…而…)，这是实现男女平等的一大阻碍。

6.　A：既然网络暴力的危害这么大，为什么还要让人们在网上发表自己的看法呢？

B：_____。（不能因为…而…）

7.　对于莱温斯基的演讲，有人认为_____，而有人却认为_____。（没有/有资格）

8.　A：美国觉得中国没有言论自由，可是中国政府认为_____。（没有资格）

9. A：面对"网络暴力"问题，个人可以做些什么？

　　B：_____。（呼吁）

10. 面对全球变暖(Global Warming) 的问题，科学家_____。（呼吁）

11. A: 为什么说莱温斯基也是"网络暴力"的"受害者"？

　　B：_____。(没有经过…同意…)

12. A: 美国有哪些保护个人隐私的规定？

　　B: 美国法律规定，_____。(经过…同意…)

13. A: 这几课我已经学过了，不用再练习了。

　　B：_____。（不等于）

14. A: 我想说什么说什么，这是我的自由。

　　B: _____。（不等于）

15. 发展中国家的环境问题，主要是因为_____。(…过分注意…，而忽视了…)

四、回答问题 (Answer the questions)

1. 什么是"网络暴力"？网络暴力会给人们带来什么样的伤害？

2. 名人是不是更容易成为网络暴力的受害者？为什么？

3. 莱温斯基算不算是网络暴力的受害者？

4. 莱温斯基讲了一个男大学生因为网络暴力而自杀的故事，你觉得这个大学生是不是心理太脆弱了？

5. 为什么会出现网络暴力？

6. 一个人做错了事，只要真诚道歉，就可以被原谅吗？请用例子来说明你的看法。

7. 莱温斯基说："现在人们过分注意言论自由的权利，而忽视了言论自由背后的责任。"你同意她的看法吗？

第 22 课

隐私与安全

A：美国学生　　　　**B：中国学生**

A：我今天坐地铁去了一趟天安门，麻烦死了！

B：怎么了？

A：虽然我早就料到地铁站、天安门这些地方会十分拥挤，可是万万没想到这些地方竟然需要安检。检查还挺严格的，除了查包以外，如果游客手上拿着饮料，也得喝一口，安检人员才会让游客通过。有的时候，安检人员还在我的身上摸来摸去，让我很不舒服。

B：安全检查不是挺正常的吗？

A：才不是呢！要是警察滥用"安全检查"的权力，人们的权利就会受到侵害。最近苹果公司和 FBI 就因为安全检查的问题要打官司了。

天安门	Tiān'ān mén	n.	Gate of Heavenly Peace
料到	liàodào	v.	to foresee; to expect
拥挤	yōngjǐ	adj.	crowded; packed
安检	ānjiǎn	n.	security check
游客	yóukè	n.	tourists
饮料	yǐnliào	n.	beverage
正常	zhèngcháng	n.	normal; regular
滥用	lànyòng	v.	to abuse (one's power, privilege, authority)
权力	quánlì	n.	power

B：是吗？！谁告谁？

A：是 FBI 告苹果公司。

B：你开玩笑吧？FBI 不是美国的政府部门吗？他们权力那么大，他们的话谁敢不听？还需要打官司吗？

A：FBI 的权力大是大，可是美国毕竟是法治国家，无论谁要做什么事，都必须遵守美国的法律，即使是 FBI 也不例外。

B：好吧。那你快告诉我，他们为什么要打官司？

A：一个月以前，一对夫妇用枪杀死了 14 个人。这对夫妇在跟警察的枪战中也被警察打死。后来，警察在他们的车里找到了一部苹果手机。警察怀疑，这部手机里面可能有恐怖组织的信息。可是，他们没有办法解开这部手机的电子锁。于是，FBI 马上向法院申请许可，要求苹果公司提供

告	gào	v.	to sue
部门	bùmén	n.	department
例外	lìwài	n.	exception
夫妇	fūfù	n.	couple
枪	qiāng	n.	gun
枪战	qiāngzhàn	n.	gunfight
部	bù	m.w.	(for phone)
怀疑	huáiyí	v.	to suspect; to doubt
恐怖组织	kǒngbùzǔzhī	n.	terrorist organization
信息	xìnxī	n.	information
解开	jiěkāi	v.	to unlock
电子锁	diànzǐsuǒ	n.	electronic lock
于是	yúshì	conj.	consequently

解开手机电子锁的密码。出人意料的是，苹果公司拒绝了 FBI 的要求。为了得到解开电子锁的密码，FBI 不得不跟苹果公司打官司。

　　B：原来是这么回事啊。我觉得，FBI 的要求挺合理的，苹果公司为什么要拒绝？要是 FBI 怀疑一座房子里有坏人，只要他们有法院的许可，无论房子的主人允不允许，他们都可以进入那座房子。

　　A：问题没那么简单。FBI 想拿到的密码不但能解开恐怖分子手机的电子锁，而且也能解开所有苹果手机的电子锁。一旦 FBI 拿到这样的密码，那普通老百姓的隐私就没有保障了。

　　B：隐私能跟生命安全相提并论吗？这一对夫妇不是普通的小偷，而是恐怖分子！恐怖袭击造成的伤害是非常大的，它威胁着所有人的生命安全。难道你忘了 911 了吗？你不希望这样的悲剧再次发生吧？

　　A：使用手机的这对夫妇已经死了。他们手机里的信息也就没什么用了。

许可	xǔkě	n.	warrant; permission
密码	mìmǎ	n.	password
拒绝	jùjué	v.	to refuse
合理	hélǐ	adj.	reasonable
恐怖分子	kǒngbù fènzǐ	n.	terrorist
一旦	yídàn	conj.	once/as soon as (sth. happens)
保障	bǎozhàng	v./n.	to ensure; to guarantee
生命	shēngmìng	n.	life
恐怖袭击	kǒngbù xíjī	n.	terrorist attack
威胁	wēixié	v./n.	to threaten; threat
悲剧	bēijù	n.	tragedy

B：那可不一定！万一这部手机还有恐怖组织的其他计划，那我们不就错过了防止下一次袭击的机会了吗？生命比什么都重要！苹果公司应该接受 FBI 的要求。

A：可是，苹果公司一旦把密码给了 FBI，FBI 就可以侵犯老百姓的隐私权了。他们不需要法院的许可就可以随便解开任何一部苹果手机，查看手机里的信息。隐私权是美国宪法赋予美国人的最重要的权利之一，无论是谁都不能侵犯，即使是美国政府也不例外。

B：在我看来，保护隐私权只是苹果公司的借口。苹果公司不能只顾自己的利益，而不管老百姓的生命安全。还有，苹果公司也可能想利用这个官司来为自己做广告。这个官司打完以后，人们会觉得苹果公司非常注重保护人们的隐私权，也就会更信任苹果公司，相信他们的产品的安全性。其实他们完全可以先把密码给 FBI，然后再升级他们的电子锁。

万一	wànyī	conj.	if by any chance; in case
错过	cuòguò	v.	to miss (e.g. an opportunity)
防止	fángzhǐ	v.	to prevent
下一次	xià yícì	n.	next time
侵犯	qīnfàn	v.	to infringe on
查看	chákàn	v.	to examine; to check
宪法	xiànfǎ	n.	constitution (of a country)
赋予	fùyǔ	v.	(of the law) to confer; to vest
利益	lìyì	n.	interest; benefit
信任	xìnrèn	v./n.	to trust; trust
安全性	ānquánxìng	n.	security; safety (the state of not being dangerous or harmful)
升级	shēngjí	v.	to upgrade

A：可是苹果公司一旦把密码给了 FBI，就会失去顾客的信任，这对苹果公司来说是一个沉重的打击。而且，有了第一次，就会有第二次，第三次……，以后苹果公司就没有理由拒绝 FBI 的要求了。其实，我觉得这次 FBI 的确有滥用权力的嫌疑。

B：话可不能这么说！反恐是一项艰巨的任务。现在恐怖主义活动在世界各地频繁发生，每个国家的政府不但需要国内老百姓、公司的积极配合，也需要跟其他国家的政府合作。加强安全检查就是为了防止恐怖袭击，给我们一个安全的环境。作为老百姓，我对各种形式的安全检查是非常支持的。

顾客	gùkè	n.	customer
沉重	chénzhòng	adj.	heavy; hard; serious
打击	dǎjī	n./v.	blow; hit; to take strong measures against
理由	lǐyóu	n.	reason; justification; argument
嫌疑	xiányí	n.	suspicion
反恐	fǎn kǒng	n./v.	anti-terrorism; to fight terrorism
项	xiàng	m.w.	measure word for tasks, projects, etc.
艰巨	jiānjù	adj.	arduous
恐怖主义	kǒngbù zhǔyì	n.	terrorism
频繁	pínfán	adj.	frequent
配合	pèihé	v.	to coordinate with; to act in concert with; to provide assistance
合作	hézuò	v.	to collaborate; to cooperate
加强	jiāqiáng	v.	to reinforce; to strengthen

I. 词语搭配 *Collocation*

1. 滥用+权力

   to abuse one's power

2. A 跟 B 打官司

   A brings a lawsuit against B

3. A 告 B

   A sues B

4. 解开+电子锁

   to unlock the electronic lock

5. 原来是这么回事啊!

   "Ah, that's it!" (used to express a sudden realization of sth.)

6. 要求+合理

   the demands/requests are reasonable

7. 拒绝/接受+要求

   to decline/accept a demand or request

8. 威胁+sb.的生命/安全/利益

   to threaten one's life/safety or security/interest

9. 防止+……问题/恐怖主义活动

   to prevent the problem of… (from happening)/terrorism activities

10. 侵犯+隐私权/权利

    to infringe on or to invade one's privacy/rights

11. 查看+…信息

    to check the information of…

12. 宪法/法律+赋予…people…权利

    The constitution/law vests in people the right of…

13. 为…sth.…做广告

    to advertise sth.

14. 沉重的打击

a heavy blow to sb.

15. sb. 有……的嫌疑

sb. is suspected of...

16. 话可不能这么说！

That's not right! (to express your disapproval of what one just said)

17. 一项艰巨的任务

an arduous mission or task

18. 加强+安全检查 / 合作

to reinforce, strengthen security check/cooperation

II. 句型结构 Sentence Pattern and Structure

1. 虽然……早就料到……，可是万万没想到……

Although...have already foreseen that..., ... never would have expected....

虽然我早就料到地铁站、天安门这些地方十分拥挤，可是万万没想到这些地方竟然需要安检。

2. 无论……，都……，即使…extreme example…也不例外。

"No matter what/when/who..., (Subj.) all...., even for..."

This structure stresses that the situation applies to all and there is no exception.

无论谁要做什么事，都必须遵守美国的法律，即使是 FBI 也不例外。

在这里，无论是谁，都不可以迟到，即使老板也不例外。

3. ……，后来，……　　"later," used in a narration of the past

一个月以前，一对夫妇用枪杀死了 14 个人。这对夫妇在跟警察的枪战中也被警察杀死。后来，警察在他们的车里找到了一部苹果手机。

老板和他的同事发生了婚外关系，后来，这件事被他的太太发现了。他太太非常生气，马上跟他离婚了。

4. ……，于是，……

于是，meaning "thereupon" is often used to describe consequential events in an narration of the past.

FBI 没有办法解开这部手机的电子锁。于是，FBI 马上向法院申请许可，要求苹果公司提供解开苹果手机电子锁的密码。

苹果公司拒绝了 FBI 的要求，于是，FBI 就把苹果公司告到法院去了。

5. 只要……，无论……，…都…

"As long as…, no matter…, the subject can still…"

要是 FBI 怀疑一座房子里有坏人，只要他们有法院的许可，无论房子的主人允不允许，他们都可以进入那座房子。

只要是你说的话，无论是什么，我都相信。

6. A(不)允许 B V.P.

A (does not) allow B to do sth.

在美国，如果主人不允许，你不可以随便进入别人家。

他的父母不允许他去美国留学，因为他们觉得美国太危险了。

7. ……一旦……，……就……

This structure, meaning "once/as soon as (sth. happens), then…" is often used to 1) make a prediction, or 2) to warn people about the finality of the potential result/consequences.

一旦 FBI 拿到这样的密码，那普通老百姓的隐私就没有保障了。

一旦你的同事开始怀疑你，你们就很难在一起工作了。

8. 万一……，那……就……

万一: one ten thousandth; a very small percentage

This structure, meaning "If by any chance/just in case…, then…"is often used to talk about the result or effect of something that may happen or be true.

万一这部手机还有恐怖组织的其他计划，那我们不就错过了防止下一次恐怖主义活动的机会了吗？

"找到我的手机"这个 APP 很有用，万一你的苹果手机丢了，那你就可以用其他苹果设备帮你找到手机。

9. Subj. 没有理由+V.P.

    Subj. has no cause to… or there is no reason for the subject to…

    可是有了第一次，就会有第二次，第三次……，以后苹果公司就没有理由拒绝 FBI 的要求了。

    请你相信我，我没有理由骗你。

10. A 不能只顾…noun phrase 1…，而不管…noun phrase 2…

    A cannot only think of…and neglect…

    苹果公司不能只顾自己的利益，而不管老百姓的生命安全。

    中国父母不能只顾赚钱，而不管孩子的学习。

III. 词语辨析 *Synonym Differentiation*

1. 注重+abstract noun：to put emphasis on; to pay attention to

    重视+abstract noun/sb./sb.的看法 or 意见：(lit) to regard sth. as important; to value; to take…seriously

    很多大公司更注重年轻大学生的能力和热情，因为经验是可以慢慢积累的。

    老板很重视他，也非常重视他的意见，每次有问题都要先找他谈话。

2. 信任：to trust sb.

    相信：to believe

    他是我最值得信任的朋友，我什么话都可以跟他说。

    你一定要相信我，我说的都是真的。

3. 理由：reason or excuse; it is often subjective and used to express one's opinion or to give an explanation.

原因：reason; it is often objective, describing a fact

苹果拒绝 FBI 的理由是他们要保护顾客。我觉得这个理由没有什么道理。

苹果公司成功的原因是他们的产品设计很好看，使用起来也很方便。

4. A 配合 B：A acts in accordance with B. In many cases, B plays the dominant role, while A provides assistance to B.

A 与 B 合作：A and B collaborate/cooperate, each playing an equally important role.

老百姓应该配合政府，做好反恐的工作。

中国愿意跟美国合作，一起打击恐怖主义活动。

隱私與安全

A：美國學生　　　　　　B：中國學生

A：我今天坐地鐵去了一趟天安門，麻煩死了！

B：怎麼了？

A：雖然我早就料到地鐵站、天安門這些地方會十分擁擠，可是萬萬沒想到這些地方竟然需要安檢。檢查還挺嚴格的，除了查包以外，如果遊客手上拿著飲料，也得喝一口，安檢人員才會讓遊客通過。有的時候，安檢人員還在我的身上摸來摸去，讓我很不舒服。

B：安全檢查不是挺正常的嗎？

A：才不是呢！要是警察濫用"安全檢查"的權力，人們的權利就會受到侵害。最近蘋果公司和 FBI 就因為安全檢查的問題要打官司了。

B：是嗎？！誰告誰？

A：是 FBI 告蘋果公司。

B：你開玩笑吧？FBI 不是美國的政府部門嗎？他們權力那麼大，他們的話誰敢不聽？還需要打官司嗎？

A：FBI 的權力大是大，可是美國畢竟是法治國家，無論誰要做什麼事，都必須遵守美國的法律，即使是 FBI 也不例外。

B：好吧。那你快告訴我，他們為什麼要打官司？

A：一個月以前，一對夫婦用槍殺死了 14 個人。這對夫婦在跟警察的槍戰中也被警察殺死了。後來，警察在他們的車裏找到了一部蘋果手機。警察懷疑，這部手機裏面可能有恐怖組織的信息。可是，他們沒有辦法解開這部手機的電子鎖。於是，FBI 馬上向法院申請許可，要求蘋果公司提供解開手機電子鎖的密碼。出人意料的是，蘋果公司拒絕了 FBI 的要求。為了得到解開電子鎖的密碼，FBI 不得不跟蘋果公司打官司。

B：原來是這麼回事啊。我覺得，FBI 的要求挺合理的，蘋果公司為什麼要拒絕？要是 FBI 懷疑一座房子裏有壞人，只要他們有法院的許可，無論房子的主人允不允許，他們都可以進入那座房子。

A：問題沒那麼簡單。FBI 想拿到的密碼不但能解開恐怖分子手機的電子鎖，而且也能解開所有蘋果手機的電子鎖。一旦 FBI 拿到這樣的密碼，那普通老百姓的隱私就沒有保障了。

B：隱私能跟生命的安全相提並論嗎？這一對夫婦不是普通的小偷，而是恐怖分子！恐怖襲擊造成的傷害是非常大的，它威脅著所有人的生命安全。難道你忘了 911 了嗎？你不希望這樣的悲劇再次發生吧？

A：使用手機的這對夫婦已經死了。他們手機裏的信息也就沒什麼用了。

B：那可不一定！萬一這部手機還有恐怖組織的其他計劃，那我們不就錯過了防止下一次恐怖襲擊的機會了嗎？生命比什麼都重要！蘋果公司應該接受 FBI 的要求。

A：FBI 只是懷疑這部手機裏有恐怖組織的信息，並不是真的確定。可是，一旦蘋果公司把密碼給了 FBI，FBI 就可以侵犯老百姓的隱私權了。他們不需要法院的許可就可以隨便解開任何一部蘋果手機，查看手機裏的信息。隱私權是美國憲法賦予美國人的最重要的權利之一，無論是誰都不能侵犯，即使是美國政府也不例外。你想想，要是一個國家的人民沒有隱私權，老百姓與政府之間，人和人之間就不會有信任感。沒有信任感，人民的生活還會幸福嗎？

B：在我看來，保護隱私權只是蘋果公司的藉口。蘋果公司不能只顧自己的利益，而不管老百姓的生命安全。還有，蘋果公司可能也想利用這個官司來為自己做廣告。這個官司打完以後，人們會覺得蘋果公司非常注重保護人們的隱私權，也就會更信任蘋果公司，相信他們的產品的安全性。其實，他們完全可以先把密碼給 FBI，然後再升級他們的電子鎖。

A：可是蘋果公司一旦把密碼給了 FBI，就會失去顧客的信任，這對蘋果公司來說無疑是一個沉重的打擊。而且，有了第一次，就會有第二次，第三次……，以後蘋果公司就沒有理由拒絕 FBI 的要求了。其實，我覺得這次 FBI 的確有濫用權力的嫌疑。

B：話可不能這麼說！反恐是一項艱巨的任務。現在恐怖主義活動在世界各地頻繁發生，每個國家的政府不但需要國內老百姓、公司的積極配合，也需要跟其他國家的政府合作。加強安全檢查就是為了防止恐怖襲擊，給我們一個安全的環境。作為老百姓，我對各種形式的安全檢查是非常支持的。

课后习题
第 22 课

一、词语搭配 (Please pair the term in the left column with the most appropriate term in the right column. Then use the completed phrases to complete the sentences. You can change the order of the words and add more information if needed.)

（1）

(　　) 滥用　　　　A 信息

(　　) 加强　　　　B 安检

(　　) 查看　　　　C 要求

(　　) 拒绝　　　　D 权力

1. 如果缺乏监督,政府官员就会为了实现个人利益而_____。

2. 2008 年奥运会之前,为了保证安全,政府在地铁站_____。

3. 但也有人对政府的安检表示不满,他们_____。

4. 经过机场安检时,工作人员一般会要求你拿出护照(hùzhào, passport),_____。

（2）

(　　) 沉重的　　　A 隐私

(　　) 防止　　　　B 打击

(　　) 侵犯　　　　C 任务

(　　) 艰巨的　　　D 恐怖袭击

1. 2000 年以前,美国经济发达,社会安定,但 911 事件_____。

2. 911 事件以后,所有机场都加强了安检,希望_____。

3. 据说,FBI 可以监听(to monitor)每个人的电话,有人认为这样做是为了防止恐怖袭击,可是也有人担心_____。

4. 怎么在保护公共安全的同时不侵害个人权利,仍然是一个_____。

二、选择填空 (Complete the sentences by choosing the most appropriate term.)

1. 注重　　重视

随着生活水平的提高，人们不再只要求"吃饱"，也更_____食物的质量。

媒体曝光了这个社会问题，希望可以引起有关部门的_____。

2. 信任　　相信

如果苹果公司接受 FBI 的要求，交出密码，很可能会失去用户的_____。因为

用户有理由_____，苹果公司今天可以交出这部手机的密码，明天就可能会交出

所有手机的密码。

3. 原因　　理由

失败并不可怕，重要的是找到失败的_____，避免再犯同样的错误。

有时候，政府会以保护国家安全、社会稳定为_____来侵犯个人隐私。

4. 配合　　合作

恐怖主义对全世界造成了巨大的威胁，各国应该_____来解决这个问题。

在这个过程中，个人和公司应该积极_____政府完成这个艰巨的任务。

三、完成句子 (Complete the sentence or dialogue with the given item in parentheses.)

1. 《隐私与安全》这篇文章很有意思，_____。

（虽然…早就…，可是万万没想到…）

2. A：美国真的很重视个人隐私吗？

B：_____。

（无论…，都…，即使…也不例外）

3. 人们常说美国是一个法制社会，因为_____。

（无论…，都…，即使…也不例外）

4. FBI 在恐怖分子的车里找到了一个苹果手机，＿＿＿＿＿＿＿＿＿＿＿＿＿＿＿＿＿＿（于是），

可是苹果公司拒绝与政府合作，＿＿＿＿＿＿＿＿＿＿＿＿＿＿＿＿＿＿（于是）。

5. 美国法律赋予公民很多权利，比方说，＿＿＿＿＿＿＿＿＿。（只要…，无论…，…都…）

6. 我很信任这个朋友，＿＿＿＿＿＿＿＿＿＿＿＿＿。（只要…，无论…，…都…）

7. 在美国，如果＿＿＿＿＿＿＿＿＿＿＿＿＿＿，是不可以进入别人家的。(允许)

8. 中文课上有一些严格的规定，比如，＿＿＿＿＿＿＿＿＿＿＿＿。(不允许)

9. 开车的时候千万要小心，因为＿＿＿＿＿＿＿＿＿＿＿＿。(…一旦…，…就…)

10. 所有的权利都需要监督，＿＿＿＿＿＿＿＿＿＿＿＿。(…一旦…，…就…)

11. 我支持 FBI 的做法，必须解开恐怖分子手机的电子锁，＿＿＿＿＿＿＿＿＿。

（万一…，那…就…）

12. A 中国的环境污染已经很严重了，政府＿＿＿＿＿＿。(不能只顾…，而不管…)

13. 有人认为 FBI 不应该要求苹果公司解开电子锁，因为＿＿＿＿＿＿＿＿＿。可
是也有人不同意，他们认为＿＿＿＿＿＿＿＿＿。(不能只顾…，而不管…)

四、回答问题 (Answer the questions.)

1. 美国是不是一个法治国家？请举例说明你的看法。

2. 隐私与安全，哪个更重要？

3. 你觉得怎么才能有效防止恐怖袭击？

4. FBI 跟苹果公司打官司，你支持谁？

5. 苹果公司拒绝了 FBI 的要求，是为了保护自己的利益还是用户的隐私？

6. 法律为什么要保护个人的隐私权？隐私权对人们有什么意义？

第 23 课

深圳、城镇化与中国的海上发展

深圳在中国近代的移民史和城市发展史上都是一个成功的例子。

改革开放以前，深圳只是广东省沿海的一个小渔村，在经过不到 40 年的发展之后，深圳已经成了一个人口超过一千万的现代化大城市，和北京、上海、广州并列为中国的"一线城市"。深圳也可以说是一个由各省移民组成的城市，城里的人口来自全国各地，通行的语言不是广东话，而是普通话。这和邻近的香港和广州比起来是很不同的，在香港、广州，许多地方通行的还是广东话，但在深圳通行的却是普通话，因此，

近代	jìndài	n.	modern times
沿海	yánhǎi	adj.	along the coast; coastal
渔村	yúcūn	n.	fishing village
并列	bìngliè	v.	(lit.) to stand side by side; be ranked together with…; tied for…
组成	zǔchéng	v.	to make up; to constitute; to form
来自	láizì	v.	to come from
通行	tōngxíng	adj.	common (language or currency)
邻近	línjìn	attr.	neighboring

深圳没有很浓的地方色彩，也显得特别包容。对外地人和外国人来说，深圳是个适宜生活、创业的城市。

深圳的发展反映了全中国正在快速进行的城镇化，农村人口向城市集中。就 20 世纪后半期来说，中国是世界上城镇化规模最大的国家。随着快速的城镇化，中国社会也出现了许多问题，城乡差距的扩大是当前中国急需解决的问题。

有人说，从中国东南沿海向西北走去，你会发现三个不同的中国，在几个一线的大城市里，你看到的是发达国家，在中部地区，你看到的是发展中国家，到了西北的农村，你看到的是落后国家。许多外国人到了中国，主要的活动只局限在北京、上海，于是，他们以为全中国都像这两个城市这么繁荣、进步，这样的了解是不够全面的。我利用这次假

浓	nóng	adj.	strong
显得	xiǎndé	v.	to appear to be
外地人	wàidì rén	n.	non-local people; non-native
适宜	shìyí	v.	suitable (for living)
城镇化	chéngzhèn huà	n.	urbanization
后半期	hòubàn qī	n.	latter half (of a century)
规模	guīmó	n.	scale; scope
扩大	kuòdà	v.	to expand
当前	dāngqián	t.w.	present time
急需	jíxū	v.	in urgent need
局限于	júxiàn yú	v.	be limited to; be confined to
繁荣	fánróng	adj.	prosperous; booming; flourishing
全面	quánmiàn	adj.	comprehensive; all-round (opp.:片面 biased)

期，去了一趟甘肃的农村，这些地方和北京、上海的差距不但是经济上的，也是时间上的，我想甘肃的农村和几十年以前的情况大概没有太大的不同。

1949 年之后，中国政府为了有效地管理和控制人口的流动，建立了严格的户籍制度。每一个中国人的身份认定，除了身份证以外，还有户籍。每个人的工作、健康保险和子女的教育都和户籍有密切的关系。一个有北京、上海户口的人能享受到许多外地人所享受不到的福利。这个制度一方面保障了城市居民的福利，但另一方面却使许多进城打工的农民工在医疗保险和子女教育等问题上，面临解决不了的困难。户籍制

甘肃	Gānsù	n.	Gansu province in (in northwest China)
管理	guǎnlǐ	v.	to manage; to govern; to administer
控制	kòngzhì	v.	to control
流动	liúdòng	v.	(of water, air, etc.) to flow; to go from place to place; (of people) to move, migrate
户籍	hùjí	n.	residence registration system
认定	rèndìng	v.	to determine (a fact, identity)
身份证	shēnfèn zhèng	n.	identification card
保险	bǎoxiǎn	n.	insurance
密切	mìqiè	adj.	close (relationship)
福利	fúlì	n.	welfare; benefit
居民	jūmín	n.	residents

度像一道无形的长城，给城市和农村之间的交流造成了许多人为的障碍。

　　深圳快速崛起的另一个意义是中国加强了面向海洋的发展。明代早期，一个叫做郑和（1371-1433）的宦官组织了一支由两万多人、两百多艘船组成的舰队，七次远航到越南、印度尼西亚、泰国、印度南部及锡兰等国家，做了不少经济和文化上的交流。可惜，这个面向海外

道	dào	m.w.	measure word for walls, doors, etc.
无形	wúxíng	adj.	invisible; intangible
人为	rénwéi	adj.	man-made; artificial
崛起	juéqǐ	v.	to rise to prominence
面向	miànxiàng	v.	to turn in the direction of…
海洋	hǎiyáng	n.	ocean
明代	Mín dài	n.	The Ming dynasty (1368-1644)
早期	zǎoqī	n.	early stage; initial stage
宦官	huànguān	n.	eunuch
组织	zǔzhī	v.	to organize
支	zhī	m.w.	measure word for teams, troops, etc
艘	sōu	m.w.	measure word for ships
舰队	jiànduì	n.	fleet
远航	yuǎnháng	v.	to take a long (sea) voyage
越南	Yuènán	n.	Vietnam
印度尼西亚	Yìndùníxīyà	n.	Indonesia
泰国	Tàiguó	n.	Thailand
印度	Yìndù	n.	India
锡兰	Xīlán	n.	former name of Sri Lanka (until 1972)

发展的计划，15 世纪中期 以后就中止 了。最近中国在南海 建设岛礁，扩建 海军，建造 航空母舰和核潜艇，这都是有意把中国转型 成为一个海上大国的证明。

许多人都知道中国古代有陆上 的丝绸之路，是中国和中亚、西亚的交通枢纽，其实除了陆上 的丝绸之路，还有一条海上的丝绸之路。中国

中期	zhōngqī	n.	middle period
中止	zhōngzhǐ	v.	to suspend; to discontinue
南海	Nánhǎi	n.	South China Sea
岛礁	dǎojiāo	n.	reef
扩建	kuòjiàn	v.	to expand (armed forces/the navy)
海军	hǎijūn	n.	navy
建造	jiànzào	v.	to build
核潜艇	hé qiántǐng	n.	nuclear-powered submarine
转型	zhuǎnxíng	v.	(of a socioeconomic structure, cultural practices, etc.) transform; evolve
陆上	lùshàng	attr.	land (based); on land
丝绸	sīchóu	n.	silk
中亚	zhōngyà	n.	Central Asia
西亚	xīyà	n.	Southwest Asia
枢纽	shūniǔ	n.	pivot, hub

今天的建设正是要重建这两条中国与中亚、西亚、欧洲交流的道路。我们相信：在这个过程中，深圳将会扮演一个交通枢纽的角色。

重建	chóngjiàn	v.	to rebuild
扮演	bànyǎn	v.	to play (the role of...)
交通枢纽	jiāotōng shūniǔ	n.	transportation hub
角色	juésè	n.	role (in a play, movie, etc.)

I. 词语搭配 *Collocation*

1. 由……组成

   …is made up by…

2. 通行的语言/货币

   common language/currency

3. 很浓的+政治/地方色彩

   to have a strong political/local color

4. 适宜+生活/居住

   suitable for living/ (livable)

5. ……向 place 集中/聚集

   to converge on…

6. 急需+解决/提高

   in urgent need to solve (a problem)/improve

7. 建立+制度

   to establish a system

8. 保障+福利/权利/安全/生活/稳定

   to guarantee the welfare/rights; to ensure the safety/livelihood/social stability

9. 人为的+障碍

   artificial barrier

10. 计划+中止

    to suspend a project/plan

11. 建设+岛礁

    to construct reefs

12. 扩建+军队/海军

    to expand the armed forces/the navy

13. 建造+航母/核潜艇

    to build craft-carriers/nuclear-powered submarine

II. 句型结构 *Sentence Pattern and Structure*

1. 经过……的发展/努力/奋斗，subj.….(成了/变得/越来越) …

   Through/after…… (time duration) …development/effort,……

   改革开放以前，深圳只是广东省沿海的一个小渔村，在经过不到 40 年的发展
   之后，深圳已经成了一个人口超过一千万的现代化的大城市

   经过长期的奋斗，他们终于实现了他们的理想。

2. 显得+adj.

   appears to be (an implied comparison)

   在香港、广州，许多地方通行的还是广东话，但在深圳通行的却是普通话，
   从这一点上来说，深圳没有很浓的地方色彩，也显得特别包容。

   她虽然已经 40 多岁了，可是穿这件衣服显得特别年轻。

3. 就……来说，……

   Based solely on…

   就 20 世纪后半期来说，中国是世界上城镇化规模最大的国家。

   就经济的发展来说，这个地方的进步是有目共睹的。

4. ……只局限在……　　　　　　　to be limited to; be confined to

   ……不能 / 不应该只局限在……　…shouldn't be confined to…

   许多外国人到了中国，主要的活动只局限在北京、上海，于是，他们以为全
   中国都像这两个城市这么繁荣，进步。

   一个国家的发展不能只局限在经济方面，政治、文化方面也应该有进步。

5. A 和 B 有密切的关系

   A is closely related to B

   每个人的工作、健康保险和子女的教育都和户籍有密切的关系。

338

研究发现，学习的效率跟休息的质量有密切的关系。

III. 词语辨析 *Synonym Differentiation*

1. 适宜：适宜+生活 / 居住 / 创业

   适合：适合+生活 / 居住 / 创业 / sb. (of shoes, dress, a partner, etc.) just right for sb.

   深圳是一个适宜 / 适合居住和创业的城市。

   他不适合你，你们的价值观太不一样了，以后一定会有很多问题。

2. 显得：(usually after a comparison) …appears to be

   看起来：it seems that…

   你该理发了，头发太长会让你显得没有精神。

   你今天看起来有点儿没精神，生病了吗？

深圳、城鎮化與中國的海上發展

深圳在中國近代的移民史和城市發展史上都是一個成功的例子。

改革開放以前，深圳只是廣東省沿海的一個小漁村，在經過不到 40 年的發展之後，深圳已經成了一個人口超過一千萬的現代化的大城市，和北京、上海、廣州並列為中國的“一線城市”。深圳也可以說是一個由各省移民組成的城市，城裏的人口來自全國各地，通行的語言不是廣東話，而是普通話。這和鄰近的香港和廣州比起來是很不同的，在香港、廣州，許多地方通行的還是廣東話，但在深圳通行的卻是普通話，因此，深圳沒有很深的地方色彩，也顯得特別包容。對外地人和外國人來說，深圳是個適宜生活、創業的城市。

深圳的發展反映了全中國正在快速進行的城鎮化，農村人口向城市集中。就 20 世紀後半期來說，中國是世界上城鎮化規模最大的國家。隨著快速的城鎮化，中國社會也出現了許多問題，城鄉差距的擴大是當前中國急需解決的問題。

有人說，從中國東南沿海向西北走去，你會發現三個不同的中國，在幾個一線的大城市裏，你看到的是發達國家，在中部地區，你看到的是發展中國家，到了西北的農村，你看到的是落後國家。許多外國人到了中國，主要的活動就局限在北京、上海，於是，他們以為全中國都像這兩個城市這麼繁榮、進步，這樣的了解是不夠全面的。我利用這次假期，去了一趟甘肅的農村，這些地方和北京、上海的差距不但是經濟上的，也是時間上的，我想甘肅的農村和幾十年以前的情況大概沒有太大的不同。

1949 年之後，中國政府為了有效地管理和控制人口的流動，建立了嚴格的戶籍制度。每一個中國人的身份認定，除了身份證以外，還有戶籍。每個人的工作、健康保險和子女的教育都和戶籍有密切的關係。一個有北京、上海戶口的人能享受到許多外地人所享受不到的福利。這個制度一方面保障了城市居民的福利，但另一方面卻使許多進城打工的農民工在醫療保險和子女教育等問題上，面臨解決不了的困難。戶籍制度像一道無形的長城，給城市和農村之間的交流造成了許多人為的障礙。

　　深圳快速崛起的另一個意義是中國加強了面向海洋的發展。明代早期，一個叫做鄭和（1371-1433）的宦官組織了一支由兩萬多人、兩百多艘船組成的艦隊，七次遠航到越南、印度尼西亞、泰國、印度南部及錫蘭等國家，做了不少經濟和文化上的交流。可惜，這個面向海外發展的計劃，15 世紀中期以後就中止了。最近中國在南海建設島礁，擴建海軍，建造航空母艦和核潛艇，這都是有意把中國轉型成為一個海上大國的證明。

　　許多人都知道中國古代有陸上的絲綢之路，是中國和中亞西亞的交通樞紐，其實除了陸上的絲綢之路，還有一條海上的絲綢之路。中國今天的建設正是要重建這兩條中國與中亞、西亞、歐洲交流的道路。我們相信：在這個過程中，深圳將會扮演一個交通樞紐的角色。

课后习题

第 23 课

一、词语搭配 (Please pair the term in the left column with the most appropriate term in the right column. Then use the completed phrases to complete the sentences. You can change the order of words and add more information if needed.)

（1）

（　　）急需　　　　A ...制度

（　　）建立　　　　B 福利

（　　）扩建　　　　C 军队

（　　）保障　　　　D 解决

1. 腐败问题越来越严重，影响到了政府的形象和信用，这个问题＿＿＿＿＿＿＿。

2. 解决腐败问题必须＿＿＿＿＿＿＿，有了监督，官员就不能贪污，也不敢贪污。

3. 中国有意转型成海上大国，建造航母，＿＿＿＿＿＿＿＿＿＿＿＿＿，就是证明。

4. 中国的户口制度一方面＿＿＿＿＿＿＿，但另一方面也给外来人口造成了困难。

（2）

（　　）通行的　　　　A 生活

（　　）计划　　　　　B 语言

（　　）很浓的　　　　C ...色彩

（　　）适宜　　　　　D 中止

1. 英语是全世界＿＿＿＿＿＿＿＿＿＿＿，只要学会了英语，就能和各国人交流。

2. 美国原来计划建造航天飞机(space shuttle)，后来由于资金问题，＿＿＿＿＿＿＿。

3. 这个小城和其他地方不同，他们的语言、饮食和文化都有＿＿＿＿＿＿＿＿。

4. 深圳是一个沿海城市，环境好，机会多，＿＿＿＿＿＿＿＿＿。

二、选择填空 (Complete the sentences by choosing the most appropriate term.)

1. 适宜　　适合

一线城市的就业机会虽然多，但污染严重，交通堵塞，并不_____居住。

找一份工作并不难，难的是找到一份_____自己的工作。

2. 显得　　看起来

跟这座新建成的大楼相比，旁边的房子都_____很矮小。

你今天_____不太高兴，遇到有什么麻烦事了吗？

三、完成句子 (Complete the sentence or dialogue with the given item in parentheses.)

1. 改革开放以前，中国只是一个普通的发展中国家，_____，

中国在世界上扮演的角色越来越重要了。（经过…的发展/努力/奋斗，…）

2. 几年前，他还只是一个来城里打工的农民工，_____，

他终于_____。（经过…的发展/努力/奋斗，…）

3. A：你觉得年轻人应该选择在深圳这样的大城市工作，还是在小城市工作？

B：_____。(就…来说)

4. A：你在中美两国都生活过，你更喜欢哪个国家？

B：_____。(就…来说)

5. 一国的发展_____，政治、文化方面也应该有进步。（不能只局限在…）

6. 学习的时候，_____，书本以外的知识也很重要。（不能只局限在…）

7. 在中国，户籍制度很重要，因为_____。（A 和 B 有密切的关系）

8. 许多国家都很重视军事，因为_____。（A 和 B 有密切的关系）

四、回答问题 (Answer the questions.)

1. 改革开放以前和以后的深圳有什么不同？

2. 为什么说深圳是一个特别包容的城市？

3. 城镇化对中国有什么影响？

4. 中国各个地区的发展一样快吗？你的国家存在发展不平衡的问题吗？

5. 中国政府为什么要建立户籍制度？这个制度现在还有存在的必要吗？

6. 有哪些事情可以证明中国加强了面向海洋的发展？美国政府对这件事有什么看法？你同意美国政府的看法吗？

7. 请你上网了解一下中国的"一带一路"(One Belt, One Road)计划，说说你的看法。

第 24 课

工人都去哪儿了?

　　以前，谈到中国劳动力的时候，人们就自然地想到"廉价"这个词。廉价的劳动力吸引了成千上万的外国公司来中国投资开厂。于是，中国成了全球公认的"世界工厂"。

　　中国劳动力之所以廉价，主要是因为这些劳动力大都来自农村。农村缺乏就业机会，农村人不得已，离开家乡，到广东、福建、浙江等地区的沿海城市打工。这些工人就是所谓的"农民工"。上个世纪八、九十年代，如果工厂需要招聘工人，只要到就业市场贴一个招聘广告，马上就有一大批农民工来应聘。然而，这种情况在不知不觉中发生了改变。

　　最近几年，广东省不断出现"工厂招聘不到工人"的现象。据报道，在广东省的很多地方，工厂的老板都在为招聘不到工人发愁。招聘广告上的

谈到	tándào	conj./v.-c.	in speaking of; to touch on; to mention
劳动力	láodòng lì	n.	labor force
廉价	liánjià	adj.	low-priced; cheap (derogatory term)
成千上万	chéngqiān shàngwàn	idm.	thousands of
就业	jiùyè	n.	employment (modifier)
不得已	bùdéyǐ	adj.	have no alternative but to
农民工	nóngmín gōng	n.	migrant workers
招聘	zhāopìn	v.	to recruit
应聘	yìngpìn	v.	to apply for (an advertised position)
发愁	fāchóu	v.	to worry about; to fret about; be anxious

工资一个月比一个月高，可即使是这样还是没有什么人来应聘。偶尔有一两个年轻人进来，可是一听说不提供吃住，就立刻掉头离开了。

广东省是中国经济最发达的地区之一。由于广东离香港、台湾都很近，容易吸引香港、台湾的商人来投资，"改革开放"政策就是从这里开始推行的。政府为投资的商人提供很多优惠条件，比方说，可以免费租用土地，可以少交税等等。于是，大量的工厂在广东出现。对很多中西部的农村人来说，广东可以说是一个充满机会和希望的地方。但现在，为什么广东省会不断出现招聘不到工人的问题呢？

造成广东招聘不到工人的原因是多方面的。首先，工厂的待遇没有真正提高。表面上，现在每个月的工资比以前提高了不少，但是，如果考虑到最近几年飞快上涨的物价，实际上工资根本没提高。十年前去超市 100 块钱可以买不少东西，可是现在 100 块钱，还没买什么东西就差不多花完了。

偶尔	ǒu'ěr	adv.	occasionally; once in a while
掉头	diàotóu	v.	to turn around
优惠	yōuhuì	adj./n.	preferential; discount
租用	zūyòng	v.	to rent and use
交税	jiāoshuì	v-o.	to pay taxes
中西部	zhōngxī bù	n.	central and western part (of a country)
充满	chōngmǎn	v.	to be full of; to brim with
待遇	dàiyù	n.	treatment; wages and benefits
上涨	shàngzhǎng	v.	(of price) to rise
物价	wùjià	n.	price of commodities

其次，年轻一代的农民工要求提高了。这些年轻人都是 80 年代末90年代初出生的，他们不像上一代农民工那样吃苦耐劳。上一代的农民工可以接受长时间的工作，也可以忍受非常恶劣的工作环境，而且由于自卑心理，即使受到压迫，也不会反抗。相反，年轻一代的农民工不但要求有更高的工资，也希望有医疗保险、养老保险等。这一代农民工也开始有了平等意识，在城里人面前，他们不再像上一代农民工那样自卑。他们都希望能通过自己的努力奋斗留在大城市里生活。另外，这一代农民工很多都有一定的技能。他们相信，只要有一技之长，就不怕找不到工作。

另外，中西部的发展也让一小部分的农民工留在自己的家乡工作。现在，中国政府为了缩小中西部与沿海地区的差距，加大了对中西部地区的投资力度。像河南、湖北、四川，逐渐出现了新兴的工业区。这些工业区

年轻一代	niánqīng yídài	n.	the young generation
末	mò	suffix.	the end of (a century or decade)
初	chū	suffix.	the beginning of (a century or decade)
吃苦耐劳	chīkǔ nàiláo	idm.	(lit.) to bear hardships and stand hard work
上一代	shàng yídài	n.	last generation
自卑	zìbēi	adj.	be self-abased
压迫	yāpò	v.	to oppress
反抗	fǎnkàng	v.	to react against (oppression)
医疗保险	yīliáo bǎoxiǎn	n.	medical insurance
养老保险	yǎnglǎo bǎoxiǎn	n.	retirement insurance
意识	yìshi	n.	consciousness; awareness
一技之长	yíjì zhīcháng	idm.	(lit.) skill in a specialized area; professional skill
逐渐	zhújiàn	adv.	gradually
新兴	xīnxīng	attr.	emerging (as a modifier); up-and-coming
工业区	gōngyè qū	n.	industrial area

也吸引了一部分中西部的农村人来找工作。虽然现在中西部的发展才刚刚开始，但这是中国未来发展的一个方向，对解决中国的很多问题是很有帮助的。

未来	wèilái	t.w.	in the future
方向	fāngxiàng	n.	direction

I. 词语搭配 *Collocation*

1. 就业+机会/情况

   job opportunities /the employment situation

2. 招聘+工人

   to hire workers

3. 优惠+条件/政策/措施

   preferential or favorable terms/policies/measures

4. 充满+希望/机会

   (a place) of hope/opportunities

5. 提高+待遇

   to improve wages and benefits

6. 物价/房价/费用+上涨

   (commodity) prices/housing prices/expenses rise or go up

7. 反抗+压迫

   to react against oppression/ to rise against oppression

8. 新兴（的）+工业区/行业/市场/城市

   an up-and-coming industrial park/profession/market/city

II. 句型结构 *Sentence Pattern and Structure*

1. ……都……？

   Dōu 都 is used as an adverb and denotes that the speaker assumes the existence of more than one thing, referring to either the subject or the object.

   （以前广东省有非常多工人，）现在工人都去哪儿了？

   你的包鼓鼓的，你的包里都有什么东西？

2. 谈到……，……就自然想到……

   When speaking of…, people will naturally think of…

   以前，谈到中国劳动力的时候，人们就自然地想到"廉价"这个词。

很多外国人谈到中国，就自然想到长城、故宫。

3. A 成了/是……公认+最 adj. 的 noun/title

   A became/is known as the most…

   廉价的劳动力吸引了成千上万的外国公司来中国投资开厂。于是，中国成了全球公认的"世界工厂"。

   上海是全国公认经济最发达的城市。

4. ……之所以……，主要是因为……

   The reason why…is primarily because…

   中国劳动力之所以非常廉价，主要是因为这些劳动力大都来自农村。

   他之所以决定不出国，主要是因为父母的身体不太好，需要人照顾。

5. Subj. 不得已+……V.P.……

   Subj. + V.P.是不得已(的)

   The subj. had no alternative but to do sth.

   农村缺乏就业机会，农村人不得已离开家乡，到广东、福建、浙江等地区的沿海城市打工。

   她跟那个有钱的老头儿结婚是不得已的，因为她需要钱。

6. Sb. 为……发愁　　　　sb. worries/frets/be anxious about…

   据报道，在广东省的很多地方，工厂的老板都在为招聘不到工人发愁。

   以前，中国人为吃不饱饭发愁；现在生活好了，人们又开始为吃什么发愁。

7. ……，可即使是这样，还是……

   …but even so, still…

   招聘广告上的工资一个月比一个月高，可即使是这样还是没有什么人来应聘。

   中文有声调（tones），还有很多汉字，非常难学。可即使是这样，还是有很多外国学生对学中文很感兴趣。

8. 造成……的原因是多方面的：首先，……，其次……，另外……

The reasons for…are manifold: first…, second, …, in addition…

造成广东招聘不到工人的原因是多方面的。首先，工厂的待遇没有真正提高。其次，年轻一代的农民工要求提高了。另外，中西部的发展也让一小部分的农民工留在自己的家乡工作。

9. …Subj…还没…A…就…B…了

B happened even before the subject had time to do A. This structure is used to indicate that B happened prematurely.

十年前去超市 100 块钱可以买不少东西，可是现在 100 块钱，还没买什么东西就差不多花完了。

这个老师太没有耐心（impatient）了，学生常常还没说完话，他就请别的学生回答问题了。

10. A 不像 B 那样 adj.

A is not as …(adj.)… as B

这些年轻人都是 80 年代末 90 年代初出生的，他们不像上一代农民工那样吃苦耐劳。

这个地方的生活不像大城市那样方便。

11. ……通过（自己的）努力/奋斗+achieve a goal

to achieve a goal through one's own effort/struggle

年轻人都希望能通过自己的努力奋斗留在大城市里生活。

她不靠关系、不走后门，而是通过自己的努力进入了一所好大学。

III. 词语辨析 *Synonym Differentiation*

1. 不得已：*adj.* to act against one's will; have no alternative but to…(it can be used as predicate in a sentence).

他们不得已，离开了家乡。

他们离开家乡是不得已(的)。

不得不: *adv.* have to

他们不得不离开家乡。

2. 廉价：low-priced; cheap (written language, often derogatory); (fig.) worthless, valueless

便宜：cheap, petty advantages (more colloquial, can be neutral or derogatory)

太好了，这里的 DVD 真便宜，我要多买几张带回美国。

这件衣服看起来很廉价，穿去比较正式的场合，恐怕不太合适。

过去，中国靠廉价的劳动力吸引海外投资。

工人都去哪兒了？

以前，談到中國勞動力的時候，人們就自然地想到"廉價"這個詞。廉價的勞動力吸引了成千上萬的外國公司來中國投資開廠。於是，中國成了世界公認的"世界工廠"。

中國勞動力之所以廉價，主要是因為這些勞動力大都來自農村。農村缺乏就業機會，農村人不得已，離開家鄉，到廣東、福建、浙江等地區的沿海城市打工。這些工人就是所謂的"農民工"。上個世紀八、九十年代，如果工廠需要招聘工人，只要到就業市場貼一個招聘廣告，馬上就有一大批農民工來應聘。然而，這種情況在不知不覺中發生了改變。

最近幾年，廣東省不斷出現"工廠招聘不到工人"的現象。據報導，在廣東省的很多地方，工廠的老闆都在為招聘不到工人發愁。招聘廣告上的工資一個月比一個月高，可即使是這樣還是沒有什麼人來應聘。偶爾有一兩個年輕人進來，可是一聽說不提供吃住，就立刻掉頭離開了。

廣東省是中國經濟最發達的地區之一。由於廣東離香港，臺灣都很近，容易吸引香港、臺灣的商人來投資，"改革開放"政策就是從這裏開始推行的。政府為投資的商人提供很多優惠條件，比方說，可以免費租用土地，可以少交稅等等。於是，大量的工廠在廣東出現。對很多中西部的農村人來說，廣東可以說是一個充滿機會和希望的地方。但現在，為什麼廣東省會不斷出現招聘不到工人的問題呢？

造成廣東招聘不到工人的原因是多方面的。首先，工廠的待遇沒有真正提高。表面上，現在每個月的工資比以前提高了不少，但是，如果考慮到最近幾年飛快上漲的物價，實際上工資根本沒提高。十年前去超市 100 塊錢可以買不少東西，可是現在 100 塊錢，還沒買什麼東西就差不多花完了。

其次，年輕一代的農民工要求提高了。這些年輕人都是 80 年代末 90 年代初出生的，他們不像上一代農民工那樣吃苦耐勞。上一代的農民工可以接受長時間的工作，也可以忍受非常惡劣的工作環境，而且由於自卑心理，即使受到壓迫，也不會反抗。相反，年輕一代的農民工不但要求有更高的工資，也希望有醫療保險、養老保險等。這一代農民工也培養出了平等意識，在城裏人面前，他們不再像上一代農民工那樣自卑。他們都希望能通過自己的努力奮鬥留在大城市裏生活。另外，這一代農民工很多都有一定的技能。他們相信，只要有一技之長，就不怕找不到工作。

另外，中西部的發展也讓一小部分的農民工留在自己的家鄉工作。現在，中國政府為了縮小中西部與沿海地區的差距，加大了對中西部地區的投資力度。像河南、湖北、四川，逐漸出現了新興的工業區。這些工業區也吸引了一部分中西部的農村人來找工作。雖然現在中西部的發展才剛剛開始，但這是中國未來發展的一個方向，對解決中國的很多問題是很有幫助的。

课后习题

第24课

一、词语搭配 (Please pair the term in the left column with the most appropriate term in the right column. Then use the completed phrases to complete the sentences. You can change the order of the words and add more information if needed.)

(1)

(　) 就业　　　A 行业

(　) 优惠　　　B 上涨

(　) 房价　　　C 政策

(　) 新兴　　　D 机会

1. 为了推动经济发展,提供_____,美国政府鼓励本国公司把工厂搬回美国。

2. 为了吸引投资,政府提供了一系列_____,包括免费租用土地,减税等等。

3. 近年来,一线城市_____,刚毕业的学生只能与人合租,或者和父母挤在一起。

4. 随着科技的发展,出现了一些_____,比如,无人汽车,绿色能源等等。

(2)

(　) 招聘　　　A 压迫

(　) 充满　　　B 工人

(　) 提高　　　C 机会

(　) 反抗　　　D 待遇

1. 过去,工厂每年都会_____,只要广告一贴出去,就有大批工人来应聘。

2. 那时,农村的年轻人都希望能到大城市里工作,因为那里_____。

3. 现在,很多工厂出现了"招工难"的情况,为了吸引工人,许多工厂_____。

4. 一方面,工人要求得到更好的待遇,另一方面,他们也学会了保护自己。如果工厂要求他们长时间工作,不提供保险,工人们也会_____。

二、选择填空 (Complete the sentences by choosing the most appropriate term.)

1. 不得已　不得不

因为家里穷，没有钱让他上学，他_____离开家乡去城里打工。

谁不希望孩子有个好的未来？他的父母这样做，也是_____的。

2. 廉价　　便宜

_____的劳动力是发展中国家能吸引到外国投资的一个重要原因。

"中国制造"的产品不但质量好，而且价格_____，对世界经济有很大的贡献。

三、完成句子 (Complete the sentence or dialogue with the given item in parentheses.)

1. 以前是"有人没活儿干"，现在是"有活儿没人干"，工人_____？（…都…）

2. 很多人_____ (谈到…，就自然想到…)，其实美国也有很多不同的方面。

3. 成千上万的外国公司来中国投资开厂，于是，中国_____。(公认)

4. A: 为什么世界各地的学生都想来美国留学？

   B:_____。(公认)

5. A: 为什么欧美公司都喜欢把工厂建在发展中国家呢？

   B: _____。(…之所以…，主要是因为…)

6. 过去，中国人吃不饱，穿不暖，整天_____ （为……发愁）；现在生活越来越好了，可是人们又开始_____（为……发愁）。

7. 许多沿海城市出现"招工难"的现象，因此工厂_____。

   （…，可即使是这样，还是…）

8. 面对"贫富不均"问题，各国政府_____。

   （…，可即使是这样，还是…）

9. A: 为什么现在很多工厂招不到工人呢？

   B: _____。

   （造成…的原因是多方面的：首先，…，其次…，另外…）

10. A: 为什么中国的中西部地区和东部沿海的差距（东西差距）那么大呢？

　　　　B: _____。

　　　　　　　　（造成…的原因是多方面的：首先，…，其次…，另外…）

11. A：你为什么总说现在的钱 "不值钱"？

　　　　B: _____。(还没…就…了)

12. A：在美国，大学生毕业以后才开始工作吗？

　　　　B: _____。(还没…就…了)

13. A: 很多学生上了大学后抱怨（bàoyuàn, to complain）作业多，考试压力大。难道高中的时候没有考试、作业吗？

　　　　B: _____。（A 不像 B 那样 adj.）

14. 很多中老年人总是看不惯年轻人的生活方式，觉得_____。其实，每一代人都有自己的特点，没有必要要求他们和上一代一样。（A 不像 B 那样 adj.）

15. A：什么是 "美国梦" 呢？

　　　　B:　美国梦就是_____。(…通过…努力/奋斗…..)

　　　　B: 那什么又是 "中国梦" 呢？

　　　　A: _____。(…通过…努力/奋斗…..)

四、回答问题 (Answer the questions.)

1. 中国为什么能成为 "世界工厂"？

2. 广东为什么能成为中国经济最发达的地区之一？

3. 现在中国沿海城市的工厂为什么会出现招聘不到工人的情况？

4. 上一代工人和年轻一代有什么不同？

5. 有人说，现在 "招工难" 反映了中国的进步。你同不同意这个看法？

6. 你觉得中国工业未来发展的方向是什么？

第 25 课

谁来救 救孩子？

　　几天前电视上的一个新闻震惊了全国。贵州 农村的四个孩子喝农药自杀了。其中，最大的孩子 13 岁，最小的孩子 5 岁。这四个孩子的父母在大城市打工，爷爷奶奶已经去世，外公 外婆 因为年纪太大没有办法照顾这四个孩子。这个悲剧再一次引起了人们对"留守儿童"的注意。

　　所谓的"留守儿童"，就是被到大城市打工的父母留在农村老家 的孩子。留守儿童一般跟祖父母住在一起。要是祖父母年纪太大，孩子就会交给亲戚。最糟糕 的情况就是孩子自己照顾自己。目前 全中国的留守儿童超过

救	jiù	v.	to save
震惊	zhènjīng	v.	to shock
贵州	Guìzhōu	n.	a province in southwest China
其中	qízhōng	p.w.	among which
去世	qùshì	v.	to pass away
外公	wàigōng	n.	maternal grandpa
外婆	wàipó	n.	maternal grandma
留守儿童	liúshǒu értóng	n.	left-behind children
老家	lǎojiā	n.	hometown
交给	jiāogěi	v.	to give to; to entrust sb. with
亲戚	qīnqi	n.	relatives
糟糕	zāogāo	adj.	awful; terrible
目前	mùqián	t.w.	at present; at the moment

6000 万，占农村儿童总数的三分之一，占全国儿童总数的五分之一。这几个数字反映了留守儿童问题的严重性。

留守儿童的父母到城市里工作，一般都是在制造衣服、鞋子、玩具等商品的工厂打工。他们平时的工作非常忙碌，常常一天工作十几个小时。由于工资不高，加上火车票比较贵，大部分父母一年只回一次家，有时候为了省钱，有些父母甚至两三年才回一次家。长时间不跟父母生活在一起，给留守儿童造成了一系列问题。

留守儿童面临着什么问题？首先是心理问题。孩子没有独立生活的能力，他们在成长的过程中常常碰到各种各样的问题。这时候他们最需要的是父母的关心和爱护。要是父母在身边，不但能帮助他们解决问题，而且能给他们安全感，让他们勇敢面对生活中的困难。然而，留守儿童的父母长时间不在他们的身边，让这些孩子觉得他们被父母抛弃了。他们常常觉得很孤独，很无助。他们开始不喜欢跟别人交流，性格变得越来越孤僻。

总数	zǒngshù	n.	total; sum
数字	shùzì	n.	number
严重性	yánzhòng xìng	n.	seriousness
玩具	wánjù	n.	toy
省钱	shěngqián	v.-o.	to save money
成长	chéngzhǎng	v./n.	to grow; growth
碰到	pèngdào	v.	to encounter; to come across
这时候	zhèshíhou	interj.	at this point; at this time
身边	shēnbiān	n.	(by) one's side
安全感	ānquán gǎn	n.	sense of security
勇敢	yǒnggǎn	adj.	brave
孤独	gūdú	adj.	lonely

其次是讨厌上学。孩子的学习往往需要学校和家长的合作。学校教给孩子知识，帮助孩子了解自己的兴趣，家长在鼓励孩子努力学习的同时也需要对孩子进行适当的约束。由于没有父母陪在身边，留守儿童缺乏必要的约束，再加上心理问题，他们开始讨厌上学。他们常常不做作业，逃课，最后甚至不再去学校上学。

另外，留守儿童中的一部分女孩儿受到过性侵犯。因为没有父母的保护，学校又缺乏必要的性教育，有些女孩儿经常面临性侵犯的问题。让人震惊的是，这些侵犯留守女童的男人大都是熟人，有的甚至是学校里的老师。这些男人常常假装要帮助留守女童，实际上却是要侵犯她们。这些留守女童也因为认识这些男人而对他们没有防备。被侵犯以后，她们也不敢告诉别人。因此，这个问题越来越严重。

无助	wúzhù	adj.	helpless
性格	xìnggé	n.	character
孤僻	gūpì	adj.	unsociable and eccentric
讨厌	tǎoyàn	v.	to dislike
上学	shàngxué	v-o.	to attend school
鼓励	gǔlì	v.	to encourage
适当	shìdàng	adj.	appropriate; proper (in degree)
约束	yuēshù	v.	to discipline
陪	péi	v.	to accompany; to spend time with
必要	bìyào	adj.	necessary
逃课	táokè	v.-o.	to skip classes
性侵犯	xìng qīnfàn	n.	sexual assault; sexual abuse
熟人	shúrén	n.	acquaintance
防备	fángbèi	v./n.	to guard against; precaution

　　值得注意的是，有些留守儿童一方面是受害者，但同时也是少年犯。有缺 零花钱 偷东西的，有跟同学吵架打伤同学的，还有加入 黑社会 的。留守儿童由于没有父母的教育，不知道什么是道德，更不知道什么是法律。因此常常做出违反 道德标准甚至是法律的事情。

　　留守儿童的父母不能常常回家，可是把孩子带到大城市也有问题。一方面，大城市的生活费用太高，把孩子带到大城市生活会加重父母的负担；另一方面农村人没有城市户口，他们的孩子根本进不了城里的学校，没有办法接受教育。

　　留守儿童是中国城市化 带来的一个大问题。孩子是国家的未来。留守儿童的问题已经不只是对农村人有影响，而关系到这个国家的发展。虽然解决这个问题需要相当长的时间，但政府必须意识到 这个问题的严重性和解决这个问题的迫切性。

少年犯	shàonián fàn	n.	juvenile delinquent
缺	quē	v.	to lack
零花钱	línghuā qián	n.	allowance; pocket money
吵架	chǎojià	v-o.	to quarrel
加入	jiārù	v.	to join (an organization)
黑社会	hēi shèhuì	n.	gang; criminal underworld
违反	wéifǎn	v.	to violate; to break (e.g. moral standards/the law/traffic rules/regulations)
加重	jiāzhòng	v.	to aggravate; to increase (e.g. the burden)
负担	fùdān	n.	burden
城市化	chéngshì huà	n.	urbanization
意识到	yìshi dào	v.-c.	to become aware of; to be conscious of
迫切性	pòqiè xìng	n.	urgency

I. 词语搭配 *Collocation*

1. 震惊＋全国 / 社会 / 世界

   to shock the nation/the society/the world

2. 年纪＋很大 / 很小 / 很轻

   (of a person) old/very young (i.e. children & teenagers)/young (i.e. young people)

3. 性格＋孤僻

   (of a person) unsociable and eccentric

4. A 陪在 B 身边　　　A stays with B.

   A 陪 B + Vp　　　A accompanies B to do sth.

5. 缺乏＋机会/了解/交流 / 沟通 / 教育（abstract noun）

   to lack opportunities/ basic understanding/communication/interaction/education

6. A 受到 B 的性侵犯/B 侵犯 A

   A was sexually assaulted by B/B (sexually) assaulted A

7. A 对 B 没有防备（心）

   A takes no precautions against B.

8. 缺＋sth. concrete（e.g. 零花钱）

   to be in short of (e.g. pocket money)

9. 加入＋an organization（e.g. 黑社会）

   to join an organization (e.g. gang)

10. 违反＋道德标准 / 法律 / 交通规则 / 规定

    to break moral standards/the law/traffic rules/regulations

11. 加重＋负担

    to increase the burden

II. 句型结构 *Sentence Pattern and Structure*

1. ……，其中，……

   …, among which, …

   几天前电视上的一个新闻震惊了全国。在贵州农村的四个孩子喝农药自杀了。其中，最大的孩子 13 岁，最小的孩子 5 岁。

这学期我选了四门课，其中，最难的课是经济课。

2.　……反映……严重性 / 重要性 / 生活 / 现实 / clause

to reflect the seriousness or the importance of…/to reflect real life/reality…

这几个数字反映了留守儿童问题的严重性。

美国电影其实并不能反映美国人的生活。所以通过美国电影了解美国社会不是一个好办法。

3.　由于……，（再）加上……，（所以）……

Due to the fact that/because of…, in addition/on top of that…, (therefore)…

由于工资不高，加上火车票比较贵，大部分父母一年只回一次家。

由于没有父母陪在身边，留守儿童缺乏必要的约束，再加上心理问题，他们开始讨厌上学。

4.　Time duration V num.次　object（frequency）

Time duration　才　V　一次　object　（low frequency）

These two patterns are used to describe the frequency of an action. The adverb 才 cái in the second pattern stresses the low frequency of the action.

大部分父母一年只回一次家，有时候为了省钱，有些父母甚至两三年才回一次家。

上大学以前，我每天运动一次。上了大学以后，我一个月才运动一次。

5.　长时间不 VP，…bad consequence…

Not doing sth. /without doing sth. for a long time led or will lead to an undesirable result.

长时间不跟父母生活在一起，给留守儿童造成了一系列问题。

长时间不跟别人交流，会让你变得越来越孤僻。

6.　……在……的同时，也应该 / 需要……

While doing…, the subject should also do… (it is used to make suggestions)

家长在鼓励孩子努力学习的同时，也需要对孩子进行适当的约束。

政府在发展经济的同时，也应该注意保护环境。

7. ……对 object 进行＋disyllabic verb（e.g.批评/教育/约束/研究/改革）

The verb 进行 jìnxíng, literally means "to conduct, to carry out," and is often used with disyllabic verbs to create a very formal tone (such as in a news report, an academic paper or talk, etc.).

家长在鼓励孩子努力学习的同时也需要对孩子进行适当的约束。

留守儿童问题很严重，政府必须对这个问题进行研究，然后提出解决办法。

8. A 假装+V.P.　　　A pretends to do…

A 假装+成 B　　　A pretends to be B; A acts B.

这些男人常常假装要帮助留守女童，实际上却是要侵犯她们。

为了进入图书馆，他常常穿上学生的衣服，假装成这个学校的学生。

9. 值得注意的是，……

It is worthwhile/important to note that…

值得注意的是，有些留守儿童一方面是受害者，但同时也是少年犯。

值得注意的是，对留守女童进行性侵犯的往往是熟人。

10. ……一方面……，但同时……

On one hand…, but at the same time/meanwhile…

This structure is often used to introduce an opposing opinion, or another aspect of a given topic.

有些留守儿童一方面是受害者，但同时也是少年犯。

到外国学习一方面会给你提供更多机会练习，但同时你也会遇到很多困难。

11. ……关系到+…的发展/进步/成长/幸福/未来…

364

to concern, to have a bearing on

留守儿童的问题已经不只是对农村人有影响，而关系到这个国家的发展。

你的决定关系到你一辈子的幸福，你一定要想清楚。

12. ……意识到……严重性 / 重要性 / 迫切性 / clause

to be conscious of or to awake to the seriousness/importance/urgency of…

虽然解决这个问题需要相当长的时间，但政府必须意识到这个问题的严重性和解决这个问题的迫切性。

越来越多人意识到只有努力工作才能为自己带来成功。

III. 词语辨析 *Synonym Differentiation*

1. 变得+adj.　　to become

   变成+n.　　to become/transform into

   他的性格现在变得很孤僻，跟我以前认识的他完全不一样。

   他现在变成了一个性格孤僻的人，跟我以前认识的他完全不一样。

2. 适当+约束/改革/提高/降低/…　　proper (in degree)

   合适的 noun:　suitable (matching the size, length, occasion, etc.)

   我们应该适当提高工人的工资，这样，他们才会努力工作。

   我想找个合适的机会，跟他好好谈谈他的问题。

3. 认识到 to realize, to bear in on (the truth, principle, hows and whys, etc.)

   意识到 to become conscious of (a fact, or the truth, hows and whys, etc.)

   年轻人现在都已经认识到 / 意识到：只有努力工作才能成功。

   我来到教室，发现一个人都没有，我才意识到今天是星期天，我们没有课！

誰來救救孩子？

　　幾天前電視上的一個新聞震驚了全國。貴州農村的四個孩子喝農藥自殺了。其中，最大的孩子 13 歲，最小的孩子 5 歲。這四個孩子的父母在大城市打工，爺爺奶奶已經去世，外公外婆因為年紀太大沒有辦法照顧這四個孩子。這個悲劇再一次引起了人們對"留守兒童"的注意。

　　所謂的"留守兒童"，就是被到大城市打工的父母留在農村老家的孩子。留守兒童一般跟祖父母住在一起。要是祖父母年紀太大，孩子就會交給親戚。最糟糕的情況就是孩子自己照顧自己。目前全中國的留守兒童超過 6000 萬，占農村兒童總數的三分之一，占全國兒童總數的五分之一。這幾個數字反映了留守兒童問題的嚴重性。

　　留守兒童的父母到城市裏工作，一般都是在製造衣服、鞋子、玩具等商品的工廠打工。他們平時的工作非常忙碌，常常一天工作十幾個小時。由於工資不高，加上火車票比較貴，大部分父母一年只回一次家，有時候為了省錢，有些父母甚至兩三年才回一次家。長時間不跟父母生活在一起，給留守兒童造成了一系列問題。

　　留守兒童面臨著什麼問題？首先是心理問題。孩子沒有獨立生活的能力，他們在成長的過程中常常碰到各種各樣的問題。這時候他們最需要的是父母的關心和愛護。要是父母在身邊，不但能幫助他們解決問題，而且能給他們安全感，讓他們勇敢面對生活中的困難。然而，留守兒童的父母長時間不在他們的身邊，讓這些孩子覺得他們被父母拋棄了。他們常常覺得很孤獨，很無助。他們開始不喜歡跟別人交流，性格變得越來越孤僻。

　　其次是討厭上學。孩子的學習往往需要學校和家長的合作。學校教給孩子知識，幫助孩子瞭解自己的興趣，家長在鼓勵孩子努力學習的同時也需要對孩子進行適當的約束。由於沒有父母陪在身邊，留守兒童缺乏必要的約束，再加上心理問題，他們開始討厭上學。他們常常不做作業，逃課，最後甚至不再去學校上學。

　　另外，留守兒童中的一部分女孩兒受到過性侵犯。因為沒有父母的保護，學校又缺乏必要的性教育，有些女孩兒經常面臨性侵犯的問題。讓人震驚的是，這些侵犯留守女童的男人大都是熟人，有的甚至是學校裡的老師。這些男人常常假裝要幫助留守女童，實際上卻是要侵犯她們。這些留守女童也因為認識這些男人而對他們沒有防備。被侵犯以後，她們也不敢告訴別人。因此，這個問題越來越嚴重。

值得注意的是，有些留守兒童一方面是受害者，但同時也是少年犯。有缺零花錢偷東西的，有跟同學吵架打傷同學的，還有加入黑社會的。留守兒童由於沒有父母的教育，不知道什麼是道德，更不知道什麼是法律。因此常常做出違反道德標準甚至是法律的事情。

留守兒童的父母不能常常回家，可是把孩子帶到大城市也有問題。一方面，大城市的生活費用太高，把孩子帶到大城市生活會加重父母的負擔；另一方面農村人沒有城市戶口，他們的孩子根本進不了城裏的學校，沒有辦法接受教育。

留守兒童是中國城市化帶來的一個大問題。孩子是國家的未來。留守兒童的問題已經不只是對農村人有影響，而關係到這個國家的發展。雖然解決這個問題需要相當長的時間，但政府必須意識到這個問題的嚴重性和解決這個問題的迫切性。

课后习题

第 25 课

一、词语搭配 (Please pair the term in the left column with the most appropriate term in the right column. Then use the completed phrases to complete the sentences. You can change the order of the words and add more information if needed.)

（1）

(　　) 震惊　　　A 孤僻

(　　) 性格　　　B 了解

(　　) 受到　　　C 侵犯

(　　) 缺乏　　　D 全国

1. 最近，"留守儿童"自杀事件＿＿＿＿＿＿＿＿，引起了人们对这些孩子的关注。

2. 这些孩子因为长期缺乏父母的照顾，＿＿＿＿＿＿＿＿＿＿，不爱和人打交道。

3. 一些留守女童，由于没有父母的保护，又缺乏必要的性教育，＿＿＿＿＿＿＿。

4. 以前，人们对留守儿童受到性侵犯的问题＿＿＿＿＿＿＿＿＿，直到最近才意识到问题的严重性。

（2）

(　　) 陪在　　　A …组织

(　　) 加入　　　B …身边

(　　) 违反　　　C 负担

(　　) 加重　　　D 法律

1. 孩子小时候特别需要父母的照顾，这个时候父母应该尽量＿＿＿＿＿＿＿＿＿。

2. 如果缺乏教育和约束，孩子可能＿＿＿＿＿＿＿，做出一些＿＿＿＿＿的事。

3. 解决"留守儿童"问题的一个方法是让父母把孩子带到他们打工的城市，但这样做无疑会＿＿＿＿＿＿＿＿＿＿＿＿＿＿＿＿。

二、选择填空 (Complete the sentences by choosing the most appropriate term.)

1. 变得　　变成

   深圳以前只是一个小渔村，现在已经_____了中国"一线大城市"。

   随着交流的增加，这个城市也_____越来越包容。

2. 适当　　合适

   父母应该_____对孩子进行约束，不能让孩子想做什么就做什么。

   父母往往希望孩子上好大学，找好工作，却很少考虑这条路是否_____孩子。

3. 认识到　　　意识到

   经历了这次失败以后，我充分_____了沟通的重要性。

   他一直说，完全没有_____身边的人对这个话题并不感兴趣。

三、完成句子 (Complete the sentence or dialogue with the given item in parentheses.)

1. 中国目前有几千万"留守儿童"，_____。（其中）

2. _____了留守儿童问题的严重性。（反映）

3. A: 如果在中国的学生想了解美国社会，应该读什么书？

   B: _____。（反映）

4. A: 据你了解，为什么会出现少年犯的问题？

   B: _____。(由于…，（再）加上…，（所以）…)

5. 为了省钱，在外打工的父母_____。（Time duration 才 V 一次 object）

6. 以前，我_____，上了大学以后，我_____。(Time duration V…次…)

7. 因为_____（长时间不 VP），他已经不习惯和家人住在一起了。

8. Tazarn 这个电影里的孩子，由于_____。(长时间不 VP)

9. 作为 21 世纪的大学生，_____。(…在…的同时，也应该／需要…)

10. 如果孩子犯了错，父母应该_____。(对…进行…)

11. 现在少年犯的问题很严重，政府必须_____。(对…进行…)

12. 有的时候，人们会＿＿＿＿＿＿＿＿＿＿＿＿＿＿＿＿＿（假装），这往往是因为不自信。

13. 路上有一个老人摔倒了，可是＿＿＿＿＿＿＿＿＿＿，没有一个人帮助他。（假装）

14. 留守儿童的问题越来越严重，＿＿＿＿＿＿＿＿＿＿＿＿＿＿。（值得注意的是，…）

15. 政府的责任是多方面的，＿＿＿＿＿＿＿＿＿＿＿＿＿＿。（…一方面…，但同时…）

16. 政府近年来＿＿＿＿＿＿＿＿＿（意识到…），因此在这方面投入了很大的努力。

17. A: 为什么中国人这么重视孩子的教育？

　　 B:＿＿＿＿＿＿＿＿＿＿＿＿＿＿＿＿＿＿＿＿＿＿＿＿＿。（…关系到…）

18. A: 你觉得美国目前急需解决的问题时什么？

　　 B: 我觉得是＿＿＿＿＿＿＿＿，因为这个问题＿＿＿＿＿＿＿＿＿（…关系到…）。

四、回答问题 (Answer the questions.)

1. 什么是"留守儿童"？在你的国家有没有类似的现象？

2. 造成"留守儿童"问题的原因有哪些？

3. 留守儿童面临什么样的问题？

4. 怎么帮助留守儿童解决心理问题？

5. 孩子讨厌上学是很普遍的现象，怎么解决这个问题？

6. 留守儿童为什么容易受到性侵害？

7. 为什么有的留守儿童会变成少年犯？

8. 农民工为什么不把孩子带到大城市里跟他们一起生活？

9. 如果政府通过法律规定父母双方至少得有一方陪在孩子身边,这是不是一个解决"留守儿童"问题的好办法？

10. 你觉得"留守儿童"的问题应该由谁来解决？怎么解决？

第 26 课

学生偷窃跳楼，谁的过错？

　　前不久，甘肃省一个 13 岁的女中学生到一家超市去买矿泉水。她趁超市的售货员不注意的时候，偷偷地把几包零食放进了裤子的口袋里。当她结完账通过超市防盗报警门的时候，警报响了起来。超市收银员把女学生拦住，让女学生再次通过防盗报警门，警报再次响起。随后，收银员

偷窃	tōuqiè	v.	to steal
跳楼	tiàolóu	v.-o.	to jump off a building (to commit suicide)
过错	guòcuò	n.	fault
前不久	qiánbùjiǔ	t.w.	not long ago
甘肃	Gānsù	n.	Gansu province (in northwest China)
矿泉水	kuàngquánshuǐ	n.	mineral water
售货员	shòuhuòyuán	n.	salesperson; shop assistant
偷偷	tōutōu	adv.	secretly
零食	língshí	n.	snack
口袋	kǒudài	n.	pocket
结账	jiézhàng	v.-o.	to pay the check; to check out
防盗	fángdào	v	to guard against theft
报警	bàojǐng	v	to report (an incident) to the police
安检门	ānjiǎn mén	n.	the security gates
警报	jǐngbào	n.	alarm
响	xiǎng	v.	to ring; (of a bell/phone) to shrill
收银员	shōuyínyuán	n.	cashier
拦	lán	v.	to stop sb. and not let him/her go

在女学生的身上发现了几包薯片和几块巧克力，价值100多块钱。收银员马上把超市经理请过来处理这个问题。

　　经理把女学生带到二楼的一个房间进行批评教育。据说，在批评教育的过程中，经理说了一些讥讽的话。最后，经理要求女学生给家长打电话，让家长交100元的罚金，要不然就打电话叫警察，告诉女学生的学校。女学生的母亲很快就到了超市。见到经理和女儿以后，这个又气又急的母亲先是给经理道歉，然后就打了女儿两巴掌。经理劝住女学生的母亲，让她交100元罚金就放她女儿走。可是这个母亲只带了95块钱。但经理坚持要求她们交100元罚金，一块钱都不能少。女学生的母亲只好去找在街边卖爆米花的丈夫拿钱。凑够钱以后，超市终于同意放女学生离开。在整个过程中，女学生一直低着头，一句话都没有说。半个小时以后，悲剧发生

随后	suíhòu	interj.	subsequently; soon afterwards
价值	jiàzhí	n.	value
经理	jīnglǐ	n.	manager
请	qǐng	v.	to ask (sb. to do sth. politely)
讥讽	jīfěng	v.	to ridicule and satirize
罚金	fájīn	n.	fine; forfeit
又气又急	yòuqìyòují	phr.	angry and anxious; furious
巴掌	bāzhǎng	n.	palm
劝住	quànzhù	v.-c.	to persuade sb. not to do sth.
坚持	jiānchí	v.	to insist
爆米花	bàomǐhuā	n.	popcorn
凑钱	còuqián	v.-o.	to scrape together money
终于	zhōngyú	adv.	finally
低头	dītóu	v.-o.	to lower one's head

了。警察接到报警电话，说有一个女孩儿从 17 楼跳了下来，当场死亡。

　　女学生跳楼的第二天，她的父母到超市讨说法。很快，超市周围就聚集了上千人。人们都谴责超市经理不该为了几块巧克力就逼死一个年轻的生命。人们情绪越来越激动，可是超市经理一直没有出来解释。最后，在一些人的带领下，聚集的群众打砸了这个超市。第三天，有人在超市门口摆放花圈，引起群众围观。当地政府出动警察维持秩序，下午超市再次聚集了上千人，并与维持秩序的警察发生了激烈冲突，市长甚至因此受伤。

接电话	jiē diànhuà	v.-o.	to answer the phone
当场	dāngchǎng	adv.	on the spot
讨说法	tǎo shuōfǎ	v.-o.	to seek justice; to seek an answer/explanation
周围	zhōuwéi	n.	surrounding
谴责	qiǎnzé	v.	to condemn
逼死	bīsǐ	v.-c.	to hound sb. to death
激动	jīdòng	adj.	to become hysterical; (of one's emotion) become extreme and uncontrolled
解释	jiěshì	v.	to explain
带领	dàilǐng	v.	to lead
群众	qúnzhòng	n.	the crowd; the masses
打砸	dǎzá	v.	to beat and smash
摆放	bǎifàng	v.	to display
花圈	huāquān	n.	wreath
围观	wéiguān	v.	(of a crowd of people) to gather and watch; to look on
维持	wéichí	v.	to maintain
秩序	zhìxù	n.	order
冲突	chōngtū	n.	conflict

这个事件的结果是，带头打砸超市的 59 人被逮捕。据调查，这 59 个人中有 28 人以前有过犯罪记录。另一方面，超市与女学生家长达成协议，超市赔偿女学生家长 85 万人民币。

对这个结果，网友们发表了截然不同的看法。有人认为，超市经理没有权利扣留偷东西的女学生，更不应该对女学生进行讥讽、罚款。超市侵害女学生人格尊严的行为是导致女学生跳楼的直接原因，超市应该赔偿。也有人认为，超市批评教育偷东西的女学生是应该的，超市没有选择报警，也是为了给女学生留点儿面子。超市并没有什么错。还有人认为，女学生的父母应该对孩子的死负主要责任。首先，孩子偷东西，说明父母平时没有注意孩子的道德培养，没有教育孩子什么事应该做，什么事不应该做。其次，孩子因为偷东西被发现就自杀，说明孩子心理很脆弱，也间接说明

市长	shìzhǎng	n.	mayor
受伤	shòushāng	v.-o.	to get hurt
事件	shìjiàn	n.	incident
逮捕	dàibǔ	v.	to arrest
犯罪	fànzuì	v.-o.	to commit a crime
记录	jìlù	v./n.	to record; record
达成	dáchéng	v.	to reach (an agreement)
协议	xiéyì	n.	agreement
赔偿	péicháng	v./n.	to compensate; compensation
截然不同	jiérán bùtóng	idm.	completely different
扣留	kòuliú	v.	to detain
罚款	fákuǎn	v./n.	to impose a fine or forfeit; fine or forfeit
侵害	qīnhài	v.	to infringe on
人格尊严	réngé zūnyán	n.	human dignity
间接	jiànjiē	adv.	indirectly

父母从来不注意孩子的心理健康。最后，母亲一到超市就打了孩子两巴掌，使孩子的人格尊严受到进一步损害。这可能才是导致孩子自杀的真正原因。

　　还有一些人认为，最可恨的是那些打砸超市的人，他们利用人们的同情心来发泄自己对社会的不满，这种行为严重影响了中国的法治，必须严厉地惩罚这些人。

进一步	jìnyībù	adv.	further
损害	sǔnhài	v.	to damage; to impair (one's health/reputation)
惩罚	chéngfá	v./n.	to punish; punishment

I. 词语搭配 *Collocation*

1. 通过+安检门　　to pass through a security gate
2. A 把 B 拦住　　A stops/waylays B
3. Sth.响了起来　　(of a bell/phone) rang or shrilled
4. 把 sb.请过来　　to invite sb. to come over/ to politely ask sb. to come over
5. 交+罚金　　to pay the fine
6. 打 sb.两巴掌　　to give sb. *several* slaps (on the face)
7. 凑+够+钱　　to gather together/scrape up enough money
8. 放 sb.走/离开　　to release sb.
9. 接+电话　　to answer the phone
10. A 向 B 讨+说法　　A seeks an answer/explanation from B
11. 情绪+激动　　to become hysterical; (of one's emotion) become extreme and uncontrolled
12. 维持+秩序　　to maintain order
13. 发生+（激烈）冲突　　to clash; to come into (violent) conflict
14. 达成+协议　　to reach a settlement/agreement
15. A 赔偿 B + sth.　　A compensates B (for the loss) with sth.
16. 截然不同+的 abstract noun（看法/意见/……）

    (views/opinions) that are completely different/in striking contrast
17. 侵害+人格尊严　　to infringe on sb.'s human dignity
18. 给 sb.留点儿面子 to save sb. a little face

II. 句型结构 *Sentence Pattern and Structure*

1. Subj. 趁……的时候+V.P.

   Subj. (seized the opportunity) and did sth. while…

   她趁超市的售货员不注意的时候，偷偷地把几包零食放进了裤子的口袋里。

   小时候，我常常趁父母不在家的时候偷偷看电视。

376

2. ……，一 mw noun 都不/没……

By emphasizing an extremely small amount of something (一块钱, 一分钟, etc.),
this structure conveys a negative meaning.

经理坚持要求她们交 100 元罚金，一块钱都不能少。

昨天他非常忙，一分钟都没休息，一直在工作。

3. ……，终于……了　　　　　in the end (in a narration of the past)

……现在/今天终于……了。　Finally (This is used to express that something has

finally resulted in a new and desirable change.)

凑够钱以后，超市终于同意放女学生离开（了）。

昨天堵车堵得很厉害，堵了一个小时以后，我的车终于能走动了。

以前他总是被迫听父母的话，今天他终于有自己做决定的自由了。

4. ……不该/不能为了……就……

should not do sth. simply for…

人们都谴责超市经理不该为了几块巧克力就逼死一个年轻的生命。

你不该为了一点儿钱就去做损害别人利益的事。

5. 上百/上千/上万

up to/ as many as a hundred/thousand/ten thousand or so

很快，超市周围就聚集了上千人。

我的家里有上百本中文书。要是你想看，你可以来我家。

6. 在……disyllabic verb（帮助/保护/带领/照顾）……下

under the help/protection/lead/care of…

最后，在一些人的带领下，聚集的群众打砸了这个超市。

在老师的帮助下，我的中文进步了很多。

7. ……，……因此…V.P.…　　　　　　…because of this/thus, …

Cǐ 此　refers to the aforementioned reason or factor in the first clause.

下午超市再次聚集了上千人，并与维持秩序的警察发生了激烈冲突，市长甚至因此受伤。

昨天雨下得很大，领导因此取消了本来安排好的会。

8. ……没有权利……，更不应该……

…does not have the right to…, much/still less…

In this pattern, the adverb 更 gèng is used to introduce and emphasize something as being even less likely or suitable than the thing already mentioned in the first clause.

有人认为，超市经理没有权利扣留偷东西的女学生，更不应该对女学生进行讥讽、罚款。

虽然他是你的爸爸，但是他没有权利管你怎么花钱，更不应该干涉你的婚姻。

9. A 是导致 B 的直接原因

A is the direct/immediate cause of B

超市侵害女学生人格尊严的行为是导致女学生跳楼的直接原因。

汽车过多，是导致交通堵塞的直接原因。

10. 进一步+disyllabic verb（分析/研究/了解/讨论）

to further analyze/study/understand/discuss (disyllabic verb)

最后，母亲到了超市就打了孩子两巴掌，使孩子的人格尊严受到进一步损害。

这个问题我们需要进一步分析、讨论，明天我们会告诉大家结果。

III. 词语辨析 *Synonym Differentiation*

1. 维持：to maintain (a low level or unsatisfactory status) with difficulty

e.g. 维持婚姻 to hold one's marriage together；维持生活 to scrape along；维持秩序 to maintain order

保持：to keep; to maintain,

e.g. 保持水平 to keep a (high) level；保持原来的生活方式/习惯 to keep (one's original) living style/habit; to stay the same as before 保持老样子

为了维持生活，他不得不每天去饭馆打工。

在中国学了两个月以后，我的中文有了很大的进步，可是回美国以后，怎么保持中文水平呢？

2. 侵犯：1) to violate or infringe (other's rights) 侵犯+权利；

   2) to invade (a country) 侵犯+国家；

   3) to (sexually) assault sb. 侵犯+sb.

侵害：1) to infringe on (others' rights/interest) 侵害+权利／利益

言论自由是宪法赋予人民的权利，谁都不可以侵犯／侵害。

要是别的国家敢侵犯我们，我们一定会全力(with all one's strength)反抗。

有的熟人假装要帮助小女孩儿，其实这些人是想侵犯她们。

3. 惩罚：punishment (in general); suffering, pain or loss that serves as retribution

处罚：a penalty inflicted on an offender usually through judicial procedure

我们来玩个游戏吧，输了的人得接受惩罚。

不遵守交通规则的司机应该受到交警（交通警察）的／法律处罚。

學生偷竊跳樓，誰的過錯？

前不久，甘肅省的一個 13 歲的女中學生到一家超市去買礦泉水。她趁超市的售貨員不注意的時候，偷偷地把幾包零食放進了褲子的口袋裡。當她結完賬通過超市防盜報警門的時候，警報響了起來。超市收銀員把女學生攔住，讓女學生再次通過防盜報警門，警報再次響起。隨後，收銀員在女學生的身上發現了幾包薯片和幾塊巧克力，價值 100 多塊錢。收銀員馬上把超市經理請過來處理這個問題。

經理把女學生帶到二樓的一個房間進行批評教育。據說，在批評教育的過程中，經理說了一些譏諷的話。最後，經理要求女學生給家長打電話，讓家長交 100 元的罰金，要不然就打電話叫警察，告訴女學生的學校。女學生的母親很快就到了超市。見到經理和女兒以後，這個又氣又急的母親先是給經理道歉，然後就打了女兒兩巴掌。經理勸住女學生的母親，讓她交 100 元罰金就放她女兒走。可是這個母親只帶了 95 塊錢。但經理堅持要求她們交 100 元罰金，一塊錢都不能少。女學生的母親只好去找在街邊賣爆米花的丈夫拿錢。湊夠錢以後，超市終於同意放女學生離開。在整個過程中，女學生一直低著頭，一句話都沒有說。半個小時以後，悲劇發生了。警察接到報警電話，說有一個女孩兒從 17 樓跳了下來，當場死亡。

女學生跳樓的第二天，她的父母到超市討說法。很快，超市周圍就聚集了上千人。人們都譴責超市經理不該為了幾塊巧克力就逼死一個年輕的生命。人們情緒越來越激動，可是超市經理一直沒有出來解釋。最後，在一些人的帶領下，聚集的群眾打砸了這個超市。第三天，有人在超市門口擺放花圈，引起群眾圍觀。當地政府出動警察維持秩序，下午超市再次聚集了上千人，並與維持秩序的警察發生了激烈衝突，市長甚至因此受傷。這個事件的結果是，帶頭打砸超市的 59 人被逮捕。據調查，這 59 個人中有 28 人以前有過犯罪記錄。另一方面，超市與女學生家長達成協議，超市賠償女學生家長 85 萬人民幣。

對這個結果，網友們發表了截然不同的看法。有人認為，超市經理沒有權利扣留偷東西的女學生，更不應該對女學生進行譏諷、罰款。超市侵害女學生人格尊嚴的行為是導致女學生跳樓的直接原因，超市應該賠償。也有人認為，超市批評教育偷東西的女學生是應該的，超市沒有選擇報警，也是為了給女學生留點兒面子。超市並沒有什麼錯。還有人認為，女學生的父母應該對孩子的死負主要責任。首先，孩子偷東西，說明父母平時沒有注意孩子的道德培養，沒有教育孩子什麼事應該做，什麼事不應該做。其次，孩子因為偷東西被發現就自殺，說明孩子心理很脆弱，也間接說明父母從來不注意孩子的心理健康。最後，母親一到超市就打了孩子兩巴掌，使孩子的人格尊嚴受到進一步損害。這可能才是導致孩子自殺的真正原因。

還有一些人認為，最可恨的是那些打砸超市的人，他們利用人們的同情心來發洩自己對社會的不滿，這種行為嚴重影響了中國的法治，必須嚴屬地懲罰這些人。

课后习题
第26课

一、词语搭配 (Please pair the term in the left column with the most appropriate term in the right column. Then use the completed phrases to complete the sentences. You can change the order of the words and add more information if needed.)

（1）

（　　）交　　　　A 面子
（　　）接　　　　B 罚金
（　　）讨　　　　C 电话
（　　）留　　　　D 说法

1. 今天早上妈妈＿＿＿＿＿＿＿＿＿＿＿＿＿＿，可是完全听不出来电话那头的人是谁。
2. 电话是从一个超市打来的，对方说孩子在超市里偷了东西，为了＿＿＿＿＿＿＿＿＿＿，他们并没通知学校，也没有报警。
3. 妈妈马上赶到了超市，但是经理坚持必须＿＿＿＿＿＿＿＿＿＿＿＿才放孩子走。
4. 孩子后来跳楼自杀了，于是妈妈把超市告上了法庭，希望＿＿＿＿＿＿＿＿＿＿＿。

（2）

（　　）情绪　　　　A 秩序
（　　）维持　　　　B 激动
（　　）发生　　　　C 协议
（　　）达成　　　　D 冲突

1. 女孩儿自杀以后，父母来到了这家超市，他们大哭大叫，＿＿＿＿＿＿＿＿＿＿＿。
2. 很多市民也聚集到了超市附近，谴责超市的做法，政府派出了警察＿＿＿＿＿＿＿。
3. 没想到，聚集的群众越来越多，并且和警察＿＿＿＿＿＿＿＿＿＿＿＿＿。
4. 为了解决这个问题，超市最后与孩子的父母＿＿＿＿＿＿，答应道歉并赔偿85万元。

二、选择填空 (Complete the sentences by choosing the most appropriate term.)

1. 维持　　保持

　　这对夫妻的感情并不好,但是为了不影响孩子,他们决定努力_____婚姻。

　　如果你希望_____中文水平就应该坚持每天练习。

2. 惩罚　　处罚

　　孩子因为看电视忘记了做作业,作为_____,妈妈决定一个星期不让他看电视。

　　他多次违反交通规则,交警对他进行了_____。

三、完成句子 (Complete the sentence or dialogue with the given item in parentheses.)

1. 这个小偷_____。(趁...的时候...)

2. 我试着跟老板讲价,可是老板说 _____。(一...都不/没...)

3. 经过几年的努力,我_____。(终于)

4. A: 我觉得超市经理让偷东西的女孩交罚金并没有什么问题。

　　B: _____。(...不该为了...就...)

5. 一些美国的名校,很受学生欢迎,每年都有_____。(上百/上千/上万)

6. _____,我的中文有了很大的进步。(在...帮助/保护/带领/照顾下)

7. 超市经理对偷东西的孩子进行了批评教育,没想到_____。(因此)

8. A: 我觉得这个故事里的母亲并没有做错,作为母亲,她当然可以批评孩子。

　　B: _____。(...没有权利...,更不应该...)

9. A: 你觉得故事里的女孩子到底为什么会跳楼自杀?

　　B: _____。(A是导致B的直接原因)

　　但是想完全搞清楚事情的真相,还需要_____。(进一步)

10. 经过一个学期的学习,我们对中国已经有了一定的了解,但是如果想

　　_____, 还得_____。(进一步)

四、回答问题　(Answer the questions.)

1. 请你从超市经理和女学生的角度讲一讲这个故事。

2. 发现女学生偷窃，超市经理是怎么处理的？他的处理方法有没有问题？为什么？

3. 你觉得女学生的母亲有没有错？为什么？

4. 在整个事件的处理过程中，为什么那个女孩一句话都没说？她在想什么？

5. 后来，女学生的父母为什么要去超市讨说法？超市经理为什么一直都没有出来解释？

6. 最后，超市赔偿了女学生父母 85 万元。你对这个结果有什么看法？

7. 你认为，是什么导致了女学生跳楼自杀？

8. 为什么会出现千人打砸超市的情况？这件事说明了什么问题？

第 27 课

台湾的政治与认同

（一）台湾的历史与现状

最近系 里请了一位从台湾来的教授给同学们做了一个演讲，题目是《台湾的政治与认同》。我对这个题目很感兴趣。这位教授的英文不太流利，但是因为有英文翻译，他的演讲，我基本上 都听懂了。

我的父母是从台湾来的，从我懂事 以来，他们就告诉我，我们是中国人，而台湾是中国的一部分。所以，我从小就认为：台湾人就是中国人。可是这位台湾教授在演讲的时候却说，台湾人认为自己是中国人的比例越来越低了，尤其是 80、90 以后出生的台湾人，百分之八十以上，觉得自己就是台湾人，跟中国人完全没有关系。这让我觉得很惊讶。

据他说，台湾人在认同上离中国越来越远，既有历史原因，也跟大陆、台湾的政策有关系。1895 年，中国和日本发生了"甲午战争"，中国被日本

现状	xiànzhuàng	n.	current situation
系	xì	n.	department (in a university)
流利	liúlì	adj.	fluent
翻译	fānyì	v./n.	to translate; translation
基本上	jīběnshang	adv.	basically; on the whole; by and large
懂事	dǒngshì	v.	(of a child) to be able to make judgments; be sensible
比例	bǐlì	n.	percentage; rate
甲午战争	Jiǎwǔ Zhànzhēng	n.	The Sino-Japanese War (1894-1895)

打败了。清朝政府除了赔款以外，还把台湾割让给了日本，从此，台湾开始了 50 年的殖民地历史。有些台湾人对这段历史的解释是：清朝政府根本没把台湾当回事，打了败仗，就把台湾当一件礼物一样送给日本。让台湾成了"亚洲的孤儿"。1945 年，二战结束了，日本战败了，台湾又还给了中国。

二战结束以后，中国发生了内战，蒋介石领导的国民党非常腐败，短短几年(1945-1949)就被毛泽东领导的共产党打败了。1949 年，国民政府退到了台湾。

看看这一百多年的历史，台湾从 1895 到 1945 年，是日本人的殖民地，1945 以后，台湾又一直在国民党的统治底下。台湾人总觉得自己没有管理过自己，而总是接受别人的管理。这种感觉是很不好的。对这段历史有了一些了解以后，我对台湾人的认同，多了一些同情。

赔款	péikuǎn	n.	reparations; indemnity
割让	gēràng	v.	to cede
败仗	bàizhàng	n.	a lost battle; defeat
当	dāng	v.	to treat sth. /sb. as …
亚洲	Yàzhōu	n.	Asia
孤儿	gū'ér	n.	orphan
二战	Èrzhàn	n.	World War II
战败	zhànbài	v.	to be defeated
内战	nèizhàn	n.	civil war
退	tuì	v.	to retreat
统治	tǒngzhì	v.	to govern
管理	guǎnlǐ	v./n.	to manage; management
同情	tóngqíng	v./n.	to sympathize; sympathy

　　1945 年之后，国民党在台湾表面上推行民主，但实际上是一党独裁。言论和新闻的自由是非常有限的。台湾老百姓对这样的政治制度越来越不满，他们要求成立新的政党。1975 年蒋介石死了，他的儿子蒋经国很快就成了台湾的领导人，他比他父亲开明，并有计划地从事经济和政治的改革，使台湾在短短几年之内成了"亚洲四小龙"之一。台湾的经济起飞带来了政治上的改革。

（二）台湾问题是中国问题，还是国际问题？

　　中国大陆在过去 30 年来，经济上改革开放的成绩是有目共睹的。中国从一个贫穷落后的农业国家，成了世界第二大经济体，仅次于美国。有些人以为，台湾的发展模式也可以应用在中国大陆。我想这样的估计有些

民主	mínzhǔ	n./adj.	democracy; democratic　民主+制度/国家
独裁	dúcái	n.	dictatorship
有限	yǒuxiàn	adj.	limited
政党	zhèngdǎng	n.	party
领导人	lǐngdǎorén	n.	leader of a country or party
开明	kāimíng	n.	liberal; open-minded
从事	cóngshì	v.	to undertake; to take up (as a profession)
起飞	qǐfēi	v./n.	to take off; (economic) take-off
大陆	dàlù	n.	Mainland China
有目共睹	yǒumùgòngdǔ	idm.	widely recognized; to be perfectly obvious
经济体	jīngjìtǐ	n.	economy
模式	móshì	n.	model
应用	yìngyòng	v.	to apply
估计	gūjì	v.	to estimate

不切实际，也不了解两岸的实际情况。台湾是个小岛，南北长约 400 公里，人口只有两千多万，而大陆无论就面积还是就人口来说，都是台湾的几十倍，甚至几百倍。在台湾能做的事，在大陆不一定能做。

　　这位台湾教授说："美国人基本上是同情台湾，而不支持中国统一的。"这个说法，当然有它的道理，但是我觉得，与其说美国人支持台湾独立是为了让台湾人享受民主自由，不如说中国统一对美国是不利的。中国不统一，台湾是美国在太平洋上一艘"不沉的航空母舰"，对美国在太平洋上势力的扩张和发展是非常有帮助的。要是两岸统一了，这艘航空母舰就是中国的了，更何况，台湾的价值哪里是一艘航空母舰可以相提并论的呢？对美国来说，台湾在军事上的价值，比夏威夷更重要。

不切实际	búqièshíjì	adj.	unrealistic; impractical
两岸	liǎng'àn	n.	both sides of the Taiwan Strait (i.e. Taiwan and mainland China)
岛	dǎo	n.	island
面积	miànjī	n.	area; size
统一	tǒngyī	v.	to unite
太平洋	Tàipíngyáng	n.	the Pacific Ocean
沉	chén	v.	to sink
势力	shìlì	n.	power; influence
扩张	kuòzhāng	v.	to aggrandize (one's power/influence)
更何况	gènghékuàng	adv.	let alone …; not to mention…
夏威夷	Xiàwēiyí	n.	Hawaii

　　这位台湾教授还说："台湾问题实在很复杂，对中国大陆来说，这是一个国家主权的问题，但对台湾来说，却是个独立自主的问题，台湾人应该有权利决定自己的生活方式和政治结构。"

　　听了演讲以后，我觉得台湾问题是个中国问题，而不是国际问题，台湾问题应该由中国人来解决，美国人不应该插手。美国政府常常觉得自己是国际警察，世界上任何地区发生了冲突，美国都得出兵干涉。我想，美国人得慢慢地适应：中国已经不是 19 世纪的中国，而是一个强大的现代国家。至于美国式的民主也不一定适合每一个国家，没有美国的历史背景，却勉强地要实行民主，结果往往造成社会的大混乱。我想每个国家都得选择他们自己的生活方式，走自己的道路。

复杂	fùzá	adj.	complicated
独立自主	dúlìzìzhǔ	adj.	independent and autonomous
结构	jiégòu	n.	structure
由	yóu	prep.	by
插手	chāshǒu	v.	to meddle in; to get involved in (an unwanted involvement)
出兵	chūbīng	v.	to dispatch/send out troops
干涉	gānshè	v.	to interfere
背景	bèijǐng	n.	background
勉强	miǎnqiǎng	adv.	with difficultly; forcefully
实行	shíxíng	v.	to put into practice; to carry out
混乱	hùnluàn	adj./n.	messy; disorder
道路	dàolù	n.	path; road

Notes:

蒋介石　　　　Jiǎng Jièshí, or Chiang Kai-shek (1887-1975), was a Chinese political and military leader who served as the leader of the Republic of China between 1928 and 1975.

国民党　　　　Guómín dǎng; The Kuomintang of China was once the ruling political party of the Republic of China in Mainland China and later in Taiwan.

毛泽东　　　　Máo Zédōng (1893-1976), commonly referred to as Chairman Mao, was a Chinese communist revolutionary and the founding father of the People's Republic of China.

亚洲四小龙　　Yàzhōu sì xiǎolóng, or the Four Little Dragons of Asia, is a term used in reference to Hong Kong, Singapore, South Korea and Taiwan.

蒋经国　　　　Jiǎng Jīngguó (1910-1988), the eldest son of Chiang Kai-shek and his successor in Taiwan

I. 词语搭配 *Collocation*

1. 比例+高/低

   a high/low percentage

2. A 和 B 发生+战争

   A goes to war with B

3. A 把 place 割让给 B

   A cedes (part of its territory) to B

4. A 被 B 打败了

   A is defeated by B

5. A 战败了

   A lost the war/was defeated in a war.

6. Sb.根本没把……当回事

   Sb. does not take sth. seriously at all

7. A 对 B（很）不满

   A harbors a (deep) grievance against B/ A is dissatisfied with B.

8. ……的想法/估计/计划+不切实际

   The idea/estimate/plan of… is impractical

9. 享受+民主/自由/权利

   to enjoy democracy/freedom/rights

10. 扩张+势力

    to aggrandize one's power/influence (disapproving)

11. 适应+新情况/新环境/新生活

    to adapt to a new situation/new environment/new life

II. 句型结构 *Sentence Pattern and Structure*

1. 从……以来……就……

   Ever since…, …

In this structure, the adverb 就 stresses the earliness of the action described, "as early as."

我的父母是从台湾来的，从我懂事以来，他们就告诉我，我们是中国人，而台湾是中国的一部分。

从我上大学以来，就不靠家里了，我一直自己打工赚钱。

2. ……，既有…历史/政治/意识形态…（的）原因，也跟……有关系。

There is a historical/political/ideological…reason for…, but it also has something to do with… This structure is often used to introduce more reasons or contributing factors to a given fact.

据他说，台湾人在认同上离中国越来越远，既有历史原因，也跟大陆、台湾的政策有关系。

美国插手台湾问题，既有意识形态（ideological）的原因，也跟美国的国家利益有关系。

3. ……，从此，……　　　　from then on/ since then

Here *cǐ* 此 refers back to an aforementioned time point.

1895 年，中国和日本发生了甲午战争，中国被日本打败了。清朝政府除了赔款以外，还把台湾割让给了日本，从此，台湾开始了 50 年的殖民地历史。

18 岁那年，他离开了家，从此他就没有再回过家。

4. ……短短几年+之间/之内+就……

…within only a few years…

二战结束以后，中国发生了内战，蒋介石领导的国民党非常腐败，短短几年之间就让毛泽东领导的共产党打败了。

中国的高铁短短几年之内就发展起来了。现在中国的高铁是全世界最发达的。

5. 表面上，……，但实际上……

On the surface…, but in reality/in fact, …

This structure is often used to reveal true or hidden problems, feelings, etc.

1945 年之后，国民党在台湾表面上推行民主，但实际上是一党独裁。

一些美国人表面上很开放，但实际上他们在很多方面也很保守。

6. 有计划地 V.P.

in a planned way; according to plan

1976 年蒋介石死了，他的儿子蒋经国很快就成了台湾的领导人，他比他父亲开明，并有计划地从事经济和政治的改革。

为了解决交通问题，政府应该有计划地发展城市的交通建设。

7. …成绩/成就/发展/进步…是有目共睹的。

(lit.) …is obvious to anyone (who has eyes); this structure is often used to say that the achievement/accomplishment/development/progress of…is completely obvious or speaks for itself.

中国大陆在过去 30 年来，经济上改革开放的成绩是有目共睹的。

我们学生的进步是有目共睹的，他们从开始的一句话都说不好，到现在可以说出很长的一段话。他们的进步让我们很骄傲。

8. 就……来说，……

Based solely on…; speaking solely from the perspective of…

Note that this structure is often used to introduce, and contrast two related aspects of a given topic.

台湾是个小岛，南北长约 400 公里，人口只有两千多万，而大陆无论就面积还是就人口来说，都是台湾的几十倍，甚至几百倍。

吸引外国公司来投资开工厂，就经济发展来说，这是一件好事；但就环境保护来说，它带来的负面影响也是不可以忽视的。

9. 与其说…A…，不如说…B…。

This structure is often used to say that B is a better or more accurate way of saying sth. than A. It is often used to provide a new interpretation or explanation that is different from the conventional or commonly held beliefs.

我觉得，与其说美国人支持台湾独立是为了让台湾人享受民主自由，不如说中国统一对美国是不利的。

离婚问题与其说是一个道德问题，不如说是一个法律问题。

10. ……，更何况，……

"Moreover; besides;" it is often used to add another perspective (e.g. reason) to the aforementioned topic.

中国不统一，台湾是美国在太平洋上一艘 "不沉的航空母舰"，对美国在太平洋上势力的扩张和发展是非常有帮助的。要是两岸统一了，这艘航空母舰就是中国的了，更何况，台湾的价值哪里是一艘航空母舰可以相提并论的呢？

你不要去那个公司工作了，在那里你没有什么发展的机会，更何况，它给你的待遇也不好。

11. A 的价值/能力/贡献/地位+哪里是 B 可以相提并论的呢？

This structure is used as a rhetorical question to stress the superiority of A in terms of value, contribution, ability or importance. It literally means "how could B even be comparable to A (in terms of values/abilities/contributions/social status)?" Note that *nǎlǐ* 哪里 is used to form a rhetorical question.

台湾的价值哪里是一艘航空母舰可以相提并论的呢？

George Washington 总统被叫做美国的 "国父"，他的地位和贡献哪里是现在的美国总统可以相提并论的呢？

12. Object 由 subject+ (来) disyllabic verb（解决/处理/决定/安排…）

The object is solved/handled/decided/arranged (disyllabic verbs) by the subject.

Note that yóu 由 introduces the doer of the action and the object should be placed at the beginning of the sentence.

我觉得台湾问题是中国问题，而不是国际问题，台湾问题应该由中国人来解决。
家里的大事应该由夫妻双方共同来决定。

13. 没有……，却勉强要……，结果往往……

Without…, yet forcefully attempting…, the result is often that…

没有美国的历史背景，却勉强地要实行民主，结果往往造成社会的大混乱。

没有爱情，却勉强要生活在一起，结果往往是婚姻不幸福。

III. 词语辨析 *Synonym Differentiation*

1. 与其…A…不如…B…：It is better to do B than to do A (often used when making a suggestion)

与其说…A…, 不如说…B…：B is a better or more accurate way of saying sth. (often used in providing a new interpretation or explanation)

你与其天天在宿舍里写字，不如多出去跟中国人说话。

美国帮助台湾，与其说是因为他们同情台湾，不如说是为了他们自己的利益。

2. 插手：*v.o.* to meddle in; to get involved in (disapproving; an unwanted involvement in a specific thing)

干涉：*verb obj.* (the object is usually abstract nouns: 自由，生活，决定，etc.); to interfere (disapproving)

这是他们的事，请你不要插手，这样只会带来更多麻烦。

即使是父母，也不能干涉孩子的生活，干涉孩子的决定。

臺灣的政治與認同

（一）臺灣的歷史與現狀

最近系裏請了一位從臺灣來的教授給同學們做了一個演講，題目是《臺灣的政治與認同》。我對這個題目很感興趣。這位教授的英文不太流利，但是因為有英文翻譯，他的演講，我基本上都聽懂了。

我的父母是從臺灣來的，從我懂事以來，他們就告訴我，我們是中國人，而臺灣是中國的一部分。所以，我從小就認為：臺灣人就是中國人。可是這位臺灣教授在演講的時候卻說，臺灣人認為自己是中國人的比例越來越低了，尤其是 80、90 以後出生的臺灣人，百分之八十以上，覺得自己就是臺灣人，跟中國人完全沒有關係。這讓我覺得很驚訝。

據他說，臺灣人在認同上離中國越來越遠，既有歷史原因，也跟大陸、臺灣的政策有關係。1895 年，中國和日本發生了"甲午戰爭"，中國被日本打敗了。清朝政府除了賠款以外，還把臺灣割讓給了日本，從此，臺灣開始了 50 年的殖民地歷史。有些臺灣人對這段歷史的解釋是：清朝政府根本沒把臺灣當回事，打了敗仗，就把臺灣當一件禮物一樣送給日本。讓臺灣成了"亞洲的孤兒"。1945 年，二戰結束了，日本戰敗了，臺灣又還給了中國。

二戰結束以後，中國發生了內戰，蔣介石領導的國民黨非常腐敗，短短幾年(1945-1949)就被毛澤東領導的共產黨打敗了。1949 年，國民政府退到了臺灣。

看看這一百多年的歷史，臺灣從 1895 到 1945 年，是日本人的殖民地，1945 以後，臺灣又一直在國民黨的統治底下。臺灣人總覺得自己沒有管理過自己，而總是接受別人的管理。這種感覺是很不好的。對這段歷史有了一些瞭解以後，我對臺灣人的認同，多了一些同情。

1945 年之後，國民黨在臺灣表面上推行民主，但實際上是一黨獨裁。言論和新聞的自由是非常有限的。臺灣老百姓對這樣的政治制度越來越不滿，他們要求成立新的政黨。1975 年蔣介石死了，他的兒子蔣經國很快就成了臺灣的領導人，他比他父親開明，並有計劃地從事經濟和政治的改革，使臺灣在短短幾年之內成了"亞洲四小龍"之一。臺灣的經濟起飛帶來了政治上的改革。

（二）臺灣是中國問題，還是國際問題？

中國大陸在過去 30 年來，經濟上改革開放的成績是有目共睹的。中國從一個貧窮落後的農業國家，成了世界第二大經濟體，僅次於美國。有些人以為，臺灣的發展模式也可以應用在中國大陸。我想這樣的估計有些不切實際，也不瞭解兩岸的實際情況。臺灣是個小島，南北長約 400 公里，人口只有兩千多萬，而大陸無論就面積還是就人口來說，都是臺灣的幾十倍，甚至幾百倍。在臺灣能做的事，在大陸不一定能做。

這位臺灣教授說："美國人基本上是同情臺灣，而不支持中國統一的。"這個說法，當然有它的道理，但是我覺得，與其說美國人支持臺灣獨立是為了讓臺灣人享受民主自由，不如說中國統一對美國是不利的。中國不統一，臺灣是美國在太平洋上一艘"不沉的航空母艦"，對美國在太平洋上勢力的擴張和發展是非常有幫助的。要是兩岸統一了，這艘航空母艦就是中國的了，更何況，臺灣的價值哪裏是一艘航空母艦可以相提並論的呢？對美國來說，臺灣在軍事上的價值，比夏威夷更重要。

這位臺灣教授還說："臺灣問題實在很複雜，對中國大陸來說，這是一個國家主權的問題，但對臺灣來說，卻是個獨立自主的問題，臺灣人應該有權利決定自己的生活方式和政治結構。"

聽了演講以後，我覺得臺灣問題是個中國問題，而不是國際問題，臺灣問題應該由中國人來解決，美國人不應該插手。美國政府常常覺得自己是國際警察，世界上任何地區發生了衝突，美國都得出兵干涉。我想，美國人得慢慢地適應：中國已經不是 19 世紀的中國，而是一個強大的現代國家。至於美國式的民主也不一定適合每一個國家，沒有美國的歷史背景，卻勉強地要實行民主，結果往往造成社會的大混亂。我想每個國家都得選擇他們自己的生活方式，走自己的道路。

课后习题
第 27 课

一、词语搭配 (Please pair the term in the left column with the most appropriate term in the right column. Then use the completed phrases to complete the sentences. You can change the order of the words and add more information if needed.)

（1）

(　　) 发生　　　A 民主自由
(　　) 享受　　　B 战争
(　　) 扩张　　　C 环境
(　　) 适应　　　D 势力

1. 1895 年中国和日本_____，结果中国被打败了，割让了台湾。

2. 有人认为,美国支持台湾独立是为了让台湾人民_____，也有人认为这只是为了美国的国家利益。台湾对美国有很大的军事价值，有了台湾，美国就可以在亚洲和太平洋上_____。

3. 到了一个新地方,刚开始可能不太习惯,需要慢慢_____。

二、选择填空 (Complete the sentences by choosing the most appropriate term.)

1. 插手　　　干涉

有人认为,台湾问题是中国问题,应由中国大陆和台湾来解决,美国不应该_____。如果美国出兵_____中国的内政，就等于侵犯了中国的主权。

和谁结婚是孩子的自由，父母不应该_____孩子的决定。同样，结婚以后如果夫妻有了矛盾，应该让他们自己解决。父母也不应该_____。

三、完成句子 (Complete the sentence or dialogue with the given item in parentheses.)

1. 民主在美国很有基础，因为_____（从...以来...就...），而中国的情况有些不同，_____（从...以来...就...），所以，有人认为美式民主不适合中国。

2. 读了这篇文章，我觉得台湾问题的产生，_____。
（既有...的原因，也跟...有关系）

3. A：为什么中国和日本常常会有矛盾呢？

   B：_____。（既有...的原因，也跟...有关系）

4. A：台湾是怎么变成殖民地的？

   B：_____。(..., 从此...)

5. A：美国是怎么变成一个独立的国家的？

   B：_____。(..., 从此...)

6. 中国的高铁发展得真快，_____。(...短短几年+之间/之内+就...)

7. 有些国家不喜欢美国这个"国际警察"，他们认为美国_____。
（表面上，...，但实际上...）

8. 要想解决环境问题，政府应该_____。（有计划地 V.P.）

9. 过去三十年，中国_____。（有目共睹）

10. A：你觉得中国算不算是一个发达国家？

    B：_____。（就......来说）

11. A：你怎么看美国在台湾问题上的态度？

    B：_____。（与其说...，不如说...）

12. A：现在离婚的人这么多，社会的道德水平真是越来越低了！

    B：_____。（与其说...，不如说...）

13. A：你觉得美国应不应该继续扮演"世界警察"的角色？

    B：_____。(..., 更何况,...)

14. A：你为什么决定要学中文？

    B：_____。(..., 更何况,...)

15. A：你觉得中国算不算一个世界强国？

    B：_____。（相提并论）

16. A: 你觉得谁应该来解决台湾问题？为什么？

B: _____。（由… (来) Verb）

17. A: 我觉得夫妻即使感情不好，为了孩子，也应该维持婚姻。你觉得呢？

B: 我不这样看，_____。（没有…，却勉强要…，结果往往…）

18. 每个人都应该了解自己有多少能力，_____。

（没有…，却勉强要…，结果往往…）

四、回答问题　(Answer the questions.)

1. 台湾是一个独立的国家还是中国的一部分，对这个问题，有哪些不同的看法？

2. 所谓的"台湾问题"是怎么形成的？有哪些历史和政治的原因？

3. 国民党政府退到台湾以后，对台湾产生了什么影响？

4. 台湾为什么可以成为"亚洲四小龙"之一？台湾在政治和经济上的成功经验可不可以应用在中国大陆？

5. 作者认为，台湾比大陆小得多，所以在台湾能做成的事，在大陆不一定能实现。你同意不同意这样的看法？

6. 美国政府希望不希望两岸统一，为什么？

7. 如果台湾现在要独立，你觉得美国政府会不会支持台湾？为什么？

8. 你认为"台湾问题"是中国问题，还是国际问题？应该由谁来解决？

9. 为什么人们把美国叫做"国际警察"？美国应不应该继续当"国际警察"？

10. 每个国家都应该追求民主政治吗？请举例说明你的看法。

第 28 课

剩女、二奶、小鲜肉

在过去 100 多年，中国现代化的过程中，妇女解放 的成绩是有目共睹的。100 年前，还有不少中国妇女 是缠脚 的，女子学堂 的成立，自由恋爱的兴起和女子走出家庭去工作都是 20 世纪才有的新现象。但看看现在中国的妇女，各行各业都有女人参加工作，几乎已经没有只有男人能做的工作了。从国家领导人 到公交车的司机，从跨国大公司的总经理 到服务员都有男有女。我读的大学，校党委书记 就是女的，党委书记是

剩女	shèngnǚ	n.	leftover woman (mainland internet slang for a woman who is successful career-wise, but remains unsuccessful romantically)
二奶	èrnǎi	n.	mainland internet slang for mistress
小鲜肉	xiǎo xiānròu	n.	(lit.) little fresh meat (mainland internet slang for young, good-looking males; boy toys)
解放	jiěfàng	v.	to liberate
妇女	fùnǚ	n.	women in general
缠脚	chánjiǎo	v.	(of girls) to bind one's feet; boot-binding
学堂	xuétáng	n.	(an old term for) school; college
领导人	lǐngdǎo rén	n.	leader
跨国	kuàguó	adj.	transnational (company)
总经理	zǒng jīnglǐ	n.	general manager; CEO
校党委书记	xiào dǎngwěi shūjì		Secretary of the Party Committee of a school

每个中国单位里，地位最高，权力最大的一个人。这100年来，妇女所争取到的权利和平等，是中国女人最值得骄傲的地方。

（一）剩女

虽然妇女解放有这么好的成绩，但让我不能理解的是：一个在学习和工作上已经彻底解放的中国女人，在面对婚姻的时候却表现得很不自信，一个过了30岁还没有结婚的女人，在中国所受到的家庭和社会压力远比在美国要大得多。最能体现这种压力的是"剩女"这个词，"剩"是"剩下"，"剩女"也就是"剩下来没人要的女人"。这对年过30而未婚的女人是极大的侮辱，然而这个词却在中国广泛流行，并为女人所接受。我想，这样的一个不尊重女性并带着强烈贬义的词，在美国是不可能被人们接受的，在中国却经常出现在报纸和电视上。

单位	dānwèi	n.	work unit (place of employment, esp. in the PRC prior to 1978).
争取	zhēngqǔ	v.	to fight for; strive for
地方	dìfang	n.	part; aspect; place
彻底	chèdǐ	adv.	down to the bottom; thoroughly
体现	tǐxiàn	v.	to embody
未婚	wèihūn	adj.	unmarried
极大	jídà	adv.	extremely big
侮辱	wǔrǔ	v.	to insult
然而	ránér	conj.	however
广泛	guǎngfàn	adj./adv.	widespread

　　在家庭和社会极大的压力下，中国女人几乎没有不结婚的自由，绝大多数过了适婚年龄而仍是单身的女人，都不是自己的选择，而是不得已的结果。社会对剩女的态度是同情而又带着些鄙视的，在父母看来，家里有个剩女，简直是一件丢脸和不体面的事，会想方设法把剩女嫁出去，最常见的就是安排"相亲"，也就是为了结婚而介绍男/女朋友。这在一个美国人看来，是一件非常尴尬的事。

　　然而，从另一个角度来看，剩女往往是高学历、高收入的群体。正因为她们学历高，收入高，她们在经济上不需要依靠男人，所以在婚姻

适婚年龄	shìhūn niánlíng	N.P.	proper age for marriage
仍	réng	adv.	still
单身	dānshēn	adj.	single
鄙视	bǐshì	v.	to despise; to look down upon
丢脸	diūliǎn	v.o.	to lose face
不体面	bùtǐmiàn	adj.	shameful
嫁	jià	v.	(of a woman) to marry (a man)
相亲	xiāngqīn	v.	to size up a prospective mate in an arranged meeting
尴尬	gān'gà	adj.	embarrassing, awkward
群体	qúntǐ	n.	social group
经济	jīngjì	n.	financial status/position (在~上，~独立); economy
依靠	yīkào	v.	to depend on

上，就不愿意轻易妥协。除非能找到年龄、学识、收入都理想的男人，要不然，她们宁可单身。

（二）二奶

"二奶"指的是自愿当已婚男人的情人的女人。当然，这个现象每个国家都有，但在中国却特别普遍，尤其是有钱有地位的男人，有个二奶是很平常的事。中国虽然实行一夫一妻制，但实际上，许多已婚男人都在妻子之外，还有二奶，这也是半公开的事实。二奶的泛滥似乎又说明中国还有许多女人需要依靠男人来生活。

从剩女和二奶的现象来看，中国妇女解放也还有可以努力的空间。婚姻不应该是每个女人唯一的归宿，工作和事业至少和结婚生子有相

妥协	tuǒxié	v.	to compromise
学识	xuéshí	n.	learning
自愿	zìyuàn	adv.	voluntarily
已婚	yǐhūn	adj.	married
情人	qíngrén	n.	lover; mistress
一夫一妻制	yì fū yì qī	n.	monogamy
半公开	bàn gōngkāi	adj.	semi-public; more or less open
事实	shìshí	n.	fact
似乎	sìhū	adv.	as if; seemingly
唯一	wéiyī	adj.	the only; sole
归宿	guīsù	n.	a lasting or permanent place/stage in life; (of girls) to be happily married
事业	shìyè	n.	career

同的意义和价值。等到中国女人有了不结婚和不生孩子的自由，中国的妇女解放才算是上了新的台阶。

（三）小鲜肉与颜值

"小鲜肉"是过去两三年才流行起来的一个新词。刚开始的时候，指的是年轻帅气而又缺乏社会经验的男歌星或男演员，往往是中/老年女子喜欢追捧的对象，并带着强烈的性暗示，因此，有着一定的贬义。和"小鲜肉"类似的另一个词是"小白脸"，指的都是能取悦女人的男人。"小鲜肉"的出现，从女权意识的发展角度来看，说明女人也可以把男人当成一种玩物，甚至是一种消费的对象。

台阶	táijiē	n.	steps; (of career) level, stage
颜值	yánzhí	n.	(mainland Internet slang) attractiveness index (rating of how good-looking sb. is)
指	zhǐ	v.	refer to
帅气	shuàiqì	adj.	(of young men) handsome; good-looking
歌星	gēxīng	n.	singer
演员	yǎnyuán	n.	actor
追捧	zhuīpěng	v.	to chase after (a celebrity)
性暗示	xìng ànshì	n.	sexual overture
类似	lèisì	adj.	similar
小白脸	xiǎo báiliǎn	n.	young fair face—handsome, effeminate young man
取悦	qǔyuè	v.	to please (sb.)
女权	nǚquán	adj.	feminism
玩物	wánwù	n.	plaything; doll

与小鲜肉同时流行起来的另一个词是"颜值"，"颜"是容貌，"值"是数值，说白了，"颜值"就是长相的好坏，长得漂亮叫颜值高，不漂亮就是颜值低。以前对一个人容貌的判断，往往是主观的，而颜值这个词，却让主观的审美，变成了可以量化的客观的数值。一个人长相的美丑，似乎也可以精确测量，互相比较，甚至也可以进行市场交易，与商品没有什么不同。

有人说，颜值这个词的出现，说明中国社会有越来越重视一个人外表的趋势。小鲜肉无非就是又年轻又漂亮的男人，至于这样的人到底有没有学识，有没有能力，好像并不很重要，只要他年轻帅气，就有成千

容貌	róngmào	n.	facial appearance and expression
数值	shùzhí	n.	number
长相	zhǎngxiàng	n.	looks
判断	pànduàn	v.	to judge
主观	zhǔguān	adj.	subjective
审美	shěnměi	n.	aesthetics
量化	liànghuà	v.	to quantify
客观	kèguān	adj.	objective
美丑	měichǒu	n.	beauty and ugliness
精确	jīngquè	adj.	precise
测量	cèliáng	v.	to measure
外表	wàibiǎo	n.	external appearance
趋势	qūshì	n.	trend; tendency

上万的粉丝。正是在这样的压力底下，很多人都去做美容或整形的手术。整个社会除了追逐声色名利，还弥漫着一股虚浮的气息。其实，我倒并不担心这样的潮流，因为这种追逐声色名利的风气是每个时代，每个社会都有的，只是在不同的时代，有不同的方式罢了。在网络时代，任何时髦的潮流，起来得快，消失得更快，是用不着特别担心的。

剩女、二奶、小鲜肉、颜值这些新词的出现充分反映了中国社会多样并存，并在许多价值和观念上正在快速地改变。

粉丝	fěnsī	n.	fans
美容	měiróng	n./v.	beauty treatment; to improve one's looks
整形手术	zhěngxíng shǒushù	n.	plastic surgery
追逐	zhuīzhú	v.	to blindly pursue
声色名利	shēngsè mínglì	n.	sensual pleasures, fame and wealth
弥漫	mímàn	v.	(of feeling, smell) to pervade
股	gǔ	m.w.	measure word for strength, smell
虚浮	xūfú	adj.	superficial; ostentatious
气息	qìxī	n.	smell; breath; flavor
潮流	cháoliú	n.	trend; tide
风气	fēngqì	n.	ethos; the general mood (of a society, etc.)
用不着	yòng bu zháo	v.c.	there is no need for…
充分	chōngfèn	adv.	fully
多样并存	duōyàng bìngcún	idm.	many styles and kinds coexist; to have great diversity

I. 词语搭配 *Collocation*

1. 为 sb.争取+权利 / 平等 / 机会 / 时间

   to fight for rights/equality/opportunities for sb.; to race against time

2. A 是 B 最值得骄傲的地方

   A is something to be proud of (for B).

3. 年过+三十 / 四十 / 半百

   Sb. is already over thirty/forty/fifty (years old)

4. 广泛+流行 / 传播; 广泛（的）影响

   widespread; wide-ranging influence

5. 带着+（强烈的）贬义

   with (a strong) derogatory sense/connotation

6. 女人+嫁给+男人 / 父母+把+女儿+嫁出去

   a woman marries a man

7. A 向 B 妥协

   A compromises with B (A submits to B)

8. 半公开的+事实 / 关系 / 秘密

   Semi-public, semi-open facts/relations/secrets

9. ……还有可以努力 / 进步的空间

   There is still room for improvement

10. …事业…上了新的台阶

    (of one's career) comes to a new phase/level

11. 追捧+明星

    to chase after +a celebrity

12. 充分+说明/反映/体现/证明

    fully demonstrate/reflect/show (a full show of)/prove

II. 句型结构 *Sentence Pattern and Structure*

1. 所+V

This structure is often used to modify a noun, meaning "...that which..." 所 is marker of nominalization.

这 100 年来，妇女所争取到的权利和平等，是中国女人最值得骄傲的地方。

他所做的贡献不是普通人可以相提并论的。

2. A 远比 B（要）adj. 得多

A is far more...than B

一个过了 30 岁还没有结婚的（中国）女人，在中国所受到的家庭和社会压力远比在美国要大得多。

高铁的速度远比一般火车快得多。

3. ……为/被+…社会/大家/人们…所+接受/批评

Sth. is accepted/criticized by the society/people.

这对年过 30 而未婚的女人是极大的侮辱，然而这个词却在中国广泛流行，并为女人所接受。

中国的环境污染问题过去常常为世界各国所批评。

4. ……，然而，……

However, …

"剩女"这个词儿对年过 30 而未婚的女人是极大的侮辱，然而却在中国广泛流行，并为女人所接受。

小鲜肉受到很多人的追捧，然而，他们的能力却也常常受到质疑。

5. ……，但是 / 然而，从另一个角度来看，……

However, (looking) from another perspective, …..

绝大多数过了适婚年龄而仍是单身的女人，都不是自己的选择，而是不得已的结果。……，然而，从另一个角度来看，剩女往往是高学历，高收入的群体。正因为她们学历高，收入高，她们在经济上不需要依靠男人，所以在婚姻上，就不愿意轻易妥协。

中国父母常常强迫孩子学习，好像对孩子并不好。但是，从另一个角度看，孩子小的时候不知道什么是应该做的，父母的"强迫"可能对孩子的发展有一定的好处。

6. 等到…(condition)…的时候，…才（可以说/才算是）…(realization of a goal/dream)…

Only when……can subj. truly say/finally say that…

In this structure, *děngdào* 等到 introduces the time when sth. happens or the condition needed for it to happen.

等到中国女人有了不结婚和不生孩子的自由，中国的妇女解放才算是上了新的台阶。

等到上海人不说上海话，广东人不说广东话了，普通话的普及才算是真的成功了。

7. ……，说白了，……

To put it in plain language, ……

与小鲜肉同时流行起来的另一个词是"颜值"，"颜"是容貌，值是数值，说白了，"颜值"就是长相的好坏，长得漂亮叫颜值高，不漂亮就是颜值低。

他总是喜欢在新闻上批评别人，说白了，这只是他吸引别人注意的手段，并不一定是他真正的看法。

8. ……无非就是……

……is nothing but…; no more than…

小鲜肉无非就是又嫩又漂亮的男人，至于这样的人到底有没有学识，有没有能力，好像并不很重要。

这个中文培训班的要求虽然很严，但是并不多，无非就是多说多练，不说英文。

9. ……，只是……罢了

often used at the end of a declarative sentence, meaning, "it's only that…and that's all, nothing else."

其实，我倒并不担心这样的潮流，因为这种追逐声色名利的风气是每个时代，每个社会都有的，只是在不同的时代，有不同的方式罢了。

不要只批评别人，我们每个人都有缺点，只是有时候自己看不见罢了。

10. 用不着+V.P.

There is no need to; it is not worthwhile to…

在网络时代，任何时髦的潮流，起来得快，消失得更快，是用不着特别担心的。

想吃北京烤鸭，在中国城就可以吃到，用不着专门跑去北京吃。

III. 词语辨析 *Synonym Differentiation*

1. 用不着：用不着+V.P.

there is no need to; it is not worthwhile to…

用不了：用不了+N.P.

do not need all… (when you have more than is needed)

在美国，找工作用不着给领导送礼。

我平常都是自己在家做饭，用不了什么钱。

剩女、二奶、小鮮肉

在過去 100 多年，中國現代化的過程中，婦女解放的成績是有目共睹的。100 年前，還有不少中國婦女是纏腳的，女子學堂的成立，自由戀愛的興起，和女子走出家庭去工作都是 20 世紀才有的新現象。但看看現在中國的婦女，各行各業都有女人參加工作，幾乎已經沒有只有男人能做的工作了。從國家領導人到公交車的司機，從跨國大公司的總經理到服務員都有男有女。我讀的大學，校黨委書記就是女的，黨委書記是每個中國單位裏，地位最高，權力最大的一個人。這 100 年來，婦女所爭取到的權利和平等，是中國女人最值得驕傲的地方。

（一）剩女

雖然婦女解放有這麼好的成績，但讓我不能理解的是：一個在學習和工作上已經徹底解放的中國女人，在面對婚姻的時候卻表現得很不自信，一個過了 30 歲還沒有結婚的女人，在中國所受到的家庭和社會壓力遠比在美國要大得多。最能體現這種壓力的是"剩女"這個詞，"剩"是"剩下"，"剩女"也就是"剩下來沒人要的女人"。這對年過 30 而未婚的女人是極大的侮辱，然而這個詞卻在中國廣泛流行，並為女人所接受。我想，這樣的一個不尊重女性並帶著強烈貶義的詞，在美國是不可能被人們接受的，在中國卻經常出現在報紙和電視上。

在家庭和社會極大的壓力下，中國女人幾乎沒有不結婚的自由，絕大多數過了適婚年齡而仍是單身的女人，都不是自己的選擇，而是不得已的結果。社會對剩女的態度是同情而又帶著些鄙視的，在父母看來，家裏有個剩女，簡直是一件丟臉和不體面的事，會想方設法把剩女嫁出去，最常見的就是安排"相親"，也就是為了結婚而介紹男/女朋友。這在一個美國人看來，是一件非常尷尬的事。

然而，從另一個角度來看，剩女往往是高學歷，高收入的群體。正因為她們學歷高，收入高，她們在經濟上不需要依靠男人，所以在婚姻上，就不願意輕易妥協。除非能找到年齡、學識、收入都理想的男人，要不然，她們寧可單身。

（二）二奶

"二奶"指的是自願當已婚男人的情人的女人。當然，這個現象每個國家都有，但在中國卻特別普遍，尤其是有錢有地位的男人，有個二奶是很平常的事。中國雖然實行一夫一妻制，但實際上，許多已婚男人都在妻子之外，還有二奶，這也是半公開的事實。二奶的泛濫似乎又說明中國還有許多女人需要依靠男人來生活。

從剩女和二奶的現象來看，中國婦女解放也還有可以努力的空間。婚姻不應該是每個女人唯一的歸宿，工作和事業至少和結婚生子有相同的意義和價值。等到中國女人有了不結婚和不生孩子的自由，中國的婦女解放才算是上了新的臺階。

（三）小鮮肉與顏值

"小鮮肉"是過去兩三年才流行起來的一個新詞。剛開始的時候，指的是年輕帥氣而又缺乏社會經驗的男歌星或男演員，往往是中/老年女子喜歡追捧的對象，並帶著強烈的性暗示，因此，有著一定的貶義。和"小鮮肉"類似的另一個詞是"小白臉"，指的都是能取悅女人的男人。小鮮肉的出現，從女權意識的發展角度來看，說明女人也可以把男人當成一種玩物，甚至是一種消費的對象。

與小鮮肉同時流行起來的另一個詞是"顏值"，"顏"是容貌，"值"是數值，說白了，"顏值"就是長相的好壞，長得漂亮叫顏值高，不漂亮就是顏值低。以前對一個人容貌的判斷，往往是主觀的，而顏值這個詞，卻讓主觀的審美，變成了可以量化的客觀的數值。一個人長相的美醜，似乎也可以精確測量，互相比較，甚至也可以進行市場交易，與商品沒有什麼不同。

有人說，顏值這個詞的出現，說明中國社會有越來越重視一個人外表的趨勢。小鮮肉無非就是又年輕又漂亮的男人，至於這樣的人到底有沒有學識，有沒有能力，好像並不很重要，只要他年輕帥氣，就有成千上萬的粉絲。正是在這樣的壓力底下，很多人都去做美容或整形的手術。整個社會除了追逐聲色名利，還彌漫著一股虛浮的氣息。其實，我倒並不擔心這樣的潮流，因為這種追逐聲色名利的風氣是每個時代，每個社會都有的，只是在不同的時代，有不同的方式罷了。在網絡時代，任何時髦的潮流，起來得快，消失得更快，是用不著特別擔心的。

剩女、二奶、小鮮肉、顏值這些新詞的出現充分反映了中國社會多樣並存，並在許多價值和觀念上正在快速地改變。

课后习题
第 28 课

一、词语搭配 (Please pair the term in the left column with the most appropriate term in the right column. Then use the completed phrases to complete the sentences. You can change the order of words and add more information if needed.)

（1）

（　）争取	A 说明
（　）值得	B 流传
（　）广泛	C 骄傲
（　）充分	D 权利

1. 100 年来中国女性不断＿＿＿＿＿，从恋爱自由到经济权、政治权，成绩有目共睹。

2. 其中最＿＿＿＿＿＿＿＿的是女性渐渐有了和男性一样的教育和工作机会。

3. 1949 年后，"妇女能顶半边天"(Women hold up half the sky)这个说法，＿＿＿＿＿。

4. 这个说法＿＿＿＿＿＿＿＿＿＿＿＿＿女性在中国的地位有了显著的提高。

（2）

（　）半公开的	A 台阶
（　）努力的	B 事实
（　）年过	C 空间
（　）上	D 半百

1. 美国法律规定 21 岁以下不可以喝酒，但是大学生喝酒在有的学校是＿＿＿＿＿＿＿＿＿＿＿＿＿。

2. 近几年，各行各业出现了不少女性领导人，这说明妇女解放又＿＿＿＿＿＿。

3. 但在有些方面，女性还受到歧视，在这些方面还有＿＿＿＿＿＿＿＿。

4. 这对夫妻_____才生了第一个孩子，所以他们对孩子非常溺爱。

二、选择填空 (Complete the sentences by choosing the most appropriate term.)

1. 用不着　　　用不了

   在美国，过了三十岁还没结婚，也_____担心。没有人会看不起你。

   这只是一个普通手术，_____多少钱。

三、完成句子 (Complete the sentence or dialogue with the given item in parentheses.)

1. 女性为家庭、社会_____是巨大的。(所+V)

2. 我以前觉得_____，后来才发现

   _____。（A 远比 B（要）adj. 得多）

3. 以前，离过婚的女人是_____的(为...所...)，

   现在人们越来越开放，离婚，单身都渐渐_____(为...所...)。

4. "剩女" 这个词儿对年过 30 而未婚的女人是极大的侮辱，

   _____。（然而）

5. 今天，女性在经济和政治上已经争取到了一定的权利，_____。(然而)

6. 离婚人数的增加似乎说明_____,然而，_____（从另一个角度来看）。

7. 高考制度造成了很多问题,不过,_____（从另一个角度来看）。

8. 我觉得"小鲜肉"既没有能力也没有学问，_____(无非就是...)，

   不值得追捧。

9. 其实,要学好一门外语并不难,_____（无非就是...）。

10. A：他这个人真是一无是处！

    B：其实，_____（只是...罢了）。

11. A：中国有很多 "拉关系，走后门" 的事情，而美国就公平多了！

    B：其实，_____（只是...罢了）。

12. A：我真担心网络上的新潮流会破坏文化传统。

　　B：＿＿＿＿＿＿＿＿＿＿（用不着），因为＿＿＿＿＿＿＿＿＿＿＿＿＿＿＿＿＿＿＿＿＿＿＿＿。

13. A："颜值"到底是什么意思？

　　B：＿＿＿＿＿＿＿＿＿＿＿＿＿＿＿＿＿＿＿＿＿＿＿＿＿＿＿＿。（…，说白了…）

14. A：你觉得美国实现了男女平等吗？

　　B：还没有，＿＿＿＿＿＿＿＿＿（等到…的时候），我们才可以说男女完全平等了。

15. A：你觉得你现在独立了吗？

　　B：还没有，＿＿＿＿＿＿＿＿＿＿＿＿＿＿（等到…的时候），才算是真正独立了。

四、回答问题（Answer the questions.）

1. 过去一百年来，中国女性的地位是提高了，还是下降了？

2. 美国的妇女解放运动是什么时候开始的？女性争取到了哪些权利？你觉得哪个权利是最重要的？

3. 什么是"剩女"？中国社会对"剩女"的态度是什么？"剩女"不结婚，是嫁不出去还是自己的选择？

4. "二奶"现象说明了什么问题？美国有没有类似的现象？

5. 有人说，"婚姻是女人最好的归宿"，你同意这个说法吗？

6. "小鲜肉"指的是什么？为什么作者认为"小鲜肉"这个词的出现反映了女性地位的提高？你同意这个说法吗？

7. 什么是"女权主义"？怎么才能彻底实现"妇女解放"、"男女平等"？

8. 我们的社会好像越来越重视外表，这是不是一个好趋势？你担心不担心这个问题？

417

第 29 课

北京大学与现代中国

　　北京大学成立于1898年，和欧洲、美国的大学比起来，历史很短。但是北京大学在中国近代史上的地位却不是任何欧美大学可以相提并论的。在中国现代化的进程中，北京大学代表了中国知识分子追求民主科学的里程碑，是19世纪末期到20世纪中期，中国思想自由和学术独立的象征。学者们把这个象征叫做"北大精神"。

　　中国近代史上的几件大事和北京大学是分不开的。1917年的白话文运动让中国人的书面语言渐渐地由古代汉语转化到了现代汉语；1919年的五四运动和新文化运动开始大量介绍西方文化到中国来；1921年中国共产党的成立更是改变了中国往后历史的发展。北京大学的老师和

于	yú	prep.	(indicating time, place) in; on; at
进程	jìnchéng	n.	course; process
里程碑	lǐchéng bēi	n.	milestone (usu. in the course of historical development)
精神	jīngshén	n.	spirit
白话文运动	Báihuàwén Yùndòng	n.	The Vernacular Movement (1917-1919)
书面语言	shūmiàn yǔyán	n.	written language
转化	zhuǎnhuà	v.	to change; to transform
大量	dàliàng	adv.	in great quantities; in volume
往后	wǎnghòu	n.	later on; henceforth

学生不但参与而且领导了这些运动。北京大学是中国现代化运动的发源地。

北京大学原来的校园在离王府井不远的沙滩，主要的建筑只是一栋面积并不很大的红楼。毛泽东还在红楼里当过图书馆员。我每次经过红楼，总忍不住想起这栋小小的建筑竟是近代中国新思想产生的摇篮啊！从北京大学早期的历史来看，最能看出知识分子对社会发展的影响。

1949 年，中国"解放"了，但是中国人却失去了思想自由和学术独立。至少有 30 年，人人都得学习马克思列宁主义和毛泽东思想。20 世纪初期以来，北大精神的优良传统，在 1949 年之后受到了最彻底的摧毁。五四运动前后，北大是中国改革的原动力，1949 年以后，北大成了被改

发源地	fāyuán dì	n.	(of a river, historical event) place of origin; source
栋	dòng	m.w.	measure word for buildings
面积	miànjī	n.	area (of a floor, piece of land, etc.)
图书馆员	túshūguǎn yuán	n.	librarian
经过	jīngguò	v.	to go through; to experience
摇篮	yáolán	n.	cradle; (fig.) place of origin
摧毁	cuīhuǐ	v.	to destroy; to smash into pieces; to wreck (buildings, enemy forces, etc.)
原动力	yuán dònglì	n.	motive power; prime mover; first cause

革的对象，北大的许多教授和学者都在文化大革命期间受到迫害，这是中国学术界重大的损失！

　　现在北京大学的校园其实是当年的燕京大学，燕京大学的创办人是美国的传教士司徒雷登(John Leighton Stuart, 1876-1962)。他在中国生活了 50 年，也是 1949 年中美断绝外交关系之前，美国最后一任的驻华大使。他对近代中国的教育事业做出过重大的贡献。可惜，1949 年之后，中国经历了一段长时期全面的反美，使司徒雷登这样一位对中国教育

迫害	pòhài	v.	to persecute
重大	zhòngdà	adj.	major, significant (discoveries, contributions, loss, etc.)
损失	sǔnshī	n.	loss
当年	dāngnián	n.	those years/days; back then
燕京大学	Yānjīng Dàxué	n.	Yenching University (1919-1952)
创办人	chuàngbàn rén	n.	founder
传教士	chuánjiào shì	n.	missionary
断绝	duànjué	v.	to sever; to break off
任	rèn	m.w.	measure word for the number of terms served on an official post
驻华大使	zhūhuá dàshǐ	n.	ambassador to China
经历	jīnglì	n.	experience
段	duàn	m.w.	measure word for (time, experience, relation, passage, paragraph)
长时期	cháng shíqī	adj./adv.	(over) a long period of time

现代化有过重要贡献的人物，竟成了中国人民的敌人。这种盲目的排外和仇外 对中国社会发展所带来的伤害，并不亚于盲目的崇洋媚外。

　　就思想和学术的发展来说，五四运动前后是现代中国的黄金时代，在这段时期，自由主义、社会主义、共产主义、无政府主义 都能在中国发表他们的意见，进行辩论。中国的人文科学 和自然科学 的发展在这 30 年中都有巨大的飞跃。我们很希望北大思想自由，学术独立的优良传统，能很快地在改革开放的中国重新建立起来。一旦失去了思想自由和学术独立的保障，大学就成了一个训练官僚 和技师 的场所，这不但会让大学破产，也会让国家社会的发展停滞 下来。

排外	páiwài	v.-o.	to exclude or resist anything foreign; exclusionary; anti-foreign
仇外	chóuwài	v.-o	to feel animosity towards anything foreign; xenophobia
不亚于	bú yàyú	v.	to not be inferior to
黄金时代	huángjīn shídài	n.	golden age
无政府主义	wúzhèngfǔ zhǔyì	n.	anarchism
辩论	biànlùn	n.	debate
人文科学	rénwén kēxué	n.	humanities
自然科学	zìrán kēxué	n.	science
飞跃	fēiyuè	n./v.	leap; rapid progress
官僚	guānliáo	n.	bureaucrat
技师	jìshī	n.	technician; technical expert
场所	chǎngsuǒ	n.	place (of meeting or assembly)
破产	pòchǎn	v.	(of a plan) to fail; to go bankrupt
停滞	tíngzhì	v.	to stagnate; to come to a standstill

I. 词语搭配 *Collocation*

1. 现代化/西方化/历史+进程

   the course or progress of modernization/westernization/history

2. 彻底+摧毁/解决/破坏

   completely destroy/solve/damage

3. 重大的+贡献/决定/缺陷/损失

   major/significant + contribution/decision/deficiency/loss

4. 断绝+外交/父子/师生/朋友/…+关系

   to sever diplomatic relations; to break off father-son/teacher-student/friend relations

5. 盲目+排外/仇外/崇拜/追求/相信

   blind opposition/animosity towards everything foreign;

   blindly worship/purse/believe

6. 实现/有+巨大的飞跃

   to realize/have great leaps; to grow by leaps and bounds

7. 发展+停滞

   (Economic) development/growth stagnates.

II. 句型结构 *Sentence Pattern and Structure*

1. 和 A 比起来，B……，但 B 的……却不是 A 可以相提并论的。

   Comparing with A, B is… (not as good) …, yet in terms of……A cannot be mentioned in the same breath with B.

   北京大学成立于 1898 年，和欧洲、美国的大学比起来，历史很短。但是北京大学在中国近代史上的地位却不是任何欧美大学可以相提并论的。

2. …time/event…以来　　　　Since…

20 世纪初期以来，北大精神的优良传统，在 1949 年之后受到了最彻底的摧毁。

改革开放以来，中国社会的各个方面都有了巨大的进步。

3. A 的 abstract noun (重要性/价值/影响) 并不亚于 B

   Contrary to what people might think, A is not inferior to B

   这种盲目的排外和仇外对中国社会发展所带来的伤害，并不亚于盲目的崇洋媚外。

   言论自由的重要性并不亚于人身自由。

4. 停滞/停/慢+下来　　come to a standstill/stop; slow down

   下来, as a verb complement, indicates motioning towards a lower or nearer position.

   一旦失去了思想自由和学术独立的保障，大学就成了一个训练官僚和技师的场所，这不但会让大学破产，也会让国家社会的发展停滞下来。

   他的车已经开始慢了下来，我想，用不了多久，就会停下来的。

III. 词语辨析 *Synonym Differentiation*

1. 经历：to go through (v.); experience (n., countable noun); the conscious events that make up an individual life.

   经验：experience (uncountable noun), practical knowledge, skill derived from direct observation of, or participation in events or a particular activity.

   1949 年之后，中国经历了一段长时期的排外与仇外。

   两年前，我去过一次英国，我永远也忘不了那次经历。

   他当了十年的老师，非常有经验。

北京大學與現代中國

　　北京大學成立在 1898 年。和歐洲、美國的大學比起來，歷史很短。但是北京大學在中國近代史上的地位卻不是任何歐美大學可以相提並論的。在中國現代化的進程中，北京大學代表了中國知識分子追求民主科學的里程碑，是 19 世紀末期到 20 世紀中期，中國思想自由和學術獨立的象徵。學者們把這個象徵叫做"北大精神"。

　　中國近代史上的幾件大事和北京大學是分不開的。1917 年的白話文運動讓中國人的書面語言漸漸地由古代漢語轉化到了現代漢語；1919 年的五四運動和新文化運動開始大量介紹西方文化到中國來；1921 年中國共產黨的成立更是改變了中國往後歷史的發展。北京大學的老師和學生不但參與而且領導了這些運動。北京大學是中國現代化運動的發源地。

　　北京大學原來的校園在離王府井不遠的沙灘，主要的建築只是一棟面積並不很大的紅樓。毛澤東還在紅樓裏當過圖書館員。我每次經過紅樓，總忍不住想起這棟小小的建築竟是近代中國新思想產生的搖籃啊！從北京大學早期的歷史來看，最能看出知識分子對社會發展的影響。

　　1949 年，中國"解放"了，但是中國人卻失去了思想自由和學術獨立。至少有 30 年，人人都得學習馬克思/列寧主義和毛澤東思想。20 世紀初期以來，北大精神的優良傳統，在 1949 年之後受到了最徹底的摧毀。五四運動前後，北大是中國改革的原動力，1949 年以後，北大成了被改革的對象，北大的許多教授和學者都在文化大革命期間受到迫害，這是中國學術界重大的損失！

　　現在北京大學的校園其實是當年的燕京大學，燕京大學的創辦人是美國的傳教士司徒雷登(John Leighton Stuart, 1876-1962)。他在中國生活了 50 年，也是 1949 年中美斷絕外交關係之前，美國最後一任的駐華大使。他對近代中國的教育事業作出過重大的貢獻。可惜，1949 年之後，中國經歷了一段長時期全面的反美。使司徒雷登這樣一位對中國教育現代化有過重要貢獻的人物，竟成了中國人民的敵人。這種盲目的排外和仇外對中國社會發展所帶來的傷害，並不亞於盲目的崇洋媚外。

　　就思想和學術的發展來說，五四運動前後是現代中國的黃金時代，在這段時期，自由主義、社會主義、共產主義、無政府主義都能在中國發表他們的意見，進行辯論。中國的人文科學和自然科學的發展在這 30 年中都有巨大的飛躍。我們很希望北大思想自由，學術獨立的優良傳統，能很快地在改革開放的中國重新建立起來。一旦失去了思想自由和學術獨立的保障，大學就成了一個訓練官僚和技師的場所，這不但會讓大學破產，也會讓國家社會的發展停滯下來。

课后习题

第 29 课

一、词语搭配 (Please pair the term in the left column with the most appropriate term in the right column. Then use the completed phrases to complete the sentences. You can change the order of the words and add more information if needed.)

（1）

(　　) 彻底　　　　A 关系

(　　) 盲目　　　　B 相信

(　　) 断绝　　　　C 解决

1. 限制私家车的数量可以缓解交通堵塞的问题,但是并不能_____。

2. 我们要学习书上的知识,但是也不能_____,要多问几个"为什么"。

3. 1949 年新中国刚成立的时候,很多西方国家排斥这个"红色中国",纷纷_____。

（2）

(　　) 实现　　　　A 进程

(　　) 发展　　　　B 飞跃

(　　) 现代化　　　C 停滞

1. 美国是一个移民国家。移民为_____做出过重大贡献。

2. 比如说,早年的中国工人为美国建设了铁路,让西部的经济_____。

3. 今天,有些美国人很排斥移民。其实,如果没有移民,美国_____。

二、选择填空 (Complete the sentences by choosing the most appropriate term.)

1. 经历　　经验

    这位老人出生在 1919 年，＿＿＿＿＿＿＿＿＿了"民国"时代、"新中国"成立、"文化大革命"和"改革开放"这些重要的历史时期。

    大学生打工不但可以赚钱，还可以积累一些工作＿＿＿＿＿＿＿。

三、完成句子　(Complete the sentence or dialogue with the given item in parentheses.)

1. A: 北京大学只有 100 多年的历史，可为什么中国学生都那么向往这所大学？

    B: ＿＿＿＿＿＿＿＿＿＿＿＿＿＿＿＿＿＿＿＿＿＿＿＿。

    （和 A 比起来，B……，但 B 的……却不是 A 可以相提并论的)。

2. A: 美国只是一个很"年轻"的国家，为什么世界各国都这么尊重美国？

    B: ＿＿＿＿＿＿＿＿＿＿＿＿＿＿＿＿＿＿＿＿＿＿＿＿。

    （和 A 比起来，B……，但 B 的……却不是 A 可以相提并论的)。

3. A: 为什么有人说"改革开放"是新中国发展的里程碑？

    B: ＿＿＿＿＿＿＿＿＿＿＿＿＿＿＿＿＿＿＿＿＿＿＿＿。

    （…time/event…以来　　）

4. A: 为什么美国这么尊重个人的自由和权利？

    B: ＿＿＿＿＿＿＿＿＿＿＿＿＿＿＿＿＿＿＿＿＿＿＿＿。

    （…time/event…以来　　）

5. A: 中国的年轻人太崇洋媚外了，我觉得应该防止西方文化对年轻人的影响。

    B: 你这个看法很危险。＿＿＿＿＿＿＿＿＿＿＿＿＿＿＿＿＿＿＿。

    （A 的 abstract noun　并不亚于 B）

6. 雾霾严重的时候你千万别在外面跑步，＿＿＿＿＿＿＿＿＿＿＿＿＿＿＿＿。

    （A 的 abstract noun　不亚于 B）

四、回答问题　(Answer the questions)

1. 什么是 "北大精神"？

2. 北京大学与现代中国历史有什么关系？

3. 1949 年以后，北大发生了什么改变？

4. "盲目排外"和"崇洋媚外"，哪一个坏处更大？

5. 中国在哪些历史时期比较"排外"，美国呢？为什么

6. 思想自由、学术独立对一个大学来说为什么特别重要？

7. 你觉得今天的大学在社会中应该扮演什么样的角色？

第 30 课

"旧中国"与"老北京"

——现代中国的三个"三十年"

　　对一个学习汉语的外国学生来说，"旧中国"和"老北京"这两个词是不容易理解的。

　　这两个词看起来结构相同，但"旧中国"是贬义的，而"老北京"却是褒义的。和"旧中国"联系在一起的往往是"封建"、"独裁"、"黑暗"、"腐败"等这些带有负面意义的词；而和老北京联想在一起的，却是"人情味"、"淳朴"、"礼让"等这些褒义的词。

　　我常问我的中国朋友：没有旧中国，哪有老北京？旧中国如果真的那么可怕，那么一无是处，怎么能建立起这么可爱的"老北京"呢？我的

结构	jiégòu	n.	(sentence, phrase) structure
褒义	bāoyì	adj.	commendatory; complimentary
封建	fēngjiàn	n.	feudalism
人情味	rénqíngwèi	n.	genuine human warmth
淳朴	chúnpǔ	adj.	simple and honest; unsophisticated
礼让	lǐràng	v.	to give precedence to sb. out of courtesy or thoughtfulness
一无是处	yīwúshìchù	n.	(lit.) without a single redeeming feature (devoid of any merit)

中国朋友也不能给我满意的回答。后来我特别注意这两个词的用法，现在总算有了一点了解。

"旧中国"是相对"新中国"来说的，是个政治概念，而"老北京"则是文化概念。新中国是 1949 年以后共产党建立的中华人民共和国，而旧中国则是 1912 年由孙中山创建的中华民国，1949 年以后搬到了台湾。当然，"旧中国"也可以指 1912 年以前的中国。

我在美国大学学了中国历史，我们把 1912 年到 1949 年的中华民国叫做现代中国，而把 1949 以后叫做当代中国。这样的分法只是就时代的先后来说，并没有政治上的含义，是比较容易理解的。

据我的美国教授说：中华民国在大陆的时间虽然不到 40 年，但是在文化上的成就是很高的。二十世纪三十年代也是中国现代文学的黄金时代，重要的作家像鲁迅、巴金和老舍都在这段时期发表了他们最重要的作品。所以旧中国在文化上其实是很辉煌的。

满意	mǎnyì	adj.	satisfactory
总算	zǒngsuàn	adv.	at long last
概念	gàiniàn	n.	concept
创建	chuàngjiàn	v.	to found; establish
当代	dāngdài	adj.	contemporary
分法	fēnfǎ	n.	periodization; division
时代	shídài	n.	era; epoch; the times
含义	hányì	n.	connotation
成就	chéngjiù	n.	huge achievement
辉煌	huīhuáng	adj.	glorious; shining

民国时期，最大的不幸是日本从 1931 年起就开始侵略中国， 1937年中国开始了长达八年的全面抗战，这样长期的战争使中国在工业和经济的发展上受到了严重的打击。日本的侵略使中国的发展至少落后了 50年！

最近中国学术界常把中华人民共和国成立以后的历史分成两个 30年：1949-1979 是第一个 30 年；1979-2009 是第二个 30 年。第一个 30 年的代表人物是毛泽东，他的理想是要在最短的时间之内让中国变成一个公有制的共产主义社会。在这 30 年里，他发动了大跃进、人民公社和文化大革命等多次影响深远的运动。结果造成了中国长时期的大饥荒，饿死了千千万万的中国人。1966-1976 十年的文化大革命更是严重地破

民国	Mínguó	n.	Republic of China (1912-1949, the government moved to Taiwan after 1949).
抗战	Kàngzhàn	n.	abbr. for 抗日战争 The War of Resistance against Japanese Aggression (1937-1945)
长期	chángqī	attr./adv.	long period of time; long-term
学术界	xuéshù jiè	n.	academia
人物	rénwù	n.	(public, historical) figure
公有制	gōngyǒu zhì	n.	public ownership (of means of production)
发动	fādòng	v.	to start or initiate (a movement, war); to mobilize (people)
大跃进	Dà yuèjìn	n.	The Great Leap Forward (1958-1962)
人民公社	Rénmín gōngshè	n.	People's Commune (1958-1982)
文化大革命	Wénhuà dà gémìn	n.	The Cultural Revolution (1966-1976)
深远	shēnyuǎn	adj.	deep and profound; far-reaching
饥荒	jīhuāng	n.	famine

坏了中国的传统文化、社会稳定和教育制度，中国知识分子更是受到了
最残酷的迫害，许多人发疯，自杀。这 10 年是中国近代史上最黑暗，
最恐怖，最混乱的十年。八十年代有一首非常流行的摇滚乐叫做"一无
所有"。这四个字多么形象地说明了这一代的中国人！

　　中国政府对这 30 年的历史所采取的态度是避重就轻，始终没有公
开诚恳地承认过共产党的错误，而是尽可能地让老百姓忘掉这 30 年悲
惨的历史。许多小学生、中学生已经不知道大跃进、人民公社、文化大
革命是怎么回事了。一直到今天，中国还没有一个文化大革命博物馆。
我觉得为了不让这样悲惨的历史重演，成立一个文化大革命博物馆是刻
不容缓的事。

残酷	cánkù	adj.	cruel; brutal
发疯	fāfēng	v.	to go crazy; to become insane
摇滚乐	yáogǔn yuè	n.	Rock and Roll
避重就轻	bìzhòng jiùqīng	idm.	(lit.) to evade major responsibilities and choose minor, easier or lighter task or way; to keep silent about major charges while admitting minor ones
诚恳	chéngkěn	adj.	sincere
错误	cuòwù	n.	mistake
尽可能	jǐn kěnéng	adv.	to the best of one's ability
悲惨	bēicǎn	n.	tragic
重演	chóngyǎn	v.	(of disaster, tragedy) to recur; repeat
刻不容缓	kèbùrónghuǎn	idm.	of great urgency; demand immediate attention

　　第二个 30 年的主导思想是改革开放，代表人物是邓小平。他结束了第一个 30 年空想的社会主义。把集体生产的农村经济改为"包产到户"，也就是由"公有制"慢慢地恢复到"私有制"。这一转变大大地提高了农民的积极性。在思想的控制上也稍稍放宽，增加了与西方国家多方面的交流，并开始派遣留学生出国留学。这个改变奠定了 1990 年以后中国经济快速发展的基础。

主导	zhǔdǎo	adj.	dominant; guiding
空想	kōngxiǎng	attr.	Utopian; unrealistic
集体	jítǐ	n.	collective (opp. 个人 individual)
包产到户	bāochǎn dàohù	n.	a system of farm output quotas; production contracted to each household
公有制	gōngyǒu zhì	n.	public ownership (of means of production)
恢复	huīfù	v.	to resume; 恢复到: to return to (normal, an earlier state, etc.)
私有制	sīyǒuzhì	n.	private ownership (of means of production)
稍稍	shāoshāo	adv.	slightly
放宽	fàngkuān	v.	to relax (restrictions)
派遣	pàiqiǎn	v.	to send out; dispatch
奠定	diàndìng	v.	to lay (the basis/foundations)

　　近来，中国大陆有所谓"民国热"，也就是对民国时期的历史、文化和生活方式都表现出一种向往 和缅怀。看来，旧中国并不是一无可取，而是有许多值得当代中国人学习的地方。

向往	xiàngwǎng	v.	to be attracted toward; yearn for
缅怀	miǎnhuái	v.	to think of or cherish the memory of (the past, history, a person)
一无可取	yīwúkěqǔ	idm.	(lit.) (of a person, course of action) without anything to recommend

I. 词语搭配 *Collocation*

1. Sb./Sth. +一无是处 / 一无可取

   (lit.) Sb./Sth. is without a single redeeming feature (devoid of any merit); good for nothing; worthless

2. 成就+高/大

   high/huge achievement

3. 大规模+发展/扩大/改变

   large scale or extensive development/expansion/change

4. 辉煌的成就/成绩/未来/时代/历史

   glorious, shining achievements/results/future/era/history

5. A 使 B 受到了很大的打击

   A dealt B a mighty blow

6. 影响+深远

   profound and lasting effect

7. 发动+运动

   to start a (social/political) movement

8. 残酷的迫害/竞争/现实

   brutal, cruel persecution/competition/reality

9. 诚恳地+承认错误/接受批评

   sincerely admit one's mistake/accept others' criticism

10. 悲惨的历史/人生

    tragic history/life

11. （不）知道……是怎么回事

    have no idea of…..; don't know what's the matter/how sth. happened…

12. ……是刻不容缓的事。

    be of great urgency; demand immediate attention

13. 提高+积极性

to mobilize people; to instill in them enthusiasm

14. 放宽+控制

to relax restrictions

15. 多方面的+交流/影响/贡献/合作/发展

to have communication/influence/contribution/cooperation /development in many

ways

16. (为…) 奠定+基础

to lay the foundations for…

17. 向往……的生活/生活方式

to be attracted toward/long for …life/the living style of…

18. 缅怀+过去/历史

to cherish the memory or think of the past/history

II. 句型结构 *Sentence Pattern and Structure*

1. 没有 A，哪有 B？

Without…A…, how can there be…B…

没有旧中国，哪有老北京？

我在中国，常听到一句口号，"没有共产党，哪有新中国？"

2. …(some great effort)…，总算… (an acceptable result)…　　　　At long last…

后来我特别注意这两个词的用法，现在总算有了一点了解。

这种药太难找了，我找了半天，总算找到了一点儿。

3. Subj. 长/高/重/多+达+ amount + mw

Subj. is up to …in (length/height/weight/number);

Subj. is as (long/high/heavy/many) as…

中国的抗战长达 8 年。

这个城市的人口多达 2000 万。

III. 词语辨析 *Synonym Differentiation*

1.　成就：major, great achievement

成绩：accomplishment in school; grade

中华民国在大陆的时间虽然不到 40 年，但是在文化上的成就是很高的。

他的学习成绩一直都很好。

我今天能在工作上有这么一点儿成绩，都是因为有您的帮助。

2.　总算：at long last; on the whole, by and large. It is often used to say that after many

complications, the result is not ideal but acceptable.

终于：finally; often used to stress great accomplishments achieved after a long

period of time.

(我一直不懂 "旧中国" 和 "老北京" 的含义) 后来我特别注意这两个词的用

法，现在总算有了一点了解。

经过几年的建设，政府终于建成了世界上最长的高速铁路。

"舊中國"與"老北京"
——現代中國的三個"三十年"

對一個學習漢語的外國學生來說，"舊中國"和"老北京"這兩個詞是不容易理解的。

這兩個詞看起來結構相同，但"舊中國"是貶義的，而"老北京"卻是褒義的。和"舊中國"聯繫在一起的往往是"封建"、"獨裁"、"黑暗"、"腐敗"等這些帶有負面意義的詞；而和"老北京"聯想在一起的，卻是"人情味"、"淳樸"、"禮讓"等這些褒義的詞。

我常問我的中國朋友：沒有"舊中國"，哪有"老北京"？"舊中國"如果真的那麼可怕，那麼一無是處，怎麼能建立起這麼可愛的"老北京"呢？我的中國朋友也不能給我滿意的回答。後來我特別注意這兩個詞的用法，現在總算有了一點了解。

"舊中國"是相對"新中國"來說的，是個政治概念，而"老北京"則是文化概念。新中國是 1949 年以後共產黨建立的中華人民共和國，而舊中國則是 1912 年由孫中山創建的中華民國，1949 年以後搬到了臺灣。當然，"舊中國"也可以指 1912 年以前的中國。

我在美國大學學了中國歷史，我們把 1912 年到 1949 年的中華民國叫做現代中國，而把 1949 以後叫做當代中國。這樣的分法只是就時代的先後來說，並沒有政治上的含義，是比較容易理解的。

據我的美國教授說：中華民國在大陸的時間雖然不到 40 年，但是在文化上的成就是很高的。二十世紀三十年代也是中國現代文學的黃金時代，重要的作家像魯迅，巴金和老舍都在這段時期發表了他們最重要的作品。所以舊中國在文化上其實是很輝煌的。

　　民國時期，最大的不幸是日本從 1931 年起就開始侵略中國，1937 年中國開始了長達 8 年的全面抗戰，這樣長期的戰爭使中國在工業和經濟的發展上受到了嚴重的打擊。日本的侵略使中國的發展至少落後了 50 年！

　　最近中國學術界常把中華人民共和國成立以後的歷史分成兩個 30 年：1949-1979 是第一個 30 年；1979-2009 是第二個 30 年。第一個 30 年的代表人物是毛澤東，他的理想是要在最短的時間之內讓中國變成一個公有制的共產主義社會。在這 30 年裏，他發動了大躍進、人民公社和文化大革命等多次影響深遠的運動。結果造成了中國長時期的大饑荒，餓死了千千萬萬的中國人。1966-1976 十年的文化大革命更是嚴重地破壞了中國的傳統文化、社會穩定和教育制度，中國知識分子更是受到了最殘酷的迫害，許多人發瘋，自殺。這 10 年是中國近代史上最黑暗，最恐怖，最混亂的 10 年。1980 年代有一首非常流行的搖滾樂叫做“一無所有”。這 4 個字多麼形象地說明了這一代的中國人！

　　中國政府對這 30 年的歷史所採取的態度是避重就輕，始終沒有公開誠懇地承認過共產黨的錯誤，而是盡可能的讓老百姓忘掉這 30 年悲慘的歷史。許多小學生、中學生已經不知道大躍進、人民公社、文化大革命是怎麼回事了。一直到今天，中國還沒有一個文化大革命博物館。我覺得為了不讓這樣悲慘的歷史重演，成立一個文化大革命博物館是刻不容緩的事。

　　第二個 30 年的主導思想是改革開放，代表人物是鄧小平。他結束了第一個 30 年空想的社會主義。把集體生產的農村經濟改為“包產到戶”，也就是由“公有制”恢復到“私有制”。這一轉變大大地提高了農民的積極性。在思想的控制上也稍稍放寬，增加了與西方國家多方面的交流，並開始派遣留學生出國留學。這個改變奠定了 1990 年以後中國經濟快速發展的基礎。

　　近來，中國大陸有所謂“民國熱”，也就是對民國時期的歷史、文化和生活方式都表現出一種向往和緬懷。看來，“舊中國”並不是一無可取，而是有許多值得當代中國人學習的地方。

课后习题

第 30 课

一、词语搭配 (Please pair the term in the left column with the most appropriate term in the right column. Then use the completed phrases to complete the sentences. You can change the order of the words and add more information if needed.)

（1）

(　) 辉煌　　　　A 影响
(　) 深远　　　　B 发展
(　) 大规模　　　C 成就
(　) 很大的　　　D 打击

1. 中国古代的科学技术非常发达，取得过＿＿＿＿＿＿＿＿＿＿＿＿＿＿＿＿＿。
2. 现在，中国政府＿＿＿＿＿＿＿＿＿＿绿色能源、人工智能(A.I.)这样的新技术。
3. 每个国家都应该重视教育，因为教育会对一个人＿＿＿＿＿＿＿＿＿＿＿＿。
4. 在中国，高考的竞争非常激烈，考得不好对学生来说＿＿＿＿＿＿＿＿＿＿＿。

（2）

(　) 发动　　　　A 道歉
(　) 诚恳地　　　B 历史
(　) 残酷的　　　C 竞争
(　) 悲惨的　　　D 战争

1. 过去，为了得到土地和资源，帝国主义国家＿＿＿＿＿＿＿＿＿＿＿＿＿＿。
2. 对于很多犹太人(Jewish people)来说，二战是一段＿＿＿＿＿＿＿＿＿＿＿。
3. 战争造成了很大的伤害，很多人认为发动战争的国家＿＿＿＿＿＿＿＿＿＿。
4. 今天的社会，压力越来越大，很多人从小就要面对＿＿＿＿＿＿＿＿＿＿。

（3）

（　　）提高　　　A 基础

（　　）放宽　　　B 限制

（　　）奠定　　　C 生活

（　　）向往　　　D 积极性

1. 家长不能强迫孩子学习,相反,应该想办法_____,让孩子变得爱学习。

2. 以前,中国实行"一家一个孩子"的政策,现在_____。

3. 1978 年的改革开放,为中国后来的发展_____。

4. 80 年代,中国人在电视上开到美国人家家有房有车,_____。

二、选择填空 (Complete the sentences by choosing the most appropriate term.)

1. 成就　　　成绩

在学校,学生最关心的往往是考试的_____。其实,在成绩之外,还有很多重要的事情。

他年纪轻轻就取得了很大的_____,真了不起。可是,他总是说,"我能取得今天的一点点_____,是和家人朋友的帮助分不开的。"

2. 总算　　　终于

国家强大一直是中国人的梦想。经过 40 年的努力,中国_____成为了世界第二经济体。

毕业以后,他一直没有找到工作,现在他在网上卖东西,_____有了一点儿收入。

三、完成句子 (Complete the sentence or dialogue with the given item in parentheses.)

1. A：你觉得什么是 20 世纪最伟大的发明 (invention, creation)，为什么？

   B：_____。（没有 A，哪有 B）

2. A：我们为什么要学习历史呢，我觉得有点儿浪费时间？

   B：_____。（没有 A，哪有 B）

3. 第 30 课真难，我_____。（总算）

4. 她以前是一个"剩女"，_____。（总算）

5. 纽约是一个大城市，_____。（长/高/重/多+达）

6. 中国的高考竞争很激烈，_____。（长/高/重/多+达）

四、回答问题 (Answer the questions)

1. "旧中国" 会让人想到什么？"老北京"呢？

2. 没有"旧中国"，哪有"老北京"，你同意这个说法吗？

3. 如果你是一个历史老师，你会选择给学生介绍"旧中国"和"老北京"这两个概念，还是"现代中国"和"当代中国"？

4. 中华人民共和国成立以后的第一个 30 年，中国经历了哪些事情？中国政府对这段历史的态度是什么？

5. 第二个 30 年跟第一个 30 年有什么不同？你觉得今天的中国人更怀念哪个时期？

6. 什么是"民国热"？为什么近来会出现所谓的"民国热"？

7. 如果可以选择，你愿意生活在现代中国的第一个"三十年"，第二个"三十年"还是现在？为什么？

8. 今天的人为什么要了解历史？我们应该怎么给下一代人讲历史？

Pinyin Index

出入，chūrù, *n.*, discrepancy (compared to one's estimation), L. 16, p. 228

初五，Chū Wǔ, *tw.*, the fifth day of a month (of the Chinese lunar calendar), L. 16, p. 226

出行，chūxíng, *v./n.*, travel; travel, L. 17, p. 239

出于，chūyú, *prep.*, out of; stem from, L. 15, p. 210

初中，chūzhōng, *n.*, middle school, L. 14, p. 191

初中生，chūzhōngshēng, *n.*, junior high school students, L. 12, p. 162

处罚，chǔfá, *n./v.*, punishment; to punish, L. 5, p. 54

处理，chǔlǐ, *v.*, handle (a problem); to deal with, L. 6, p. 65

传，chuán, *v.*, to pass on (orally), L. 18, p. 255

传播，chuánbō, *v.*, disseminate; propagate, L. 20, p. 286

传教士，chuánjiào shì, *n.*, missionary, L. 29, p. 420

传说，chuánshuō, *n.*, legend; folklore, L. 2, p. 18

传闻，chuánwén, *n.*, hearsay, L. 21, p. 301

窗口，chuāngkǒu, *n.*, window, L. 11, p. 146

闯红灯，chuǎng hóngdēng, *v.o.*, run a red light, L. 11, p. 146

创办人，chuàngbàn rén, *n.*, founder, L. 29, p. 420

创建，chuàngjiàn, *v.*, found; establish, L. 30, p. 430

创新，chuàngxīn, *v./n.*, bring forth new ideas; innovate, L. 14, p. 193

创业，chuàngyè, *v.*, start an enterprise, L. 15, p. 209

创意，chuàngyì, *n.*, original idea, L. 15, p. 210

创造，chuàngzào, *v.*, create, L. 8, p. 99

创作，chuàngzuò, *v.*, (of work of art) create, L. 18, p. 253

吹，chuī, *v.*, blow, L. 11, p. 147

春季，chūnjì, *n.*, spring (formal), L. 16, p. 228

春节，Chūnjié, *n.*, the Spring Festival, L. 16, p. 227

淳朴，chúnpǔ, *adj.*, simple and honest; unsophisticated, L. 30, p. 429

刺激，cìjī, *v./n.*, stimulate; stimulus, L. 17, p. 238

从事，cóngshì, *v.*, undertake; take up (as a profession); go in for, L. 14, p. 190; L. 27, p. 387

凑钱，còuqián, *v.-o.*, scrape together money, L. 26, p. 372

粗略，cūlüè, *adj.*, rough, L. 10, p. 131

促进，cùjìn, *v.*, boost; stimulate, L. 20, p. 288

摧毁，cuīhuǐ, *v.*, destroy; smash into pieces; wreck, L. 29, p. 419

脆弱，cuìruò, *adj.*, (mentally or psychologically) fragile, L. 21, p. 302

村，cūn, *n.*, village, L. 9, p. 112

存在，cúnzài, *v.*, exist, L. 12, p. 161

错过，cuòguò, *v.*, miss (e.g. an opportunity), L. 22, p. 318

措施，cuòshī, *n.*, measures, L. 15, p. 211; L. 17, p. 238

错误，cuòwù, *n.*, error; mistake, L. 5, p. 56; L. 30, p. 432

D

搭，dā, *v.*, take (a subway, ship, car, etc.), L. 11, p. 147

达成，dáchéng, *v.*, reach (an agreement), L. 26, p. 374

达到，dádào, *v.*, achieve or attain (a goal), L. 16, p. 228

打败，dǎbài, *v.*, defeat, L. 7, p. 82

打的，dǎdī, *v.o.*, take a taxi, L. 11, p. 147

打工，dǎgōng, *v.-o.*, work (physical work; temporary or casual job), L. 14, p. 190

打击，dǎjī, *v./n.*, take strong measures against; crack down on (corruption, crimes); blow; hit, L. 19, p. 270; L. 22, p. 319

打交道，dǎ jiāodào, *v.-o.*, come into contact with; have dealings with, L. 6, p. 65

打砸，dǎzá, *v.*, beat and smash, L. 26, p. 373

打仗，dǎzhàng, *v.*, go to war, L. 6, p. 66

打字，dǎzì, *v.-o.*, type, L. 12, p. 160

大打折扣，dàdǎ zhékòu, *idm.*, fall short of a requirement or promise, L. 6, p. 67

大都市，dà dūshì, *n.*, metropolis, L. 9, p. 117

大幅，dàfú, *adv.*, by a big margin; substantially, L. 17, p. 239

大规模，dàguīmó, *adj.*, large-scale (usu. as a modifier), L. 16, p. 226

大量，dàliàng, *adj./adv.*, a large amount of; in great quantities; in volume, L. 4, p. 44; L. 29, p. 418

大陆，dàlù, *n.*, Mainland China, L. 4, p. 44; L. 27, p. 387

大炮，dàpào, *n.*, cannon; artillery, L. 3, p. 31

大跃进，Dà yuèjìn, *n.*, The Great Leap Forward (1958-1962), L. 30, p. 431

戴，dài, *v.*, put on (eyewear, headgear), L. 1, p. 2

代表，dàibiǎo, *v./n.*, represent; representation, L. 2, p. 18

代表作，dàibiǎozuò, *n.*, representative works; masterpiece, L. 9, p. 114

逮捕，dàibǔ, *v.*, arrest, L. 26, p. 374

带动，dàidòng, *v.*, bring along or to give an impetus to, L. 10, p. 133

代价，dàijià, *n.*, cost, L. 1, p. 4

带领，dàilǐng, *v.*, lead, L. 26, p. 373

带薪假期，dàixīnjiàqī, *n.*, paid vacation, L. 17, p. 240

待遇，dàiyù, *n.*, treatment; wages and benefits, L. 24, p. 346

单车，dānchē, *n.*, bicycle, L. 13, p. 173

单身，dānshēn, *adj.*, single, L. 28, p. 403

单位，dānwèi, *n.*, work unit (place of employment, esp. in the PRC prior to 1978)., L. 28, p. 402

当，dāng, *v.*, treat sth. /sb. as …, L. 27, p. 386

当场，dāngchǎng, *adv.*, on the spot, L. 26, p. 373

当代，dāngdài, *n./adj.*, the contemporary era; the present age; contemporary, L. 9, p. 115; L. 13, p. 173; L. 30, p. 430

当地，dāngdì, *n.*, local area, L. 4, p. 44

当年，dāngnián, *n.*, those years/days; back then, L. 29, p. 420

当前，dāngqián, *t.w.*, present time, L. 23, p. 332

当天，dāngtiān, *n.*, the same day, L. 13, p. 175

党，dǎng, *n.*, political part, L. 1, p. 4

岛，dǎo, *n.*, island, L. 27, p. 388

岛礁，dǎojiāo, *n.*, reef, L. 23, p. 335

道，dào, *m.w.*, measure word for doors, walls, etc., L. 2, p. 20; L. 23, p. 334

到达，dàodá, *v.*, arrive, L. 10, p. 132

道教，Dàojiào, *n.*, Daoism, L. 16, p. 225

道理, dàolǐ, *n.*, reason; sense; principle; hows and whys, L. 4, p. 43

道路, dàolù, *n.*, path; road, L. 27, p. 389

道歉, dàoqiàn, *v.*, apologize, L. 21, p. 303

稻田, dàotián, *n.*, rice field, L. 10, p. 130

得民心, dé mínxīn, *v.-o.*, win the support of the people, L. 5, p. 54

瞪, dèng, *v.*, stare; glare, L. 2, p. 19

等于, děngyú, *v.*, equal to, L. 21, p. 303

低估, dīgū, *v.*, underestimate, L. 21, p. 302

低龄化, dīlíng huà, *adj.*, skew toward the younger end of the spectrum; tend to be younger, L. 14, p. 192

低头, dītóu, *v.-o.*, to lower one's head, L. 26, p. 372

的确, díquè, *adv.*, indeed, L. 15, p. 207

敌人, dírén, *n.*, enemy, L. 2, p. 20

地方, dìfang, *n.*, part; aspect; place, L. 7, p. 82; L. 28, p. 402

帝国主义, dìguó zhǔyì, *n.*, imperialism, L. 7, p. 82

地域性, dìyù xìng, *n.*, local or regional peculiarity, L. 9, p. 115

点击量, diǎnjī liàng, *n.*, (of websites) number of clicks; web traffic, L. 21, p. 302

奠定, diàndìng, *v.*, lay (the basis/foundations), L. 30, p. 433

店面, diànmiàn, *n.*, shop front; sales floor, L. 13, p. 174

电视剧, diànshì jù, *n.*, TV show; TV series, L. 3, p. 30

电梯, diàntī, *n.*, lift; elevator, L. 11, p. 145

电子, diànzǐ, *adj.*, electronic, L. 13, p. 176

电子锁, diànzǐsuǒ, *n.*, electronic lock, L. 22, p. 316

雕刻, diāokè, *v.*, carve; engrave; 雕刻家: sculptor, L. 18, p. 253

掉头, diàotóu, *v.*, turn around, L. 24, p. 346

盯, dīng, *v.*, fix one's eyes on; keep a close watch on, L. 5, p. 56

订餐, dìngcān, *v.o.*, order food, L. 18, p. 254

订购, dìnggòu, *v.*, order (goods); place an order for, L. 11, p. 146

定为, dìngwéi, *v.*, establish as; recognize as, L. 3, p. 32

丢脸, diūliǎn, *v.o.*, lose face, L. 28, p. 403

懂得, dǒngdé, *v.*, to understand, L. 6, p. 67

懂事, dǒngshì, *v.*, (of a child) be able to make judgments; sensible, L. 27, p. 385

栋, dòng, *m.w.*, measure word for buildings, L. 29, p. 419

动力, dònglì, *n.*, motive; driving force, L. 20, p. 284

独裁, dúcái, *n.*, dictatorship, L. 27, p. 387

独立, dúlì, *adj.*, independent, L. 7, p. 82

独立自主, dúlì zìzhǔ, *adj.*, independent and autonomous, L. 27, p. 389

读书, dúshū, *v.-o.*, attend school; study, L. 7, p. 81

独特, dútè, *adj.*, unique; distinctive, L. 18, p. 256

堵塞, dǔsè, *v.*, stop up; block up, L. 18, p. 256

度过, dùguò, *v.*, to spend time, L. 18, p. 257

镀金, dùjīn, *v.*, gild; cover or coat with gold, L. 14, p. 192

端午节, Duānwǔ jié, *n.*, Dragon Boat Festival, L. 3, p. 32; L. 16, p. 226;

段, duàn, *m.w.*, measure word for passage, paragraph, time, experience, relation, L. 19, p. 270; L. 29, p. 420

断绝, duànjué, *v.*, sever; to break off, L. 29, p. 420

堆, duī, *m.w.*, pile, L. 19, p. 271

对比, duìbǐ, *v.*, compare (side by side), L. 20, p. 287

对策, duìcè, *n.*, the way to deal with a situation, L. 3, p. 31

对待, duìdài, *v.*, treat, L. 20, p. 286

对外汉语教学, duìwài hànyǔ jiàoxué, *n.*, Teaching Chinese as a Second Language, L. 12, p. 163

对象, duìxiàng, *n.*, target; a potential marriage partner, L. 1, p. 2

多年前, duōnián qián, *t.w.*, many years ago, L. 19, p. 272

多数, duōshù, *n.*, the majority, L. 11, p. 144

多样并存, duōyàng bìngcún, *idm.*, many styles and kinds coexist; to have a great diversity, L. 28, p. 407

堕胎, duòtāi, *n./v.*, abortion; to induce abortion, L. 19, p. 273

E

恶毒, èdú, *adj.*, vicious, L. 21, p. 301

恶化, èhuà, *v.*, deteriorate; worsen, L. 1, p. 4

恶劣, èliè, *adj.*, hostile, L. 1, p. 3

摁, èn, *v.*, press, L. 12, p. 162

二奶, èrnǎi, *n.*, mainland internet slang for mistress, L. 28, p. 401

二手烟, èrshǒu yān, *n.*, second-hand smoke, L. 11, p. 145

二战, Èrzhàn, *n.*, World War II, L. 27, p. 386

F

发表, fābiǎo, *v.*, to express; to put forward, L. 19, p. 269

发愁, fāchóu, *v.*, worry about; fret about; be anxious, L. 24, p. 345

发动, fādòng, *v.*, to start or initiate (a movement, war); to mobilize (people), L. 30, p. 431

发疯, fāfēng, *v.*, go crazy; become insane, L. 30, p. 432

发挥, fāhuī, *v.*, give full play to (one's ability), L. 8, p. 97

发泄, fāxiè, *v.*, vent (one's anger or dissatisfaction), L. 21, p. 302

发育, fāyù, *n./v.*, (of a child) development; growth; to grow, L. 4, p. 45

发源地, fāyuán dì, *n.*, (of a river, historical event) place of origin, L. 29, p. 419

发展, fāzhǎn, *n./v.*, development; develop, L. 15, p. 210

罚金, fájīn, *n.*, fine; forfeit, L. 26, p. 372

罚款, fákuǎn, *v./n.*, impose a fine or forfeit; fine or forfeit, L. 26, p. 374

法定假日, fǎdìng jiàrì, *n.*, official holidays, L. 3, p. 32

法家, Fǎjiā, , Legalists (a school of thought in ancient China), L. 6, p. 68

法治, fǎzhì, *n.*, the rule of law; govern by law, L. 6, p. 67

翻墙, fānqiáng, *v.-o.*, climb over the wall; to breach the Great Firewall, L. 7, p. 84

翻译, fānyì, *n./v.*, translation; to translate, L. 6, p. 67; L. 27, p. 385

繁荣, fánróng, *adj.*, prosperous; booming; flourishing, L. 23, p. 332

反腐, fǎnfǔ, *v.-o.*, to fight corruption, L. 5, p. 54

反抗, fǎnkàng, *v.*, react against (oppression), L. 24, p. 347

反恐, fǎn kǒng, v., anti-terrorism; fight terrorism, L. 22, p. 319

反思, fǎnsī, v., reflect; rethink, L. 15, p. 210

反贪, fǎn tān, v.-o., to fight embezzlement, L. 5, p. 56

反映, fǎnyìng, v., reflect; mirror, L. 4, p. 43

泛滥, fànlàn, v., overflow; spread unchecked, L. 4, p. 43

贩卖, fànmài, v., peddle, L. 10, p. 133

犯罪, fànzuì, v.-o., commit a crime, L. 26, p. 374

方方面面, fāngfāng miànmiàn, idm., all aspects; all sides, L. 15, p. 208

方式, fāngshì, n., way; manner; style, L. 10, p. 128

方向, fāngxiàng, n., direction, L. 24, p. 348

方言, fāngyán, n., dialect, L. 9, p. 113

妨碍, fáng'ài, v., hamper (one's relationship with others), L. 9, p. 116

防备, fángbèi, v./n., to guard against; precaution, L. 25, p. 360

防盗, fángdào, v, guard against theft, L. 26, p. 371

房价, fángjià, n., price of a house, L. 8, p. 96

防御, fángyù, v., defend; guard, L. 2, p. 20

防止, fángzhǐ, v., prevent, L. 3, p. 31; L. 22, p. 318

房租, fángzū, n., rent, L. 8, p. 96

仿冒, fǎngmào, v., counterfeit, L. 4, p. 42

放过, fàngguo, v.-c., let sb. off, L. 5, p. 54

放假, fàngjià, v.-o., give sb. a vacation; have a holiday, L. 16, p. 228

放宽, fàngkuān, v., relax (restrictions), L. 30, p. 433

放弃, fàngqì, v., give up; abandon, L. 8, p. 98

放学, fàngxué, v.-o., (of school) let out or close, L. 1, p. 2

非法, fēifǎ, adj., illegal, L. 6, p. 65

飞快, fēikuài, adv., very fast; at lightning speed, L. 12, p. 162

飞跃, fēiyuè, n./v., leap; rapid progress, L. 29, p. 421

废气, fèiqì, n., waste gas or steam; exhaust, L. 1, p. 4

废弃, fèiqì, adj., abandoned, L. 18, p. 255

费用, fèiyòng, n., expenses; cost, L. 8, p. 96

分辨, fēnbiàn, v., distinguish; differentiate, L. 4, p. 42

分不清, fēnbùqīng, v-c., cannot distinguish (A from B), L. 16, p. 226

分法, fēnfǎ, n., periodization; division, L. 30, p. 430

纷纷, fēnfēn, adv., (of comments, falling objects, etc.) numerous and in succession, L. 20, p. 287

分界线, fēnjiè xiàn, n., line of demarcation; boundary, L. 10, p. 131

分配, fēnpèi, v., allocate, L. 19, p. 272

分析, fēnxī, v./n., analyze; analysis, L. 1, p. 4

份, fèn, m.w., classifier for gifts, newspaper, etc., L. 6, p. 66

奋斗, fèndòu, v., strive, fight for; struggle hard (for success), L. 7, p. 81; L. 8 p. 95

分量, fènliàng, n., (to carry) weight; significance, L. 12, p. 163

粉丝, fěnsī, n., fans, L. 28, p. 407

封闭, fēngbì, adj., closed, L. 2, p. 20

丰厚, fēnghòu, adj., generous, L. 15, p. 210

封建, fēngjiàn, n., feudalism, L. 30, p. 429

风景, fēngjǐng, n., scenery (usually a view of natural features), L. 10, p. 129

风气, fēngqì, n., ethos; the general mood (of a society), L. 19, p. 271; L. 28, p. 407

风趣, fēngqù, adj., witty, L. 1, p. 3

讽刺, fěngcì, adj./v., ironic; satirize/ridicule, L. 12, p. 161

佛教, Fójiào, n., Buddhism, L. 16, p. 225

否认, fǒurèn, v., deny, L. 8, p. 98

否则, fǒuzé, conj., otherwise; or else, L. 12, p. 161; L. 13, p. 173

夫妇, fūfù, n., couple, L. 22, p. 316

福利, fúlì, n., welfare; benefit, L. 23, p. 333

服装, fúzhuāng, n., clothing; costume, L. 3, p. 30

腐败, fǔbài, n/adj., corruption; corrupt, L. 5, p. 56

负担, fùdān, n., burden, L. 25, p. 361

复古, fùgǔ, v.-o., revert to or restore old/ancient ways, L. 3, p. 32

复活, fùhuó, v./n., come back to life; resurrect; resurrection, L. 16, p. 225

复活节, Fùhuó jié, n., Easter, L. 16, p. 225

付款, fùkuǎn, v.o., pay a sum of money, L. 13, p. 176; L. 18, p. 254

负面, fùmiàn, adj., negative, L. 20, p. 288

妇女, fùnǚ, n., women in general, L. 28, p. 401

复兴, fùxīng, v., revitalize; revive, L. 17, p. 242

富裕, fùyù, adj., rich; wealthy, L. 7, p. 82

赋予, fùyǔ, v., (of the law) confer; vest, L. 22, p. 318

复杂, fùzá, adj., complicated; complex, L. 6, p. 67; L. 27, p. 389

G

改进, gǎijìn, v./n., improve (methods); improvement, L. 10, p. 128

改为, gǎiwéi, v., change into, L. 17, p. 238

改用, gǎiyòng, v., use (sth. else) instead; switch to, L. 9, p. 113

改造, gǎizào, v., to transform; to remodel, L. 18, p. 255

概括, gàikuò, v., to summarize, L. 19, p. 269

概念, gàiniàn, n., concept, L. 30, p. 430

敢, gǎn, aux., dare, L. 4, p. 45

尴尬, gān'gà, adj., embarrassing; awkward, L. 13, p. 178; L. 28, p. 403

干涉, gānshè, v., interfere, L. 27, p. 389

甘肃, Gānsù, n., Gansu province (in northwest China), L. 23, p. 333; L. 26, p. 371

感到, gǎndào, v.c., feel; sense, L. 7, p. 82

感动, gǎndòng, v., move or touch (sb. emotionally), L. 20, p. 284

感恩节, Gǎnēn jié, n., Thanksgiving Day, L. 16, p. 228

赶上, gǎnshàng, v.-c., catch up with, L. 11, p. 149

赶时髦, gǎn shímáo, v.o., follow the fashion; be in style, L. 15, p. 210

感受, gǎnshòu, n./v., experience; feeling, L. 3, p. 30; L. 7, p. 82

感兴趣, gǎnxìngqu, v.-o., be interested in..., L. 3, p. 32

干部, gànbu, n., cadres; government officials, L. 19, p. 270

447

港口，gǎngkǒu, *n.*, port; harbor, L. 2, p. 21

高端，gāoduān, *adj.*, high-end; upscale; up-market, L. 15, p. 211

高额，gāoé, *n.*, huge amount, L. 14, p. 193

高官，gāoguān, *n.*, high officials, L. 5, p. 54

高价，gāojià, *n.*, high price, L. 4, p. 42

高楼，gāo lóu, *n.*, tall building; skyscraper, L. 1, p. 1

高速，gāosù, *adj.*, high-speed (modifier), L. 2, p. 21

高效，gāoxiào, *adj.*, highly efficient, L. 13, p. 175

高薪，gāoxīn, *adj.*, high-paying (jobs), L. 15, p. 209

高雅，gāoyǎ, *adj.*, elegant; refined; tasteful, L. 13, p. 177

高原，gāoyuán, *n.*, plateau, L. 10, p. 130

告，gào, *v.*, sue, L. 22, p. 316

歌剧，gējù, *n.*, opera, L. 18, p. 257

哥伦比亚大学，Gēlún bǐyà dàxué, *n.*, Columbia University, L. 15, p. 209

割让，gēràng, *v.*, cede, L. 27, p. 386

歌星，gēxīng, *n.*, singer, L. 28, p. 405

革命性，gémìng xìng, *adj.*, revolutionary, L. 13, p. 176

各，gè, *pron.*, each, L. 17, p. 238

各不相同，gèbùxiāngtóng, *adj.*, have nothing in common with each other, L. 16, p. 228

个人，gèrén, *n./adj.*, individual, L. 7, p. 80

更何况，gènghékuàng, *adv.*, let alone …; not to mention…, L. 27, p. 388

共产党，Gòngchǎndǎng, *n.*, The Communist Party, L. 1, p. 4

功夫熊猫，Gōngfu Xióngmāo, *n.*, Kung Fu Panda, L. 2, p. 19

公共，gōnggòng, *adj.*, public; common, L. 11, p. 145

公共事务，gōnggòng shìwù, *n.*, public affairs, L. 20, p. 287

攻击性，gōngjī xìng, *n.*, aggressiveness; combativeness, L. 2, p. 19

工匠，gōngjiàng, *n.*, artisan; craftsman, L. 18, p. 255

工具，gōngjù, *n.*, tool, L. 5, p. 56; L. 6, p. 68

公立，gōnglì, *adj.*, public (school, hospital, etc.), L. 8, p. 98

公历，gōnglì, *n.*, Western calendar, L. 16, p. 227

公民，gōngmín, *n.*, citizen, L. 7, p. 81

公认，gōngrèn, *v.*, generally acknowledged; universally accepted, L. 10, p. 131

恭喜发财，gōngxǐfācái, *idm.*, Have a happy and prosperous New Year! L. 17, p. 240

工业，gōngyè, *n.*, industry, L. 1, p. 4

工业化，gōngyè huà, *n.*, industrialization, L. 7, p. 82

工业区，gōngyè qū, *n.*, industrial area, L. 24, p. 347

工艺，gōngyì, *n.*, craftsmanship; technical skill, L. 18, p. 255

公有制，gōngyǒu zhì, *n.*, public ownership (of means of production), L. 30, p. 431, 433

供奉，gòngfèng, *v.*, to enshrine and worship, L. 16, p. 226

贡献，gòngxiàn, *n./v.*, contribution; to contribute, L. 8, p. 99

沟通，gōutōng, *v./n.*, communicate; communication, L. 12, p. 160

购买，gòumǎi, *v.*, purchase, L. 4, p. 44

购买力，gòumǎi lì, *n.*, purchasing power, L. 15, p. 210

购物，gòuwù, *v.o.*, go shopping, L. 18, p. 254

购物节，gòuwùjié, *n.*, shopping festival; retail holiday, L. 17, p. 241

孤儿，gū'ér, *n.*, orphan, L. 27, p. 386

孤独，gūdú, *adj.*, lonely, L. 25, p. 359

估计，gūjì, *v.*, estimate, L. 27, p. 387

孤僻，gūpì, *adj.*, unsociable and eccentric, L. 25, p. 360

股，gǔ, *m.w.*, measure word for strength, smell, L. 28, p. 407

古代，gǔdài, *adj.*, ancient, L. 2, p. 18

谷歌，gǔgē, *n.*, Google, L. 7, p. 84

鼓励，gǔlì, *v.*, encourage, L. 25, p. 360

顾客，gùkè, *n.*, customer, L. 22, p. 319

顾虑，gùlǜ, *n.*, concern, L. 3, p. 31

顾问，gùwèn, *n.*, consultant, L. 14, p. 190

故乡，gùxiāng, *n.*, hometown, L. 9, p. 115

故意，gùyì, *adv.*, on purpose, L. 21, p. 302

怪不得，guàibude, *adv.*, no wonder, L. 10, p. 130

观察，guānchá, *n./v.*, observation; to observe, L. 7, p. 81

官僚，guānliáo, *n.*, bureaucrat, L. 29, p. 421

观念，guānniàn, *n.*, concept; notion, L. 6, p. 68

关心，guānxīn, *v.*, care about, L. 16, p. 227

官员，guānyuán, *n.*, official, L. 5, p. 56

关注，guānzhù, *v.*, pay close attention to, L. 7, p. 80

管理，guǎnlǐ, *v./n.*, manage; govern; administer; management, L. 23, p. 333; L. 27, p. 386

广东，Guǎngdōng, *n.*, Guangdong Province, L. 15, p. 208

广泛，guǎngfàn, *adj./adv.*, widespread; wide ranging, L. 13, p. 178; L. 28, p. 402

广告，guǎnggào, *n.*, advertisement, L. 7, p. 80

广告费，guǎnggào fèi, *n.*, advertising expense, L. 21, p. 303

规定，guīdìng, *n.*, regulation; stipulation, L. 6, p. 67

规模，guīmó, *n.*, scale; scope, L. 23, p. 332

归宿，guīsù, *n.*, a lasting or permanent place/stage in life; (of girls) to be happily married, L. 28, p. 404

规则，guīzé, *n.*, regulation; rule, L. 11, p. 145

贵州，Guìzhōu, *n.*, a province in southwest China, L. 25, p. 358

国际化，guójì huà, *adj.*, internationalized, L. 15, p. 208

国旗，guóqí, *n.*, national flag, L. 20, p. 284

国营，guóyíng, *adj.*, state-run, L. 13, p. 176; L. 18, p. 254

过程，guòchéng, *n.*, course; process, L. 7, p. 80

过错，guòcuò, *n.*, fault, L. 26, p. 371

H

海军，hǎijūn, *n.*, navy, L. 23, p. 335

海洋，hǎiyáng, *n.*, ocean, L. 23, p. 334

寒假，hánjià, *n.*, winter break, L. 16, p. 228

含义，hányì, *n.*, connotation, L. 19, p. 269; L. 30, p. 430

罕见，hǎnjiàn, *adj.*, seldom seen; rare, L. 1, p. 1

航空，hángkōng, *n.*, aviation, L. 9, p. 117

航空母舰，hángkōng mǔjiàn, *n.*, aircraft carrier, L. 7, p. 83

行业，hángyè, *n.*, trade; profession; industry, L. 13, p. 175

豪宅，háozhái, *n.*, mansion, L. 18, p. 253

好色，hàosè, *adj.*, lustful; lecherous; lascivious, L. 19, p. 270

合法化，héfǎ huà, *v.*, legalize; legitimize, L. 15, p. 209

合理，hélǐ, *adj.*, reasonable, L. 22, p. 317

河流，héliú, *n.*, rivers (collective noun), L. 10, p. 130

核潜艇，hé qiántǐng, *n.*, nuclear-powered submarine, L. 23, p. 335

合影，héyǐng, *v.*, take (joint/group) photo with…, L. 20, p. 284

合作，hézuò, *v.*, collaborate; to cooperate, L. 22, p. 319

黑暗面，hēi'àn miàn, *n.*, the dark side, L. 20, p. 287

黑社会，hēi shèhuì, *n.*, gang; criminal underworld, L. 25, p. 361

恨不得，hènbudé, *v.*, dying to; wish one could, L. 15, p. 208

轰炸机，hōngzhàjī, *n.*, bomber (aircraft), L. 7, p. 83

喉咙，hóulong, *n.*, throat, L. 1, p. 1

后半期，hòubàn qī, *n.*, latter half (of a century), L. 23, p. 332

忽视，hūshì, *v.*, to ignore, L. 21, p. 304

呼吸，hūxī, *v.*, breathe, L. 7, p. 84

呼吁，hūyù, *v.*, appeal, L. 21, p. 303

胡同，hútong, *n.*, lane; alley, L. 11, p. 144

湖泊，húpō, *n.*, lakes (collective noun), L. 10, p. 130

胡子，húzi, *n.*, barbel; beard; mustache, L. 2, p. 18

户籍，hùjí, *n.*, residence registration system, L. 23, p. 333

户口，hùkǒu, *n.*, registered permanent residence, L. 8, p. 98

花圈，huāquān, *n.*, wreath, L. 26, p. 373

华尔街，Huá'ěr jiē, *n.*, Wall Street, L. 15, p. 209

滑稽，huájī, *adj.*, funny-looking; comical, L. 12, p. 161

划分，huàfēn, *v.*, divide, L. 10, p. 131

话剧，huàjù, *n.*, modern drama; stage play, L. 18, p. 257

画室，huàshì, *n.*, studio, L. 18, p. 255

话题，huàtí, *n.*, topic, L. 7, p. 80

画展，huàzhǎn, *n.*, exhibition of paintings, L. 18, p. 255

化妆品，huàzhuāng pǐn, *n.*, cosmetics; makeup product, L. 4, p. 43

淮河，Huáihé, *n.*, The Huai River, L. 10, p. 131

怀念，huáiniàn, *v.*, to remember fondly; to reminisce, L. 11, p. 144

怀疑，huáiyí, *v.*, suspect; doubt, L. 22, p. 316

欢迎，huānyíng, *v.*, to welcome, L. 11, p. 144

环卫工人，huánwèi gōngrén *n.*, sanitation worker, L. 20, p. 285

缓解，huǎnjiě, *v.*, alleviate; ease; relieve, L. 11, p. 146; L. 17, p. 240

宦官，huànguān, *n.*, eunuch, L. 23, p. 334

换句话说，huànjùhuàshuō, *interj.*, in other words, L. 3, p. 31

皇帝，huángdì, *n.*, emperor, L. 2, p. 19

黄金时代，huángjīn shídài, *n.*, golden age, L. 23, p. 421

恢复，huīfù, *v.*, resume, L. 30, p. 433

辉煌，huīhuáng, *adj.*, glorious; shining, L. 30, p. 430

灰蒙蒙，huī méngméng, *adj.*, dusky; overcasting; , L. 1, p. 1

回报，huíbào, *v.*, repay; reciprocate, L. 15, p. 210

毁坏，huǐhuài, *v.*, to destroy; to damage, L. 17, p. 240

贿赂，huìlù, *n./v.*, bribes; to bribe, L. 5, p. 55

会议，huìyì, *n.*, conference; meeting, L. 1, p. 3; L. 10, p. 129

婚外关系，hūnwài guānxi, *n.*, extramarital affairs, L. 21, p. 299

馄饨，húndùn, *n.*, wonton, L. 9, p. 115

浑身，húnshēn, *adv.*, whole body; from head to foot, L. 20, p. 286

混乱，hùnluàn, *adj./n.*, messy; disorder, L. 27, p. 389

活动，huódòng, *n.*, event; activity, L. 1, p. 3

火，huǒ, *n.*, fire, L. 2, p. 18

火鸡，huǒjī, *n.*, turkey, L. 16, p. 228

获得，huòdé, *v.*, gain (opportunity; experience, etc.), L. 8, p. 97

或许，huòxǔ, *adv.*, perhaps; maybe, L. 18, p. 257

J

基本，jīběn, *adj./adv.*, fundamental; basic; basically, L. 7, p. 80; L. 19, p. 270

基本上，jīběn shang, *adv.*, basically; mainly; on the whole, L. 6, p. 68; L. 27, p. 385

基础，jīchǔ, *n.*, foundation, L. 18, p. 258

激动，jīdòng, *adj.*, become hysterical; (of one's emotion) become extreme and uncontrolled, L. 26, p. 373

讥讽，jīfěng, *v.*, to ridicule and satirize, L. 26, p. 372

机构，jīgòu, *n.*, organization; institution, L. 4, p. 45; L. 14, p. 190

几乎，jīhū, *adv.*, almost, L. 4, p. 42

饥荒，jīhuāng, *n.*, famine, L. 30, p. 431

积极，jījí, *adj.*, active; positive; enthusiastic, L. 20, p. 284

积累，jīlěi, *v.*, accumulate, L. 8, p. 97

激烈，jīliè, *adj.*, fierce (competition), L. 8, p. 95

激情，jīqíng, *n.*, intense emotion; passion; enthusiasm, L. 8, p. 95

极大，jídà, *adv.*, extremely big, L. 28, p. 402

集体，jítǐ, *n.*, collective (opp. 个人 individual), L. 30, p. 433

急需，jíxū, *v.*, in urgent need, L. 23, p. 332

籍贯，jíguàn, *n.*, place of one's origin, L. 9, p. 113

集中，jízhōng, *v.*, concentrate, L. 8, p. 98

记录，jìlù, *v./n.*, record, L. 26, p. 374

技能，jìnéng, *n.*, skill, L. 12, p. 160

纪念，jìniàn, *v.*, commemorate, L. 16, p. 225

纪念品，jìniàn pǐn, *n.*, souvenir, L. 10, p. 133

技师，jìshī, *n.*, technician; technical expert, L. 29, p. 421

技术，jìshù, *n.*, technology, L. 13, p. 173

计算，jìsuàn, *v.*, to calculate, L. 16, p. 226

记者，jìzhě, *n.*, reporter; journalist, L. 5, p. 56

加大，jiādà, *v.*, enlarge; augment; increase, L. 11, p. 145

假货，jiǎhuò, *n.*, fakes; counterfeit goods, L. 4, p. 42

加拿大，Jiānádà, *n.*, Canada, L. 21, p. 300

加强，jiāqiáng, *v.*, reinforce; strengthen, L. 22, p. 319

加入，jiārù, *v.*, join (an organization), L. 25, p. 361

家乡，jiāxiāng, *n.*, hometown, L. 9, p. 113

家用电器，jiāyòng diànqì, *n.*, household electronics, L. 4, p. 43

夹杂, jiāzá, v., mixed with; mingled with, L. 15, p. 208

家长, jiāzhǎng, n., parent or guardian of a child, L. 1, p. 2

加重, jiāzhòng, v., aggravate; increase (e.g. the burden), L. 25, p. 361

甲午战争, Jiǎwǔ Zhànzhēng, n., The Sino-Japanese War (1894-1895), L. 27, p. 385

假装, jiǎzhuāng, v., pretend; feign, L. 6, p. 66

嫁, jià, v., (of a woman) marry (a man), L. 28, p. 403

假期, jiàqī, n., holiday, L. 16, p. 227

价值, jiàzhí, n., value, L. 26, p. 372

价值观, jiàzhí guān, n., values, L. 3, p. 31

兼, jiān, v., hold two or more posts or to play two roles at the same time, L. 19, p. 271

坚持, jiānchí, v., to insist, L. 26, p. 372

监督, jiāndū, v., supervise, L. 4, p. 45

艰巨, jiānjù, adj., arduous, L. 22, p. 319

坚强, jiānqiáng, adj., (of a person's character) strong; tough, L. 21, p. 300

监狱, jiānyù, n., jail, L. 5, p. 54

捡, jiǎn, v., pick up (someone else' lost article), L. 20, p. 285

简称, jiǎnchēng, n., abbreviation, L. 10, p. 128

简化, jiǎnhuà, v., simplify, L. 15, p. 211

剪纸, jiǎnzhǐ, n., papercutting (traditional Chinese folk art form), L. 3, p. 32

建, jiàn, v., build, L. 2, p. 20

舰队, jiànduì, n., fleet, L. 23, p. 334

间接, jiànjiē, adv., indirectly, L. 26, p. 374

建立, jiànlì, v., establish (connections; an institute), L. 8, p. 97

见面礼, jiànmiàn lǐ, n., a present given to sb. upon first meeting, L. 6, p. 66

键盘, jiànpán, n., keyboard, L. 12, p. 162

健全, jiànquán, adj., sound and perfect (system), L. 4, p. 45

建设, jiànshè, v./n., construct; construction, L. 10, p. 128

建议, jiànyì, v., suggest; propose, L. 3, p. 31

建造, jiànzào, v., build, L. 23, p. 335

建筑, jiànzhù, n., structure; building; architecture, L. 2, p. 20

将来, jiānglái, n., future, L. 14, p. 193

江南, Jiāngnán, n., south of the Yangtze River, L. 10, p. 130

讲究, jiǎngjiū, v., particular about (food and clothing/manners/hygiene), L. 6, p. 66

酱油, jiàngyóu, n., soy sauce, L. 15, p. 208

骄傲, jiāo'ào, adj., proud (of sb.); take pride in; arrogant, L. 7, p. 82

交给, jiāogěi, v., give to; entrust sb. with, L. 25, p. 358

交税, jiāoshuì, v-o., pay taxes, L. 24, p. 346

交谈, jiāotán, v., converse; have a conversation (formal), L. 9, p. 113

交通工具, jiāotōng gōngjù, n., means of transportation, L. 13, p. 177

交通枢纽, jiāotōng shūniǔ, n., transportation hub, L. 23, p. 336

交往, jiāowǎng, v./n., in contact with; to associate with, L. 9, p. 116

交易, jiāoyì, n., deal; trade, L. 6, p. 66

角度, jiǎodù, n., perspective; point of view; angle, L. 7, p. 81

教堂, jiàotáng, n., church, L. 16, p. 225

接, jiē, v., pick up (from school, airport, etc.), L. 1, p. 2

接触, jiēchù, v., come into contact with; get in touch with, L. 6, p. 68; L. 9, p. 117

接电话, jiē diànhuà, v.-o., answer the phone, L. 26, p. 373

阶段, jiēduàn, n., stage; phase, L. 13, p. 176; L. 15, p. 211

阶段性, jiēduànxìng, adj., staged (used as a modifier), L. 17, p. 240

阶级, jiējí, n., (social) class, L. 5, p. 55

接近, jiējìn, v., similar to (quality, interests, opinions), L. 10, p. 131

接下来, jiēxiàlai, int., next; then, L. 9, p. 112

结构, jiégòu, n., structure, L. 27, p. 389; L. 30, p. 429

结合, jiéhé, v., combine; unite, L. 13, p. 173

节假日, jiéjià rì, n., holiday and vacations, L. 16, p. 228; L. 17, p. 238

节日, jiérì, n., festival, L. 3, p. 32; L. 16, p. 225

截然不同, jiérán bùtóng, idm., completely different, L. 26, p. 374

结账, jiézhàng, v.-o., pay the check; check out, L. 26, p. 371

解放, jiěfàng, v., to liberate, L. 28, p. 401

解雇, jiěgù, v., fire, L. 8, p. 96

解开, jiěkāi, v., unlock, L. 22, p. 316

解释, jiěshì, v., explain, L. 26, p. 373

介绍, jièshào, v./n., introduce; introduction, L. 3, p. 32

斤, jīn, m.w., a traditional unit of weight, equivalent to 0.5 kilograms, L. 20, p. 286

金钱, jīnqián, n., money (collective noun), L. 19, p. 270

仅次于, jǐncìyú, v., second only to; only inferior to, L. 9, p. 113

尽管, jǐnguǎn, conj., although, L. 17, p. 241

尽可能, jǐn kěnéng, adv., to the best of one's ability, L. 30, p. 432

进程, jìnchéng, n., course; process, L. 29, p. 418

近代, jìndài, n., modern times, L. 23, p. 331

近几年, jìn jǐ nián, t.w., in recent years, L. 1, p. 1

进口, jìnkǒu, v./adj., import; imported, L. 4, p. 44

尽快, jǐnkuài, adv., as quickly as possible, L. 13, p. 173

禁烟, jìnyān, v.o., ban smoking (in public areas), L. 11, p. 145

进一步, jìnyíbù, adv., further, L. 26, p. 375

禁止, jìnzhǐ, v., forbid, L. 19, p. 271

经费, jīngfèi, n., funds, L. 14, p. 194

经过, jīngguò, prep./v., with (one's permission); go through; experience, L. 21, p. 303; L. 29, p. 419

经济, jīngjì, n., financial status/position; economy, L. 28, p. 403

经济体, jīngjìtǐ, n., economy, L. 27, p. 387

京剧, jīngjù, n., Beijing opera, L. 18, p. 257

经历, jīnglì, n., experience, L. 29, p. 420

经理, jīnglǐ, n., manager, L. 26, p. 372

精确, jīngquè, adj., precise, L. 28, p. 406

精神, jīngshén, n., spirit; essence, L. 6, p. 67; L. 29, p. 418

惊喜，jīngxǐ, *adv./v.*, (pleasantly) surprised, L. 18, p. 256

惊讶，jīngyà, *v.*, feel surprised, L. 4, p. 44

经营，jīngyíng, *v.*, run (a business), L. 13, p. 174

精英，jīngyīng, *n.*, elite, L. 8, p. 99

警报，jǐngbào, *n.*, alarm, L. 26, p. 371

景点，jǐngdiǎn, *n.*, scenery spot; place of interest; attraction, L. 10, p. 133

景观，jǐngguān, *n.*, landscape; (natural/tourist) sight, L. 10, p. 133; L. 11, p. 146

景区，jǐngqū, *n.*, attractions; scenic area, L. 17, p. 239

景象，jǐngxiàng, *n.*, scene; phenomenon, L. 17, p. 239

旧，jiù, *adj.*, used; worn; old, L. 18, p. 255

救，jiù, *v.*, save, L. 25, p. 358

就业，jiùyè, *n.*, employment (modifier), L. 24, p. 345

救灾，jiùzāi, *v.*, provide disaster relief, L. 20, p. 285

居民，jūmín, *n.*, residents, L. 23, p. 333

居然，jūrán, *adv.*, unexpectedly; surprisingly; to one's surprise, L. 11, p. 146; L. 18, p. 256

局限于，júxiàn yú, *v.*, limited to; confined to, L. 23, p. 332

举办，jǔbàn, *v.*, to run or hold (an event), L. 18, p. 255

举行，jǔxíng, *v.*, hold (a meeting, ceremony, etc.), L. 1, p. 3

举止，jǔzhǐ, *n.*, manner; bearing, L. 18, p. 258

举足轻重，jǔzúqīngzhòng, *idm.*, play a decisive role, L. 17, p. 241

巨大，jùdà, *adj.*, huge; tremendous, L. 8, p. 96

聚会，jùhuì, *n.*, gather-together; gathering, L. 16, p. 228

聚集，jùjí, *v.*, gather; assemble, L. 18, p. 254

拒绝，jùjué, *v.*, to refuse, L. 22, p. 317

距离，jùlí, *n.*, distance, L. 12, p. 161

具体，jùtǐ, *adj.*, concrete; specific, L. 11, p. 144

具有，jùyǒu, *v.*, possess or have (sth. immaterial), L. 11, p. 146

绝大多数，juédàduōshù, *pron.*, the overwhelming majority, L. 12, p. 160

绝对，juéduì, *adv.*, absolutely; definitely, L. 7, p. 82

崛起，juéqǐ, *v.*, to rise to prominence, L. 23, p. 334

角色，juésè, *n.*, role (in a play, movie, etc.), L. 23, p. 336

决心，juéxīn, *n.*, determination; resolve, L. 5, p. 55

军队，jūnduì, *n.*, troops, L. 20, p. 285

军费，jūnfèi, *n.*, military expending, L. 20, p. 286

军事，jūnshì, *n.*, military, L. 3, p. 30; L. 7, p. 83

K

开除，kāichú, *v.*, expel; dismiss, L. 14, p. 194

开发，kāifā, *v.*, start up and develop, L. 10, p. 133

开明，kāimíng, *n.*, liberal; open-minded, L. 27, p. 387

开设，kāishè, *v.*, offer (a course in college, a service), L. 15, p. 209

开学，kāixué, *v.*, school begins, L. 16, p. 228

扛，káng, *v.*, shoulder; carry on the shoulder, L. 20, p. 286

抗战，Kàngzhàn, *n.*, abbr. for 抗日战争 the War of Resistance against Japanese Aggression (1937-1945), L. 30, p. 431

考虑，kǎolù, *v.*, consider; to think over, L. 8, p. 95

考研，kǎoyán, *v.*, take the graduate entrance examination, L. 14, p. 191

考验，kǎoyàn, *n./v.*, test; ordeal; put to the test, L. 12, p. 160

科技，kējì, *n.*, science and technology, L. 12, p. 161; L. 13, p. 174

科学，kēxué, *n.*, science, L. 1, p. 4

科研，kēyán, *n.*, scientific research, L. 15, p. 211

科目，kēmù, *n.*, subject (in a curriculum), L. 14, p. 191

咳嗽，késòu, *v.*, cough, L. 1, p. 2

可恨，kěhèn, *adj.*, hateful; detestable, L. 21, p. 300

可怕，kěpà, *adj.*, fearful; terrifying, L. 2, p. 18

可想而知，kěxiǎng érzhī, *idm.*, one can well imagine that…, L. 14, p. 191

刻不容缓，kèbùrónghuǎn, *idm.*, of great urgency; demand immediate attention, L. 30, p. 432

客观，kèguān, *adj.*, objective, L. 28, p. 406

客观性，kèguān xìng, *n.*, objectivity, L. 20, p. 287

客满，kèmǎn, *n.*, (of a theater, cinema, etc.) to have a full house, L. 18, p. 257

课外活动，kèwài huódòng, *n.*, extracurricular activity, L. 14, p. 191

肯定，kěndìng, *n.*, (give or receive) recognition, L. 18, p. 258

恐怖分子，kǒngbù fènzǐ, *n.*, terrorist, L. 22, p. 317

恐怖袭击，kǒngbù xíjī, *n.*, terrorist attack, L. 22, p. 317

恐怖主义，kǒngbù zhǔyì, *n.*, terrorism, L. 22, p. 319

恐怖组织，kǒngbùzǔzhī, *n.*, terrorist organization, L. 22, p. 316

空间，kōngjiān, *n.*, room; space, L. 10, p. 129

空气，kōngqì, *n.*, air, L. 1, p. 1

空前，kōngqián, *adj.*, unprecedented, L. 12, p. 160

空想，kōngxiǎng, *attr.*, Utopian; unrealistic, L. 30, p. 433

孔子学院，Kǒngzǐ Xuéyuàn, *n.*, Confucius Institute, L. 3, p. 33

控制，kòngzhì, *v.*, to control, L. 23, p. 333

口，kǒu, *m.w.*, a mouthful of (food, water, etc.), L. 11, p. 147

口袋，kǒudài, *n.*, pocket, L. 26, p. 371

口罩，kǒuzhào, *n.*, gauze mask, L. 1, p. 2

扣掉，kòudiào, *v.*, deduct…from…, L. 8, p. 96

扣留，kòuliú, *v.*, detain, L. 26, p. 374

苦中作乐，kǔzhōngzuòlè, *idm.*, have fun amidst hardships, L. 1, p. 3

夸张，kuāzhāng, *adj.*, exaggerated; overstated, L. 1, p. 2

跨国，kuàguó, *adj.*, transnational (company), L. 28, p. 401

快递，kuàidì, *n.*, express delivery, L. 13, p. 175

快速，kuàisù, *adv.*, fast; rapidly, L. 9, p. 117

宽容，kuānróng, *adj.*, tolerant; open-minded, L. 21, p. 300

宽松，kuānsōng, *adj.*, (of policy) flexible, relaxed, L. 15, p. 211

款式，kuǎnshì, *n.*, design; style, L. 20, p. 287

矿泉水，kuàngquánshuǐ, *n.*, mineral water, L. 26, p. 371

困，kùn, *v.*, trap; strand, L. 2, p. 21

困惑，kùnhuò, *v.*, feel perplexed; puzzled, L. 4, p. 44

困扰，kùnrǎo, *v.*, bother; trouble, L. 21, p. 301

扩大, kuòdà, v., expand, L. 23, p. 332

扩建, kuòjiàn, v., expand (armed forces/the navy), L. 23, p. 335

扩张, kuòzhāng, v., aggrandize (one's power/influence), L. 27, p. 388

L

拉大, lādà, v., widen, L. 8, p. 99

拉动, lādòng, v., promote; boost, L. 17, p. 238

来往, láiwǎng, v., have contact or dealings with sb., L. 10, p. 128

来自, láizì, v., come from, L. 23, p. 331

拦, lán, v., stop sb. and not let him/her go, L. 26, p. 371

蓝天, lántiān, n., blue sky, L. 1, p. 3

滥用, lànyòng, v., abuse (one's power, privilege, authority), L. 22, p. 315

劳动, láodòng, v./n., do physical work; to labor; work; labor, L. 17, p. 238

劳动力, láodòng lì, n., labor force, L. 24, p. 345

老话, lǎohuà, n., old saying; adage, L. 6, p. 65

老家, lǎojiā, n., hometown, L. 25, p. 358

老鼠, lǎoshǔ, n., mouse; rat, L. 19, p. 272

老死, lǎosǐ, v., die (of old age), L. 9, p. 116

老乡, lǎoxiāng, n., fellow-townsman/villager, L. 9, p. 112

乐观, lèguān, adj., optimistic, L. 20, p. 284

乐意, lèyì, v., be happy to do sth., L. 14, p. 194

类似, lèisì, adj., similar, L. 28, p. 405

里, lǐ, n., traditional unit of length, equal to 0.5 kilometers, L. 2, p. 20

里程碑, lǐchéng bēi, n., milestone (in the course of historical development), L. 29, p. 418

礼节, lǐjié, n., protocol; etiquette, L. 18, p. 258

理解, lǐjiě, v., understand; comprehend, L. 7, p. 83

礼让, lǐràng, v., give precedence to sb. out of courtesy or thoughtfulness, L. 30, p. 429

礼尚往来, lǐshàngwǎnglái, idm., courtesy/friendly politeness demands reciprocity, L. 6, p. 66

理所当然, lǐsuǒdāngrán, idm., It is only right and proper, L. 13, p. 178

理想, lǐxiǎng, n., ideal; aspiration (career related), L. 8, p. 98

礼仪, lǐyí, n., etiquette, L. 17, p. 241

理由, lǐyóu, n., reason; justification; argument, L. 22, p. 319

力度, lìdù, n., strength; force, L. 11, p. 145

历法, lìfǎ, n., calendar; calendric system, L. 16, p. 227

立刻, lìkè, adv., immediately, L. 5, p. 56

力量, lìliàng, n., (physical) strength, ability, power, L. 3, p. 30

例外, lìwài, n., exception, L. 6, p. 67; L. 22, p. 316

利益, lìyì, n., interest; benefit, L. 22, p. 318

利用, lìyòng, v., utilize; take advantage of, L. 14, p. 190

廉价, liánjià, adj., low-priced; cheap (derogatory term), L. 24, p. 345

连累, liánlèi, v., implicate; cause or bring trouble to another, L. 14, p. 194

联系, liánxì, v., connect; link; relate, L. 7, p. 84; L. 9, p. 117

脸书, liǎnshū, n., Facebook, L. 7, p. 83

恋人, liànrén, n., loved one; girlfriend or boyfriend, L. 1, p. 2

亮, liàng, adj., bright, L. 16, p. 227

良好, liánghǎo, adj., (of one's performance, habit, etc.) good, L. 20, p. 286

两岸, liǎng'àn, n., both sides of the Taiwan Strait (i.e. Taiwan and mainland), L. 27, p. 388

两者, liǎng zhě, pron., both sides, both parties, L. 10, p. 133

量化, liànghuà, v., quantify, L. 28, p. 406

了不起, liǎobuqǐ, adj., extraordinary; terrific, L. 16, p. 226

了解, liǎojiě, v., know (a fact); find out about, L. 4, p. 44

料到, liàodào, v., foresee; expect, L. 22, p. 315

劣质, lièzhì, adj., poor or low quality; inferior (modifier), L. 4, p. 42; L. 10, p. 133

邻近, línjìn, attr., neighboring, L. 23, p. 331

零花钱, línghuā qián, n., allowance; pocket money, L. 25, p. 361

零食, língshí, n., snack, L. 26, p. 371

领导, lǐngdǎo, v./n., lead; exercise leadership, L. 1, p. 4

领导人, lǐngdǎo rén, n., leader of a country or party, L. 27, p. 387; L. 28, p. 401

领域, lǐngyù, n., field, L. 17, p. 241

流动, liúdòng, v., (of water, air, etc.) to flow; migrate, L. 23, p. 333

流利, liúlì, adj., fluent; fluently, L. 27, p. 385

留守儿童, liúshǒu értóng, n., left-behind children, L. 25, p. 358

流行, liúxíng, v./adj., popular or prevalent, L. 8, p. 95

留学热, liúxué rè, n., craze of studying abroad, L. 14, p. 190

流失, liúshī, v., lose or drain, L. 15, p. 212

龙, lóng, n., dragon, L. 2, p. 18

龙的传人, lóng de chuánrén, n., Descendants of the Dragon, L. 2, p. 18

录取, lùqǔ, v., admit, L. 14, p. 194

陆上, lùshàng, attr., land (based); on land, L. 23, p. 335

绿卡, lùkǎ, n., "Green Card," permanent residence permit for foreigners, L. 15, p. 209

旅游, lǚyóu, n./v., traveling; tourism, L. 3, p. 33

论坛, lùntán, n., forum for discussion, L. 21, p. 299

落后, luòhòu, adj., backward; behind the times, L. 7, p. 81

M

骂, mà, v., verbally abuse; curse, L. 21, p. 299

埋头, máitóu, v., bury one's head in; immerse oneself in (work, study), L. 12, p. 162

买卖, mǎimài, n., buy and sell; business, L. 6, p. 66

满意, mǎnyì, adj., satisfactory, L. 30, p. 430

漫画, mànhuà, n., comic; cartoon, L. 7, p. 80

忙碌, mánglù, adj., busy (formal), L. 8, p. 99

盲目, mángmù, adv., blindly, L. 14, p. 194

蟒蛇, mǎngshé, n., serpent; python, L. 2, p. 18

毛病, máobìng, n., defect; shortcoming; bad habit, L. 11, p. 147

冒犯, màofàn, *v.*, offend (superiors, gods, taboos); incur, L. 19, p. 273

媒体, méitǐ, *n.*, media, L. 5, p. 56

美丑, měichǒu, *n.*, beauty and ugliness, L. 28, p. 406

美丽, měilì, *adj.*, beautiful; pretty, L. 10, p. 133

美容, měiróng, *n./v.*, beauty treatment; to improve one's looks, L. 28, p. 407

美术, měishù, *n.*, the fine arts, L. 18, p. 255

弥漫, mímàn, *v.*, (of feeling, smell) to pervade, L. 28, p. 407

秘书, mìshu, *n.*, secretary, L. 19, p. 271

密码, mìmǎ, *n.*, password, L. 22, p. 317

密切, mìqiè, *adj.*, close (relationship), L. 23, p. 333

缅怀, miǎnhuái, *v.*, to think of or cherish the memory of (the past, history, a person), L. 30, p. 434

勉强, miǎnqiǎng, *adv.*, with difficultly; forcefully, L. 27, p. 389

面对, miànduì, *v.*, face; confront, L. 1, p. 3

面积, miànjī, *n.*, area (of a floor, piece of land, etc.); size, L. 27, p. 388; L. 29, p. 419

面貌, miànmào, *n.*, appearance (of things); look; aspect, L. 19, p. 272

面向, miànxiàng, *v.*, to turn in the direction of…, L. 23, p. 334

描述, miáoshù, *v.*, describe and narrate, L. 19, p. 271

描写, miáoxiě, *v.*, describe, L. 19, p. 270

明代, Míng dài, *n.*, The Ming dynasty (1368-1644), L. 23, p. 334

民国, Mínguó, *n.*, Republic of China (1912-1949, the government moved to Taiwan after 1949)., L. 30, p. 431

民营, mínyíng, *adj.*, privately run; run by private citizens, L. 18, p. 255

民主, mínzhǔ, *n./adj.*, democracy; democratic (country 民主国家, system 民主制度), L. 27, p. 387

民族, mínzú, *n.*, people; nationality, L. 1, p. 3

民族主义, mínzú zhǔyì, *n.*, nationalism, L. 7, p. 82

闽南话, Mǐnnán huà , *n.*, Southern Fujian dialect, L. 11, p. 148

名车, míngchē, *n.*, luxury car, L. 18, p. 253

名贵, míngguì, *adj.*, famous and precious, L. 18, p. 253

名牌, míngpái, *adj.*, brand name (modifier), L. 4, p. 42

名人, míngrén, *n.*, famous figures; celebrity, L. 16, p. 225; L. 21, p. 301

名声, míngshēng, *n.*, reputation, L. 21, p. 301

明显, míngxiǎn, *adj./adv*, obvious; obviously, L. 10, p. 130

明星, míngxīng, *n.*, star; celebrity, L. 21, p. 301

模式, móshì, *n.*, model, L. 27, p. 387

摩天大楼, mótiān dàlóu, *n.*, skyscraper, L. 11, p. 144

末, mò, *suffix.*, the end of (a century or decade), L. 24, p. 347

陌生人, mòshēng rén, *n.*, stranger, L. 1, p. 2

目的地, mùdì dì, *n.*, destination, L. 10, p. 132

目前, mùqián, *t.w.*, at present; at the moment, L. 25, p. 358

N

奶粉, nǎifěn, *n.*, milk powder, L. 4, p. 44

难得, nándé, *adj.*, rare, hard-earned (chance, opportunity), L. 1, p. 3

难怪, nánguài, *adv.*, no wonder, L. 4, p. 44

南海, Nánhǎi, *n.*, South China Sea, L. 23, p. 335

内容, nèiróng, *n.*, content, L. 10, p. 128

内需, nèixū, *n.*, domestic demand, L. 17, p. 238

内战, nèizhàn, *n.*, civil war, L. 27, p. 386

泥土, nítǔ, *n.*, earth; soil, L. 9, p. 114

匿名, nìmíng, *adj.*, anonymous, L. 21, p. 302

年代, niándài, *n.*, a decade; era, L. 12, p. 161

年久失修, niánjiǔshīxiū, *idm.*, (of a building) worn down by years, L. 18, p. 254

年轻一代, niánqīng yídài, *n.*, young generation, L. 24, p. 347

牛仔裤, niúzǎi kù, *n.*, jeans, L. 3, p. 30

纽约时报, Niǔyuē Shíbào, *n.*, The New York Times, L. 7, p. 84

浓, nóng, *adj.*, strong, L. 23, p. 332

农历, nónglì, *n.*, lunar calendar, L. 16, p. 226

农民工, nóngmín gōng, *n.*, migrant workers, L. 24, p. 345

农药, nóngyào, *n.*, pesticide, L. 7, p. 84

农业, nóngyè, *adj./n.*, agricultural; agriculture, L. 7, p. 81

女权, nǚquán, *adj.*, feminism, L. 28, p. 405

O

偶尔, ǒu' ěr, *adv.*, occasionally; once in a while, L. 24, p. 346

P

拍, pāi, *v.*, swat, L. 5, p. 54

排, pái, *v.*, rank… (a particular position) …in…, L. 10, p. 132

排放, páifàng, *v.*, emit; discharge, L. 1, p. 4

排挤, páijǐ , *v.*, push aside; exclude, L. 13, p. 173

排外, páiwài, *v.o.*, exclude or resist anything foreign; exclusionary; anti-foreign, L. 29, p. 421

牌子, páizi, *n.*, plate, sign, L. 11, p. 145

派遣, pàiqiǎn, *v.*, send out; dispatch, L. 30, p. 433

判断, pànduàn, *v.*, judge, L. 28, p. 406

抛弃, pāoqì , *v.*, to abandon, L. 17, p. 240

炮友, pàoyǒu, *n.*, friend with benefits, L. 13, p. 177

陪, péi, *v.*, accompany, L. 25, p. 360

赔偿, péicháng, *v./n.*, compensate; compensation, L. 26, p. 374

赔款, péikuǎn, *n.*, reparations; indemnity, L. 27, p. 386

培训, péixùn, *v./n.*, train; training, L. 14, p. 190

培养, péiyǎng, *v.*, cultivate; foster (a certain spirit) in sb., L. 14, p. 193

佩服, pèifú, *v.*, to admire from the heart, L. 18, p. 256

配合, pèihé, *v.* (*n.*), 1) cooperate; cooperation; 2) coordinate with, act in concert with, 1) L. 12, p. 162; 2) L. 22, p. 319

喷, pēn, *v.*, shoot; spurt; spout, L. 2, p. 18

蓬勃发展, péngbó fāzhǎn, *V.P.*, flourish; boom in development, L. 18, p. 253

碰, pèng, *v.*, touch, L. 19, p. 270

碰到, pèngdào, v., encounter; come across, L. 25, p. 359

皮鞋, píxié, n., leather shoes, L. 4, p. 43

片, piàn, m.w., measure word for stretches of land or scenery, L. 18, p. 256

偏僻, piānpì, adj., remote, L. 10, p. 128

偏远, piānyuǎn, adj., remote (modifier), L. 10, p. 133

漂, piāo, v., float (on the water); to drift (down the stream), L. 8, p. 98

票价, piàojià, n., ticket price, L. 18, p. 257

拼命, pīnmìng, adv., exert the utmost strength; give it one's all, L. 8, p. 96

频繁, pínfán, adj., frequent, L. 22, p. 319

贫穷, pínqióng, adj., poor; impoverished, L. 7, p. 81

品牌, pǐnpái, n., brand; make, L. 15, p. 210

品质, pǐnzhì, n., quality (of life, of a product or service), L. 1, p. 4

平安, píng'ān, adj., safe and sound, L. 16, p. 226

平常, píngcháng, adj., ordinary; common, L. 11, p. 145

平衡, pínghéng, v./n., balance, L. 10, p. 133

平均, píngjūn, adj./adv., average; equally, L. 10, p. 128

平时, píngshí, t.w., ordinarily; in regular times, L. 8, p. 99

平原, píngyuán, n., plain, L. 10, p. 130

破产, pòchǎn, v., (of a plan) fail; go bankrupt, L. 29, p. 421

迫害, pòhài, v., persecute, L. 29, p. 420

破坏, pòhuài, v., destroy (environment/traditional cultures); do great damage to; sabotage, L. 11, p. 144; L. 17, p. 239

破旧不堪, pòjiùbùkān, adj., (of a house) unbearably or extremely broken down, L. 18, p. 254

破落, pòluò, adj., dilapidated, L. 11, p. 144

迫切, pòqiè, adj., urgent; pressing, L. 7, p. 82

迫切性, pòqiè xìng, n., urgency, L. 25, p. 361

普及, pǔjí, v., popularize; make widely available, L. 12, p. 160

普通人, pǔtōng rén, n., ordinary person; average people, L. 8, p. 96

Q

欺负, qīfu, v., bully, L. 2, p. 19

期盼, qīpàn, v./n., yearn for; yearning, L. 7, p. 81

奇迹, qíjì, n., miracle; wonder, L. 2, p. 20

歧视, qíshì, v./n., discriminate; discrimination, L. 19, p. 271

其中, qízhōng, p.w., among which, L. 13, p. 175; L. 25, p. 358

起飞, qǐfēi, v./n., take off; (economic) take-off, L. 27, p. 387

起跑线, qǐpǎo xiàn, n., starting line, L. 14, p. 192

起先, qǐxiān, conj., at first; in the beginning, L. 5, p. 54

企业, qǐyè, n., enterprise; business, L. 13, p. 176; L. 18, p. 255

气愤, qìfèn, v., feel indignant, L. 5, p. 55

器官, qìguān, n., organ, L. 5, p. 56

气息, qìxī, n., smell; breath; flavor, L. 28, p. 407

恰恰, qiàqià, adv., exactly; precisely, L. 6, p. 67

千千万万, qiānqiān wànwàn, idm., thousands upon thousands, L. 3, p. 30

前不久, qiánbùjiǔ, t.w., not long ago, L. 26, p. 371

谴责, qiǎnzé, v., condemn, L. 26, p. 373

枪, qiāng, n., gun, L. 22, p. 316

枪战, qiāngzhàn, n., gunfight, L. 22, p. 316

枪支控制, qiāngzhī kòngzhì, N.P., gun control, L. 19, p. 273

强大, qiángdà, adj., powerful; strong, L. 3, p. 30

强调, qiángdiào, v., stress, L. 7, p. 80

强国梦, qiángguó mèng, n., the dream to be a strong nation, L. 7, p. 82

强烈, qiángliè, adj., strong; intense, L. 7, p. 82

抢, qiǎng, v., scramble for; vie for; to snatch, L. 11, p. 146

抢购, qiǎnggòu, v., rush to purchase (anticipating scarcity), L. 4, p. 43

悄悄, qiāoqiāo, adv., secretly, L. 11, p. 146

瞧, qiáo, v., Look! L. 1, p. 3

侵犯, qīnfàn, v., infringe on, L. 22, p. 318

侵害, qīnhài, v., infringe on, L. 26, p. 374

侵略, qīnlüè, v., invade, L. 7, p. 82

亲戚, qīnqi, n., relatives, L. 25, p. 358

亲切, qīnqiè, adj., warm; (a thing) feels near and dear to sb., L. 9, p. 113

亲友, qīnyǒu, n., family and friends, L. 17, p. 240

亲嘴, qīnzuǐ, v.-o., kiss (no object), L. 1, p. 2

情感, qínggǎn, n., emotion, L. 20, p. 284

清明节, Qīngmíng jié, n., Tomb Sweeping Day, L. 3, p. 32

轻松, qīngsōng, adj., relaxed; at ease, L. 6, p. 66

倾向, qīngxiàng, n., tendency; inclination, L. 3, p. 32; L. 14, p. 192

清新, qīngxīn, adj., pure and fresh, L. 10, p. 133

轻易, qīngyì, adv., easily, L. 10, p. 129

情人, qíngrén, n., lover; mistress, L. 28, p. 404

情人节, Qíngrén jié, n., Valentine's Day, L. 16, p. 228

情形, qíngxíng, n., situation, L. 20, p. 285

情绪, qíngxù, n., feelings; sentiment, L. 7, p. 82

请, qǐng, v., to ask (sb. to do sth. politely), L. 26, p. 372

请勿吸烟, qǐng wù xīyān, phr., No smoking, L. 11, p. 145

庆祝, qìngzhù, v., celebrate, L. 16, p. 225

区分, qūfēn, v., differentiate; distinguish, L. 10, p. 131

趋势, qūshì, n., trend; tendency, L. 28, p. 406

取代, qǔdài, v., replace, L. 12, p. 160

取得, qǔdé, v., obtain; gain, L. 10, p. 133; L. 15, p. 212

取消, qǔxiāo, v., cancel; abolish, L. 17, p. 238

取悦, qǔyuè, v., please (sb.), L. 28, p. 405

去世, qùshì, v., pass away, L. 25, p. 358

圈子, quānzi, n., circle; clique, L. 9, p. 116

权力, quánlì, n., power, L. 22, p. 315

全面, quánmiàn, adj., comprehensive; all-round (opp. 片面 biased), L. 23, p. 332

劝, quàn, v., urge; try to persuade, L. 1, p. 2

劝住, quànzhù, v.-c., to persuade sb. not to do sth., L. 26, p. 372

缺, quē, v., lack, L. 25, p. 361

454

缺乏, quēfá, *v.*, lack; be deficient in; be short of, L. 6, p. 65

群山, qúnshān, *n.*, mountain range, L. 2, p. 20

群体, qúntǐ, *n.*, social group, L. 28, p. 403

群众, qúnzhòng, *n.*, the crowd; the masses, L. 26, p. 373

群众心理, qúnzhòng xīnlǐ, *n.*, mentality of the masses, L. 11, p. 146

R

然而, rán' ér, *conj.*, however, L. 17, p. 239; L. 28, p. 402

热潮, rècháo, *n.*, great mass fervor; all the rage, L. 14, p. 191

人才, réncái, *n.*, talented person; talent; human resources, L. 8, p. 99

人才外流, réncái wàiliú, *idm.*, brain drain; outflow of talented people, L. 15, p. 208

人格尊严, réngé zūnyán, *n.*, human dignity, L. 26, p. 374

人际关系, rénjì guānxi, *n.*, interpersonal relations, L. 8, p. 96

人类, rénlèi, *n.*, humans; mankind, L. 2, p. 20

人脉, rénmài, *n.*, connections; social network, L. 8, p. 97

人民公社, Rénmín gōngshè, *n.*, People's Commune (1958-1982), L. 30, p. 431

人情, rénqíng, *n.*, a favor done for someone, L. 6, p. 65

人情味, rénqíngwèi, *n.*, genuine human warmth, L. 30, p. 429

人山人海, rénshānrénhǎi, *idm.*, huge crowds of people in the open air, L. 17, p. 239

人为, rénwéi, *adj.*, man-made; artificial, L. 23, p. 334

人文科学, rénwén kēxué, *n.*, humanities, L. 29, p. 421

人物, rénwù, *n.*, (public, historical) figure, L. 30, p. 431

人心, rénxīn, *n.*, the will of the people; public feeling, L. 3, p. 31

人员, rényuán, *n.*, personnel, L. 15, p. 211

忍受, rěnshòu, *v.*, endure; put up with, L. 21, p. 301

任, rèn, *m.w.*, measure word for the number of terms served on an official post, L. 29, p. 420

认, rèn, *v.*, try to recognize, L. 1, p. 2

认得, rèndé, *v.*, know; to recognize, L. 1, p. 1

认定, rèndìng, *v.*, to determine (a fact, identity), L. 23, p. 333

认同, rèntóng, *v.*, identify with (values/cultures/ideas), L. 3, p. 31; L. 9, p. 113

任务, rènwù, *n.*, task, L. 12, p. 161

仍, réng, *adv.*, still, L. 28, p. 403

日常生活, rìcháng shēnghuó, *n.*, daily life, L. 3, p. 30

日益, rìyì, *adv.*, day by day, L. 17, p. 239

容貌, róngmào, *n.*, facial appearance and expression, L. 28, p. 406

入手, rùshǒu, *v.*, start with; begin with, L. 12, p. 162

软弱, ruǎnruò, *adj.*, weak; soft (of character), L. 2, p. 19

软实力, ruǎn shílì, *n.*, soft power, L. 3, p. 30

S

散布, sànbù, *v.*, spread; disseminate (rumors), L. 21, p. 301

丧失, sàngshī, *v.*, lose (ambition, ability, senses, etc.), L. 15, p. 208

色彩, sècǎi, *n.*, color, L. 9, p. 115

沙袋, shādài, *n.*, sandbag, L. 20, p. 286

删掉, shāndiào, *v.*, delete, L. 20, p. 286

煽情, shānqíng, *v.*, arouse emotions and sentiment, L. 20, p. 286

山寨产品, shānzhài chǎnpǐn, *n.*, knockoff products, L. 4, p. 42

擅长, shàncháng, *v.*, be good at; master in, L. 14, p. 193

扇子, shànzi, *n.*, fan, L. 18, p. 256

伤害, shānghài, *n.*, harm, L. 1, p. 2

商品, shāngpǐn, *n.*, commodity; merchandise, L. 4, p. 43

商人, shāngrén, *n.*, merchant; businessman, L. 4, p. 43

上当受骗, shàngdàng shòupiàn, *idm.*, be duped and swindled, L. 13, p. 174

上学, shàngxué, *v.-o.*, attend school, L. 25, p. 360

上一代, shàng yídài, *n.*, last generation, L. 24, p. 347

上涨, shàngzhǎng, *v.*, (of price) rise, L. 24, p. 346

稍稍, shāoshāo, *adv.*, slightly, L. 30, p. 433

少数, shǎoshù, *pron.*, minority, L. 12, p. 160

少年犯, shàonián fàn, *n.*, juvenile delinquent, L. 25, p. 361

奢侈品, shēchǐ pǐn, *n.*, luxuries, L. 4, p. 44

舌头, shétou, *n.*, tongue, L. 5, p. 56

设备, shèbèi, *n.*, equipment, L. 10, p. 129

社会主义, shèhuì zhǔyì, *n.*, socialism, L. 19, p. 272

设计, shèjì, *n./v.*, design; to design, L. 4, p. 43

设立, shèlì, *v.*, establish; to set up, L. 8, p. 97

摄像头, shèxiàngtóu, *n.*, webcam, L. 21, p. 301

摄影, shèyǐng, *n.*, photography, L. 18, p. 255

身边, shēnbiān, *n.*, (by) one's side, L. 25, p. 359

身份, shēnfèn, *n.*, identity, L. 9, p. 113

身份证, shēnfèn zhèng, *n.*, identification card, L. 23, p. 333

深刻, shēnkè, *adj.*, deep; profound, L. 18, p. 257; L. 19, p. 269

深远, shēnyuǎn, *adj.*, deep and profound; far-reaching, L. 30, p. 431

深圳, Shēnzhèn, *n.*, Shenzhen is a major city and financial center in South China, L. 8, p. 98

神, shén, *n.*, deity, L. 16, p. 226

审美, shěnměi, *n.*, aesthetics, L. 28, p. 406

生产, shēngchǎn, *v.*, produce (milk powder/rice/food...), L. 4, p. 44

生动, shēngdòng, *adj./adv.*, lively; vividly, L. 19, p. 270

升级, shēngjí, *v.*, upgrade, L. 22, p. 318

生命, shēngmìng, *n.*, life, L. 21, p. 302; L. 22, p. 317

声色名利, shēngsè mínglì, *n.*, sensual pleasures, fame and wealth, L. 28, p. 407

生意, shēngyì, *n.*, business, L. 13, p. 174

省, shěng, *n.*, province, L. 9, p. 110

省钱, shěngqián, *v.-o.*, save money, L. 25, p. 359

圣诞节, Shèngdàn jié, *n.*, Christmas, L. 16, p. 225

胜利, shènglì, *n.*, victory; triumph, L. 11, p. 148

剩女, shèngnǚ, *n.*, leftover woman, L. 28, p. 401

剩下, shèngxià, *v.-c.*, left (over); remain, L. 8, p. 96

诗，shī, *n.*, poem; verse, L. 9, p. 114

诗人，shīrén, *n.*, poet, L. 9, p. 114

湿透，shītòu, *v.c.*, wet through; drenched, L. 20, p. 286

失主，shīzhǔ, *n.*, owner of lost property, L. 20, p. 285

时代，shídài, *n.*, era; epoch; the times, L. 30, p. 430

拾金不昧，shíjīn búmèi, *idm.*, one does not pocket the money he/she finds but returns it to its owner., L. 20, p. 285

时髦，shímáo, *adj.*, fashionable, L. 17, p. 241

食品，shípǐn, *n.*, food, L. 4, p. 45

时尚，shíshàng, *n./adj.*, fashion; fashionable, L. 3, p. 30

时速，shísù, *n.*, speed (per hour), L. 10, p. 128

食堂，shítáng, *n.*, canteen, L. 11, p. 146

实体，shítǐ, *n.*, physical (brick and mortar), L. 13, p. 174

实习，shíxí, *v./n.*, internship, L. 14, p. 190

实现，shíxiàn, *v.*, realize (one's ideal/dream/a plan), L. 7, p. 81

实行，shíxíng, *v.*, put into practice; carry out, L. 27, p. 389

—史，shǐ, *suffix*, the history of..., L. 2, p. 20

使用，shǐyòng, *v.*, use, L. 13, p. 176

始终，shǐzhōng, *adv.*, from the beginning to the end, L. 7, p. 83

士兵，shìbīng, *n.*, soldiers, L. 20, p. 285

市场，shìchǎng, *n.*, market, L. 4, p. 42

适当，shìdàng, *adj.*, appropriate; proper (in degree); suitable, L. 6, p. 67; L. 25, p. 360

适合，shìhé, *v.*, suit; fit, L. 14, p. 195

适婚年龄，shìhūn niánlíng, , proper age for marriage, L. 28, p. 403

实际，shíjì, *adj.*, practical; realistic, L. 16, p. 226

识字，shízì, *v.-o.*, learn to read; recognize characters; become literate, L. 12, p. 161

世纪，shìjì, *n.*, century, L. 6, p. 68

事件，shìjiàn, *n.*, incident, L. 26, p. 374

世界各地，shìjiè gèdì , *idm.*, all parts of the world; all over the world, L. 3, p. 33

势力，shìlì, *n.*, power; influence, L. 27, p. 388

视频，shìpín, *n.*, video, L. 21, p. 300

事实，shìshí, *n.*, fact, L. 28, p. 404

事业，shìyè, *n.*, career, L. 28, p. 404

适宜，shìyí, *v.*, suitable (for living), L. 23, p. 332

适应，shìyìng, *v.*, acclimatize; adapt to, L. 9, p. 114

市长，shìzhǎng, *n.*, mayor, L. 26, p. 374

收，shōu, *v.*, 1) accept or take (bribes/gifts/money); 2) charge (fees), 1) L. 5, p. 55; 2) L. 21, p. 302

收藏，shōucáng, *v./n.*, collect; collection, L. 18, p. 253

收取，shōuqǔ, *v.*, to take (bribes), L. 19, p. 270

收养，shōuyǎng, *v.*, adopt (a child/pet), L. 20, p. 285

收银员，shōu yíng yuán , *n.*, cashier, L. 13, p. 174; L. 26, p. 371

首，shǒu, *m.w.*, measure word for songs or poems, L. 9, p. 114

手表，shǒubiǎo, *n.*, wrist watch, L. 4, p. 43

手段，shǒuduàn, *n.*, (illegal) measures, mean or dirty tactics, L. 6, p. 65

手法，shǒufǎ, *n.*, technique, L. 18, p. 256

手提包，shǒutí bāo, *n.*, handbag, L. 4, p. 42

手续，shǒuxù, *n.*, procedure; formality, L. 15, p. 211

手指，shǒuzhǐ, *n.*, finger, L. 12, p. 162

守法，shǒufǎ, *v.-o.*, abide by the law, L. 4, p. 43

受害者，shòuhàizhě, *n.*, victim, L. 21, p. 301

售货员，shòuhuò yuán, *n.*, shop assistant; salesperson, L. 13, p. 174; L. 26, p. 371

受伤，shòushāng, *v.-o.*, get hurt, L. 26, p. 374

输，shū, *v.*, lose; defeated (opp. 赢 yíng), L. 14, p. 192

书法，shūfǎ, *n.*, calligraphy, L. 3, p. 32

书法家，shūfǎjiā, *n.*, calligrapher, L. 12, p. 160

书面语言，shūmiàn yǔyán, *n.*, written language, L. 29, p. 418

枢纽，shūniǔ, *n.*, pivot, hub, L. 23, p. 335

输入，shūrù, *v.*, input, L. 12, p. 161

书写，shūxiě, *v.*, write (formal), L. 12, p. 160

熟人，shúrén, *n.*, acquaintance, L. 25, p. 360

属于，shǔyú, *v.*, belong to, L. 18, p. 256

树立，shùlì, *v.*, set (an example), L. 20, p. 286

树叶，shùyè, *n.*, leaves (of a tree), L. 8, p. 98

数值，shùzhí, *n.*, number, L. 28, p. 406

数字，shùzì, *n.*, number, L. 25, p. 359

帅气，shuàiqì, *adj.*, (of young men) handsome; good-looking, L. 28, p. 405

双方，shuāngfāng, *pron.*, both sides; the two parties involved, L. 9, p. 112

爽朗，shuǎnglǎng, *adj.*, hearty; frank and open, L. 10, p. 132

水土不服，shuǐtǔ bùfú , *v.*, unaccustomed to the environment and climate of a new place, L. 9, p. 114

水灾，shuǐzāi, *n.*, flood, L. 20, p. 285

顺口溜儿，shùnkǒuliūér, *n.*, jingle; doggerel, L. 19, p. 269

顺序，shùnxù, *n.*, order; sequence, L. 12, p. 163

说，shuō, *v.*, criticize; to blame, L. 8, p. 99

说唱，shuōchàng, *n.*, rap (music style), L. 19, p. 269

说到底，shuō dàodǐ, *adv.*, after all; simply put, L. 15, p. 210

说明，shuōmíng, *v.*, show; to illustrate, L. 7, p. 81

硕士，shuòshì, *n.*, Master (of Science or Arts), L. 14, p. 192

丝绸，sīchóu, *n.*, silk, L. 23, p. 335

思考，sīkǎo, *v.*, consider; contemplate, L. 14, p. 190

私人，sīrén, *adj.*, private, L. 21, p. 300

思乡，sīxiāng, *v-o.*, to be homesick, L. 9, p. 113

私有制，sīyǒuzhì, *n.*, private ownership (of means of production), L. 30, p. 433

死亡，sǐwáng, *v./n.*, die, L. 4, p. 45

四川，Sìchuān, *n.*, a province in the southwest of China, L. 9, p. 112

四合院，sìhéyuàn, *n.*, a compound with houses around a square courtyard, L. 11, p. 144

似乎，sìhū, *adv.*, as if; seemingly, L. 28, p. 404

寺庙，sìmiào, *n.*, temple, L. 16, p. 225

四通八达, sìtōng bādá , *idm.*, extend in all directions, L. 2, p. 21

送达, sòngdá, *v.*, deliver, L. 13, p. 175

艘, sōu, *m.w.*, measure word for ships, L. 23, p. 334

俗话, súhuà, *n.*, common saying; proverb, L. 15, p. 212

俗气, súqì, *adj.*, vulgar; tacky; gaudy, L. 10, p. 133

素质, sùzhì, *n.*, quality (of citizens), L. 14, p. 193

随便, suíbiàn, *adv.*, casual; random, L. 13, p. 178

随地吐痰, suídì tǔtán, *phr.*, spit indiscriminately, L. 11, p. 146

随后, suíhòu, *interj.*, subsequently; soon afterwards, L. 26, p. 372

损害, sǔnhài, *v.*, damage; impair (one's health/reputation), L. 26, p. 375

损失, sǔnshī, *n.*, loss, L. 29, p. 420

缩小, suōxiǎo, *v.*, narrow (a gap); reduce (in width, size, scope), L. 8, p. 99

T

台阶, táijiē, *n.*, steps; (of career) level, stage, L. 28, p. 404

态度, tàidù, *n.*, attitude, L. 1, p. 3

泰国, Tàiguó, *n.*, Thailand, L. 23, p. 334

太平洋, Tàipíngyáng, *n.*, the Pacific Ocean, L. 27, p. 388

贪, tān, *v.*, embezzle (a certain amount of money), L. 5, p. 54

贪财, tāncái, *adj.*, avaricious; greedy, L. 19, p. 270

贪腐, tānfǔ, *n.*, embezzlement and corruption, L. 6, p. 65

贪官, tānguān, *n.*, corrupt officials, L. 5, p. 54

瘫痪, tānhuàn, *v.*, paralyzed, L. 1, p. 4

贪污, tānwū, *v.*, embezzle, L. 5, p. 55

贪污腐化, tānwū fǔhuà, *v.*, embezzle and be corrupt, L. 5, p. 56

谈到, tándào, *conj./v.-c.*, in speaking of; to touch on; to mention, L. 24, p. 345

糖, táng, *n.*, candy, L. 4, p. 42

唐朝, Táng cháo, *n.*, The Tang Dynasty (618-907), L. 9, p. 113

趟, tàng, *mw.*, (for trips), L. 10, p. 129

套, tào, *m.w.*, measure word for an apartment or suite, L. 8, p. 95

逃课, táokè, *v.-o.*, skip classes, L. 25, p. 360

讨说法, tǎo shuōfǎ, *v.-o.*, seek justice; seek an answer/explanation, L. 26, p. 373

讨厌, tǎoyàn, *v.*, dislike, L. 25, p. 360

套, tào, *m.w.*, measure word for an apartment or suite, L. 8, p. 95

特定, tèdìng, *adj.*, particular; given, L. 17, p. 241

特权, tèquán, *n.*, privilege; prerogative, L. 5, p. 55

特殊, tèshū, *adj.*, special, L. 19, p. 269

提笔忘字, tíbǐ wàngzì, *idm.*, forget how to write words by hand, L. 12, p. 162

提笔写字, tíbǐ xiězì, *idm.*, take up a pen and write, L. 12, p. 160

提倡, tíchàng, *v.*, advocate; promote, L. 3, p. 31

提出, tíchū, *v.*, lodge (a challenge), put forward, L. 7, p. 83

提前, tíqián, *adv.*, in advance; to be earlier than planned or expected, L. 16, p. 228

提升, tíshēng, *v.*, improve (quality), L. 13, p. 174

体现, tǐxiàn, *v.*, embody, L. 13, p. 177; L. 28, p. 402

天安门, Tiān'ān mén, *n.*, Gate of Heavenly Peace, L. 22, p. 315

天地, tiāndì, *n.*, heaven and earth; a little world in itself, L. 18, p. 256

挑战, tiǎozhàn, *n./v.*, challenge, L. 7, p. 83

跳楼, tiàolóu, *v.-o.*, jump off a building (to commit suicide), L. 26, p. 371

跳跃式, tiàoyuè shì, *adj.*, by leaps and bounds, L. 13, p. 176

贴, tiē, *v.*, put up (a poster, notice, etc.), L. 11, p. 145

贴标签, tiē biāoqiān, *v.o.*, label sth.as; stereotype, L. 20, p. 284

帖子, tiězi, *n.*, (forum) post, thread on Internet, L. 21, p. 299

停放, tíngfàng, *v.*, park (a vehicle), L. 18, p. 258

停滞, tíngzhì, *v.*, stagnate; come to a standstill, L. 29, p. 421

停止, tíngzhǐ, *v.*, stop, L. 21, p. 303

通过, tōngguò, *v.*, pass (an exam), L. 12, p. 161

通奸, tōngjiān, *v.-o.*, commit adultery, L. 19, p. 270

通行, tōngxíng, *adj.*, common (language or currency), L. 23, p. 331

通用, tōngyòng, *v.*, in common use, L. 16, p. 227

同情, tóngqíng, *v./n.*, sympathize; sympathy, L. 27, p. 386

同情心, tóngqíng xīn, *n.*, compassion; sympathy, L. 21, p. 302

同乡, tóngxiāng, *n.*, a person from the same village, town or province, L. 9, p. 112

同音词, tóngyīn cí, *n.*, homonym, L. 12, p. 161

统一, tǒngyī, *adj./v.*, unified; unitary; unite, L. 11, p. 148; L. 27, p. 388

统治, tǒngzhì, *v.*, govern, L. 27, p. 386

偷拍, tōupāi, *v.*, take a picture of a person without his/her permission or without his/her knowledge., L. 21, p. 301

偷窃, tōuqiè, *v.*, steal, L. 26, p. 371

偷偷, tōutōu, *adv.*, secretly, L. 26, p. 371

投入, tóurù, *v.*, invest; input, L. 8, p. 99

突出, tūchū, *v.*, protrude; to stick out, L. 2, p. 18

突飞猛进, tūfēi měngjìn, *idm.*, make a sudden stride in progress; advance by leaps and bounds, L. 10, p. 128

突然, tūrán, *adv.*, suddenly; abruptly, L. 1, p. 3

图书馆员, túshūguǎn yuán, *n.*, librarian, L. 29, p. 419

土地, tǔdì, *n.*, land; territory, L. 3, p. 31

团聚, tuánjù, *v.*, (of a family) reunite, L. 17, p. 239

团圆, tuányuán, *v./n.*, reunite; family reunion, L. 16, p. 227

推荐信, tuījiàn xìn, *n.*, recommendation letter, L. 14, p. 194

推行, tuīxíng, *v.*, promote (system, ideas); carry into effect (laws), L. 11, p. 148

退, tuì, *v.*, retreat, L. 27, p. 386

退步, tuìbù, *v.*, retrogress; lag behind, L. 1, p. 4

退休, tuìxiū, *v.*, retire, L. 8, p. 97

妥协, tuǒxié, *v.*, compromise, L. 28, p. 403

W

外表, wàibiǎo, *n.*, external appearance, L. 28, p. 406

外地人, wàidì rén, *n.*, non-local people; non-native; people from out of town, L. 8, p. 98; L. 23, p. 332

外公, wàigōng, n., maternal grandpa, L. 25, p. 358

外国货, wàiguóhuò, n., foreign goods, L. 4, p. 44

外教, wàijiào, n., foreign teacher, L. 14, p. 191

外界, wàijiè, n., the external or outside world, L. 10, p. 128

外卖, wàimài, n., take-out, L. 13, p. 175

外婆, wàipó, n., maternal grandma, L. 25, p. 358

玩具, wánjù, n., toy, L. 25, p. 359

玩物, wánwù, n., plaything; doll, L. 28, p. 405

晚点, wǎndiǎn, v., late (for trains/flights); behind schedule, L. 10, p. 132

万一, wànyī, conj., if by any chance; in case, L. 22, p. 318

往返, wǎngfǎn, v., to shuttle; to take a roundtrip, L. 10, p. 129

往后, wǎnghòu, n., later on; henceforth, L. 29, p. 418

网络, wǎngluò, n., Internet, L. 5, p. 56; L. 21, p. 301

网络暴力, wǎngluò bàolì, n., cyber bullying; online trolling, L. 21, p. 299

网络约车, wǎngluò yuēchē, n., online taxi reservation, L. 15, p. 209

网友, wǎngyǒu, n., fellow netizen, L. 20, p. 286

网站, wǎngzhàn, n., website, L. 21, p. 302

威胁, wēixié, v./n., to threaten; threat, L. 22, p. 317

维持, wéichí, v., maintain, L. 26, p. 373

违反, wéifǎn, v., violate; break (e.g. moral standards, the law, etc.), L. 25, p. 361

围观, wéiguān, v., (of a crowd of people) gather and watch; look on, L. 26, p. 373

违规, wéiguī, v.o., violate regulations; break the rules, L. 11, p. 145

唯一, wéiyī, adj., the only; sole, L. 28, p. 404

伟大, wěidà, adj., great (worthy of the greatest admiration), L. 2, p. 20

萎缩, wěisuō, v., (of a market, economy, etc.) to shrink, sag, L. 13, p. 174

伪劣产品, wěiliè chǎnpǐn, n., fake and inferior products, L. 4, p. 43

未婚, wèihūn, adj., unmarried, L. 28, p. 402

未来, wèilái, t.w., in the future, L. 24, p. 348

未免, wèimiǎn, adv., a bit too…, L. 15, p. 207

温哥华, Wēngēhuá, n., Vancouver, L. 21, p. 300

温和, wēnhé, adj., mild; gentle, L. 2, p. 19

温柔, wēnróu, adj., gentle; sweet, L. 10, p. 132

文化大革命, Wénhuà dà gémìn, n., The Cultural Revolution (1966-1976), L. 17, p.240; L. 30, p. 431

文明, wénmíng, adj., civilized, L. 18, p. 258

文物, wénwù, n., cultural and historical relics, L. 17, p. 240

文学, wénxué, n., literature, L. 3, p. 33

文娱活动, wényú huódòng, n., recreational activities, L. 18, p. 257

文章, wénzhāng, n., essay; article, L. 4, p. 43

文字, wénzì, n., writing system; characters, L. 12, p. 160

稳定, wěndìng, adj., stable, L. 7, p. 81

污染, wūrǎn, n./v., pollution, L. 1, p. 1

无处不在, wúchù búzài, idm., everywhere; ubiquitous, L. 3, p. 31

无法, wúfǎ, v., unable, L. 13, p. 174; L. 16, p. 229

无奈, wúnài, adj., grudgingly; have no alternative, L. 1, p. 3

无所不有, wúsuǒbùyǒu, idm., have everything; all-inclusive; all-embracing, L. 7, p. 81

无形, wúxíng, adj., invisible; intangible, L. 23, p. 334

无政府主义, wúzhèngfǔ zhǔyì, n., anarchism, L. 29, p. 421

无助, wúzhù, adj., helpless, L. 25, p. 360

午餐, wǔcān, n., lunch, L. 6, p. 65

武汉, Wǔhàn, n., the capital of Hubei 湖北 province, L. 20, p. 285

武器, wǔqì, n., weapon, L. 7, p. 83

侮辱, wǔrǔ, v., to insult, L. 28, p. 402

午夜, wǔyè, n., midnight, L. 10, p. 129

雾, wù, n., fog, L. 1, p. 1

物产, wùchǎn, n., products; produce, L. 10, p. 130

误导, wùdǎo, v./n., mislead; misguide, L. 2, p. 19

物价, wùjià, n., price of commodities, L. 24, p. 346

雾霾, wùmái, n., smog, haze, L. 1, p. 1

物美价廉, wùměi jiàlián, idm., good value for money, L. 4, p. 42

X

锡兰, Xīlán, n., former name of Sri Lanka (until 1972), L. 23, p. 334

西化, xīhuà, v./n., westernize; Westernization, L. 3, p. 31

西亚, xīyà, n., Southwest Asia, L. 23, p. 335

西洋, xīyáng, adj., Western, L. 17, p. 241

吸引, xīyǐn, v., attract, L. 8, p. 99

西元, xīyuán, n., the Christian era, L. 16, p. 227

习俗, xísú, n., custom; convention, L. 17, p. 240

喜好, xǐhào, n., what sb. likes or loves, L. 18, p. 253

系, xì, n., department (in a university), L. 27, p. 385

系统, xìtǒng, n., system, L. 13, p. 173; L. 17, p. 239

下单, xiàdān, v., place an order online, L. 13, p. 175

下功夫, xià gōngfu, v., put in time and energy, L. 15, p. 209

下令, xiàlìng, v.-o., give an order; command, L. 4, p. 44

夏威夷, Xiàwēiyí, n., Hawaii, L. 27, p. 388

下一次, yícì, n., next time, L. 22, p. 318

先进, xiānjìn, adj., advanced, L. 7, p. 81

先决条件, xiānjué tiáojiàn, n., prerequisite, L. 12, p. 162

咸水鸭, xiánshuǐ yā, n., brine duck, L. 9, p. 115

嫌疑, xiányí, n., suspicion, L. 22, p. 319

显得, xiǎnde, v., appear to be, L. 23, p. 332

显然, xiǎnrán, adv., obviously; evidently, L. 1, p. 2

显示, xiǎnshì, v., show; display; demonstrate, L. 11, p. 147

显著, xiǎnzhù, adj., notable; remarkable, L. 11, p. 145

县, xiàn, n., county, L. 9, p. 112

县城, xiànchéng, n., town, L. 8, p. 95

宪法, xiànfǎ, n., constitution (of a country), L. 22, p. 318

现金, xiànjīn, *n.*, cash, L. 13, p. 176; L. 18, p. 254

羡慕, xiànmu, *v.*, admire (a person); envy, L. 18, p. 256

现实, xiànshí, *adj.*, practical, L. 16, p. 226

现象, xiànxiàng, *n.*, phenomenon, L. 4, p. 43

限制, xiànzhì, *v.*, to restrict; to limit, L. 4, p. 44

现状, xiànzhuàng, *n.*, current situation, L. 27, p. 385

相当于, xiāngdāngyú, *v.*, equivalent to, L. 16, p. 227

相反, xiāngfǎn, *adj.*, opposite; on the contrary (conj.), L. 6, p. 67

相亲, xiāngqīn, *v.*, size up a prospective mate in an arranged meeting, L. 28, p. 403

相提并论, xiāngtí bìnglùn, *idm.*, [usu. in the negative] to mention in the same breath, L. 16, p. 229

乡下人, xiāngxià rén, *n.*, country folk; hick, L. 11, p. 147

乡谊, xiāngyí, *n.*, fellow-villager's mutual affection, L. 9, p. 113

响, xiǎng, *v.*, ring; (of a bell/phone) shrill, L. 26, p. 371

想方设法, xiǎngfāng shèfǎ, *idm.*, do everything possible; try every means, L. 14, p. 194

想象, xiǎngxiàng, *v./n.*, imagine; imagination, L. 10, p. 129

项, xiàng, *m.w.*, measure word for tasks, projects, etc., L. 22, p. 319

向往, xiàngwǎng, *v.*, be attracted toward; yearn for, L. 30, p. 434

象征, xiàngzhēng, *v./n.*, symbolize; symbol, L. 2, p. 19; L. 17, p. 242

消费, xiāofèi, *v./n.*, consume; consumption, L. 13, p. 177; L. 17, p. 238

消失, xiāoshī, *v.*, disappear, L. 3, p. 32; L. 13, p. 176

销售量, xiāoshòu liàng, *n.*, sales, L. 1, p. 4

萧条, xiāotiáo, *adj.*, (of business) very dull; (of general conditions) depressed, L. 13, p. 175

逍遥法外, xiāoyáo fǎwài, *idm.*, get off scot-free, L. 5, p. 54

小白脸, xiǎo báiliǎn, *n.*, young fair face—handsome, effeminate young man, L. 28, p. 405

小贩, xiǎofàn, *n.*, small peddler, L. 18, p. 255

小摊, xiǎotān, *n.*, vendor's stall, L. 13, p. 176

小鲜肉, xiǎo xiānròu, *n.*, little fresh meat; boy toy, L. 28, p. 401

校党委书记, xiào dǎngwěi shūjì, *n.*, Secretary of the Party Committee of a school, L. 28, p. 401

效果, xiàoguǒ, *n.*, effect, result, L. 15, p. 212

协议, xiéyì, *n.*, agreement, L. 26, p. 374

辛苦, xīnkǔ, *adj./adv.*, (of life) hard; toilsome; laborious, L. 8, p. 95

心理, xīnlǐ, *n.*, mentality; psychology, L. 14, p. 193

欣赏, xīnshǎng, *v.*, appreciate or enjoy (art/literature/acrobatics), L. 3, p. 33

薪水, xīnshuǐ, *n.*, wage, L. 19, p. 270

心态, xīntài, *n.*, psychology; mentality, L. 15, p. 208

新鲜, xīnxian, *adj.*, fresh; new; novel; strange, L. 7, p. 84; L. 16, p. 227

新型, xīnxíng, *adj.*, new type; new pattern (modifier), L. 13, p. 175

新兴, xīnxīng, *attr.*, emerging (as a modifier); up-and-coming, L. 24, p. 347

新意, xīnyì, *n.*, original and creative ideas, L. 15, p. 210

信任, xìnrèn, *v./n.*, trust, L. 22, p. 318

信息, xìnxī, *n.*, information, L. 22, p. 316

信仰, xìnyǎng, *n.*, creed; belief; conviction, L. 19, p. 273

信用卡, xìnyòng kǎ, *n.*, credit card, L. 13, p. 176

兴起, xīngqǐ, *v.*, rise; spring up, L. 13, p. 175; L. 14, p. 191

行, xíng, *adj.*, capable; competent, L. 1, p. 4

形成, xíngchéng, *v.*, form; come into being, L. 1, p. 4

行程, xíngchéng, *n.*, itinerary, L. 10, p. 129

行李, xínglǐ, *n.*, luggage, L. 9, p. 115

形容, xíngróng, *v.*, describe, L. 11, p. 146

形式, xíngshì, *n.*, form, L. 19, p. 269

行为, xíngwéi, *n.*, behavior, L. 18, p. 258; L. 19, p. 270

形象, xíngxiàng, *n./adj./adv.*, 1) image; 2) vivid; vividly, 1) L. 2, p. 20; 2) L. 9, p. 115; L. 19, p. 270

性暗示, xìng ànshì, *n.*, sexual overture, L. 28, p. 405

性别, xìngbié, *n.*, gender, L. 19, p. 271

幸福, xìngfú, *adj./n.*, happy; happiness, L. 8, p. 97

性格, xìnggé, *n.*, character, L. 25, p. 360

性关系, xìng guānxi, *n.*, sexual relationship, L. 13, p. 178

性侵犯, xìng qīnfàn, *n.*, sexual assault; sexual abuse, L. 25, p. 360

性情, xìngqíng, *n.*, disposition; temperament, L. 10, p. 132

凶猛, xiōngměng, *adj.*, fierce, L. 2, p. 19

熊猫, xióngmāo, *n.*, panda, L. 2, p. 18

羞辱, xiūrǔ, *v.*, humiliate, L. 21, p. 300

绣, xiù, *v.*, embroider, L. 2, p. 19

虚浮, xūfú, *adj.*, superficial; ostentatious, L. 28, p. 407

虚拟, xūnǐ, *adj.*, virtual, L. 13, p. 173

虚伪, xūwěi, *adj.*, hypocritical, L. 13, p. 178

许多, xǔduō, *attr.*, many; a great deal of, L. 19, p. 273

许可, xǔkě, *n.*, warrant; permission, L. 22, p. 317

宣传, xuānchuán, *v.*, to propagate; to publicize, L. 5, p. 56; L. 18, p. 257

选修课, xuǎnxiū kè, *n.*, optional (selective) course, L. 14, p. 191

学期, xuéqī, *n.*, semester, L. 16, p. 228

学识, xuéshí, *n.*, learning, L. 28, p. 403

学术, xuéshù, *adj.*, academic, L. 15, p. 212

学术界, xuéshù jiè, *n.*, academia, L. 30, p. 431

学堂, xuétáng, *n.*, (an old term for) school; college, L. 28, p. 401

学业, xuéyè, *n.*, one's studies; school work, L. 14, p. 194

Y

压迫, yāpò, *v.*, oppress, L. 24, p. 347

押韵, yāyùn, *v-o.*, to rhyme, L. 19, p. 269

亚洲, Yàzhōu, *n.*, Asia, L. 27, p. 380

淹, yān, *v.*, flood; submerge, L. 20, p. 285

燕京大学, Yānjīng Dàxué, *n.*, Yenching University (1919-1952), L. 29, p. 420

严格, yángé, *adv./adj.*, strictly, L. 4, p. 45

459

严厉, yánlì, *adj./adv.*, severe (punishment/criticism); severely, L. 5, p. 54

言论, yánlùn, *n.*, expression of opinion; speech, L. 21, p. 302

言论自由, yánlùn zìyóu, *n.*, freedom of speech, L. 21, p. 299

沿海, yánhǎi, *adj.*, along the coast; coastal, L. 23, p. 331

沿途, yántú, *adj.*, on the way; throughout a journey, L. 10, p. 129

颜值, yánzhí, *n.*, (mainland Internet slang) attractiveness index, L. 28, p. 405

严重性, yánzhòng xìng, *n.*, seriousness, L. 25, p. 359

演出, yǎnchū, *n.*, performance, L. 18, p. 257

演讲, yǎnjiǎng, *n./v.*, speech; talk; to give a talk, L. 21, p. 300

掩饰, yǎnshì, *v.*, to cover up (one's errors/mistakes), L. 5, p. 56

演员, yǎnyuán, *n.*, actor, L. 28, p. 405

演奏, yǎnzòu, *v.*, give an instrumental performance, L. 18, p. 253

央视, Yāngshì, *abbr.*, China Central Television (CCTV), L. 20, p. 285

洋学历, yáng xuélì, *n.*, degrees obtained from abroad, L. 14, p. 192

养, yǎng, *v.*, raise (a child/a pet/livestock), L. 7, p. 81

养成, yǎngchéng, *v.*, cultivate the habit of, L. 11, p. 146

养老保险, yǎnglǎo bǎoxiǎn, *n.*, retirement insurance, L. 24, p. 347

样子, yàngzi, *n.*, appearance, L. 2, p. 18

摇, yáo, *v.*, roll (up/down the car window), L. 11, p. 147

摇滚乐, yáogǔn yuè, *n.*, Rock and Roll, L. 30, p. 432

摇篮, yáolán, *n.*, cradle; (fig.) place of origin, L. 29, p. 419

谣言, yáoyán, *n.*, rumor, L. 21, p. 301

耶稣, Yēsū, *n.*, Jesus, L. 16, p. 225

业务, yèwù, *n.*, business, L. 13, p. 175

依靠, yīkào, *v.*, depend on, L. 28, p. 403

依恋, yīliàn, *v.*, feel attached to, L. 9, p. 115

医疗保险, yīliáo bǎoxiǎn, *n.*, medical insurance, L. 24, p. 347

一无可取, yīwúkěqǔ, *idm.*, (lit.) (of a person, course of action) without anything to recommend, L. 30, p. 434

一无是处, yīwúshìchù, *n.*, without a single redeeming feature (devoid of any merit), L. 30, p. 429

一无所有, yīwúsuǒyǒu, *idm.*, not have a single thing to one's name, L. 7, p. 81

一线城市, yīxiàn chéngshì, *n.*, first-tier cities, L. 8, p. 96

医学, yīxué, *n.*, medical science, L. 11, p. 147

一战, yī zhàn, *n.*, World War I (1914-1918), L. 7, p. 83

医学, yīxué, *n.*, medical science, L. 11, p. 147

一步步, yí bùbù, *adv.*, step by step, L. 15, p. 209

一次性, yícì xìng, *adj.*, one-time; disposable (goods), L. 13, p. 177

一旦, yídàn, *conj.*, once; as soon as (sth. happens), L. 22, p. 317

一大批, yí dàpī, large quantities of, L. 15, p. 212

一技之长, yíjì zhīcháng, *idm.*, skill in a specialized area; professional skill, L. 24, p. 347

一向, yíxiàng, *adv.*, all along; consistently, L. 14, p. 192

一系列, yí xìliè, a series of, L. 15, p. 211

移民, yímín, *n./v.*, immigrant; to immigrate, L. 7, p. 80

移动, yídòng, *v.*, move, L. 17, p. 238

遗弃, yíqì, *v.*, abandon, L. 20, p. 285

一切, yíqiè, *pron.*, everything; all, L. 9, p. 116

已婚, yǐhūn, *adj.*, married, L. 28, p. 404

亿, yì, *num.*, a hundred million, L. 5, p. 54

一般, yìbān, *adj.*, average (people); ordinary, L. 7, p. 83

一夫一妻制, yì fū yì qī, *n.*, monogamy, L. 28, p. 404

一模一样, yìmú yíyàng, *idm.*, exactly the same; exactly alike, L. 4, p. 42

意识, yìshi, *n.*, consciousness; awareness, L. 24, p. 347

意识到, yìshi dào, *v.-c.*, become aware of; become conscious of, L. 25, p. 361

艺术, yìshù, *n.*, art, L. 3, p. 33

艺术品, yìshù pǐn, *n.*, work of art, L. 18, p. 253

艺术区, yìshù qū, *n.*, art zone or art district, L. 18, p. 253

意外, yìwài, *adj.*, surprised; taken by surprise, L. 1, p. 3

意味, yìwèi, *v.*, mean; signify, L. 13, p. 174

因素, yīnsù, *n.*, factor; element, L. 7, p. 81

引进, yǐnjìn, *v.*, introduce (from elsewhere); bring in, L. 15, p. 211

饮料, yǐnliào, *n.*, beverage, L. 22, p. 315

引领, yǐnlǐng, *v.*, lead (e.g. the trend), L. 3, p. 30

引起, yǐnqǐ, *v.*, lead to; bring (emphasis on), L. 17, p. 241

饮食, yǐnshí, *n.*, cuisine; food and drink, L. 3, p. 30

引用, yǐnyòng, *v.*, cite, L. 19, p. 272

印度, Yìndù, *n.*, India, L. 23, p. 334

印度尼西亚, Yìndùníxīyà , *n.*, Indonesia, L. 23, p. 334

印象, yìnxiàng, *n.*, impression, L. 2, p. 19

英特网, Yīngtèwǎng, *n.*, Internet, L. 13, p. 173

英雄, yīngxióng, *n.*, hero, L. 20, p. 286

婴儿, yīng' ér, *n.*, infant, L. 4, p. 45

婴儿用品, yīng' ér yòngpǐn, *n.*, baby products, L. 15, p. 208

影响, yǐngxiǎng, *v.*, affect; impair, L. 4, p. 45

影响力, yǐngxiǎnglì, *n.*, influence; clout, L. 3, p. 31

应酬, yìngchóu, *v./n.*, (begrudgingly) attend social events, L. 8, p. 96

应对, yìngduì, *v.*, respond (to a change), L. 3, p. 31

应聘, yìngpìn, *v.*, apply for (an advertised position), L. 24, p. 345

应试, yìngshì, *adj.*, examination-oriented, L. 14, p. 193

硬实力, yìng shílì, *n.*, hard power (military and economic power), L. 3, p. 30

应用, yìngyòng, *v.*, apply, L. 27, p. 387

拥挤, yōngjǐ, *adj.*, crowded; packed, L. 22, p. 315

拥有, yōngyǒu, *v.*, possess/command (weapon/land/people), L. 7, p. 83

勇敢, yǒnggǎn, *adj.*, brave, L. 25, p. 359

永久, yǒngjiǔ, *adj.*, permanent, L. 13, p. 177

用不着, yòng bu zháo, *v.c.*, there is no need for..., L. 28, p. 407

优惠, yōuhuì, *adj./n.*, preferential; discount, L. 24, p. 346

优良，yōuliáng, *adj.*, (of quality, grades) fine, L. 15, p. 210

幽默，yōumò, *adj./n.*, humorous; humor, L. 1, p. 3

幽默感，yōumò gǎn, *n.*, sense of humor, L. 1, p. 3

悠闲，yōuxián, *adj.*, leisurely and carefree, L. 8, p. 97

优秀，yōuxiù, *adj.*, outstanding; excellent; splendid, L. 8, p. 99

优越感，yōuyuègǎn, *n.*, sense of superiority, L. 11, p. 147

由，yóu, *prep.*, 1) from; 2) by, 1) L. 13, p. 177; 2) L. 27, p. 389

游客，yóukè, *n.*, tourists, L. 22, p. 315

尤其，yóuqí, *adv.*, in particular; especially, L. 19, p. 273

犹豫，yóuyù, *v.*, hesitate, L. 15, p. 212

油纸，yóuzhǐ, *n.*, oilpaper, L. 18, p. 255

有目共睹，yǒumùgòngdǔ, *idm.*, widely recognized; perfectly obvious, L. 27, p. 387

有限，yǒuxiàn, *adj.*, limited, L. 27, p. 387

有效，yǒuxiào, *adj.*, effective, L. 3, p. 31

有意，yǒuyì, *v.*, have a mind to; be inclined to, L. 15, p. 209

又气又急，yòuqìyòují, *phr.*, angry and anxious; furious, L. 26, p. 372

于，yú, *prep.*, (indicating time, place) in; on; at, L. 29, p. 418

渔村，yúcūn, *n.*, fishing village, L. 23, p. 331

愉快，yúkuài, *adj.*, happy; joyful; cheerful, L. 6, p. 66

娱乐，yúlè, *n.*, entertainment, L. 8, p. 99

舆论，yúlùn, *n.*, public opinion; media, L. 20, p. 287

鱼米之乡，yúmǐzhīxiāng, *idm.*, a region where the cultivation of rice and the breeding of fish flourish, L. 10, p. 130

于是，yúshì, *conj.*, consequently, L. 22, p. 316

雨衣，yǔyī, *n.*, raincoat, L. 20, p. 286

语音，yǔyīn, *n.*, pronunciation, L. 12, p. 162

与众不同，yǔzhòngbùtóng, *idm.*, different "with" (from) the others; unconventional, L. 11, p. 148

遇到，yùdào, *v.*, encounter, L. 1, p. 3

原本，yuánběn, *adj.*, original, L. 12, p. 161

原动力，yuán dònglì, *n.*, motive power; prime mover; first cause, L. 29, p. 419

原来，yuánlái, *adv.*, as it turns out; actually, L. 15, p. 207

原谅，yuánliàng, *v.*, forgive, L. 21, p. 303

远程，yuǎnchéng, *adj.*, long-range; long-distance, L. 7, p. 83

远处，yuǎnchù, *n.*, a distant place, L. 1, p. 1

远航，yuǎnháng, *v.*, to take a long (sea) voyage, L. 23, p. 334

愿望，yuànwàng, *n.*, wish (often related to personal life), L. 7, p. 84

约会，yuēhuì, *v.-o.*, date, L. 1, p. 2

约炮，yuēpào, *v.*, hook up for a one-night stand; booty call, L. 13, p. 177

约束，yuēshù, *v.*, discipline, L. 25, p. 360

月球，yuèqiú, *n.*, moon/lunar L. 18, p. 257

月亮，yuèliang, *n.*, moon, L. 15, p. 207

越南，Yuènán, *n.*, Vietnam, L. 23, p. 334

允许，yúnxǔ, *v.*, allow; if…condition…allows/permits, L. 14, p. 193

运，yùn, *v.*, to transport, L. 20, p. 286

Z

杂技，zájì, *n.*, acrobatics, L. 3, p. 33

在此之前，zàicǐzhīqián, *phr.*, before this, L. 17, p. 239

在意，zàiyì, *v.*, to mind; to take to heart, L. 16, p. 226

咱们，zánmen, *pron.*, we; us, L. 1, p. 4

攒钱，zǎnqián, *v.-o.*, save up money, L. 8, p. 96

暂时，zànshí, *adj.*, temporary, L. 13, p. 177

糟糕，zāogāo, *adj.*, awful; terrible, L. 25, p. 358

造假，zàojiǎ, *v.*, counterfeit, L. 14, p. 194

早期，zǎoqī, *n.*, early stage; initial stage, L. 23, p. 334

早晚，zǎowǎn, *adv.*, sooner or later, L. 14, p. 193

增强，zēngqiáng, *v.*, increase and strengthen (power, capability influence, etc.), L. 15, p. 210; L. 17, p. 239

展览，zhǎnlǎn, *n.*, exhibition, L. 18, p. 257

占，zhàn, *v.*, take up; occupy, L. 3, p. 32

战败，zhànbài, *v.*, defeated, L. 27, p. 386

战场，zhànchǎng, *n.*, battlefield, L. 6, p. 66

站出来，zhàn chūlai, *v.-c.*, stand up, L. 21, p. 303

占领，zhànlǐng, *v.*, capture; to ccupy, L. 7, p. 83

战争，zhànzhēng, *n.*, war, L. 16, p. 226

张，zhāng, *v.*, open (one's mouth/eyes), L. 2, p. 18

张牙舞爪，zhāngyá wǔzhǎo, *idm.*, bare fangs and brandish claws, L. 2, p. 18

长，zhǎng, *v.*, grow, L. 2, p. 18

长相，zhǎngxiàng, *n.*, looks; appearance, L. 10, p. 131; L. 28, p. 406

障碍，zhàng'ài, *n.*, obstacle, L. 6, p. 67

招聘，zhāopìn, *v.*, recruit, L. 24, p. 345

遮，zhē, *v.*, cover, L. 1, p. 2

这时候，zhèshíhou, *interj.*, at this point; at this time, L. 25, p. 359

真诚，zhēnchéng, *n.*, sincerity, L. 21, p. 303

真品，zhēnpǐn, *n.*, genuine articles/products, L. 4, p. 42

真实，zhēnshí, *adj.*, true; real, L. 13, p. 173

真实性，zhēnshí xìng, *n.*, authenticity; veracity, L. 20, p. 287

真正，zhēnzhèng, *adv./adj.*, truly; authentic, L. 19, p. 272

震惊，zhènjīng, *v.*, shock, L. 25, p. 358

睁，zhēng, *v.*, open (one's eyes), L. 6, p. 66

征服，zhēngfú, *v.*, conquer; subdue, L. 3, p. 31

争取，zhēngqǔ, *v.*, strive for; fight for, L. 19, p. 273; L. 28, p. 402

征收，zhēngshōu, *v.-o.*, levy (a tax), L. 4, p. 44

争先恐后，zhēngxiān kǒnghòu, *idm.*, strive to be the first and fear being left behind; vie for, L. 11, p. 146

整形手术，zhěngxíng shǒushù, *n.*, plastic surgery, L. 28, p. 407

正常，zhèngcháng, *adj.*, normal; regular, L. 7, p. 83

正当，zhèngdàng, *adj.*, legitimate; (of behavior, etc.) correct, proper, L. 6, p. 65

政党，zhèngdǎng, *n.*, party, L. 27, p. 387

正面，zhèngmiàn, *adj.*, positive (opp. negative 负面), L. 20, p. 284

证明, zhèngmíng, *v./n.*, prove; proof, L. 17, p. 239

正能量, zhèng néngliàng, *n.*, positive energy, L. 20, p. 284

证实, zhèngshí, *v./n.*, verify; confirm (sth. to be true), L. 21, p. 301

政治家, zhèngzhì jiā, *n.*, statesman, L. 18, p. 257

政治人物, zhèngzhì rénwù, *n.*, political figure, L. 21, p. 301

政治正确, zhèngzhì zhèngquè, *n.*, political correctness, L. 19, p. 273

支, zhī, *m.w.*, measure word for teams, troops, etc., L. 23, p. 334

支付, zhīfù, *v.*, pay (money), L. 13, p. 176

支票, zhīpiào, *n.*, check, L. 13, p. 176

之前, zhīqián, *n.*, before; prior to..., L. 20, p. 287

知识产权, zhīshi chǎnquán, *n.*, intellectual property rights, L. 4, p. 43

值得, zhídé, *v.*, worth, L. 1, p. 4

执法, zhífǎ, *v.-o.*, enforce the law, L. 4, p. 45

直接, zhíjiē, *adj.*, direct, L. 3, p. 30

值钱, zhíqián, *adj.*, valuable, L. 14, p. 192

直率, zhíshuài, *adj.*, frank; candid; straightforward, L. 10, p. 132

执行, zhíxíng, *v.*, carry out (a task); to enforce; to execute (an order), L. 6, p. 68

职业, zhíyè, *att.*, professional, L. 18, p. 253

指, zhǐ, *v.*, refer to, L. 28, p. 405

指导, zhǐdǎo, *v.*, guide; direct, L. 14, p. 190

智能手机, zhìnéng shǒujī, *n.*, smart phone, L. 12, p. 160

制裁, zhìcái, *v.*, punish (the agent/doer is "法律"), L. 5, p. 55

制定, zhìdìng, *v.*, make/draw up (the law); lay down (rules), L. 6, p. 68

治理, zhìlǐ, *v.*, govern, L. 6, p. 68

秩序, zhìxù, *n.*, order, L. 11, p. 146; L. 26, p. 373

质疑, zhìyí, *v.*, to call in question; to raise doubt, L. 20, p. 285

至于, zhìyú, *conj.*, as for; as to, L. 4, p. 45

制造, zhìzào, *v.*, manufacture, L. 4, p. 44

制作, zhìzuò, *v.*, create; manufacture, L. 18, p. 256

中国结, zhōngguó jié, *n.*, Chinese knots (traditional Chinese folk art form), L. 3, p. 32

中国梦, Zhōngguó mèng, *n.*, Chinese Dream, L. 7, p. 80

中介, zhōngjiè, *n.*, intermediate; agency, L. 14, p. 190

中考, zhōngkǎo, *n.*, entrance examination for senior high school, L. 14, p. 191

中期, zhōngqī, *n.*, middle period, L. 23, p. 335

中秋节, Zhōngqiū jié, *n.*, the Mid-Autumn Festival, L. 16, p. 227

钟头, zhōngtóu, *n.*, hour, L. 10, p. 132

中西部, zhōngxī bù, *n.*, central and western part (of a country), L. 24, p. 346

中亚, zhōngyà, *n.*, Central Asia, L. 23, p. 335

终于, zhōngyú, *adv.*, at (long) last; in the end; finally, L. 11, p. 148; L. 26, p. 372

中止, zhōngzhǐ, *v.*, suspend; discontinue, L. 23, p. 335

种族, zhǒngzú, *n.*, race, L. 19, p. 273

重大, zhòngdà, *adj.*, major, significant (discoveries, contributions, loss, etc.), L. 29, p. 420

重视, zhòngshì, *v.*, take sth. seriously; attach importance to; to value, L. 6, p. 66; L. 17, p. 241

重税, zhòng shuì, *n.*, a heavy tax, L. 4, p. 44

众所周知, zhòngsuǒzhōuzhī, *idm.*, as everyone knows; as is known to all, L. 14, p. 192

重要性, zhòngyàoxìng, *n.*, importance, L. 9, p. 113

周到, zhōudào, *adj.*, thoughtful; considerate, L. 10, p. 129

洲际弹道导弹, zhōujìdàndào dǎodàn, *n.*, intercontinental ballistic missile, L. 7, p. 83

周围, zhōuwéi, *n.*, surrounding, L. 26, p. 373

主导, zhǔdǎo, *adj.*, dominant; guiding, L. 30, p. 433

主观, zhǔguān, *adj.*, subjective, L. 28, p. 406

主权, zhǔquán, *n.*, sovereign; sovereignty, L. 7, p. 82

主食, zhǔshí, *n.*, staple food; principal food, L. 9, p. 115

主题, zhǔtí, *n.*, theme; subject, L. 7, p. 80

主张, zhǔzhāng, *v.*, advocate; stand for, L. 6, p. 68

祝, zhù, *v.*, "Wish you...", L. 17, p. 240

祝福, zhùfú, *v.*, wish sb. well; invoke a blessing, L. 20, p. 284

驻华大使, zhūhuá dàshǐ, *n.*, ambassador to China, L. 29, p. 420

注重, zhùzhòng, *v.*, lay emphasis on, L. 19, p. 272

抓, zhuā, *v.*, arrest; catch, L. 5, p. 54; L. 19, p. 272

专, zhuān, *adv.*, exclusively; (of a shop) specialized in, L. 18, p. 255

专家, zhuānjiā, *n.*, expert, L. 4, p. 42

专人, zhuānrén, *n.*, person specially assigned to a task or job, L. 13, p. 175

转变, zhuǎnbiàn, *v.*, transform; to shift, L. 7, p. 81

转化, zhuǎnhuà, *v.*, to change; to transform, L. 29, p. 418

转型, zhuǎnxíng, *v.*, (of a socioeconomic structure, culture) transform; evolve, L. 23, p. 335

赚取, zhuànqǔ, *v.*, make a profit, L. 18, p. 256

装饰, zhuāngshì, *n./v.*, ornament; decorate, L. 10, p. 133; L. 18, p. 253

追捧, zhuīpěng, *v.*, chase after (a celebrity), L. 28, p. 405

追求, zhuīqiú, *v.*, pursue; seek, L. 8, p. 97

追逐, zhuīzhú, *v.*, to blindly pursue, L. 28, p. 407

准点, zhǔndiǎn, *adj./adv.*, punctual; on time, L. 10, p. 132

准确, zhǔnquè, *adj./adv.*, accurate; accurately, L. 12, p. 163

资本主义, zīběn zhǔyì, *n.*, capitalism, L. 19, p. 272

资格, zīgé, *n.*, qualification; right, L. 21, p. 303

资金, zījīn, *n.*, fund; capital, L. 8, p. 99

资源, zīyuán, *n.*, resources, L. 3, p. 33

仔细, zǐxì, *adv.*, attentively; meticulously, L. 14, p. 193

自卑, zìbēi, *adj.*, self-abased, L. 24, p. 347

自豪, zìháo, *adj.*, be proud (of one's identity, country, etc.), L. 2, p. 20

自觉, zìjué, *adj.*, consciously; on one's own initiative, L. 11, p. 145

自来水, zìlái shuǐ, *n.*, running water; tap water, L. 7, p. 84; L. 11, p. 144

自然， zìrán, *adv.*, naturally, L. 17, p. 241

自然科学， zìrán kēxué, *n.*, science, L. 29, p. 421

自杀， zìshā, *v.*, commit suicide, L. 21, p. 301

自私， zìsī, *adj.*, selfish, L. 8, p. 99

自卫， zìwèi, *v./n.*, defend oneself; self-defense, L. 2, p. 19

自信， zìxìn, *n./adj.*, self-confidence; confident, L. 15, p. 208

字形， zìxíng, *n.*, structure and form of a Chinese character, L. 12, p. 162

自愿， zìyuàn, *adv.*, voluntarily, L. 28, p. 404

综合， zōnghé, *adj.*, comprehensive; overall, L. 14, p. 193

宗教， zōngjiào, *n.*, religion, L. 16, p. 225

宗教性， zōngjiào xìng, n./*adj.*, religious, L. 16, p. 225

总经理， zǒng jīnglǐ, *n.*, general manager; CEO, L. 28, p. 401

总数， zǒngshù, *n.*, total; sum, L. 25, p. 359

总算， zǒngsuàn, *adv.*, at long last, L. 30, p. 430

粽子， zòngzi, *n.*, a pyramid-shaped sticky rice balls made of glutinous rice and wrapped in bamboo leaves, L. 16, p. 227

租， zū, *v.*, rent, L. 13, p. 177

足够， zúgòu, *adj./adv.*, enough; sufficient; sufficiently, L. 2, p. 19

组成， zǔchéng, *v.*, make up; constitute; form, L. 23, p. 331

祖父母， zǔfùmǔ, *n.*, grandfather and grandmother, L. 9, p. 113

祖国， zǔguó, *n.*, homeland; motherland, L. 20, p. 284

租用， zūyòng, *v.*, rent and use, L. 24, p. 346

组织， zǔzhī, *v.*, to organize, L. 23, p. 334

嘴巴， zuǐbā, *n.*, mouth, L. 2, p. 18

最佳， zuìjiā, *adj.*, best (used as a modifier), L. 17, p. 241

最终， zuìzhōng, *conj.*, finally; in the end, L. 20, p. 287

遵守， zūnshǒu, *v.*, abide by; follow, L. 6, p. 68

作品， zuòpǐn, *n.*, works of (literature or art), L. 9, p. 113

作为， zuòwéi, *prep.*, as, L. 1, p. 4

作秀， zuòxiù, *v.*, put on a show; grandstand, L. 17, p. 242

English Index

464

appearance (of things); look; aspect, 面貌, miànmào, *n.*, L. 19, p. 272

apply, 应用, yìngyòng, *v.*, L. 27, p. 387

apply for (an advertised position), 应聘, yìngpìn, *v.*, L. 24, p. 345

appreciate or enjoy (art/literature/acrobatics), 欣赏, xīnshǎng, *v.*, L. 3, p. 33

appropriate; proper (in degree); suitable, 适当, shìdàng, *adj.*, L. 6, p. 67; L. 25, p. 360

arduous, 艰巨, jiānjù, *adj.*, L. 22, p. 319

area (of a floor, piece of land, etc.); size, 面积, miànjī, *n.*, L. 27, p. 388; L. 29, p. 419

arouse emotions and sentiment, 煽情, shānqíng, *v.*, L. 20, p. 286

arrest, 逮捕, dàibǔ, *v.*, L. 26, p. 374

arrest; catch, 抓, zhuā, *v.*, L. 5, p. 54; L. 19, p. 272

arrive, 到达, dàodá, *v.*, L. 10, p. 132

art, 艺术, yìshù, *n.*, L. 3, p. 33

art zone or art district, 艺术区, yìshù qū, *n.*, L. 18, p. 253

artisan; craftsman, 工匠, gōngjiàng, *n.*, L. 18, p. 255

as, 作为, zuòwéi, *prep.*, L. 1, p. 4

as everyone knows; as is known to all, 众所周知, zhòngsuǒzhōuzhī, *idm.*, L. 14, p. 192

as for; as to, 至于, zhìyú, *conj.*, L. 4, p. 45

as if; seemingly, 似乎, sìhū, *adv.*, L. 28, p. 404

as it turns out; actually, 原来, yuánlái, *adv.*, L. 15, p. 207

as quickly as possible, 尽快, jǐnkuài, *adv.*, L. 13, p. 173

Asia, 亚洲, Yàzhōu, *n.*, L. 27, p. 386

ask (sb. to do sth. politely), 请, qǐng, *v.*, L. 26, p. 372

at (long) last; in the end; finally, 终于, zhōngyú, *adv.*, L. 11, p. 148; L. 26, p. 372

at first; in the beginning, 起先, qǐxiān, *conj.*, L. 5, p. 54

at long last, 总算, zǒngsuàn, *adv.*, L. 30, p. 430

at present; at the moment, 目前, mùqián, *t.w.*, L. 25, p. 358

at this point; at this time, 这时候, zhèshíhou, *interj.*, L. 25, p. 359

attached to one's native land and unwilling to leave it, 安土重迁, āntǔ zhòngqiān, *idm.*, L. 10, p. 132

attend school, 上学, shàngxué, *v.-o.*, L. 25, p. 360

attend school; study, 读书, dúshū, *v.-o.*, L. 7, p. 81

attend social events (begrudgingly), 应酬, yìngchóu, *v./n.*, L. 8, p. 96

attentively; meticulously, 仔细, zǐxì, *adv.*, L. 14, p. 193

attitude, 态度, tàidù, *n.*, L. 1, p. 3

attract, 吸引, xīyǐn, *v.*, L. 8, p. 99

attractions; scenic area, 景区, jǐngqū, *n.*, L. 17, p. 239

attractiveness index (mainland Internet slang), 颜值, yánzhí, *n.*, L. 28, p. 405

authenticity; veracity, 真实性, zhēnshí xìng, *n.*, L. 20, p. 287

avaricious; greedy, 贪财, tāncái, *adj.*, L. 19, p. 270

average (people); ordinary, 一般, yìbān, *adj.*, L. 7, p. 83

average; equally, 平均, píngjūn, *adj./adv.*, L. 10, p. 128

aviation, 航空, hángkōng, *n.*, L. 9, p. 117

avoid, 避免, bìmiǎn, *v.*, L. 9, p. 115; L. 19, p. 273

awful; terrible, 糟糕, zāogāo, *adj.*, L. 25, p. 358

B

baby products, 婴儿用品, yīng' ér yòngpǐn, *n.*, L. 15, p. 208

background, 背景, bèijǐng, *n.*, L. 27, p. 389

backward; behind the times, 落后, luòhòu, *adj.*, L. 7, p. 81

balance, 平衡, pínghéng, *v./n.*, L. 10, p. 133

ban smoking (in public areas), 禁烟, jìnyān, *v.o.*, L. 11, p. 145

barbel; beard; mustache, 胡子, húzi, *n.*, L. 2, p. 18

bare fangs and brandish claws, 张牙舞爪, zhāngyá wǔzhǎo, *idm.*, L. 2, p. 18

basically; mainly; on the whole, 基本上, jīběn shang, *adv.*, L. 6, p. 68; L. 27, p. 385

battlefield, 战场, zhànchǎng, *n.*, L. 6, p. 66

be able to make judgments; sensible, 懂事, dǒngshì, *v.*, L. 27, p. 385

be adverse to; be detrimental to, 不利于, búlìyú, *v.*, L. 17, p. 239

be attracted toward; yearn for, 向往, xiàngwǎng, *v.*, L. 30, p. 434

be duped and swindled, 上当受骗, shàngdàng shòupiàn, *idm.*, L. 13, p. 174

be good at; master in, 擅长, shàncháng, *v.*, L. 14, p. 193

be happy to do sth., 乐意, lèyì, *v.*, L. 14, p. 194

be interested in…, 感兴趣, gǎnxìngqu, *v.-o.*, L. 3, p. 32

be proud (of one's identity, country, etc.), 自豪, zìháo, *adj.*, L. 2, p. 20

bear hardships and stand hard work, 吃苦耐劳, chīkǔ nàiláo, *idm.*, L. 24, p. 347

bear hardships; suffer a great deal, 吃苦, chīkǔ, *v.*, L. 8, p. 95

beat and smash, 打砸, dǎzá, *v.*, L. 26, p. 373

beautiful; pretty, 美丽, měilì, *adj.*, L. 10, p. 133

beauty and ugliness, 美丑, měichǒu, *n.*, L. 28, p. 406

beauty treatment; to improve one's looks, 美容, měiróng, *n./v.*, L. 28, p. 407

become aware of; become conscious of, 意识到, yìshi dào, *v.-c.*, L. 25, p. 361

become hysterical; (of one's emotion) become extreme and uncontrolled, 激动, jīdòng, *adj.*, L. 26, p. 373

before this, 在此之前, zàicǐzhīqián, *phr.*, L. 17, p. 239

before; prior to…, 之前, zhīqián, *n.*, L. 20, p. 287

beginning of (a century or decade), 初, chū, *suffix*, L. 24, p. 347

behavior, 行为, xíngwéi, *n.*, L. 18, p. 258; L. 19, p. 270

behind; back, 背后, bèihòu, *n.*, L. 14, p. 190

Beijing opera, 京剧, jīngjù, *n.*, L. 18, p. 257

belong to, 属于, shǔyú, *v.*, L. 18, p. 256

best (used as a modifier), 最佳, zuìjiā, *adj.*, L. 17, p. 241

beverage, 饮料, yǐnliào, *n.*, L. 22, p. 315

bicycle, 单车, dānchē, *n.*, L. 13, p. 173

blindly, 盲目, mángmù, *adv.*, L. 14, p. 194

blindly pursue, 追逐, zhuīzhú, *v.*, L. 28, p. 407

blow, 吹, chuī, *v.*, L. 11, p. 147

blue sky, 蓝天, lántiān, *n.*, L. 1, p. 3

bomber (aircraft), 轰炸机, hōngzhàjī, *n.*, L. 7, p. 83

boost; stimulate, 促进, cùjìn, *v.*, L. 20, p. 288

boot-binding; bind one's feet, 缠脚, chánjiǎo, *v.*, L. 28, p. 401

both sides, both parties, 两者, liǎng zhě, *pron.*, L. 10, p. 133

both sides of the Taiwan Strait (i.e. Taiwan and mainland), 两岸, liǎng'àn, *n.*, L. 27, p. 388

both sides; the two parties involved, 双方, shuāngfāng, *pron.*, L. 9, p. 112

bother; trouble, 困扰, kùnrǎo, *v.*, L. 21, p. 301

brain drain; outflow of talented people, 人才外流, réncái wàiliú, *idm.*, L. 15, p. 208

brand name (modifier), 名牌, míngpái, *adj.*, L. 4, p. 42

brand; make, 品牌, pǐnpái, *n.*, L. 15, p. 210

brave, 勇敢, yǒnggǎn, *adj.*, L. 25, p. 359

breathe, 呼吸, hūxī, *v.*, L. 7, p. 84

bribes; to bribe, 贿赂, huìlù, *n./v.*, L. 5, p. 55

bright, 亮, liàng, *adj.*, L. 16, p. 227

brine duck, 咸水鸭, xiánshuǐ yā, *n.*, L. 9, p. 115

bring along or to give an impetus to, 带动, dàidòng, *v.*, L. 10, p. 133

bring forth new ideas; innovate, 创新, chuàngxīn, *v./n.*, L. 14, p. 193

Buddhism, 佛教, Fójiào, *n.*, L. 16, p. 225

build, 建, jiàn, *v.*, L. 2, p. 20

build, 建造, jiànzào, *v.*, L. 23, p. 335

bully, 欺负, qīfu, *v.*, L. 2, p. 19

burden, 负担, fùdān, *n.*, L. 25, p. 361

bureaucrat, 官僚, guānliáo, *n.*, L. 29, p. 421

bury one's head in; immerse oneself in (work, study), 埋头, máitóu, *v.*, L. 12, p. 162

business, 生意, shēngyì, *n.*, L. 13, p. 174

business, 业务, yèwù, *n.*, L. 13, p. 175

busy (formal), 忙碌, mánglù, *adj.*, L. 8, p. 99

buy and sell; business, 买卖, mǎimài, *n.*, L. 6, p. 66

by, 由, yóu, *prep.*, 1) L. 13, p. 177; 2) L. 27, p. 389

by a big margin; substantially, 大幅, dàfú, *adv.*, L. 17, p. 239

by hook or crook (derogatory term), 不择手段, bùzéshǒuduàn, *idm.*, L. 19, p. 272

by leaps and bounds, 跳跃式, tiàoyuè shì, *adj.*, L. 13, p. 176

by one's side, 身边, shēnbiān, *n.*, L. 25, p. 359

C

cadres; government officials, 干部, gànbu, *n.*, L. 19, p. 270

calculate, 计算, jìsuàn, *v.*, L. 16, p. 226

calendar; calendric system, 历法, lìfǎ, *n.*, L. 16, p. 227

call in question; to raise doubt, 质疑, zhìyí, *v.*, L. 20, p. 285

calligrapher, 书法家, shūfǎjiā, *n.*, L. 12, p. 160

calligraphy, 书法, shūfǎ, *n.*, L. 3, p. 32

can be found everywhere; all around, 比比皆是, bǐbǐ jiēshì, *adj.*, L. 11, p. 145

Canada, 加拿大, Jiānádà, *n.*, L. 21, p. 300

cancel; abolish, 取消, qǔxiāo, *v.*, L. 17, p. 238

candy, 糖, táng, *n.*, L. 4, p. 42

cannon; artillery, 大炮, dàpào, *n.*, L. 3, p. 31

cannot distinguish (A from B), 分不清, fēnbùqīng, *v-c.*, L. 16, p. 226

canteen, 食堂, shítáng, *n.*, L. 11, p. 146

capability; ability; talent, 才能, cáinéng, *n.*, L. 7, p. 81

capable; competent, 行, xíng, *adj.*, L. 1, p. 4

capitalism, 资本主义, zīběn zhǔyì, *n.*, L. 19, p. 272

capture; occupy, 占领, zhànlǐng, *v.*, L. 7, p. 83

care about, 关心, guānxīn, *v.*, L. 16, p. 227

career, 事业, shìyè, *n.*, L. 28, p. 404

carry out (a task); to enforce; to execute (an order), 执行, zhíxíng, *v.*, L. 6, p. 68

carry weight; significance, 分量, fènliàng, *n.*, L. 12, p. 163

cars; vehicles (collective noun), 车辆, chēliàng, *n.*, L. 18, p. 258

carve; engrave; 雕刻家: sculptor, 雕刻, diāokè, *v.*, L. 18, p. 253

case, 案例, ànlì, *n.*, L. 20, p. 287

cash, 现金, xiànjīn, *n.*, L. 13, p. 176; L. 18, p. 254

cashier, 收银员, shōu yíng yuán, *n.*, L. 13, p. 174; L. 26, p. 371

casual; random, 随便, suíbiàn, *adv.*, L. 13, p. 178

catch up with, 赶上, gǎnshàng, *v.-c.*, L. 10, p. 129

cede, 割让, gēràng, *v.*, L. 27, p. 386

celebrate, 庆祝, qìngzhù, *v.*, L. 16, p. 225

central and western part (of a country), 中西部, zhōngxī bù, *n.*, L. 24, p. 346

Central Asia, 中亚, zhōngyà, *n.*, L. 23, p. 335

century, 世纪, shìjì, *n.*, L. 6, p. 68

challenge, 挑战, tiǎozhàn, *n./v.*, L. 7, p. 83

change into, 改为, gǎiwéi, *v.*, L. 17, p. 238

change; transform, 转化, zhuǎnhuà, *v.*, L. 29, p. 418

character, 性格, xìnggé, *n.*, L. 25, p. 360

charge (fees), 收, shōu, *v.*, 1) L. 5, p. 55; 2) L. 21, p. 302

chase after (a celebrity), 追捧, zhuīpěng, *v.*, L. 28, p. 405

check, 支票, zhīpiào, *n.*, L. 13, p. 176

cherish and take care of, 爱护, àihù, *v.*, L. 9, p. 116

China Central Television (CCTV), 央视, Yāngshì, *abbr.*, L. 20, p. 285

Chinese Dream, 中国梦, Zhōngguó mèng, *n.*, L. 7, p. 80

Chinese knots (traditional Chinese folk art form), 中国结, zhōngguó jié, *n.*, L. 3, p. 32

Chinese radicals, 部首, bùshǒu, *n.*, L. 12, p. 163

Christian era, 西元, xīyuán, *n.*, L. 16, p. 227

Christmas, 圣诞节, Shèngdàn jié, *n.*, L. 16, p. 225

church, 教堂, jiàotáng, *n.*, L. 16, p. 225

circle; clique, 圈子, quānzi, *n.*, L. 9, p. 116

cite, 引用, yǐnyòng, *v.*, L. 19, p. 272

citizen, 公民, gōngmín, *n.*, L. 7, p. 81

city wall, 城墙, chéngqiáng, *n.*, L. 2, p. 20

civil war, 内战, nèizhàn, *n.*, L. 27, p. 386

craftsmanship; technical skill, 工艺, gōngyì, *n.*, L. 18, p. 255

craze of studying abroad, 留学热, liúxué rè, *n.*, L. 14, p. 190

create, 创造, chuàngzào, *v.*, L. 8, p. 99

create (work of art), 创作, chuàngzuò, *v.*, L. 18, p. 253

create; manufacture, 制作, zhìzuò, *v.*, L. 18, p. 256

credit card, 信用卡, xìnyòng kǎ, *n.*, L. 13, p. 176

creed; belief; conviction, 信仰, xìnyǎng, *n.*, L. 19, p. 273

criticize; to blame, 说, shuō, *v.*, L. 8, p. 99

crowd; the masses, 群众, qúnzhòng, *n.*, L. 26, p. 373

crowded; packed, 拥挤, yōngjǐ, *adj.*, L. 22, p. 315

cruel; brutal, 残酷, cánkù, *adj.*, L. 30, p. 432

cuisine; food and drink, 饮食, yǐnshí, *n.*, L. 3, p. 30

cultivate the habit of, 养成, yǎngchéng, *v.*, L. 11, p. 146

cultivate; foster (a certain spirit) in sb., 培养, péiyǎng, *v.*, L. 14, p. 193

cultural and historical relics, 文物, wénwù, *n.*, L. 17, p. 240

Cultural Revolution (1966-1976), 文化大革命, Wénhuà dà gémìn, L.17, p.240; L. 30, p. 431

current situation, 现状, xiànzhuàng, *n.*, L. 27, p. 385

custom; convention, 习俗, xísú, *n.*, L. 17, p. 240

customer, 顾客, gùkè, *n.*, L. 22, p. 319

cyber bullying; online trolling, 网络暴力, wǎngluò bàolì, *n.*, L. 21, p. 299

D

daily life, 日常生活, rìcháng shēnghuó, *n.*, L. 3, p. 30

damage; impair (one's health/reputation), 损害, sǔnhài, *v.*, L. 26, p. 375

Daoism, 道教, Dàojiào, *n.*, L. 16, p. 225

dare, 敢, gǎn, *aux.*, L. 4, p. 45

dark side, 黑暗面, hēi'àn miàn, *n.*, L. 20, p. 287

date, 约会, yuēhuì, *v.-o.*, L. 1, p. 2

day by day, 日益, rìyì, *adv.*, L. 17, p. 239

deal; trade, 交易, jiāoyì, *n.*, L. 6, p. 66

debate, 辩论, biànlùn, *n.*, L. 29, p. 421

decade; era, 年代, niándài, *n.*, L. 12, p. 161

deduct...from..., 扣掉, kòudiào, *v.*, L. 8, p. 96

deep and profound; far-reaching, 深远, shēnyuǎn, *adj.*, L. 30, p. 431

deep; profound, 深刻, shēnkè, *adj.*, L. 18, p. 257; L. 19, p. 269

defeat, 打败, dǎbài, *v.*, L. 7, p. 82

defeated, 战败, zhànbài, *v.*, L. 27, p. 386

defect; shortcoming; bad habit, 毛病, máobìng, *n.*, L. 11, p. 147

defend oneself; self-defense, 自卫, zìwèi, *v./n.*, L. 2, p. 19

defend; guard, 防御, fángyù, *v.*, L. 2, p. 20

degree; level, 程度, chéngdù, *n.*, L. 14, p. 191

degrees obtained from abroad, 洋学历, yáng xuélì, *n.*, L. 14, p. 192

deity, 神, shén, *n.*, L. 16, p. 226

delete, 删掉, shāndiào, *v.*, L. 20, p. 286

deliver, 送达, sòngdá, *v.*, L. 13, p. 175

democracy; democratic (country 民主国家, system 民主制度), 民主, mínzhǔ, *n./adj.*, L. 27, p. 387

deny, 否认, fǒurèn, *v.*, L. 8, p. 98

department, 部门, bùmén, *n.*, L. 22, p. 316

department (in a university), 系, xì, *n.*, L. 27, p. 385

depend on, 依靠, yīkào, *v.*, L. 28, p. 403

Descendants of the Dragon, 龙的传人, lóng de chuánrén, *n.*, L. 2, p. 18

describe, 描写, miáoxiě, *v.*, L. 19, p. 270

describe, 形容, xíngróng, *v.*, L. 11, p. 146

describe and narrate, 描述, miáoshù, *v.*, L. 19, p. 271

design; style, 款式, kuǎnshì, *n.*, L. 20, p. 287

design; to design, 设计, shèjì, *n./v.*, L. 4, p. 43

despise; look down upon, 鄙视, bǐshì, *v.*, L. 13, p. 178; L. 28, p. 403

destination, 目的地, mùdì dì, *n.*, L. 10, p. 132

destroy (environment/traditional cultures); do great damage to; sabotage, 破坏, pòhuài, *v.*, L. 11, p. 144; L. 17, p. 239

destroy; damage, 毁坏, huǐhuài, *v.*, L. 17, p. 240

destroy; smash into pieces; wreck, 摧毁, cuīhuǐ, *v.*, L. 29, p. 419

detain, 扣留, kòuliú, *v.*, L. 26, p. 374

deteriorate; worsen, 恶化, èhuà, *v.*, L. 1, p. 4

determination; resolve, 决心, juéxīn, *n.*, L. 5, p. 55

determine (a fact, identity), 认定, rèndìng, *v.*, L. 23, p. 333

development; develop, 发展, fāzhǎn, *n./v.*, L. 15, p. 210

dialect, 方言, fāngyán, *n.*, L. 9, p. 113

dictatorship, 独裁, dúcái, *n.*, L. 27, p. 387

die, 死亡, sǐwáng, *v./n.*, L. 4, p. 45

die (of old age), 老死, lǎosǐ, *v.*, L. 9, p. 116

different "with" (from) the others; unconventional, 与众不同, yǔzhòngbùtóng, *idm.*, L. 11, p. 148

differentiate; distinguish, 区分, qūfēn, *v.*, L. 10, p. 131

dilapidated, 破落, pòluò, *adj.*, L. 11, p. 144

direct, 直接, zhíjiē, *adj.*, L. 3, p. 30

direction, 方向, fāngxiàng, *n.*, L. 24, p. 348

disappear, 消失, xiāoshī, *v.*, L. 3, p. 32; L. 13, p. 176

discipline, 约束, yuēshù, *v.*, L. 25, p. 360

discrepancy (compared to one's estimation), 出入, chūrù, *n.*, L. 16, p. 228

discriminate; discrimination, 歧视, qíshì, *v./n.*, L. 19, p. 271

dislike, 讨厌, tǎoyàn, *v.*, L. 25, p. 360

dispatch or send out (troops), 出动, chūdòng, *v.*, L. 20, p. 285

dispatch/send out troops, 出兵, chūbīng, *v.*, L. 27, p. 389

display, 摆放, bǎifàng, *v.*, L. 26, p. 373

display; show, 表现, biǎoxiàn, *v.*, L. 1, p. 2

disposition; temperament, 性情, xìngqíng, *n.*, L. 10, p. 132

dissatisfied; dissatisfaction, 不满, bùmǎn, *adj./n.*, L. 21, p. 302

disseminate; propagate, 传播, chuánbō, *v.*, L. 20, p. 286

distance, 距离, jùlí, *n.*, L. 12, p. 161

distant place, 远处, yuǎnchù, *n.*, L. 1, p. 1

distinguish; differentiate, 分辨, fēnbiàn, *v.*, L. 4, p. 42

divide, 划分, huàfēn, *v.*, L. 10, p. 131

do everything possible; try every means, 想方设法, xiǎngfāng shèfǎ, *idm.*, L. 14, p. 194

do physical work; to labor; work; labor, 劳动, láodòng, *v./n.*, L. 17, p. 238

domestic demand, 内需, nèixū, *n.*, L. 17, p. 238

dominant; guiding, 主导, zhǔdǎo, *adj.*, L. 30, p. 433

down to the bottom; thoroughly, 彻底, chèdǐ, *adv.*, L. 28, p. 402

downpour, 暴雨, bàoyǔ, *n.*, L. 10, p. 132

dragon, 龙, lóng, *n.*, L. 2, p. 18

Dragon Boat Festival, 端午节, Duānwǔ jié, *n.*, L. 3, p. 32; L. 16, p. 226;

dream to be a strong nation, 强国梦, qiángguó mèng, *n.*, L. 7, p. 82

dull (economy); depressed (general conditions), 萧条, xiāotiáo, *adj.*, L. 13, p. 175

dusky; overcasting, 灰蒙蒙, huī méngméng, *adj.*, L. 1, p. 1

dying to; wish one could, 恨不得, hènbudé, *v.*, L. 15, p. 208

E

each, 各, gè, *pron.*, L. 17, p. 238

early stage; initial stage, 早期, zǎoqī, *n.*, L. 23, p. 334

earth; soil, 泥土, nítǔ, *n.*, L. 9, p. 114

easily, 轻易, qīngyì, *adv.*, L. 10, p. 129

Easter, 复活节, Fùhuó jié, *n.*, L. 16, p. 225

economy, 经济体, jīngjìtǐ, *n.*, L. 27, p. 387

effect, result, 效果, xiàoguǒ, *n.*, L. 15, p. 212

effective, 有效, yǒuxiào, *adj.*, L. 3, p. 31

electronic, 电子, diànzǐ, *adj.*, L. 13, p. 176

electronic lock, 电子锁, diànzǐsuǒ, *n.*, L. 22, p. 316

elegant; refined; tasteful, 高雅, gāoyǎ, *adj.*, L. 13, p. 177

elite, 精英, jīngyīng, *n.*, L. 8, p. 99

embarrassing; awkward, 尴尬, gān'gà, *adj.*, L. 13, p. 178; L. 28, p. 403

embezzle, 贪污, tānwū, *v.*, L. 5, p. 55

embezzle (a certain amount of money), 贪, tān, *v.*, L. 5, p. 54

embezzle and be corrupt, 贪污腐化, tānwū fǔhuà, *v.*, L. 5, p. 56

embezzlement and corruption, 贪腐, tānfǔ, *n.*, L. 6, p. 65

embody, 体现, tǐxiàn, *v.*, L. 13, p. 177; L. 28, p. 402

embroider, 绣, xiù, *v.*, L. 2, p. 19

emerging (as a modifier); up-and-coming, 新兴, xīnxīng, *attr.*, L. 24, p. 347

emit; discharge, 排放, páifàng, *v.*, L. 1, p. 4

emotion, 情感, qínggǎn, *n.*, L. 20, p. 284

emperor, 皇帝, huángdì, *n.*, L. 2, p. 19

employment (modifier), 就业, jiùyè, *n.*, L. 24, p. 345

encounter, 遇到, yùdào, *v.*, L. 1, p. 3

encounter; come across, 碰到, pèngdào, *v.*, L. 25, p. 359

encourage, 鼓励, gǔlì, *v.*, L. 25, p. 360

end of (a century or decade), 末, mò, *suffix.*, L. 24, p. 347

endure; put up with, 忍受, rěnshòu, *v.*, L. 21, p. 301

enemy, 敌人, dírén, *n.*, L. 2, p. 20

enforce the law, 执法, zhífǎ, *v.-o.*, L. 4, p. 45

enlarge; augment; increase, 加大, jiādà, *v.*, L. 11, p. 145

enough; sufficient; sufficiently, 足够, zúgòu, *adj./adv.*, L. 2, p. 19

enshrine and worship, 供奉, gòngfèng, *v.*, L. 16, p. 226

ensure; guarantee, 保障, bǎozhàng, *v./n.*, L. 22, p. 317

enterprise; business, 企业, qǐyè, *n.*, L. 13, p. 176; L. 18, p. 255

entertainment, 娱乐, yúlè, *n.*, L. 8, p. 99

entrance examination for senior high school, 中考, zhōngkǎo, *n.*, L. 14, p. 191

equal to, 等于, děngyú, *v.*, L. 21, p. 303

equipment, 设备, shèbèi, *n.*, L. 10, p. 129

equivalent to, 相当于, xiāngdāngyú, *v.*, L. 16, p. 227

era; epoch; the times, 时代, shídài, *n.*, L. 30, p. 430

error; mistake, 错误, cuòwu, *n.*, L. 5, p. 56; L. 30, p. 432

essay; article, 文章, wénzhāng, *n.*, L. 4, p. 43

establish (an organization); found, 成立, chénglì, *v.*, L. 3, p. 33; L. 18, p. 254

establish (connections; an institute), 建立, jiànlì, *v.*, L. 8, p. 97

establish as; recognize as, 定为, dìngwéi, *v.*, L. 3, p. 32

establish; to set up, 设立, shèlì, *v.*, L. 8, p. 97

estimate, 估计, gūjì, *v.*, L. 27, p. 387

ethos; the general mood (of a society), 风气, fēngqì, *n.*, L. 19, p. 271; L. 28, p. 407

etiquette, 礼仪, lǐyí, *n.*, L. 17, p. 241

eunuch, 宦官, huànguān, *n.*, L. 23, p. 334

event; activity, 活动, huódòng, *n.*, L. 1, p. 3

everything; all, 一切, yíqiè, *pron.*, L. 9, p. 116

everywhere; in all aspects, 处处, chùchù, *adv.*, L. 15, p. 208

everywhere; ubiquitous, 无处不在, wúchù búzài, *idm.*, L. 3, p. 31

exactly the same; exactly alike, 一模一样, yìmú yíyàng, *idm.*, L. 4, p. 42

exactly; precisely, 恰恰, qiàqià, *adv.*, L. 6, p. 67

exaggerated; overstated, 夸张, kuāzhāng, *adj.*, L. 1, p. 2

examination-oriented, 应试, yìngshì, *adj.*, L. 14, p. 193

examine; check, 查看, chákàn, *v.*, L. 22, p. 318

exceed; go beyond, 超乎, chāohū, *v.*, L. 14, p. 191

exceed; surpass, 超过, chāoguò, *v.*, L. 1, p. 4

exception, 例外, lìwài, *n.*, L. 6, p. 67; L. 22, p. 316

exclude or resist anything foreign; exclusionary; anti-foreign, 排外, páiwài, *v.o.*, L. 29, p. 421

exclusively; (of a shop) specialized in, 专, zhuān, *adv.*, L. 18, p. 255

exert the utmost strength; give it one's all, 拼命, pīnmìng, *adv.*, L. 8, p. 96

exhibition, 展览, zhǎnlǎn, *n.*, L. 18, p. 257

exhibition of paintings, 画展, huàzhǎn, *n.*, L. 18, p. 255

exist, 存在, cúnzài, *v.*, L. 12, p. 161

expand, 扩大, kuòdà, *v.*, L. 23, p. 332

470

forgive, 原谅, yuánliàng, v., L. 21, p. 303

form, 形式, xíngshì, n., L. 19, p. 269

form; come into being, 形成, xíngchéng, v., L. 1, p. 4

former name of Sri Lanka (until 1972), 锡兰, Xīlán, n., L. 23, p. 334

forum for discussion, 论坛, lùntán, n., L. 21, p. 299

forum post, thread on Internet, 帖子, tiězi, n., L. 21, p. 299

found; establish, 创建, chuàngjiàn, v., L. 30, p. 430

foundation, 基础, jīchǔ, n., L. 18, p. 258

founder, 创办人, chuàngbàn rén, n., L. 29, p. 420

fragile (mentally or psychologically), 脆弱, cuìruò, adj., L. 21, p. 302

frank; candid; straightforward, 直率, zhíshuài, adj., L. 10, p. 132

freedom of speech, 言论自由, yánlùn zìyóu, n., L. 21, p. 299

frequent, 频繁, pínfán, adj., L. 22, p. 319

fresh, 新鲜, xīnxiān, adj., L. 7, p. 84

friend with benefits, 炮友, pàoyǒu, n., L. 13, p. 177

from, 由, yóu, prep., 1) L. 13, p. 177; 2) L. 27, p. 389

from the beginning to the end, 始终, shǐzhōng, adv., L. 7, p. 83

full of; brim with, 充满, chōngmǎn, v., L. 24, p. 346

fully, 充分, chōngfèn, adv., L. 28, p. 407

fund; capital, 资金, zījīn, n., L. 8, p. 99

fundamental; basic; basically, 基本, jīběn, adj./adv., L. 7, p. 80; L. 19, p. 270

funds, 经费, jīngfèi, n., L. 14, p. 194

funny-looking; comical, 滑稽, huájī, adj., L. 12, p. 161

further, 进一步, jìnyibù, adv., L. 26, p. 375

future, 将来, jiānglái, n., L. 14, p. 193

G

gain (opportunity; experience, etc.), 获得, huòdé, v., L. 8, p. 97

gang; criminal underworld, 黑社会, hēi shèhuì, n., L. 25, p. 361

Gansu province (in northwest China), 甘肃, Gānsù, n., L. 23, p. 333; L. 26, p. 371

gap; disparity, 差距, chājù, n., L. 8, p. 99

Gate of Heavenly Peace, 天安门, Tiān'ān mén, n., L. 22, p. 315

gather and watch; look on, 围观, wéiguān, v., L. 26, p. 373

gather; assemble, 聚集, jùjí, v., L. 18, p. 254

gather-together; gathering, 聚会, jùhuì, n., L. 16, p. 228

gauze mask, 口罩, kǒuzhào, n., L. 1, p. 2

gender, 性别, xìngbié, n., L. 19, p. 271

general manager; CEO, 总经理, zǒng jīnglǐ, n., L. 28, p. 401

generally acknowledged; universally accepted, 公认, gōngrèn, v., L. 10, p. 131

generous, 丰厚, fēnghòu, adj., L. 15, p. 210

gentle; sweet, 温柔, wēnróu, adj., L. 10, p. 132

genuine articles/products, 真品, zhēnpǐn, n., L. 4, p. 42

genuine human warmth, 人情味, rénqíngwèi, n., L. 30, p. 429

get distorted, 变味儿, biànwèir, v., L. 19, p. 272

get hurt, 受伤, shòushāng, v.-o., L. 26, p. 374

get married and start one's career, 成家立业, chéngjiā lìyè, idm., L. 16, p. 226

get off scot-free, 逍遥法外, xiāoyáo fǎwài, idm., L. 5, p. 54

get rid of; extricate from, 摆脱, bǎituō, v., L. 21, p. 302

gild; cover or coat with gold, 镀金, dùjīn, v., L. 14, p. 192

give an instrumental performance, 演奏, yǎnzòu, v., L. 18, p. 253

give an order; command, 下令, xiàlìng, v.-o., L. 4, p. 44

give full play to (one's ability), 发挥, fāhuī, v., L. 8, p. 97

give precedence to sb. out of courtesy or thoughtfulness, 礼让, lǐràng, v., L. 30, p. 429

give sb. a vacation; have a holiday, 放假, fàngjià, v.-o., L. 16, p. 228

give to; entrust sb. with, 交给, jiāogěi, v., L. 25, p. 358

give up; abandon, 放弃, fàngqì, v., L. 8, p. 98

glorious; shining, 辉煌, huīhuáng, adj., L. 30, p. 430

go crazy; become insane, 发疯, fāfēng, v., L. 30, p. 432

go dining, wining, whoring and gambling, 吃喝嫖赌, chī hē piáo dǔ, idm., L. 5, p. 55

go shopping, 购物, gòuwù, v.o., L. 18, p. 254

go to war, 打仗, dǎzhàng, v., L. 6, p. 66

golden age, 黄金时代, huángjīn shídài, n., L. 29, p. 421

good (e.g. one's performance, habit, etc.), 良好, liánghǎo, adj., L. 20, p. 286

good value for money, 物美价廉, wùměi jiàlián, idm., L. 4, p. 42

Google, 谷歌, gǔgē, n., L. 7, p. 84

govern, 统治, tǒngzhì, v., L. 27, p. 386

govern, 治理, zhìlǐ, v., L. 6, p. 68

govern by law; the rule of law, 法治, fǎzhì, n., L. 6, p. 67

grandfather and grandmother, 祖父母, zǔfùmǔ, n., L. 9, p. 113

great (worthy of the greatest admiration), 伟大, wěidà, adj., L. 2, p. 20

great mass fervor; all the rage, 热潮, rècháo, n., L. 14, p. 191

Great Leap Forward (1958-1962), 大跃进, Dà yuèjìn, L. 30, p. 431

Great Wall, 长城, Chángchéng, n., L. 2, p. 20

Green Card, permanent residence permit for foreigners, 绿卡, lùkǎ, n., L. 15, p. 209

grow, 长, zhǎng, v., L. 2, p. 18

grow; growth, 成长, chéngzhǎng, v./n., L. 25, p. 359

growth; development (of a child); to grow, 发育, fāyù, n./v., L. 4, p. 45

grudgingly; have no alternative, 无奈, wúnài, adj., L. 1, p. 3

Guangdong Province, 广东, Guǎngdōng, n., L. 15, p. 208

guard against theft, 防盗, fángdào, v, L. 26, p. 371

guard against; precaution, 防备, fángbèi, v./n., L. 25, p. 360

guide; direct, 指导, zhǐdǎo, v., L. 14, p. 190

gun, 枪, qiāng, n., L. 22, p. 316

gun control, 枪支控制, qiāngzhī kòngzhì, N.P., L. 19, p. 273

gunfight, 枪战, qiāngzhàn, n., L. 22, p. 316

H

471

hamper (one's relationship with others), 妨碍, fáng'ài, v., L. 9, p. 116

handbag, 手提包, shǒutí bāo, n., L. 4, p. 42

handle (a problem); to deal with, 处理, chǔlǐ, v., L. 6, p. 65

handle affairs; act, 办事, bànshì, v.-o., L. 6, p. 65

handsome; good-looking, 帅气, shuàiqì, adj., L. 28, p. 405

happy; happiness, 幸福, xìngfú, adj./n., L. 8, p. 97

happy; joyful; cheerful, 愉快, yúkuài, adj., L. 6, p. 66

hard power (military and economic power), 硬实力, yìng shílì, n., L. 3, p. 30

hard; toilsome; laborious, 辛苦, xīnkǔ, adj./adv., L. 8, p. 95

harm, 伤害, shānghài, n., L. 1, p. 2

hateful; detestable, 可恨, kěhèn, adj., L. 21, p. 300

have a full house, 客满, kèmǎn, n., L. 18, p. 257

Have a happy and prosperous New Year! 恭喜发财, gōngxǐfācái, idm., L. 17, p. 240

have a mind to; be inclined to, 有意, yǒuyì, v., L. 15, p. 209

have contact or dealings with sb., 来往, láiwǎng, v., L. 10, p. 128

have everything; all-inclusive; all-embracing, 无所不有, wúsuǒbùyǒu, idm., L. 7, p. 81

have fun amidst hardships, 苦中作乐, kǔzhōngzuòlè, idm., L. 1, p. 3

have no alternative but to, 不得已, bùdéyǐ, adj., L. 24, p. 345

have nothing in common with each other, 各不相同, gèbùxiāngtóng, adj., L. 16, p. 228

Hawaii, 夏威夷, Xiàwēiyí, L. 27, p. 388

hearsay, 传闻, chuánwén, n., L. 21, p. 301

hearty; frank and open, 爽朗, shuǎnglǎng, adj., L. 10, p. 132

heaven and earth; a little world in itself, 天地, tiāndì, n., L. 18, p. 256

heavy tax, 重税, zhòng shuì, n., L. 4, p. 44

heavy; hard; serious, 沉重, chénzhòng, adj., L. 22, p. 319

hegemony, 霸权, bàquán, n., L. 7, p. 83

helpless, 无助, wúzhù, adj., L. 25, p. 360

hero, 英雄, yīngxióng, n., L. 20, p. 286

hesistate, 犹豫, yóuyù, v., L. 15, p. 212

high officials, 高官, gāoguān, n., L. 5, p. 54

high price, 高价, gāojià, n., L. 4, p. 42

high-end; upscale; up-market, 高端, gāoduān, adj., L. 15, p. 211

highly efficient, 高效, gāoxiào, adj., L. 13, p. 175

high-paying (jobs), 高薪, gāoxīn, adj., L. 15, p. 209

high-speed (modifier), 高速, gāosù, adj., L. 2, p. 21

history of...-史, shǐ, suffix, L. 2, p. 20

hold (a meeting, ceremony, etc.), 举行, jǔxíng, v., L. 1, p. 3

hold two or more posts or to play two roles at the same time, 兼, jiān, v., L. 19, p. 271

holiday, 假期, jiàqī, n., L. 16, p. 227

holiday and vacations, 节假日, jiéjià rì, n., L. 16, p. 228; L. 17, p. 238

homeland; motherland, 祖国, zǔguó, n., L. 20, p. 284

homesick, 思乡, sīxiāng, v-o., L. 9, p. 113

hometown, 故乡, gùxiāng, n., L. 9, p. 115

hometown, 家乡, jiāxiāng, n., L. 9, p. 113

hometown, 老家, lǎojiā, n., L. 25, p. 358

homonym, 同音词, tóngyīn cí, n., L. 12, p. 161

hook up for a one-night stand; booty call, 约炮, yuēpào, v., L. 13, p. 177

hostile, 恶劣, èliè, adj., L. 1, p. 3

hound sb. to death, 逼死, bīsǐ, v.-c., L. 26, p. 373

hour, 钟头, zhōngtóu, n., L. 10, p. 132

household electronics, 家用电器, jiāyòng diànqì, n., L. 4, p. 43

however, 然而, rán'ér, conj., L. 17, p. 239; L. 28, p. 402

Huai River, 淮河, Huáihé, n., L. 10, p. 131

huge achievement, 成就, chéngjiù, n., L. 30, p. 430

huge amount, 高额, gāoé, n., L. 14, p. 193

huge crowds of people in the open air, 人山人海, rénshānrénhǎi, idm., L. 17, p. 239

huge; tremendous, 巨大, jùdà, adj., L. 8, p. 96

human dignity, 人格尊严, réngé zūnyán, n., L. 26, p. 374

humanities, 人文科学, rénwén kēxué, n., L. 29, p. 421

humans; mankind, 人类, rénlèi, n., L. 2, p. 20

humiliate, 羞辱, xiūrǔ, v., L. 21, p. 300

humorous; humor, 幽默, yōumò, adj./n., L. 1, p. 3

hypocritical, 虚伪, xūwěi, adj., L. 13, p. 178

I

ideal; aspiration (career related), 理想, lǐxiǎng, n., L. 8, p. 98

identification card, 身份证, shēnfèn zhèng, n., L. 23, p. 333

identify with (values/cultures/ideas), 认同, rèntóng, v., L. 3, p. 31; L. 9, p. 113

identity, 身份, shēnfèn, n., L. 9, p. 113

if by any chance; in case, 万一, wànyī, conj., L. 22, p. 318

ignore, 忽视, hūshì, v., L. 21, p. 304

illegal, 非法, fēifǎ, adj., L. 6, p. 65

image, 形象, xíngxiàng, n./adj./adv., 1) L. 2, p. 20; 2) L. 9, p. 115; L. 19, p. 270

imagine; imagination, 想象, xiǎngxiàng, v./n., L. 10, p. 129

immediately, 立刻, lìkè, adv., L. 5, p. 56

immigrant; to immigrate, 移民, yímín, n./v., L. 7, p. 80

imperialism, 帝国主义, dìguó zhǔyì, n., L. 7, p. 82

implicate; cause or bring trouble to another, 连累, liánlèi, v., L. 14, p. 194

import; imported, 进口, jìnkǒu, v./adj., L. 4, p. 44

importance, 重要性, zhòngyàoxìng, n., L. 9, p. 113

impose a fine or forfeit; fine or forfeit, 罚款, fákuǎn, v./n., L. 26, p. 374

impression, 印象, yìnxiàng, n., L. 2, p. 19

improve (quality), 提升, tíshēng, v., L. 13, p. 174

improve (methods); improvement, 改进, gǎijìn, v./n., L. 10, p. 128

in advance; to be earlier than planned or expected, 提前, tíqián, adv., L. 16, p. 228

in common use, 通用, tōngyòng, v., L. 16, p. 227

in contact with; to associate with, 交往, jiāowǎng, v./n., L. 9, p. 116

in groups; in great numbers, 成群, chéngqún, adj., L. 11, p. 146

in other words, 换句话说, huànjùhuàshuō, interj., L. 3, p. 31

in particular; especially, 尤其, yóuqí, adv., L. 19, p. 273

in recent years, 近几年, jìn jǐ nián, t.w., L. 1, p. 1

in speaking of; to touch on; to mention, 谈到, tándào, conj./v.-c., L. 24, p. 345

in the future, 未来, wèilái, t.w., L. 24, p. 348

in urgent need, 急需, jíxū, v., L. 23, p. 332

in; on; at (indicating time, place), 于, yú, prep., L. 29, p. 418

incident, 事件, shìjiàn, n., L. 26, p. 374

inclusive; tolerant; to tolerate, 包容, bāoróng, adj./v., L. 2, p. 20

inconvenience, 不便, búbiàn, n., L. 13, p. 173

increase and strengthen (power, capability influence, etc.), 增强, zēngqiáng, v., L. 15, p. 210; L. 17, p. 239

indeed, 的确, díquè, adv., L. 15, p. 207

independent, 独立, dúlì, adj., L. 7, p. 82

independent and autonomous, 独立自主, dúlì zìzhǔ, adj., L. 27, p. 389

India, 印度, Yìndù, n., L. 23, p. 334

indirectly, 间接, jiànjiē, adv., L. 26, p. 374

individual, 个人, gèrén, n./adj., L. 7, p. 80

Indonesia, 印度尼西亚, Yìndùníxīyà, n., L. 23, p. 334

industrial area, 工业区, gōngyè qū, n., L. 24, p. 347

industrialization, 工业化, gōngyè huà, n., L. 7, p. 82

industry, 工业, gōngyè, n., L. 1, p. 4

inevitable, 不可避免, bùkěbìmiǎn, idm., L. 21, p. 301

infant, 婴儿, yīng' ér, n., L. 4, p. 45

influence; clout, 影响力, yǐngxiǎnglì, n., L. 3, p. 31

information, 信息, xìnxī, n., L. 22, p. 316

infringe on, 侵犯, qīnfàn, v., L. 22, p. 318

infringe on, 侵害, qīnhài, v., L. 26, p. 374

initial stage; early days, 初期, chūqī, n., L. 15, p. 211

input, 输入, shūrù, v., L. 12, p. 161

insist, 坚持, jiānchí, v., L. 26, p. 372

insult, 侮辱, wǔrǔ, v., L. 28, p. 402

insurance, 保险, bǎoxiǎn, n., L. 23, p. 333

intellectual property rights, 知识产权, zhīshi chǎnquán, n., L. 4, p. 43

intense emotion; passion; enthusiasm, 激情, jīqíng, n., L. 8, p. 95

intercontinental ballistic missile, 洲际弹道导弹, zhōujìdàndào dǎodàn, n., L. 7, p. 83

interest; benefit, 利益, lìyì, n., L. 22, p. 318

interfere, 干涉, gānshè, v., L. 27, p. 389

intermediate; agency, 中介, zhōngjiè, n., L. 14, p. 190

internationalized, 国际化, guójì huà, adj., L. 15, p. 208

Internet, 网络, wǎngluò, n., L. 5, p. 56; L. 21, p. 301

Internet, 英特网, Yīngtèwǎng, n., L. 13, p. 173

internship, 实习, shíxí, v./n., L. 14, p. 190

interpersonal relations, 人际关系, rénjì guānxi, n., L. 8, p. 96

introduce (from elsewhere); bring in, 引进, yǐnjìn, v., L. 15, p. 211

introduce; introduction, 介绍, jièshào, v./n., L. 3, p. 32

invade, 侵略, qīnlüè, v., L. 7, p. 82

invest; input, 投入, tóurù, v., L. 8, p. 99

invisible; intangible, 无形, wúxíng, adj., L. 23, p. 334

ironic; satirize/ridicule, 讽刺, fěngcì, adj./v., L. 12, p. 161

island, 岛, dǎo, n., L. 27, p. 388

It is only right and proper, 理所当然, lǐsuǒdāngrán, idm., L. 13, p. 178

itinerary, 行程, xíngchéng, n., L. 10, p. 129

J

jail, 监狱, jiānyù, n., L. 5, p. 54

jeans, 牛仔裤, niúzǎi kù, n., L. 3, p. 30

Jesus, 耶稣, Yēsū, n., L. 16, p. 225

jingle; doggerel, 顺口溜儿, shùnkǒuliūér, n., L. 19, p. 269

join (an organization), 加入, jiārù, v., L. 25, p. 361

judge, 判断, pànduàn, v., L. 28, p. 406

jump off a building (to commit suicide), 跳楼, tiàolóu, v.-o., L. 26, p. 371

junior high school students, 初中生, chūzhōngshēng, n., L. 12, p. 162

juvenile delinquent, 少年犯, shàonián fàn, n., L. 25, p. 361

K

keep silent about major charges while admitting minor ones, 避重就轻, bìzhòng jiùqīng, idm., L. 30, p. 432

keyboard, 键盘, jiànpán, n., L. 12, p. 162

kiss (no object), 亲嘴, qīnzuǐ, v.-o., L. 1, p. 2

knockoff products, 山寨产品, shānzhài chǎnpǐn, n., L. 4, p. 42

know (a fact); find out about, 了解, liǎojiě, v., L. 4, p. 44

know; to recognize, 认得, rènde, v., L. 1, p. 1

Kung Fu Panda, 功夫熊猫, Gōngfu Xióngmāo, L. 2, p. 19

L

label sth.as; stereotype, 贴标签, tiē biāoqiān, v.o., L. 20, p. 284

labor force, 劳动力, láodòng lì, n., L. 24, p. 345

lack, 缺, quē, v., L. 25, p. 361

lack; be deficient in; be short of, 缺乏, quēfá, v., L. 6, p. 65

lakes (collective noun), 湖泊, húpō, n., L. 10, p. 130

land (based); on land, 陆上, lùshàng, attr., L. 23, p. 335

land; territory, 土地, tǔdì, n., L. 3, p. 31

landscape; (natural/tourist) sight, 景观, jǐngguān, n., L. 10, p. 133; L. 11, p. 146

lane; alley, 胡同, hútong, n., L. 11, p. 144

laptop, 笔记本电脑, bǐjìběn diànnǎo, n., L. 12, p. 160

large quantities of, 一大批, yí dàpī, n., L. 15, p. 212

large-scale (usu. as a modifier), 大规模, dàguīmó, adj., L. 16, p. 226

last generation, 上一代, shàng yídài, *n.*, L. 24, p. 347

lasting or permanent place/stage in life; (of girls) to be happily married, 归宿, guīsù, *n.*, L. 28, p. 404

late (for trains/flights); behind schedule, 晚点, wǎndiǎn, *v.*, L. 10, p. 132

later on; henceforth, 往后, wǎnghòu, *n.*, L. 29, p. 418

latter half (of a century), 后半期, hòubàn qī, *n.*, L. 23, p. 332

lay (the basis/foundations), 奠定, diàndìng, *v.*, L. 30, p. 433

lay emphasis on, 注重, zhùzhòng, *v.*, L. 19, p. 272

lead, 带领, dàilǐng, *v.*, L. 26, p. 373

lead (e.g. the trend), 引领, yǐnlǐng, *v.*, L. 3, p. 30

lead to; bring (emphasis on), 引起, yǐnqǐ, *v.*, L. 17, p. 241

lead; exercise leadership, 领导, lǐngdǎo, *v./n.*, L. 1, p. 4

leader of a country or party, 领导人, lǐngdǎo rén, *n.*, L. 27, p. 387; L. 28, p. 401

leap; rapid progress, 飞跃, fēiyuè, *n./v.*, L. 29, p. 421

learn to read; recognize characters; become literate, 识字, shízì, *v.-o.*, L. 12, p. 161

learning, 学识, xuéshí, *n.*, L. 28, p. 403

leather shoes, 皮鞋, píxié, *n.*, L. 4, p. 43

leaves (of a tree), 树叶, shùyè, *n.*, L. 8, p. 98

left (over); remain, 剩下, shèngxià, *v.-c.*, L. 8, p. 96

left-behind children, 留守儿童, liúshǒu értóng, *n.*, L. 25, p. 358

leftover woman, 剩女, shèngnǚ, *n.*, L. 28, p. 401

Legalists (a school of thought in ancient China), 法家, Fǎjiā, L. 6, p. 68

legalize; legitimize, 合法化, héfǎ huà, *v.*, L. 15, p. 209

legend; folklore, 传说, chuánshuō, *n.*, L. 2, p. 18

legitimate; (of behavior, etc.) correct, proper, 正当, zhèngdàng, *adj.*, L. 6, p. 65

leisurely and carefree, 悠闲, yōuxián, *adj.*, L. 8, p. 97

let alone …; not to mention…, 更何况, gènghékuàng, *adv.*, L. 27, p. 388

let sb. off, 放过, fàngguo, *v.-c.*, L. 5, p. 54

levy (a tax), 征收, zhēngshōu, *v.-o.*, L. 4, p. 44

liberal; open-minded, 开明, kāimíng, *n.*, L. 27, p. 387

liberate, 解放, jiěfàng, *v.*, L. 28, p. 401

librarian, 图书馆员, túshūguǎn yuán, *n.*, L. 29, p. 419

life, 生命, shēngmìng, *n.*, L. 21, p. 302; L. 22, p. 317

lift; elevator, 电梯, diàntī, *n.*, L. 11, p. 145

limited, 有限, yǒuxiàn, *adj.*, L. 27, p. 387

limited to; confined to, 局限于, júxiàn yú, *v.*, L. 23, p. 332

line of demarcation; boundary, 分界线, fēnjiè xiàn, *n.*, L. 10, p. 131

literature, 文学, wénxué, *n.*, L. 3, p. 33

little fresh meat; boy toy, 小鲜肉, xiǎo xiānròu, *n.*, L. 28, p. 401

lively; vividly, 生动, shēngdòng, *adj./adv.*, L. 19, p. 270

local, 本土, běntǔ, *adj.*, L. 14, p. 192

local area, 当地, dāngdì, *n.*, L. 4, p. 44

local or regional peculiarity, 地域性, dìyù xìng, *n.*, L. 9, p. 115

lodge (a challenge); put forward, 提出, tíchū, *v.*, L. 7, p. 83

lonely, 孤独, gūdú, *adj.*, L. 25, p. 359

long period of time, 长时期, cháng shíqī, *adj./adv.*, L. 29, p. 420

long period of time; long-term, 长期, chángqī, *attr./adv.*, L. 30, p. 431

long vacation, 长假, chángjià, *n.*, L. 17, p. 238

long-distance, 长途, chángtú, *adj.*, L. 17, p. 239

long-range; long-distance, 远程, yuǎnchéng, *adj.*, L. 7, p. 83

Look! 瞧, qiáo, *v.*, L. 1, p. 3

looks; appearance, 长相, zhǎngxiàng, *n.*, L. 10, p. 131; L. 28, p. 406

lose (ambition, ability, senses, etc.), 丧失, sàngshī, *v.*, L. 15, p. 208

lose face, 丢脸, diūliǎn, *v.o.*, L. 28, p. 403

lose or drain, 流失, liúshī, *v.*, L. 15, p. 212

lose; defeated (opp. 赢 yíng), 输, shū, *v.*, L. 14, p. 192

loss, 损失, sǔnshī, *n.*, L. 29, p. 420

lost battle; defeat, 败仗, bàizhàng, *n.*, L. 27, p. 386

loved one; girlfriend or boyfriend, 恋人, liànrén, *n.*, L. 1, p. 2

lover; mistress, 情人, qíngrén, *n.*, L. 28, p. 404

lower one's head, 低头, dītóu, *v.-o.*, L. 26, p. 372

low-priced; cheap (derogatory term), 廉价, liánjià, *adj.*, L. 24, p. 345

luggage, 行李, xínglǐ, *n.*, L. 9, p. 115

lunar calendar, 农历, nónglì, *n.*, L. 16, p. 226

lunch, 午餐, wǔcān, *n.*, L. 6, p. 65

lustful; lecherous; lascivious, 好色, hàosè, *adj.*, L. 19, p. 270

luxuries, 奢侈品, shēchǐ pǐn, *n.*, L. 4, p. 44

luxury car, 名车, míngchē, *n.*, L. 18, p. 253

M

Mainland China, 大陆, dàlù, *n.*, L. 4, p. 44; L. 27, p. 387

mainland internet slang for mistress, 二奶, èrnǎi, *n.*, L. 28, p. 401

maintain, 维持, wéichí, *v.*, L. 26, p. 373

major, significant (discoveries, contributions, loss, etc.), 重大, zhòngdà, *adj.*, L. 29, p. 420

majority, 多数, duōshù, *n.*, L. 11, p. 144

make a profit, 赚取, zhuànqǔ, *v.*, L. 18, p. 256

make a sudden stride in progress; advance by leaps and bounds, 突飞猛进, tūfēi měngjìn, *idm.*, L. 10, p. 128

make up (jokes, jingles, etc.), 编, biān, *v.*, L. 19, p. 271

make up; constitute; form, 组成, zǔchéng, *v.*, L. 23, p. 331

make/draw up (the law); lay down (rules), 制定, zhìdìng, *v.*, L. 6, p. 68

manage; govern; administer; management, 管理, guǎnlǐ, *v./n.*, L. 23, p. 333; L. 27, p. 386

manager, 经理, jīnglǐ, *n.*, L. 26, p. 372

man-made; artificial, 人为, rénwéi, *adj.*, L. 23, p. 334

manner; bearing, 举止, jǔzhǐ, *n.*, L. 18, p. 258

mansion, 豪宅, háozhái, *n.*, L. 18, p. 253

manufacture, 制造, zhìzào, *v.*, L. 4, p. 44

many styles and kinds coexist; to have a great diversity, 多样并存, duōyàng bìngcún, *idm.*, L. 28, p. 407

many years ago, 多年前, duōnián qián, *t.w.*, L. 19, p. 272

many; a great deal of, 许多, xǔduō, *attr.*, L. 19, p. 273

market, 市场, shìchǎng, *n.*, L. 4, p. 42

married, 已婚, yǐhūn, *adj.*, L. 28, p. 404

marry (a woman marries a man), 嫁, jià, *v.*, L. 28, p. 403

Master (of Science or Arts), 硕士, shuòshì, *n.*, L. 14, p. 192

maternal grandma, 外婆, wàipó, *n.*, L. 25, p. 358

maternal grandpa, 外公, wàigōng, *n.*, L. 25, p. 358

mature; ripe, 成熟, chéngshú, *adj.*, L. 14, p. 193

mayor, 市长, shìzhǎng, *n.*, L. 26, p. 374

meal and refreshments, 餐点, cāndiǎn, *n.*, L. 13, p. 175

mean; signify, 意味, yìwèi, *v.*, L. 13, p. 174

means of transportation, 交通工具, jiāotōng gōngjù, *n.*, L. 13, p. 177

measure, 测量, cèliáng, *v.*, L. 28, p. 406

measure word for songs or poems, 首, shǒu, *m.w.*, L. 9, p. 114

measure word for an apartment or suite, 套, tào, *m.w*, L. 8, p. 95

measure word for buildings, 栋, dòng, *m.w.*, L. 29, p. 419

measure word for cars, phones, 部, bù, *m.w.*, L. 18, p. 254; L. 22, p. 316

measure word for doors, walls, etc., 道, dào, *m.w.*, L. 2, p. 20; L. 23, p. 334

measure word for passage, paragraph, time, experience, relation, 段, duàn, *m.w.*, L. 19, p. 270; L. 29, p. 420

measure word for ships, 艘, sōu, *m.w.*, L. 23, p. 334

measure word for strength, smell, 股, gǔ, *m.w.*, L. 28, p. 407

measure word for stretches of land or scenery, 片, piàn, *m.w.*, L. 18, p. 256

measure word for tasks, projects, etc., 项, xiàng, *m.w.*, L. 22, p. 319

measure word for teams, troops, etc, 支, zhī, *m.w.*, L. 23, p. 334

measure word for the number of terms served on an official post, 任, rèn, *m.w.*, L. 29, p. 420

measure word for trips, 趟, tàng, *mw.*, L. 10, p. 129

measurement; limitation or tolerance (of free speech), 尺度, chǐdù, *n.*, L. 19, p. 273

measures, 措施, cuòshī, *n.*, L. 15, p. 211; L. 17, p. 238

measures, mean or dirty tactics, 手段, shǒuduàn, *n.*, L. 6, p. 65

meddle in; get involved in, 插手, chāshǒu, *v.*, L. 27, p. 389

media, 媒体, méitǐ, *n.*, L. 5, p. 56

medical insurance, 医疗保险, yīliáo bǎoxiǎn, *n.*, L. 24, p. 347

medical science, 医学, yīxué, *n.*, L. 11, p. 147

meet for the first time, 初次见面, chūcì jiànmiàn, L. 6, p. 66

mentality of the masses, 群众心理, qúnzhòng xīnlǐ, *n.*, L. 11, p. 146

mentality; psychology, 心理, xīnlǐ, *n.*, L. 14, p. 193

mention in the same breath, 相提并论, xiāngtí bìnglùn, *idm.*, L. 16, p. 229

merchant; businessman, 商人, shāngrén, *n.*, L. 4, p. 43

messy; disorder, 混乱, hùnluàn, *adj./n.*, L. 27, p. 389

metropolis, 大都市, dà dūshì, *n.*, L. 9, p. 117

Mid-Autumn Festival, 中秋节, Zhōngqiū jié, *n.*, L. 16, p. 227

middle period, 中期, zhōngqī, *n.*, L. 23, p. 335

middle school, 初中, chūzhōng, *n.*, L. 14, p. 191

midnight, 午夜, wǔyè, *n.*, L. 10, p. 129

migrant workers, 农民工, nóngmín gōng, *n.*, L. 24, p. 345

mild; gentle, 温和, wēnhé, *adj.*, L. 2, p. 19

milestone (in the course of historical development), 里程碑, lǐchéng bēi, *n.*, L. 29, p. 418

military, 军事, jūnshì, *n.*, L. 3, p. 30; L. 7, p. 83

military expending, 军费, jūnfèi, *n.*, L. 20, p. 286

milk powder, 奶粉, nǎifěn, *n.*, L. 4, p. 44

mind; take to heart, 在意, zàiyì, *v.*, L. 16, p. 226

mineral water, 矿泉水, kuàngquánshuǐ, *n.*, L. 26, p. 371

Ming dynasty (1368-1644), 明代, Mín dài, *n.*, L. 23, p. 334

minority, 少数, shǎoshù, *pron.*, L. 12, p. 160

miracle; wonder, 奇迹, qíjì, *n.*, L. 2, p. 20

mislead; misguide, 误导, wùdǎo, *v./n.*, L. 2, p. 19

miss (e.g. an opportunity), 错过, cuòguò, *v.*, L. 22, p. 318

missionary, 传教士, chuánjiào shì, *n.*, L. 29, p. 420

mixed with; mingled with, 夹杂, jiāzá, *v.*, L. 15, p. 208

model, 模式, móshì, *n.*, L. 27, p. 387

model; a good example, 榜样, bǎngyàng, *n.*, L. 15, p. 208

modern drama; stage play, 话剧, huàjù, *n.*, L. 18, p. 257

modern times, 近代, jìndài, *n.*, L. 23, p. 331

money (collective noun), 金钱, jīnqián, *n.*, L. 19, p. 270

monogamy, 一夫一妻制, yì fū yì qī, *n.*, L. 28, p. 404

moon, 月亮, yuèliang, *n.*, L. 15, p. 207

mooncake, 月饼, yuèbǐng, *n.*, L. 16, p. 227

motive power; prime mover; first cause, 原动力, yuán dònglì, *n.*, L. 29, p. 419

motive; driving force, 动力, dònglì, *n.*, L. 20, p. 284

mountain range, 群山, qúnshān, *n.*, L. 2, p. 20

mouse; rat, 老鼠, lǎoshǔ, *n.*, L. 19, p. 272

mouth, 嘴巴, zuǐbā, *n.*, L. 2, p. 18

move, 移动, yídòng, *v.*, L. 17, p. 238

move or touch (sb. emotionally), 感动, gǎndòng, *v.*, L. 20, p. 284

N

narrow (a gap); reduce (in width, size, scope), 缩小, suōxiǎo, *v.*, L. 8, p. 99

national flag, 国旗, guóqí, *n.*, L. 20, p. 284

nationalism, 民族主义, mínzú zhǔyì, *n.*, L. 7, p. 82

naturally, 自然, zìrán, *adv.*, L. 17, p. 241

navy, 海军, hǎijūn, *n.*, L. 23, p. 335

necessary, 必要, bìyào, *adj.*, L. 25, p. 360

negative, 负面, fùmiàn, *adj.*, L. 20, p. 288

neighboring, 邻近, línjìn, *attr.*, L. 23, p. 331

new type; new pattern (modifier), 新型, xīnxíng, *adj.*, L. 13, p. 175

new; novel; strange, 新鲜, xīnxian, *adj.*, L. 16, p. 227

New York Times, 纽约时报, Niǔyuē Shíbào, *n.*, L. 7, p. 84

next time, 下一次, yícì, *n.*, L. 22, p. 318

next; then, 接下来, jiēxiàlái, *int.*, L. 9, p. 112

No smoking, 请勿吸烟, qǐng wù xīyān, *phr.*, L. 11, p. 145

no wonder, 怪不得, guàibude, *adv.*, L. 10, p. 130

no wonder, 难怪, nánguài, *adv.*, L. 4, p. 44

non-local people; non-native; people from out of town, 外地人, wàidì rén, *n.*, L. 8, p. 98; L. 23, p. 332

norm; a normal part of life, 常态, chángtài, *n.*, L. 13, p. 173

normal; regular, 正常, zhèngcháng, *n.*, L. 22, p. 315

not good (e.g. one's performance, grades, image), 不佳, bùjiā, *adj.*, L. 14, p. 194

not have a single thing to one's name, 一无所有, yīwúsuǒyǒu, *idm.*, L. 7, p. 81

not inferior to, 不亚于, bú yàyú, *v.*, L. 29, p. 421

not long ago, 前不久, qiánbùjiǔ, *t.w.*, L. 26, p. 371

notable; remarkable, 显著, xiǎnzhù, *adj.*, L. 11, p. 145

nuclear-powered submarine, 核潜艇, hé qiántǐng, *n.*, L. 23, p. 335

number, 数值, shùzhí, *n.*, L. 28, p. 406

number, 数字, shùzì, *n.*, L. 25, p. 359

number of clicks; web traffic, 点击量, diǎnjī liàng, *n.*, L. 21, p. 302

numerous and in succession (of comments, falling objects, etc.), 纷纷, fēnfēn, *adv.*, L. 20, p. 287

O

objective, 客观, kèguān, *adj.*, L. 28, p. 406

objectivity, 客观性, kèguān xìng, *n.*, L. 20, p. 287

observation; to observe, 观察, guānchá, *n./v.*, L. 7, p. 81

obstacle, 障碍, zhàng'ài, *n.*, L. 6, p. 67

obtain; gain, 取得, qǔdé, *v.*, L. 10, p. 133; L. 15, p. 212

obvious; obviously, 明显, míngxiǎn, *adj./adv.*, L. 10, p. 130

obviously; evidently, 显然, xiǎnrán, *adv.*, L. 1, p. 2

occasion; situation, 场合, chǎnghé, *n.*, L. 11, p. 145

occasionally; once in a while, 偶尔, ǒu' ěr, *adv.*, L. 24, p. 346

ocean, 海洋, hǎiyáng, *n.*, L. 23, p. 334

of great urgency; demand immediate attention, 刻不容缓, kèbùrónghuǎn, *idm.*, L. 30, p. 432

offend (superiors, gods, taboos); incur, 冒犯, màofàn, *v.*, L. 19, p. 273

offer (a course in college, a service), 开设, kāishè, *v.*, L. 15, p. 209

office; agency, 办事处, bànshì chù, *n.*, L. 8, p. 97

official, 官员, guānyuán, *n.*, L. 5, p. 56

official holidays, 法定假日, fǎdìng jiàrì, *n.*, L. 3, p. 32

oilpaper, 油纸, yóuzhǐ, *n.*, L. 18, p. 255

old saying; adage, 老话, lǎohuà, *n.*, L. 6, p. 65

Olympic Games, 奥运会, Àoyùnhuì, *n.*, L. 1, p. 3

on purpose, 故意, gùyì, *adv.*, L. 21, p. 302

on the spot, 当场, dāngchǎng, *adv.*, L. 26, p. 373

on the way; throughout a journey, 沿途, yántú, *adj.*, L. 10, p. 129

once; as soon as (sth. happens), 一旦, yídàn, *conj.*, L. 22, p. 317

one can well imagine that…, 可想而知, kěxiǎng érzhī, *idm.*, L. 14, p. 191

one does not pocket the money he/she finds but returns it to its owner., 拾金不昧, shíjīn búmèi, *idm.*, L. 20, p. 285

one's studies; school work, 学业, xuéyè, *n.*, L. 14, p. 194

one-time; disposable (goods), 一次性, yícì xìng, *adj.*, L. 13, p. 177

online taxi reservation, 网络约车, wǎngluò yuēchē, *n.*, L. 15, p. 209

only; sole, 唯一, wéiyī, *adj.*, L. 28, p. 404

open (one's eyes), 睁, zhēng, *v.*, L. 6, p. 66

open (one's mouth/eyes), 张, zhāng, *v.*, L. 2, p. 18

opera, 歌剧, gējù, *n.*, L. 18, p. 257

opposite; on the contrary (conj.), 相反, xiāngfǎn, *adj.*, L. 6, p. 67

oppress, 压迫, yāpò, *v.*, L. 24, p. 347

optimistic, 乐观, lèguān, *adj.*, L. 20, p. 284

optional (selective) course, 选修课, xuǎnxiū kè, *n.*, L. 14, p. 191

order, 秩序, zhìxù, *n.*, L. 11, p. 146; L. 26, p. 373

order (goods); place an order for, 订购, dìnggòu, *v.*, L. 11, p. 146

order food, 订餐, dìngcān, *v.o.*, L. 18, p. 254

order; sequence, 顺序, shùnxù, *n.*, L. 12, p. 163

ordinarily; in regular times, 平时, píngshí, *t.w.*, L. 8, p. 99

ordinary person; average people, 普通人, pǔtōng rén, *n.*, L. 8, p. 96

ordinary; common, 平常, píngcháng, *adj.*, L. 11, p. 145

organ, 器官, qìguān, *n.*, L. 5, p. 56

organization; institution, 机构, jīgòu, *n.*, L. 4, p. 45; L. 14, p. 190

organize, 组织, zǔzhī, *v.*, L. 23, p. 334

original, 原本, yuánběn, *adj.*, L. 12, p. 161

original and creative ideas, 新意, xīnyì, *n.*, L. 15, p. 210

original idea, 创意, chuàngyì, *n.*, L. 15, p. 210

ornament; decorate, 装饰, zhuāngshì, *n./v.*, L. 10, p. 133; L. 18, p. 253

orphan, 孤儿, gū'ér, *n.*, L. 27, p. 386

otherwise; or else, 否则, fǒuzé, *conj.*, L. 12, p. 161; L. 13, p. 173

out of; stem from, 出于, chūyú, *prep.*, L. 15, p. 210

outdated; obsolete, 陈旧, chénjiù, *adj.*, L. 11, p. 144

outstanding; excellent; splendid, 优秀, yōuxiù, *adj.*, L. 8, p. 99

overflow; spread unchecked, 泛滥, fànlàn, *v.*, L. 4, p. 43

overwhelming majority, 绝大多数, juédàduōshù, *pron.*, L. 12, p. 160

owner of lost property, 失主, shīzhǔ, *n.*, L. 20, p. 285

P

Pacific Ocean, 太平洋, Tàipíngyáng, *n.*, L. 27, p. 388

packaging, 包装, bāozhuāng, *n.*, L. 4, p. 43

paid vacation, 带薪假期, dàixīnjiàqī, *n.*, L. 17, p. 240

palm, 巴掌, bāzhǎng, *n.*, L. 26, p. 372

panda, 熊猫, xióngmāo, *n.*, L. 2, p. 18

papercutting (traditional Chinese folk art form), 剪纸, jiǎnzhǐ, *n.*, L. 3, p. 32

paralyzed, 瘫痪, tānhuàn, *v.*, L. 1, p. 4

parcel, 包裹, bāoguǒ, *n.*, L. 13, p. 175

parent or guardian of a child, 家长, jiāzhǎng, *n.*, L. 1, p. 2

park (a vehicle), 停放, tíngfàng, *v.*, L. 18, p. 258

part; aspect; place, 地方, dìfang, *n.*, L. 7, p. 82; L. 28, p. 402

participate; involved in, 参与, cānyù, *v.*, L. 20, p. 287

particular about (food and clothing/manners/ hygiene), 讲究, jiǎngjiū, *v.*, L. 6, p. 66

particular; given, 特定, tèdìng, *adj.*, L. 17, p. 241

party, 政党, zhèngdǎng, *n.*, L. 27, p. 387

pass (an exam), 通过, tōngguò, *v.*, L. 12, p. 161

pass away, 去世, qùshì, *v.*, L. 25, p. 358

pass on (orally), 传, chuán, *v.*, L. 18, p. 255

password, 密码, mìmǎ, *n.*, L. 22, p. 317

path; road, 道路, dàolù, *n.*, L. 27, p. 389

pay (money), 支付, zhīfù, *v.*, L. 13, p. 176

pay a sum of money, 付款, fùkuǎn, *v.o.*, L. 13, p. 176; L. 18, p. 254

pay close attention to, 关注, guānzhù, *v.*, L. 7, p. 80

pay taxes, 交税, jiāoshuì, *v-o.*, L. 24, p. 346

pay the check; check out, 结账, jiézhàng, *v.-o.*, L. 26, p. 371

peddle, 贩卖, fànmài, *v.*, L. 10, p. 133

people; nationality, 民族, mínzú, *n.*, L. 1, p. 3

People's Commune (1958-1982), 人民公社, Rénmín gōngshè, L. 30, p. 431

percentage; rate, 比例, bǐlì, *n.*, L. 27, p. 385

performance, 演出, yǎnchū, *n.*, L. 18, p. 257

perhaps; maybe, 或许, huòxǔ, *adv.*, L. 18, p. 257

periodization; division, 分法, fēnfǎ, *n.*, L. 30, p. 430

permanent, 永久, yǒngjiǔ, *adj.*, L. 13, p. 177

persecute, 迫害, pòhài, *v.*, L. 29, p. 420

person specially assigned to a task or job, 专人, zhuānrén, *n.*, L. 13, p. 175

personnel, 人员, rényuán, *n.*, L. 15, p. 211

perspective; point of view; angle, 角度, jiǎodù, *n.*, L. 7, p. 81

persuade sb. not to do sth., 劝住, quànzhù, *v.-c.*, L. 26, p. 372

pervade, 弥漫, mímàn, *v.*, L. 28, p. 407

pesticide, 农药, nóngyào, *n.*, L. 7, p. 84

pet, 宠物, chǒngwù, *n.*, L. 2, p. 19

phenomenon, 现象, xiànxiàng, *n.*, L. 4, p. 43

photography, 摄影, shèyǐng, *n.*, L. 18, p. 255

physical (brick and mortar), 实体, shítǐ, *n.*, L. 13, p. 174

physical strength, ability, power, 力量, lìliàng, *n.*, L. 3, p. 30

pick up (from school, airport, etc.), 接, jiē, *v.*, L. 1, p. 2

pick up (someone else' lost article), 捡, jiǎn, *v.*, L. 20, p. 285

pile, 堆, duī, *m.w.*, L. 19, p. 271

pivot, hub, 枢纽, shūniǔ, *n.*, L. 23, p. 335

place (of meeting or assembly), 场所, chǎngsuǒ, *n.*, L. 29, p. 421

place an order online, 下单, xiàdān, *v.*, L. 13, p. 175

place of one's origin, 籍贯, jíguàn, *n.*, L. 9, p. 113

place of origin (of a river, historical event), 发源地, fāyuán dì, *n.*, L. 29, p. 419

plagiarize; to copy, 抄袭, chāoxí, *v.*, L. 4, p. 43

plain, 平原, píngyuán, *n.*, L. 10, p. 130

plastic surgery, 整形手术, zhěngxíng shǒushù, *n.*, L. 28, p. 407

plate, sign, 牌子, páizi, *n.*, L. 11, p. 145

plateau, 高原, gāoyuán, *n.*, L. 10, p. 130

play (the role of...), 扮演, bànyǎn, *v.*, L. 23, p. 336

play a decisive role, 举足轻重, jǔzúqīngzhòng, *idm.*, L. 17, p. 241

plaything; doll, 玩物, wánwù, *n.*, L. 28, p. 405

pleasantly surprised, 惊喜, jīngxǐ, *adv./v.*, L. 18, p. 256

please (sb.), 取悦, qǔyuè, *v.*, L. 28, p. 405

pocket, 口袋, kǒudài, *n.*, L. 26, p. 371

poem; verse, 诗, shī, *n.*, L. 9, p. 114

poet, 诗人, shīrén, *n.*, L. 9, p. 114

political correctness, 政治正确, zhèngzhì zhèngquè, *n.*, L. 19, p. 273

political figure, 政治人物, zhèngzhì rénwù, *n.*, L. 21, p. 301

political part, 党, dǎng, *n.*, L. 1, p. 4

pollution, 污染, wūrǎn, *n./v.*, L. 1, p. 1

poor or low quality; inferior (modifier), 劣质, lièzhì, *adj.*, L. 4, p. 42; L. 10, p. 133

poor; impoverished, 贫穷, pínqióng, *adj.*, L. 7, p. 81

popcorn, 爆米花, bàomǐhuā, *n.*, L. 26, p. 372

popular or prevalent, 流行, liúxíng, *v./adj.*, L. 8, p. 95

popularize; make widely available, 普及, pǔjí, *v.*, L. 12, p. 160

port; harbor, 港口, gǎngkǒu, *n.*, L. 2, p. 21

positive (opp. negative 负面), 正面, zhèngmiàn, *adj.*, L. 20, p. 284

positive energy, 正能量, zhèng néngliàng, *n.*, L. 20, p. 284

possess or have (sth. immaterial), 具有, jùyǒu, *v.*, L. 11, p. 146

possess/command (weapon/land/people), 拥有, yōngyǒu, *v.*, L. 7, p. 83

power, 权力, quánlì, *n.*, L. 22, p. 315

power; influence, 势力, shìlì, *n.*, L. 27, p. 388

powerful; strong, 强大, qiángdà, *adj.*, L. 3, p. 30

practical, 现实, xiànshí, *adj.*, L. 16, p. 226

practical; realistic, 实际, shíjì, *adj.*, L. 16, p. 226

precise, 精确, jīngquè, *adj.*, L. 28, p. 406

preferential; discount, 优惠, yōuhuì, *adj./n.*, L. 24, p. 346

prerequisite, 先决条件, xiānjué tiáojiàn, *n.*, L. 12, p. 162

present given to sb. upon first meeting, 见面礼, jiànmiàn lǐ, *n.*, L. 6, p. 66

present time, 当前, dāngqián, *t.w.*, L. 23, p. 332

press, 摁, èn, *v.*, L. 12, p. 162

pressed/dried salted duck, 板鸭, bǎnyā, *n.*, L. 9, p. 115

pretend; feign, 假装, jiǎzhuāng, *v.*, L. 6, p. 66

prevent, 防止, fángzhǐ, *v.*, L. 3, p. 31

prevent, 防止, fángzhǐ, *v.*, L. 22, p. 318

price of a house, 房价, fángjià, *n.*, L. 8, p. 96

price of commodities, 物价, wùjià, *n.*, L. 24, p. 346

477

private, 私人, sīrén, *adj.*, L. 21, p. 300

private ownership (of means of production), 私有制, sīyǒuzhì, *n.*, L. 30, p. 433

privately run; run by private citizens, 民营, mínyíng, *adj.*, L. 18, p. 255

privilege; prerogative, 特权, tèquán, *n.*, L. 5, p. 55

procedure, 程序, chéngxù, *n.*, L. 6, p. 65

procedure; formality, 手续, shǒuxù, *n.*, L. 15, p. 211

produce (milk powder/rice/food…), 生产, shēngchǎn, *v.*, L. 4, p. 44

product, 产品, chǎnpǐn, *n.*, L. 4, p. 42

products; produce, 物产, wùchǎn, *n.*, L. 10, p. 130

professional, 职业, zhíyè, *att.*, L. 18, p. 253

promote (system, ideas); carry into effect (laws), 推行, tuīxíng, *v.*, L. 11, p. 148

promote; boost, 拉动, lādòng, *v.*, L. 17, p. 238

pronunciation, 语音, yǔyīn, *n.*, L. 12, p. 162

propagate; to publicize, 宣传, xuānchuán, *v.*, L. 5, p. 56; L. 18, p. 257

proper age for marriage, 适婚年龄, shìhūn niánlíng, L. 28, p. 403

prosperous; booming; flourishing, 繁荣, fánróng, *adj.*, L. 23, p. 332

protocol; etiquette, 礼节, lǐjié, *n.*, L. 18, p. 258

protrude; to stick out, 突出, tūchū, *v.*, L. 2, p. 18

proud (of sb.); take pride in; arrogant, 骄傲, jiāo'ào, *adj.*, L. 7, p. 82

prove; proof, 证明, zhèngmíng, *v./n.*, L. 17, p. 239

provide disaster relief, 救灾, jiùzāi, *v.*, L. 20, p. 285

province, 省, shěng, *n.*, L. 9, p. 112

psychology; mentality, 心态, xīntài, *n.*, L. 15, p. 208

public (school, hospital, etc.), 公立, gōnglì, *adj.*, L. 8, p. 98

public affairs, 公共事务, gōnggòng shìwù, *n.*, L. 20, p. 287

public opinion; media, 舆论, yúlùn, *n.*, L. 20, p. 287

public or historical figure, 人物, rénwù, *n.*, L. 30, p. 431

public ownership (of means of production), 公有制, gōngyǒu zhì, *n.*, L. 30, p. 431, 433

public; common, 公共, gōnggòng, *adj.*, L. 11, p. 145

punctual; on time, 准点, zhǔndiǎn, *adj./adv.*, L. 10, p. 132

punish (the agent/doer is "法律"), 制裁, zhìcái, *v.*, L. 5, p. 55

punish; punishment, 惩罚, chéngfá, *v./n.*, L. 26, p. 375

punishment; to punish, 处罚, chǔfá, *n./v.*, L. 5, p. 54

purchase, 购买, gòumǎi, *v.*, L. 4, p. 44

purchasing power, 购买力, gòumǎi lì, *n.*, L. 15, p. 210

pure and fresh, 清新, qīngxīn, *adj.*, L. 10, p. 133

pursue; seek, 追求, zhuīqiú, *v.*, L. 8, p. 97

push aside; exclude, 排挤, páijǐ, *v.*, L. 13, p. 173

put in time and energy, 下功夫, xià gōngfu, *v.*, L. 15, p. 209

put into practice; carry out, 实行, shíxíng, *v.*, L. 27, p. 389

put on (eyewear, headgear), 戴, dài, *v.*, L. 1, p. 2

put on a show; grandstand, 作秀, zuòxiù, *v.*, L. 17, p. 242

put up (a poster, notice, etc.), 贴, tiē, *v.*, L. 11, p. 145

Q

qualification; right, 资格, zīgé, *n.*, L. 21, p. 303

quality (of citizens), 素质, sùzhì, *n.*, L. 14, p. 193

quality (of life, of a product or service), 品质, pǐnzhì, *n.*, L. 1, p. 4

quantify, 量化, liànghuà, *v.*, L. 28, p. 406

quarrel, 吵架, chǎojià, *v-o.*, L. 25, p. 361

R

race, 种族, zhǒngzú, *n.*, L. 19, p. 273

raincoat, 雨衣, yǔyī, *n.*, L. 20, p. 286

raise (a child/a pet/livestock), 养, yǎng, *v.*, L. 7, p. 81

rank… (a particular position) …in…, 排, pái, *v.*, L. 10, p. 132

rap (music style), 说唱, shuōchàng, *n.*, L. 19, p. 269

rare, hard-earned (chance, opportunity), 难得, nándé, *adj.*, L. 1, p. 3

reach (an agreement), 达成, dáchéng, *v.*, L. 26, p. 374

react against (oppression), 反抗, fǎnkàng, *v.*, L. 24, p. 347

realize (one's ideal/dream/a plan), 实现, shíxiàn, *v.*, L. 7, p. 81

reason; justification; argument, 理由, lǐyóu, *n.*, L. 22, p. 319

reason; sense; principle; hows and whys, 道理, dàolǐ, *n.*, L. 4, p. 43

reasonable, 合理, hélǐ, *adj.*, L. 22, p. 317

rebuild, 重建, chóngjiàn, *v.*, L. 23, p. 336

recite; repeat from memory, 背诵, bèisòng, *v.*, L. 9, p. 114

recognition, 肯定, kěndìng, *n.*, L. 18, p. 258

recommendation letter, 推荐信, tuījiàn xìn, *n.*, L. 14, p. 194

record, 记录, jìlù, *v./n.*, L. 26, p. 374

recreational activities, 文娱活动, wényú huódòng, *n.*, L. 18, p. 257

recruit, 招聘, zhāopìn, *v.*, L. 24, p. 345

recur; repeat (of disaster, tragedy), 重演, chóngyǎn, *v.*, L. 30, p. 432

reef, 岛礁, dǎojiāo, *n.*, L. 23, p. 335

refer to, 指, zhǐ, *v.*, L. 28, p. 405

reflect; mirror, 反映, fǎnyìng, *v.*, L. 4, p. 43

reflect; rethink, 反思, fǎnsī, *v.*, L. 15, p. 210

refuse, 拒绝, jùjué, *v.*, L. 22, p. 317

registered permanent residence, 户口, hùkǒu, *n.*, L. 8, p. 98

regulation; rule, 规则, guīzé, *n.*, L. 11, p. 145

regulation; stipulation, 规定, guīdìng, *n.*, L. 6, p. 67

relatives, 亲戚, qīnqi, *n.*, L. 25, p. 358

relax (restrictions), 放宽, fàngkuān, *v.*, L. 30, p. 433

relaxed; at ease, 轻松, qīngsōng, *adj.*, L. 6, p. 66

religion, 宗教, zōngjiào, *n.*, L. 16, p. 225

religious, 宗教性, zōngjiào xìng, *n.*, L. 16, p. 225

remember fondly; reminisce, 怀念, huáiniàn, *v.*, L. 11, p. 144

remote, 偏僻, piānpì, *adj.*, L. 10, p. 128

remote (modifier), 偏远, piānyuǎn, *adj.*, L. 10, p. 133

rent, 房租, fángzū, *n.*, L. 8, p. 96

rent, 租, zū, *v.*, L. 13, p. 177

rent and use, 租用, zūyòng, v., L. 24, p. 346

reparations; indemnity, 赔款, péikuǎn, n., L. 27, p. 386

repay; reciprocate, 回报, huíbào, v., L. 15, p. 210

repeat, 重复, chóngfù, v., L. 12, p. 163

replace, 取代, qǔdài, v., L. 12, p. 160

report (an incident) to the police, 报警, bàojǐng, v, L. 26, p. 371

report; cover (news), 报道, bàodào, v., L. 5, p. 56

reporter; journalist, 记者, jìzhě, n., L. 5, p. 56

represent; representation, 代表, dàibiǎo, v./n., L. 2, p. 18

representative works; masterpiece, 代表作, dàibiǎozuò, n., L. 9, p. 114

Republic of China (1912-1949, the government moved to Taiwan after 1949)., 民国, Mínguó, n., L. 30, p. 431

reputation, 名声, míngshēng, n., L. 21, p. 301

required (obligatory) course, 必修课, bìxiū kè, n., L. 14, p. 191

required (subject), 必考, bìkǎo, adj., L. 14, p. 191

residence registration system, 户籍, hùjí, n., L. 23, p. 333

residents, 居民, jūmín, n., L. 23, p. 333

resources, 资源, zīyuán, n., L. 3, p. 33

respond (to a change), 应对, yìngduì, v., L. 3, p. 31

restrict; limit, 限制, xiànzhì, v., L. 4, p. 44

resume, 恢复, huīfù, v., L. 30, p. 433

retire, 退休, tuìxiū, v., L. 8, p. 97

retirement insurance, 养老保险, yǎnglǎo bǎoxiǎn, n., L. 24, p. 347

retreat, 退, tuì, v., L. 27, p. 386

retrogress; lag behind, 退步, tuìbù, v., L. 1, p. 4

reunite (of a family), 团聚, tuánjù, v., L. 17, p. 239

reunite; family reunion, 团圆, tuányuán, v./n., L. 16, p. 227

revere foreign things and pander to foreign, 崇洋媚外, chóngyáng mèiwài idm., L. 15, p. 207

revert to or restore old/ancient ways, 复古, fùgǔ, v.-o., L. 3, p. 32

revitalize; revive, 复兴, fùxīng, v., L. 17, p. 242

revolutionary, 革命性, gémìng xìng, adj., L. 13, p. 176

rhyme, 押韵, yāyùn, v-o., L. 19, p. 269

rice field, 稻田, dàotián, n., L. 10, p. 130

rich; wealthy, 富裕, fùyù, adj., L. 7, p. 82

ridicule and satirize, 讥讽, jīfěng, v., L. 26, p. 372

ridicule; laugh at, 嘲笑, cháoxiào, v., L. 21, p. 303

ring; (of a bell/phone) shrill, 响, xiǎng, v., L. 26, p. 371

rise, 上涨, shàngzhǎng, v., L. 24, p. 346

rise to prominence, 崛起, juéqǐ, v., L. 23, p. 334

rise; spring up, 兴起, xīngqǐ, v., L. 13, p. 175；L. 14, p. 191

rivers (collective noun), 河流, héliú, n., L. 10, p. 130

Rock and Roll, 摇滚乐, yáogǔn yuè, n., L. 30, p. 432

role (in a play, movie, etc.), 角色, juésè, n., L. 23, p. 336

roll (up/down the car window), 摇, yáo, v., L. 11, p. 147

room; space, 空间, kōngjiān, n., L. 10, p. 129

rough, 粗略, cūlüè, adj., L. 10, p. 131

rumor, 谣言, yáoyán, n., L. 21, p. 301

run (a business), 经营, jīngyíng, v., L. 13, p. 174

run a red light, 闯红灯, chuǎng hóngdēng, v.o., L. 11, p. 146

run or hold (an event), 举办, jǔbàn, v., L. 18, p. 255

running water; tap water, 自来水, zìlái shuǐ, n., L. 7, p. 84; L. 11, p. 144

rush to purchase (anticipating scarcity), 抢购, qiǎnggòu, v., L. 4, p. 43

S

safe and sound, 平安, píng'ān, adj., L. 16, p. 226

sales, 销售量, xiāoshòu liàng, n., L. 1, p. 4

same day, 当天, dāngtiān, n., L. 13, p. 175

sandbag, 沙袋, shādài, n., L. 20, p. 286

sanitation worker, 环卫工人, huánwèi gōngrén n., L. 20, p. 285

satisfactory, 满意, mǎnyì, adj., L. 30, p. 430

save, 救, jiù, v., L. 25, p. 358

save money, 省钱, shěngqián, v.-o., L. 25, p. 359

save up money, 攒钱, zǎnqián, v.-o., L. 8, p. 96

scale; scope, 规模, guīmó, n., L. 23, p. 332

scene; phenomenon, 景象, jǐngxiàng, n., L. 17, p. 239

scenery (usually a view of natural features), 风景, fēngjǐng, n., L. 10, p. 129

scenery spot; place of interest; attraction, 景点, jǐngdiǎn, n., L. 10, p. 133

scheduled train/bus, 班车, bānchē, n., L. 10, p. 129

school begins, 开学, kāixué, v., L. 16, p. 228

school ends, 放学, fàngxué, v.-o., L. 1, p. 2

school; college (an old term), 学堂, xuétáng, n., L. 28, p. 401

science, 自然科学, zìrán kēxué, n., L. 29, p. 421

science, 科学, kēxué, n., L. 1, p. 4

science and technology, 科技, kējì, n., L. 12, p. 161; L. 13, p. 174

scientific research, 科研, kēyán, n., L. 15, p. 211

scramble for; vie for; to snatch, 抢, qiǎng, v., L. 11, p. 146

scrape together money, 凑钱, còuqián, v.-o., L. 26, p. 372

second only to; only inferior to, 仅次于, jǐncìyú, v., L. 9, p. 113

second-hand smoke, 二手烟, èrshǒu yān, n., L. 11, p. 145

secretary, 秘书, mìshu, n., L. 19, p. 271

Secretary of the Party Committee of a school, 校党委书记, xiào dǎngwěi shūjì, L. 28, p. 401

secretly, 偷偷, tōutōu, adv., L. 26, p. 371

secretly, 悄悄, qiāoqiāo, adv., L. 11, p. 146

secure and peaceful, 安稳, ānwěn, adj., L. 8, p. 97

security check, 安检, ānjiǎn, n., L. 22, p. 315

security gate, 安检门, ānjiǎn mén, n., L. 26, p. 371

security; safety, 安全性, ānquánxìng, n., L. 22, p. 318

seek justice; seek an answer/explanation, 讨说法, tǎo shuōfǎ, v.-o., L. 26, p. 373

seldom seen; rare, 罕见, hǎnjiàn, adj., L. 1, p. 1

self-abased, 自卑, zìbēi, adj., L. 24, p. 347

self-confidence; confident, 自信, zìxìn, n./adj., L. 15, p. 208

selfish, 自私, zìsī, *adj.*, L. 8, p. 99

semester, 学期, xuéqī, *n.*, L. 16, p. 228

semi-colony, 半殖民地, bàn zhímíndì, L. 7, p. 82

semi-public; more or less open, 半公开, bàn gōngkāi, *adj.*, L. 28, p. 404

send out; dispatch, 派遣, pàiqiǎn, *v.*, L. 30, p. 433

sense of fulfillment; sense of achievement, 成就感, chéngjiù gǎn, *n.*, L. 8, p. 97

sense of humor, 幽默感, yōumò gǎn, *n.*, L. 1, p. 3

sense of security, 安全感, ānquán gǎn, *n.*, L. 25, p. 359

sense of superiority, 优越感, yōuyuègǎn, *n.*, L. 11, p. 147

sensual pleasures, fame and wealth, 声色名利, shēngsè mínglì, *n.*, L. 28, p. 407

seriousness, 严重性, yánzhòng xìng, *n.*, L. 25, p. 359

serpent; python, 蟒蛇, mǎngshé, *n.*, L. 2, p. 18

set (an example), 树立, shùlì, *v.*, L. 20, p. 286

sever; to break off, 断绝, duànjué, *v.*, L. 29, p. 420

severe (punishment/criticism); severely, 严厉, yánlì, *adj./adv.*, L. 5, p. 54

sexual assault; sexual abuse, 性侵犯, xìng qīnfàn, *n.*, L. 25, p. 360

sexual overture, 性暗示, xìng ànshì, *n.*, L. 28, p. 405

sexual relationship, 性关系, xìng guānxi, *n.*, L. 13, p. 178

shameful, 不体面, bùtǐmiàn, *adj.*, L. 28, p. 403

Shenzhen, a major city and financial center in South China, 深圳, Shēnzhèn, *n.*, L. 8, p. 98

shock, 震惊, zhènjīng, *v.*, L. 25, p. 358

shoot; spurt; spout, 喷, pēn, *v.*, L. 2, p. 18

shop assistant; salesperson, 售货员, shòuhuò yuán, *n.*, L. 13, p. 174; L. 26, p. 371

shop front; sales floor, 店面, diànmiàn, *n.*, L. 13, p. 174

shopping festival; retail holiday, 购物节, gòuwùjié, *n.*, L. 17, p. 241

shoulder; carry on the shoulder, 扛, káng, *v.*, L. 20, p. 286

show; display; demonstrate, 显示, xiǎnshì, *v.*, L. 11, p. 147

show; to illustrate, 说明, shuōmíng, *v.*, L. 7, p. 81

shrink, sag, 萎缩, wěisuō, *v.*, L. 13, p. 174

shuttle; take a roundtrip, 往返, wǎngfǎn, *v.*, L. 10, p. 129

silk, 丝绸, sīchóu, *n.*, L. 23, p. 335

similar, 类似, lèisì, *adj.*, L. 28, p. 405

similar to (quality, interests, opinions), 接近, jiējìn, *v.*, L. 10, p. 131

simple and honest; unsophisticated, 淳朴, chúnpǔ, *adj.*, L. 30, p. 429

simplify, 简化, jiǎnhuà, *v.*, L. 15, p. 211

sincere, 诚恳, chéngkěn, *adj.*, L. 30, p. 432

sincerity, 真诚, zhēnchéng, *n.*, L. 21, p. 303

singer, 歌星, gēxīng, *n.*, L. 28, p. 405

single, 单身, dānshēn, *adj.*, L. 28, p. 403

sink, 沉, chén, *v.*, L. 27, p. 388

Sino-Japanese War (1894-1895), 甲午战争, Jiǎwǔ Zhànzhēng, *n.*, L. 27, p. 385

situation, 情形, qíngxíng, *n.*, L. 20, p. 285

size up a prospective mate in an arranged meeting, 相亲, xiāngqīn, *v.*, L. 28, p. 403

skew toward the younger end of the spectrum, tend to be younger 低龄化, dīlíng huà, *adj.*, L. 14, p. 192

skill, 技能, jìnéng, *n.*, L. 12, p. 160

skill in a specialized area; professional skill, 一技之长, yíjì zhīcháng, *idm.*, L. 24, p. 347

skip classes, 逃课, táokè, *v.-o.*, L. 25, p. 360

skyscraper, 摩天大楼, mótiān dàlóu, *n.*, L. 11, p. 144

slightly, 稍稍, shāoshāo, *adv.*, L. 30, p. 433

slogan, 标语, biāoyǔ, *n.*, L. 7, p. 80

small peddler, 小贩, xiǎofàn, *n.*, L. 18, p. 255

smart phone, 智能手机, zhìnéng shǒujī, *n.*, L. 12, p. 160

smell; breath; flavor, 气息, qìxī, *n.*, L. 28, p. 407

smog, haze, 雾霾, wùmái, *n.*, L. 1, p. 1

smoke (a cigarette or a pipe), 抽烟, chōuyān, *v.-o.*, L. 1, p. 1

snack, 零食, língshí, *n.*, L. 26, p. 371

social class, 阶级, jiējí, *n.*, L. 5, p. 55

social group, 群体, qúntǐ, *n.*, L. 28, p. 403

socialism, 社会主义, shèhuì zhǔyì, *n.*, L. 19, p. 272

soft power, 软实力, ruǎn shílì, *n.*, L. 3, p. 30

soldiers, 士兵, shìbīng, *n.*, L. 20, p. 285

sooner or later, 早晚, zǎowǎn, *adv.*, L. 14, p. 193

sound and perfect (system), 健全, jiànquán, *adj.*, L. 4, p. 45

South China Sea, 南海, Nánhǎi, *n.*, L. 23, p. 335

south of the Yangtze River, 江南, Jiāngnán, *n.*, L. 10, p. 130

Southern Fujian dialect, 闽南话, Mǐnnán huà, *n.*, L. 11, p. 148

Southwest Asia, 西亚, xīyà, *n.*, L. 23, p. 335

souvenir, 纪念品, jìniàn pǐn, *n.*, L. 10, p. 133

sovereign; sovereignty, 主权, zhǔquán, *n.*, L. 7, p. 82

soy sauce, 酱油, jiàngyóu, *n.*, L. 15, p. 208

special, 特殊, tèshū, *adj.*, L. 19, p. 269

speech; talk; to give a talk, 演讲, yǎnjiǎng, *n./v.*, L. 21, p. 300

speed (per hour), 时速, shísù, *n.*, L. 10, p. 128

spend time, 度过, dùguò, *v.*, L. 18, p. 257

spirit; essence, 精神, jīngshén, *n.*, L. 6, p. 67; L. 29, p. 418

spit indiscriminately, 随地吐痰, suídì tǔtán, *phr.*, L. 11, p. 146

spread; disseminate (rumors), 散布, sànbù, *v.*, L. 21, p. 301

spring (formal), 春季, chūnjì, *n.*, L. 16, p. 228

Spring Festival, 春节, Chūnjié, *n.*, L. 16, p. 227

stable, 稳定, wěndìng, *adj.*, L. 7, p. 81

stage; phase, 阶段, jiēduàn, *n.*, L. 13, p. 176; L. 15, p. 211

staged (used as a modifier), 阶段性, jiēduànxìng, *adj.*, L. 17, p. 240

stagnate; come to a standstill, 停滞, tíngzhì, *v.*, L. 29, p. 421

stand side by side; tie for, 并列, bìngliè, *v.*, L. 23, p. 331

stand up, 站出来, zhàn chūlai, *v.-c.*, L. 21, p. 303

standard, 标准, biāozhǔn, *adj.*, L. 10, p. 131

staple food; principal food, 主食, zhǔshí, *n.*, L. 9, p. 115

star; celebrity, 明星, míngxīng, *n.*, L. 21, p. 301

stare; glare, 瞪, dèng, *v.*, L. 2, p. 19

start an enterprise, 创业, chuàngyè, *v.*, L. 15, p. 209

start or initiate (a movement, war); to mobilize (people), 发动, fādòng, *v.*, L. 30, p. 431

start up and develop, 开发, kāifā, *v.*, L. 10, p. 133

start with; begin with, 入手, rùshǒu, *v.*, L. 12, p. 162

starting line, 起跑线, qǐpǎo xiàn, *n.*, L. 14, p. 192

state-run, 国营, guóyíng, *adj.*, L. 13, p. 176; L. 18, p. 254

statesman, 政治家, zhèngzhì jiā, *n.*, L. 18, p. 257

steal, 偷窃, tōuqiè, *v.*, L. 26, p. 371

step by step, 一步步, yí bùbù, *adv.*, L. 15, p. 209

steps; (of career) level, stage, 台阶, táijiē, *n.*, L. 28, p. 404

still, 仍, réng, *adv.*, L. 28, p. 403

stimulate; stimulus, 刺激, cìjī, *v./n.*, L. 17, p. 238

stop, 停止, tíngzhǐ, *v.*, L. 21, p. 303

stop sb. and not let him/her go, 拦, lán, *v.*, L. 26, p. 371

stop up; block up, 堵塞, dǔsè, *v.*, L. 18, p. 256

story; floor, 层, céng, *m.w.*, L. 11, p. 144

stranger, 陌生人, mòshēng rén, *n.*, L. 1, p. 2

strength; force, 力度, lìdù, *n.*, L. 11, p. 145

stress, 强调, qiángdiào, *v.*, L. 7, p. 80

strictly, 严格, yángé, *adv./adj.*, L. 4, p. 45

strive for; fight for, 争取, zhēngqǔ, *v.*, L. 19, p. 273; L. 28, p. 402

strive to be the first and fear being left behind; vie for, 争先恐后, zhēngxiān kǒnghòu, *idm.*, L. 11, p. 146

strive, fight for; struggle hard (for success), 奋斗, fèndòu, *v.*, L. 7, p. 80; L. 8, p. 95

stroke, 笔画, bǐhuà, *n.*, L. 12, p. 163

strong, 浓, nóng, *adj.*, L. 23, p. 332

strong; intense, 强烈, qiángliè, *adj.*, L. 7, p. 82

strong; tough, 坚强, jiānqiáng, *adj.*, L. 21, p. 300

structure, 结构, jiégòu, *n.*, L. 27, p. 389; L. 30, p. 429

structure and form of a Chinese character, 字形, zìxíng, *n.*, L. 12, p. 162

structure; building; architecture, 建筑, jiànzhù, *n.*, L. 2, p. 20

studio, 画室, huàshì, *n.*, L. 18, p. 255

subject (in a curriculum), 科目, kēmù, *n.*, L. 14, p. 191

subjective, 主观, zhǔguān, *adj.*, L. 28, p. 406

subsequently; soon afterwards, 随后, suíhòu, *interj.*, L. 26, p. 372

suddenly; abruptly, 突然, tūrán, *adv.*, L. 1, p. 3

sue, 告, gào, *v.*, L. 22, p. 316

suggest; propose, 建议, jiànyì, *v.*, L. 3, p. 31

suit; fit, 适合, shìhé, *v.*, L. 14, p. 195

suitable (for living), 适宜, shìyí, *v.*, L. 23, p. 332

summarize, 概括, gàikuò, *v.*, L. 19, p. 269

superficial; ostentatious, 虚浮, xūfú, *adj.*, L. 28, p. 407

supervise, 监督, jiāndū, *v.*, L. 4, p. 45

surprised; taken by surprise, 意外, yìwài, *adj.*, L. 1, p. 3

surrounding, 周围, zhōuwéi, *n.*, L. 26, p. 373

suspect; doubt, 怀疑, huáiyí, *v.*, L. 22, p. 316

suspend; discontinue, 中止, zhōngzhǐ, *v.*, L. 23, p. 335

suspicion, 嫌疑, xiányí, *n.*, L. 22, p. 319

swat, 拍, pāi, *v.*, L. 5, p. 54

symbolize; symbol, 象征, xiàngzhēng, *v./n.*, L. 2, p. 19; L. 17, p. 242

sympathize; sympathy, 同情, tóngqíng, *v./n.*, L. 27, p. 386

system, 系统, xìtǒng, *n.*, L. 13, p. 173; L. 17, p. 239

T

take (a subway, ship, car, etc.), 搭, dā, *v.*, L. 11, p. 147

take (bribes), 收取, shōuqǔ, *v.*, L. 19, p. 270

take (joint/group) photo with..., 合影, héyǐng, *v.*, L. 20, p. 284

take a long (sea) voyage, 远航, yuǎnháng, *v.*, L. 23, p. 334

take a picture of a person without his/her permission or without his/her knowledge., 偷拍, tōupāi, *v.*, L. 21, p. 301

take a taxi, 打的, dǎdī, *v.o.*, L. 11, p. 147

take advantage, 趁, chèn, *v.*, L. 18, p. 257

take off; (economic) take-off, 起飞, qǐfēi, *v./n.*, L. 27, p. 387

take sth. seriously; attach importance to; to value, 重视, zhòngshì, *v.*, L. 6, p. 66

take strong measures against; crack down on (corruption, crimes); blow; hit, 打击, dǎjī, *v./n.*, L. 19, p. 270; L. 22, p. 319

take the graduate entrance examination, 考研, kǎoyán, *v.*, L. 14, p. 191

take up a pen and write, 提笔写字, tíbǐ xiězì, *idm.*, L. 12, p. 160

take up; occupy, 占, zhàn, *v.*, L. 3, p. 32

take-out, 外卖, wàimài, *n.*, L. 13, p. 175

talented person; talent; human resources, 人才, réncái, *n.*, L. 8, p. 99

tall building; skyscraper, 高楼, gāo lóu, *n.*, L. 1, p. 1

Tang Dynasty (618-907), 唐朝, Táng cháo, *n.*, L. 9, p. 113

target; a potential marriage partner, 对象, duìxiàng, *n.*, L. 1, p. 2

task, 任务, rènwù, *n.*, L. 12, p. 161

tea ceremony, 茶道, chádào, *n.*, L. 3, p. 32

Teaching Chinese as a Second Language, 对外汉语教学, duìwài hànyǔ jiàoxué, *n.*, L. 12, p. 163

technician; technical expert, 技师, jìshī, *n.*, L. 29, p. 421

technique, 手法, shǒufǎ, *n.*, L. 18, p. 256

technology, 技术, jìshù, *n.*, L. 13, p. 173

temple, 寺庙, sìmiào, *n.*, L. 16, p. 225

temporary, 暂时, zànshí, *adj.*, L. 13, p. 177

tendency; inclination, 倾向, qīngxiàng, *n.*, L. 3, p. 32; L. 14, p. 192

terrorism, 恐怖主义, kǒngbù zhǔyì, *n.*, L. 22, p. 319

terrorist, 恐怖分子, kǒngbù fènzǐ, *n.*, L. 22, p. 317

terrorist attack, 恐怖袭击, kǒngbù xíjī, *n.*, L. 22, p. 317

terrorist organization, 恐怖组织, kǒngbùzǔzhī, *n.*, L. 22, p. 316

test; ordeal; put to the test, 考验, kǎoyàn, *n./v.*, L. 12, p. 160

Thailand, 泰国, Tàiguó, *n.*, L. 23, p. 334

Thanksgiving Day, 感恩节, Gǎnēn jié, *n.*, L. 16, p. 228

theme; subject, 主题, zhǔtí, *n.*, L. 7, p. 80

there is no need for..., 用不着, yòng bu zháo, *v.c.*, L. 28, p. 407

think of or cherish the memory of (the past, history, a person), 缅怀, miǎnhuái, *v.*, L. 30, p. 434

those years/days; back then, 当年, dāngnián, *n.*, L. 29, p. 420

thoughtful; considerate, 周到, zhōudào, *adj.*, L. 10, p. 129

thousands of, 成千上万, chéngqiān shàngwàn, *idm.*, L. 24, p. 345

thousands upon thousands, 千千万万, qiānqiān wànwàn, *idm.*, L. 3, p. 30

threaten; threat, 威胁, wēixié, *v./n.*, L. 22, p. 317

throat, 喉咙, hóulong, *n.*, L. 1, p. 1

ticket price, 票价, piàojià, *n.*, L. 18, p. 257

times; -fold, 倍, bèi, *n.*, L. 10, p. 128

to the best of one's ability, 尽可能, jǐn kěnéng, *adv.*, L. 30, p. 432

tolerant; open-minded, 宽容, kuānróng, *adj.*, L. 21, p. 300

Tomb Sweeping Day, 清明节, Qīngmíng jié, *n.*, L. 3, p. 32

tongue, 舌头, shétou, *n.*, L. 5, p. 56

tool, 工具, gōngjù, *n.*, L. 5, p. 56; L. 6, p. 68

topic, 话题, huàtí, *n.*, L. 7, p. 80

total; sum, 总数, zǒngshù, *n.*, L. 25, p. 359

touch, 碰, pèng, *v.*, L. 19, p. 270

tourists, 游客, yóukè, *n.*, L. 22, p. 315

town, 县城, xiànchéng, *n.*, L. 8, p. 95

toy, 玩具, wánjù, *n.*, L. 25, p. 359

trade; profession; industry, 行业, hángyè, *n.*, L. 13, p. 175

traditional unit of length, equal to 0.5 kilometers, 里, lǐ, *n.*, L. 2, p. 20

traditional unit of weight, equivalent to 0.5 kilograms, 斤, jīn, *m.w.*, L. 20, p. 286

tragedy, 悲剧, bēijù, *n.*, L. 22, p. 317

tragic, 悲惨, bēicǎn, *n.*, L. 30, p. 432

train; training, 培训, péixùn, *v./n.*, L. 14, p. 190

transcript; school report, 成绩单, chéngjì dān, *n.*, L. 14, p. 194

transform; evolve, 转型, zhuǎnxíng, *v.*, L. 23, p. 335

transform; remodel, 改造, gǎizào, *v.*, L. 18, p. 255

transform; to shift, 转变, zhuǎnbiàn, *v.*, L. 7, p. 81

translate; translation, 翻译, fānyì, *v./n.*, L. 6, p. 67; L. 27, p. 385

transnational (company), 跨国, kuàguó, *adj.*, L. 28, p. 401

transport, 运, yùn, *v.*, L. 20, p. 286

transportation hub, 交通枢纽, jiāotōng shūniǔ, *n.*, L. 23, p. 336

trap; strand, 困, kùn, *v.*, L. 2, p. 21

travel by (train, bus or air), 乘, chéng, *v.*, L. 10, p. 128

travel; travel, 出行, chūxíng, *v./n.*, L. 17, p. 239

traveling; tourism, 旅游, lǚyóu, *n./v.*, L. 3, p. 33

treat, 对待, duìdài, *v.*, L. 20, p. 286

treat sth. /sb. as ..., 当, dāng, *v.*, L. 27, p. 386

treatment; wages and benefits, 待遇, dàiyù, *n.*, L. 24, p. 346

trend; tendency, 趋势, qūshì, *n.*, L. 28, p. 406

trend; tide, 潮流, cháoliú, *n.*, L. 28, p. 407

troops, 军队, jūnduì, *n.*, L. 20, p. 285

true; real, 真实, zhēnshí, *adj.*, L. 13, p. 173

truly; authentic, 真正, zhēnzhèng, *adv./adj.*, L. 19, p. 272

trust, 信任, xìnrèn, *v./n.*, L. 22, p. 318

try to recognize, 认, rèn, *v.*, L. 1, p. 2

turkey, 火鸡, huǒjī, *n.*, L. 16, p. 228

turn around, 掉头, diàotóu, *v.*, L. 24, p. 346

turn in the direction of..., 面向, miànxiàng, *v.*, L. 23, p. 334

TV show; TV series, 电视剧, diànshì jù, *n.*, L. 3, p. 30

type, 打字, dǎzì, *v.-o.*, L. 12, p. 160

U

unable, 无法, wúfǎ, *v.*, L. 13, p. 174; L. 16, p. 229

unaccustomed to the environment and climate of a new place, 水土不服, shuǐtǔ bùfú, *v.*, L. 9, p. 114

unbearably or extremely broken down, 破旧不堪, pòjiùbùkān, *adj.*, L. 18, p. 254

unconsciously, 不知不觉, bùzhībùjué, *adv.*, L. 3, p. 31

underestimate, 低估, dīgū, *v.*, L. 21, p. 302

undergraduate student, 本科生, běnkē shēng, *n.*, L. 14, p. 192

understand, 懂得, dǒngdé, *v.*, L. 6, p. 67

understand; comprehend, 理解, lǐjiě, *v.*, L. 7, p. 83

undertake; take up (as a profession); go in for, 从事, cóngshì, *v.*, L. 14, p. 190; L. 27, p. 387

unexpectedly; surprisingly; to one's surprise, 居然, jūrán, *adv.*, L. 11, p. 146; L. 18, p. 256

unfortunate; sad, 不幸, búxìng, *adj.*, L. 2, p. 19

unified; unitary; unite, 统一, tǒngyī, *adj./v.*, L. 11, p. 148; L. 27, p. 388

unique; distinctive, 独特, dútè, *adj.*, L. 18, p. 256

unlock, 解开, jiěkāi, *v.*, L. 22, p. 316

unmarried, 未婚, wèihūn, *adj.*, L. 28, p. 402

unprecedented, 空前, kōngqián, *adj.*, L. 12, p. 160

unrealistic; impractical, 不切实际, búqièshíjì, *adj.*, L. 27, p. 388

unsociable and eccentric, 孤僻, gūpì, *adj.*, L. 25, p. 360

upgrade, 升级, shēngjí, *v.*, L. 22, p. 318

urbanization, 城市化, chéngshì huà, *n.*, L. 25, p. 361

urbanization, 城镇化, chéngzhèn huà, *n.*, L. 23, p. 332

urge; try to persuade, 劝, quàn, *v.*, L. 1, p. 2

urgency, 迫切性, pòqiè xìng, *n.*, L. 25, p. 361

urgent; pressing, 迫切, pòqiè, *adj.*, L. 7, p. 82

use, 使用, shǐyòng, *v.*, L. 13, p. 176

use (sth. else) instead; switch to, 改用, gǎiyòng, *v.*, L. 9, p. 113

used; worn; old, 旧, jiù, *adj.*, L. 18, p. 255

utilize; take advantage of, 利用, lìyòng, *v.*, L. 14, p. 190

Utopian; unrealistic, 空想, kōngxiǎng, *attr.*, L. 30, p. 433

V

Valentine's Day, 情人节, Qíngrén jié, *n.*, L. 16, p. 228

valuable, 值钱, zhíqián, *adj.*, L. 14, p. 192

value, 价值, jiàzhí, *n.*, L. 26, p. 372

value; take sth. seriously; think highly of, 重视, zhòngshì, *v.*, L. 17, p. 241

values, 价值观, jiàzhí guān, *n.*, L. 3, p. 31

Vancouver, 温哥华, Wēngēhuá, *n.*, L. 21, p. 300

vendor's stall, 小摊, xiǎotān, *n.*, L. 13, p. 176

vent (one's anger or dissatisfaction), 发泄, fāxiè, *v.*, L. 21, p. 302

verbally abuse; curse, 骂, mà, *v.*, L. 21, p. 299

verify; confirm (sth. to be true), 证实, zhèngshí, *v./n.*, L. 21, p. 301

Vernacular Movement (1917-1919), 白话文运动, Báihuà wén Yùndòng, *n.*, L. 29, p. 418

very fast; at lightning speed, 飞快, fēikuài, *adv.*, L. 12, p. 162

vicious, 恶毒, èdú, *adj.*, L. 21, p. 301

victim, 受害者, shòuhàizhě, *n.*, L. 21, p. 301

victory; triumph, 胜利, shènglì, *n.*, L. 11, p. 148

video, 视频, shìpín, *n.*, L. 21, p. 300

Vietnam, 越南, Yuènán, *n.*, L. 23, p. 334

village, 村, cūn, *n.*, L. 9, p. 112

violate regulations; break the rules, 违规, wéiguī, *v.o.*, L. 11, p. 145

violate; break (e.g. moral standards, the law, etc.), 违反, wéifǎn, *v.*, L. 25, p. 361

virtual, 虚拟, xūnǐ, *adj.*, L. 13, p. 173

vivid; vividly, 形象, xíngxiàng, *n./adj./adv.*, 1) L. 2, p. 20; 2) L. 9, p. 115; L. 19, p. 270

voluntarily, 自愿, zìyuàn, *adv.*, L. 28, p. 404

vulgar; tacky; gaudy, 俗气, súqì, *adj.*, L. 10, p. 133

W

wage, 薪水, xīnshuǐ, *n.*, L. 19, p. 270

Wall Street, 华尔街, Huá'ěr jiē, *n.*, L. 15, p. 209

war, 战争, zhànzhēng, *n.*, L. 16, p. 226

War of Resistance against Japanese Aggression (1937-1945), 抗战, Kàngzhàn, *n.*, L. 30, p. 431

warm; (a thing) feels near and dear to sb., 亲切, qīnqiè, *adj.*, L. 9, p. 113

warrant; permission, 许可, xǔkě, *n.*, L. 22, p. 317

waste gas or steam; exhaust, 废气, fèiqì, *n.*, L. 1, p. 4

way; manner; style, 方式, fāngshì, *n.*, L. 10, p. 128

way to deal with a situation, 对策, duìcè, *n.*, L. 3, p. 31

we; us, 咱们, zánmen, *pron.*, L. 1, p. 4

weak; soft (of character), 软弱, ruǎnruò, *adj.*, L. 2, p. 19

wealth, 财富, cáifù, *n.*, L. 14, p. 192

weapon, 武器, wǔqì, *n.*, L. 7, p. 83

webcam, 摄像头, shèxiàngtóu, *n.*, L. 21, p. 301

website, 网站, wǎngzhàn, *n.*, L. 21, p. 302

welcome, 欢迎, huānyíng, *v.*, L. 11, p. 144

welfare; benefit, 福利, fúlì, *n.*, L. 23, p. 333

Western, 西洋, xīyáng, *adj.*, L. 17, p. 241

Western calendar, 公历, gōnglì, *n.*, L. 16, p. 227

westernize; Westernization, 西化, xīhuà, *v./n.*, L. 3, p. 31

wet through; drenched, 湿透, shītòu, *v.c.*, L. 20, p. 286

what sb. likes or loves, 喜好, xǐhào, *n.*, L. 18, p. 253

white cloud, 白云, báiyún, *n.*, L. 1, p. 3

whole body; from head to foot, 浑身, húnshēn, *adv.*, L. 20, p. 286

widely recognized; perfectly obvious, 有目共睹, yǒumùgòngdǔ, *idm.*, L. 27, p. 387

widen, 拉大, lādà, *v.*, L. 8, p. 99

widespread; wide ranging, 广泛, guǎngfàn, *adj./adv.*, L. 13, p. 178; L. 28, p. 402

will of the people; public feeling, 人心, rénxīn, *n.*, L. 3, p. 31

win the support of the people, 得民心, dé mínxīn, *v.-o.*, L. 5, p. 54

window, 窗口, chuāngkǒu, *n.*, L. 11, p. 146

winter break, 寒假, hánjià, *n.*, L. 16, p. 228

wish (often related to personal life), 愿望, yuànwàng, *n.*, L. 7, p. 84

wish sb. well; invoke a blessing, 祝福, zhùfú, *v.*, L. 20, p. 284

Wish you..., 祝, zhù, *v.*, L. 17, p. 240

with (one's permission); go through; experience, 经过, jīngguò, *prep./v.*, L. 21, p. 303; L. 29, p. 419

without a single redeeming feature (devoid of any merit), 一无是处, yīwúshìchù, *n.*, L. 30, p. 429

without anything to recommend, 一无可取, yīwúkěqǔ, *idm.*, L. 30, p. 434

witty, 风趣, fēngqù, *adj.*, L. 1, p. 3

women in general, 妇女, fùnǚ, *n.*, L. 28, p. 401

wonton, 馄饨, húndùn, *n.*, L. 9, p. 115

work (physical work; temporary or causal job), 打工, dǎgōng, *v.-o.*, L. 14, p. 190

work of art, 艺术品, yìshù pǐn, *n.*, L. 18, p. 253

work unit (place of employment, esp. in the PRC prior to 1978), 单位, dānwèi, *n.*, L. 28, p. 402

works of (literature or art), 作品, zuòpǐn, *n.*, L. 9, p. 113

World War I (1914-1918), 一战, yī zhàn, *n.*, L. 7, p. 83

World War II, 二战, Èrzhàn, *n.*, L. 27, p. 386

worn down by years, 年久失修, niánjiǔshīxiū, *idm.*, L. 18, p. 254

worry about; fret about; be anxious, 发愁, fāchóu, *v.*, L. 24, p. 345

worth, 值得, zhídé, *v.*, L. 1, p. 4

wreath, 花圈, huāquān, *n.*, L. 26, p. 373

wrist watch, 手表, shǒubiǎo, *n.*, L. 4, p. 43

write (formal), 书写, shūxiě, *v.*, L. 12, p. 160

writing system; characters, 文字, wénzì, *n.*, L. 12, p. 160

written language, 书面语言, shūmiàn yǔyán, *n.*, L. 29, p. 418

Y

Yangtze River, 长江, Cháng Jiāng, *n.*, L. 10, p. 130

yearn for; yearning, 期盼, qīpàn, *v./n.*, L. 7, p. 81

Yenching University (1919-1952), 燕京大学, Yānjīng Dàxué, L. 29, p. 420

young fair face—handsome, effeminate young man, 小白脸, xiǎo báiliǎn, L. 28, p. 405

young generation, 年轻一代, niánqīng yídài, *n.*, L. 24, p. 347